John Donne's Physics

John Donne's Physics

Elizabeth D. Harvey & Timothy M. Harrison

The University of Chicago Press CHICAGO AND LONDON

The University of Chicago Press, Chicago 60637
The University of Chicago Press, Ltd., London
© 2024 by The University of Chicago

Published 2024
Printed in the United States of America

33 32 31 30 29 28 27 26 25 24   1 2 3 4 5

ISBN-13: 978-0-226-83350-7 (cloth)
ISBN-13: 978-0-226-83351-4 (paper)
ISBN-13: 978-0-226-83352-1 (e-book)
DOI: https://doi.org/10.7208/chicago/9780226833521.001.0001

The University of Chicago Press gratefully acknowledges the generous support of the Division of the Humanities at the University
of Chicago toward the publication of this book.

Library of Congress Cataloging-in-Publication Data

Names: Harvey, Elizabeth D., author. | Harrison,
Timothy M., author.
Title: John Donne's physics / Elizabeth D. Harvey and
Timothy M. Harrison.
Description: Chicago : The University of Chicago Press, 2024. |
Includes bibliographical references and index.
Identifiers: LCCN 2023043803 | ISBN 9780226833507 (cloth) |
ISBN 9780226833514 (paperback) | ISBN 9780226833521 (ebook)
Subjects: LCSH: Donne, John, 1572–1631. Devotions upon
emergent occasions.
Classification: LCC PR2247.D483 H37 2024 | DDC 242—dc23/
eng/20231204
LC record available at https://lccn.loc.gov/2023043803

♾ This paper meets the requirements of ANSI/NISO Z39.48-1992
(Permanence of Paper).

For Christina, Livia, and Elise
(TH)

For my students
(EH)

Contents

Figures

Abbreviations

Works by John Donne

We have chosen editions of Donne's works that are readily available. We rely primarily on the Oxford editions, since they are accessible both in hard copy and online through many libraries. We have consulted all existing editions of Donne's works, particularly the *Donne Variorum*. When significant textual differences or differences of dating between editions impinge on the work being discussed, we discuss the issue in a note. Otherwise, all the works below are cited parenthetically according to volume, page, section, and line numbers.

Ann.   *The Epithalamions, Anniversaries, and Epicedes of John Donne*, ed. Wesley Milgate (Oxford: Clarendon, 1978).

Con.   *Ignatius His Conclave*, ed. T. S. Healy (Oxford: Clarendon, 1969).

Dev.   *Devotions upon Emergent Occasions*, in *John Donne: 21st-Century Authors*, ed. Janel Mueller (Oxford: University of Oxford Press, 2015).

Div.   *The Divine Poems*, ed. Helen Gardner (Oxford: Clarendon, 1978).

Let.   *Letters to Severall Persons of Honour (1651), A Facsimile Reproduction* (Delmar, NY: Scholars' Facsimiles, 1977).

Sat.   *The Satires, Epigrams, and Verse Letters*, ed. Wesley Milgate (Oxford: Clarendon, 1967).

Ser.   *The Sermons of John Donne*, ed. Evelyn M. Simpson and George R. Potter, 10 vols. (Berkeley: University of California Press, 1953–62).

Son.   *The Elegies and The Songs and Sonnets*, ed. Helen Gardner (Oxford: Clarendon, 1966).

Other Works

Quotations that include English translation and an original language are cited parenthetically with the citation information for the English translation followed by the citation information for the original text. We have silently regularized *i/j, u/v,* and long *s* and expanded abbreviations in our quotations from early modern prose texts.

Ar.   Aristotle, *The Complete Works of Aristotle,* ed. Jonathan Barnes, 2 vols. (Princeton, NJ: Princeton University Press, 1984).

Aug. Augustine, *Confessions,* trans. Henry Chadwick (Oxford: Oxford University Press, 1991); *Confessiones,* ed. William Watts (Cambridge, MA: Harvard University Press, 1912).

Bal. R. C. Bald, *John Donne: A Life* (Oxford: Clarendon, 1970).

Mon. Michel de Montaigne, *Essays,* trans. Donald M. Frame (Stanford, CA: Stanford University Press, 1957); *Les Essais,* ed. Jean Balsamo, Michel Magnien, and Catherine Magnien-Simonin (Paris: Gallimard, 2007).

Put. George Puttenham, *The Art of English Poesy,* ed. Frank Whigham and Wayne A. Rebhorn (Ithaca, NY: Cornell University Press, 2007).

Wal. Izaak Walton, *Lives of Donne, Wotton, Hooker, Etc.* (Oxford: Oxford University Press, 1927).

Preface

John Donne is perhaps best known for his brilliant innovations in English poetry. His transformations of genre, meter, and style altered the English poetic tradition in fundamental ways. By apparent contrast, Donne's *Devotions upon Emergent Occasions* is a prose work, written toward the end of his life and typically read for its devotional, meditative, and theological qualities. It is the source of famous phrases that continue to have wider circulation and popular, if often deracinated currency: "for whom the *bell* tolls" and "No Man is an *Iland*" encapsulate in their lapidary beauty profound truths about our humanity (*Dev.* 299; 17.1). But *Devotions* is not usually considered in the way we treat it here: as a complete work with an intricate structure that is contiguous with Donne's earlier writing and responsive in complex ways to the seventeenth-century circumstances of its production. We aim to bring renewed attention to this relatively neglected masterpiece, to showcase its intellectual excitement, to examine its structure and methods, to recognize its intersections with intellectual and medical ideas, and to understand it as an expression of Donne's deep philosophical and poetic sensibility.

The first reader to be stopped short by the excellence of *Devotions* was Donne himself. We can catch a glimpse of his excitement by considering the unusual history of its composition. Born in 1572, Donne was just over fifty years old when he suffered from the debilitating and life-threatening sickness he describes in *Devotions*. Contracted sometime in late November 1623, his illness was of relatively short duration. As the metered Latin that serves as the book's table of contents registers, the crisis of his disease lasted just over seven days. But it exhausted Donne's energies for months. Although he survived the severe phase of his illness, he confronted a protracted convalescence. It was in the early days of his sickness that Donne began to write the sinewy sentences of *Devotions*. As he created order out of his jotted pages, sitting in an invalid chair alongside his sickbed, Donne must have felt the text's power, for, despite his poor health, he arranged the book's publication so effectively that it was entered in the Stationer's Register by the bookseller Thomas Jones on January 9, 1624, just over a month after its composition began. It was then printed and made available for sale sometime before February 1, 1624.

Devotions is the only work that Donne rushed into print in this way. Most of his poetry was not published during his own lifetime, circulating instead in manuscript among coterie readers. All the other works that Donne agreed to have printed were published anonymously, tied to patronage, or produced in relation to royal favor.[1] Devotions holds a special place in Donne's corpus. It is the one work that he hurried toward publication, claiming his authorship without the prompting of any external motivating force. As Donne divulged in a letter to Sir Robert Ker, his friends had "importun'd me to Print." He acquiesced to their entreaties, and he also sought Ker's advice as to whether there would be any "uncomlinesse, or unseasonablenesse" in dedicating his book to Prince Charles (Let. 249–50). His wish to see Devotions circulate in print thus responded to his friends and included a desire to thank and to solicit the interest of his royal benefactors. But friendship and patronage alone cannot account for the speedy publication of Devotions. What motivated Donne's urgency to print Devotions was his desire to communicate his encounter with dying, to share the insights gleaned from the days he had spent at the threshold.[2]

1. The list of works published during Donne's lifetime is small. Except for Devotions, all such works were published anonymously or were related to obtaining favor from those in a position to further Donne's career (or just to paying his bills). The commendatory Latin verse published along with Ben Jonson's Volpone (1607) was part of an economy of praise, reciprocated by Jonson. Pseudo-Martyr (1610) was published as part of a calculated bid to win the favor of King James. Ignatius His Conclave (1611) was published anonymously, both in Latin and in English. The Anniversaries (1611, 1612) were published to commemorate the death of Elizabeth Drury, whose parents became Donne's patrons. Likewise, the five sermons Donne published in the 1620s were all published at the request of authority figures, most notably Prince Charles. Devotions is dedicated to Charles but was not published at his request.

2. Richard Strier explores Donne's motivations to publish Devotions in "Donne and the Politics of Devotion," in Religion, Literature, and Politics in Post-Reformation England, 1540–1688, ed. Richard Strier and Donna B. Hamilton (Cambridge: Cambridge University Press, 1996), 93–114. He claims that Donne's illness prompted an urgent realization about the politics of the Church of England. Sick, trapped in bed, alone but for God and the occasional visit by his physicians, Donne was in the ideal state for devotional solitude advocated by various Protestant thinkers. Donne wrote Devotions against the Puritan impulse to favor solitude above the forms of

Throughout his life, Donne was preoccupied with the enigma of death. What does it feel like to die, and what happens as life departs from the body? He explores such questions repeatedly in many of his poems. *Devotions* continues this focus but offers the unique vantage point of having approached the very edge of life, of having prepared for an end that was then deferred and postponed. It is the firsthand account of Donne's extended sojourn in the borderland between life and death. As he asserts in *Devotions*, his illness afforded the opportunity to conduct a scrupulous examination, an anatomy of his thinking during that time, a record of his close encounter with his own mortality. Although he survived, he did not lose the urgent sense of diminished time it had afforded. In his dedicatory letter to Prince Charles in *Devotions*, he calls his returning to life in the wake of his sickness a "preter-naturall Birth" (*Dev.* 230), a reinhabitation of his life that goes beyond the bounds of nature. Outliving his almost fatal illness bequeathed an imperative to report on that journey, which he hopes will "minister some holy delight" to his readers (*Let.* 249). Although it is affiliated with multiple genres, *Devotions* belongs in a tradition that explores the art of dying, the *ars moriendi*. D. Vance Smith identifies two types of mortuary forms: first, ritual observances, prayers, and writings that depict death as a state of finitude; and second, representations of dying as a continuous action. Smith makes a crucial distinction between these conceptions. Death represents an end that is fixed in time, a resolution. Dying, on the other hand, is situated between life and death. It is a suspended state, a prolongation of a process.[3]

Two texts contemporary with *Devotions* illustrate this distinction. The first is William Drummond of Hawthornden's prose meditation on death, *A Cypress Grove*. Published in 1623, the year of Donne's illness, it provides an instructive example of a typical text from the *ars moriendi* tradition. Perhaps occasioned by the severe famine in Scotland that killed several of Drummond's close friends and associates, the meditation considers death an inevitable consequence of mortality: "This Earth is as a Table Booke, and Men are the notes, the first are washen out, that new may be written

---

ritualized togetherness promoted by the Church of England. We agree with Strier's claims, although we do not think that politics was Donne's only motivation. Donne had many reasons to want to see *Devotions* in print, which include belief in its excellence and a desire to share his explorations of style, language, thought, form, and engagement with his own earlier works. We suggest that Donne's rush to publish was generated by his strong desire to communicate insights gathered at the edge of expected death.

3. D. Vance Smith, *Arts of Dying: Literature and Finitude in Medieval England* (Chicago: University of Chicago Press, 2020), 5.

in."[4] Drummond's Christian Platonism shapes a description of death that focuses on the division between body and soul. In the extended apostrophe to his soul, Drummond calls it the "Hymen" that joins material and immaterial realms; its breakage releases the soul from the body (its "infected and leprous Inne") into the happiness and beauty of its heavenly abode (87–88). Drummond depicts death as an external force, a finite event, and despite a number of direct but unattributed quotations from or references to Donne's *Anniversaries*—the "element of fire is quite put out," the gesticulations of the executed man, elaborate similes of the lute string and ice cracking (74, 78)—his meditation is philosophically, structurally, and stylistically unlike *Devotions*. Drummond's borrowings support his portrayal of death happening in "an instant." By contrast, Donne's depiction of the beheaded man in *The Second Anniversarie* actively engages the reluctance of the soul in its departure and suggests a continuing engagement between the living and the dead through an elegiac process.

Whereas Drummond focuses on death as a final event, in *Devotions* Donne describes the extended domain of dying. We can appreciate this distinction more fully by considering the kinship between *Devotions* and another contemporary work that likewise recounts a near-death experience: Michel de Montaigne's "De l'exercitation." Recounting an event from the 1560s and first published in the 1580 *Essais*, Montaigne's account describes an almost fatal experience of being thrown from a horse. He provides an extraordinary report of what it was like to appear to be dead to those around him, even as he himself possessed a kind of otherworldly awareness of his state but remained without the capacity to speak or move.[5] Donne and Montaigne share a fascination for observation and a determination to describe their near approaches to death, what seemed to be the final moments of their dying. Montaigne claims to retain a vivid memory of each moment of his altered state, which he recounts in detail. Donne seems to have recorded his own symptoms on sheets of paper even while the fever raged, seeking to preserve the memories of his illness and his attendant thoughts while they were still vivid.

It is a measure of Donne's curiosity about himself, the process of dy-

---

4. William Drummond of Hawthornden, *Flowres of Sion, To which is adjoyned his Cypress Grove* (Edinburgh: John Hart, 1630), 68. All subsequent quotations are cited parenthetically. We are grateful to Richard Strier for calling our attention to this text. For Drummond's relation to the Scottish famine, see R. G. Spiller, "William Drummond of Hawthornden," in *Oxford Dictionary of National Biography*.

5. For a fuller treatment of Montaigne's essay, see Timothy M. Harrison, "Personhood and Impersonal Feeling in Montaigne's 'De l'exercitation,'" *Modern Philology* 114 (2016): 219–42.

ing, and the afterlife that he felt an imperative to disseminate his account while he was still convalescing. In a letter to his friend Sir Henry Goodyer, Donne provides this vision of his ideal dying:

> I would not that death should take me asleep. I would not have him meerly seise me, and onely declare me to be dead, but win me, and overcome me. When I must shipwrack, I would do it in a Sea, where mine impotencie might have some excuse; not in a sullen weedy lake, where I could not have so much as exercise for my swimming. (*Let.* 50)

Donne recognized that there were many forms of dying, including the sudden, the violent, the unexpected. It was perhaps not so much that he longed for a tender death, the gate of his "*prison . . . opened* with an *oyld key* (by a gentle and *preparing sicknes*)," as he puts it in a later sermon (*Ser.* 10:241). Rather, he wanted to be alive to his dying, to participate with his full cognition and linguistic capacities, to inhabit his exit from earthly existence as fully as he had explored and savored it while alive.

Although Donne treated *Devotions* with special attention and although it received an enthusiastic reception during his lifetime, our book, *John Donne's Physics*, published exactly four hundred years later, is only the second modern work of criticism dedicated completely to *Devotions*.[6] One explanation for this relative neglect may be that the recuperation of Donne's reputation in the late nineteenth and early twentieth centuries tended to focus on his poetry.[7] Serving first as a fraught muse for such poets as T. S. Eliot and then as a paradigm case for the critical and pedagogical value of the close reading practiced by the New Critics, Donne's poetry went, over the course of a few decades, from obscure—rarely read, never taught—to the heights of literary fashion. By contrast, the scholarly discussions of the prose in more recent years have tended to treat *Devotions*, the sermons, and much of Donne's prose principally as manifestations of a religious impulse. We also examine the text's theological and devotional elements, but our focus is the poetic and rhetorical creativity from which these religious impulses arise, the literary and philosophical thinking that drives Donne throughout his career and achieves what we

---

6. The first is Kate Frost, *Holy Delight: Typology, Numerology, and Autobiography in Donne's "Devotions upon Emergent Occasions"* (Princeton, NJ: Princeton University Press, 1990).

7. For this reception history, see, e.g., Deborah Aldrich Larson, *John Donne and Twentieth-Century Criticism* (Cranbury, NJ: Fairleigh Dickinson University Press, 1989); and Dayton Haskin, *John Donne in the Nineteenth Century* (Oxford: Oxford University Press, 2007).

see as a sustained aesthetic pitch in *Devotions*. This means that we read *Devotions* as we might a poem, examining the work's various contexts in the light shed both by its own internal workings of language and style and by its implications in the historically tumultuous intellectual currents of seventeenth-century England.

Our book pivots around the pun in our title. "Physics" denotes the study of the natural universe's fundamental laws, the principles that organize matter and such phenomena as motion, time, and sound. Physics is bound etymologically to "physick" through their common root *physis*, nature, since the study of nature also included the human body, with "physick" designating the sciences of the body, disease, and its treatments.[8] Donne was exposed to physick and medical controversy early in his life through his stepfather, John Syminges, who was a distinguished physician. Syminges was closely involved with the Royal College of Physicians, serving regularly as censor and elector from 1557 on and as president in 1569 and 1572. He married Donne's mother in 1576, and Donne's formative education with a private tutor was thus conducted in a household situated in the shadow of Saint Bartholomew's Hospital and closely aligned with physicians, medical practice, and changing beliefs about physick.[9] The traces of that immersion in medical learning overlap and intersect with Donne's explorations of inherited and new learning in astronomy and natural philosophy. These knowledge systems infuse his lived observation of his own mortally ill body, furnishing the matter for the elaborate metaphorical and conceptual world that he fashions in *Devotions*.

It is here that one reason for the relative lack of scholarly attention to *Devotions* intersects with the coauthorship of our book: the profound difficulty of seeing and understanding *Devotions* as a whole that is embedded in, but not reducible to, its varied, shifting, and overlapping contexts.[10]

8. *OED*, s.v. "physis," n., "classical Latin *physis* nature < ancient Greek φύσις nature." For an excellent study of physick as a medieval activity with cultural and literary implications, see Julie Orlemanski, *Symptomatic Subjects: Bodies, Medicine, and Causation in the Literature of Late Medieval England* (Philadelphia: University of Pennsylvania Press, 2019).

9. Baird W. Whitlock, "John Syminges, a Poet's Step-Father," *Notes and Queries* 199, no. 1 (1954): 421–24; and "The Heredity and Childhood of John Donne," *Notes and Queries* 6, no. 9 (1959): 348–54. Whitlock notes that the records of the college are inconsistent and sometimes missing, and Syminges may well have been president for five years or more. See also Bal. 38–99 and F. N. L. Poynter, "John Donne and William Harvey," *Journal of the History of Medicine and Allied Sciences* 15, no. 3 (1960): 234–35.

10. Frost, *Holy Delight*, sees both this difficulty and the importance of treating *Devotions* as a whole: "Both the *Devotions* and the [Jesuit] Spiritual Exercises are

Our collaborative endeavor stems from our attempt to position *Devotions* within the varied and diverse intellectual contexts that inform Donne's work: poetry, physics, metaphysics, theology, natural philosophy, medicine, anatomy, alchemy, devotional writing, law, rhetoric, logic, and numerous other fields. In a 1608 letter written to Goodyer, Donne claims to suffer from a "Hydroptique immoderate desire of humane learning and languages" (*Let.* 51). This thirst is apparent everywhere in his corpus, but its results are showcased with peculiar intensity in *Devotions*. It is not the case that two people are better equipped to deal with this proliferation of learning, but we have found that our distinct areas of expertise and our different stages of academic career have illuminated what would otherwise have remained opaque or even invisible to either one of us alone.

This book is the product of many years of collaborative reading, research, writing, editing, rewriting, and, most of all, conversation. We began this project in 2009 in a year-long reading course we embarked on at the University of Toronto. Our fascination with Donne's *First* and *Second Anniversaries* inaugurated an ongoing collaboration, which materialized initially in our coauthored essay on Donne's use of analogy and metonymy in his treatment of natural philosophy.[11] We began to envision a subsequent book, a larger exploration of Donne's understanding of the natural world in his writing that would include a chapter on *Devotions*. But the more we read, re-read, and re-re-read *Devotions*, the more we discussed it, puzzled over its meanings, and pored over the criticism dedicated to it, the more we realized we did not understand it well enough to write about it. So, we continued to talk about *Devotions* for over a decade, as our separate careers and lives evolved. Somewhere along the way, we realized that we were not writing a book about Donne's whole body of work. We were instead writing a book about *Devotions* that, through its focus on that one text, brought Donne's larger patterns of thought into view. Our reading of *Devotions* helped us to see that Donne's thought is most visible at the interstices that both separate and connect the text from its various contexts, the represented self from its environing worlds.

We conceive of *Devotions* as a meditative net that gathers Donne's earlier poetic and historical selves into condensed expression. His proximity

---

valid only as total entities; although both have been excerpted frequently, neither can be taken effectively in small doses" (7–8). Frost's book treats *Devotions* as a whole. We do not, however, think that her procedure for apprehending and explaining that whole—numerological investigation—is adequate to what the text demands.

11. Elizabeth D. Harvey and Timothy M. Harrison, "Embodied Resonances: Early Modern Science and Tropologies of Connection in Donne's *Anniversaries*," *ELH* 80 (2013): 981–1008.

to death and the banishment of books from his sick chamber meant that he drew on his own capacious memory. Our method follows Donne's own. We are attentive to echoes of his other writings, and we actively track affinities with his other works. We understand *Devotions* as an epitome of his thought. Moving backward and forward through his writing to understand how his earlier modes of thinking are folded into this later work, we attempt to understand the rhythms, contours, and animating principles of Donne's thought by entering the hermeneutic circle through a single text.[12] Several ideas recur in our analysis (change, style, embodiment, experience) and rather than cordoning them off in discrete sections, we deliberately cultivate repetition—understood here not as a problem, but rather as an opportunity: again but better, again but deeper.[13] Innovation is an example of one such concept to which we return. The thirst for, and fear of, novelty attracted and repelled Donne, and we examine his interest in it from multiple vantage points: the physics of change, style, the new science, language, controversies in physick, new discoveries in anatomy or geography, and so on. Donne embraced change as a central principle of the cosmos and his own mind, and to read his writings is to engage with him in his continually shifting elaborations of ideas and motifs. In *Devotions*, Donne's illness forces a pointed confrontation with the processes of change that were so radically transforming his body and his world. It is for this reason that we read *Devotions* as John Donne's physics.

12. The account of method that best captures our approach to reading *Devotions* is the description of close reading offered by Richard Strier, *Shakespearean Issues: Agency, Skepticism, and Other Puzzles* (Philadelphia: University of Pennsylvania Press, 2023), 1, 2, 251–52n1.

13. This understanding of repetition is indebted to Jonathan Lear, *Imagining the End: Mourning and Ethical Life* (Cambridge, MA: Harvard University Press, 2022).

Threshold Physics

In the darkening November days of 1623, John Donne contracted a severe illness that brought him with precipitous speed to the threshold of death. He was afflicted by high fever, pain, vertigo, rashes or spots, insomnia, and disabling weakness. Donne's symptoms were cognate with typhus or with relapsing fever, and he was probably a victim of the epidemic that overwhelmed London that autumn: some scholars estimate that as many as four hundred people died every week.[1] Donne was acutely aware that he shared his own precarious condition with fellow sufferers. Each time the nearby funeral bells from Saint Gregory's tolled to announce another death from the epidemic, he recognized the ominous import of that resonant sound. It prompted him to consider not only death's immanence in life—the fact that living is synonymous with dying—but also to recognize what Donne called our "engrafting" within a communal human body. We are all, he reminds us, chapters in the same book, waiting to be "translated" by death into another language (*Dev.* 299; 17.1). Just as Donne was surrounded by the clamorous announcements of the epidemic deaths in 1623, so too did the bells ring incessantly as coffins piled high in the churches of Bergamo in March 2020. Our own twenty-first-century COVID-19 pandemic brings Donne's circumstances and the topicality of his thought alive with new insistence.

Although his account of that illness and eventual recovery in *Devotions upon Emergent Occasions* has had a receptive readership ever since its publication in 1624, there is a fresh relevance to his ideas in a world still gripped by the pandemic. As we now know all too well, epidemic disease warps our sense of lived time, alters the sense of human community,

---

1. Derived from various parish records, so far as we know these figures were first calculated in Michael Creighton, *History of Epidemics in Britain* (Cambridge: Cambridge University Press, 1891), 1:78.

infects human contact with a fear of contagion, and disturbs our imagining of futurity. Especially pertinent is Donne's sense that the epidemic intensified the rate at which the world was changing. Donne was acutely aware of the epistemological, scientific, medical, religious, social, and cultural changes reshaping his world. His understanding of himself and his milieux was reflexively alive to historical process as a phenomenon that shapes both the objects it is possible to know and the concepts and categories through which they are known. *Devotions* is permeated with insights about this double-sided contingency that are expressed in his metaphors and the very structure of the text. In *John Donne's Physics*, we explore the complexity and urgency of Donne's thought as it is unfolded in *Devotions*: his meditations on the nature of his ailing body, the physicians who treated him, and the medical learning they possessed; his understanding of shifting astronomical knowledge and what seemed to be an altered cosmos; his intensely personal relationship with God; his muscular, wildly innovative uses of language, rhetoric, and poetic effects; and his imaginings about how his soul was bound to his body. Donne's ideas were articulated in a time of personal and social emergency, and they can furnish for readers today a powerful historical anticipation of our own preoccupations with the sweeping epistemological, cultural, scientific, and social alterations that are transforming our world four hundred years later, changes often accelerated or made newly visible by the pandemic.[2]

Donne emphasizes the importance of these varied changes in his choice of title, *Devotions upon Emergent Occasions*, the phrasing of which he had been toying with even before he fell ill. In a sermon preached at Saint Paul's Cross in 1622, Donne invited his congregation to visualize his scriptural text from the Book of Judges as two hemispheres laid out like a flat map. In the vivid image he evokes, one hemisphere holds all the knowledge of the Ancients, Europe, Asia, and Africa. The other hemisphere contains the new and recent discoveries of America. Each global region also exemplifies textual exposition, Donne suggests, with the first realm carrying the "Literall, and Historicall sense of the words," and the second zone of America, by contrast, encompassing "an emergent, a collaterall, an occasionall sense of them" (*Ser.* 4:181). The adjectives he

2. Our reading of *Devotions* in relation to the pandemic resonates with Edgar Garcia, *Emergency: Reading the* Popol Vuh *in a Time of Crisis* (Chicago: University of Chicago Press, 2022). The enthusiastic reception that Katherine Rundell's new popular biography has received also attests to the affinities readers continue to have for Donne's work and the turbulent time in which he lived: *Super-Infinite: The Transformations of John Donne* (London: Faber, 2022).

uses to describe the American hemisphere—*emergent* and *occasional* in particular—offer insight into the title of the book he would write the following autumn. The occasion of that book was, of course, the crisis of his near-fatal illness. Yet the word *occasion* denotes not only opportunity or precipitating event, but also a second, now obsolete meaning derived from its Latin root, *occidere*, to fall.[3] That archaic meaning designated the setting of the sun, and by extension, the Western geographies that are folded into the concept of the Occident.[4] Donne conjures these personal, bodily, textual, and cartological meanings in "Hymne to God My God, in my sicknesse," a poem most likely written during the same period:

> I joy, that in these straits, I see my West;
> For, though theire currants yeeld returne to none,
> What shall my West hurt me? As West and East
> In all flatt Maps (and I am one) are one,
> So death doth touch the Resurrection. (*Div.* 50; 11–15)[5]

Donne inserts himself into the map in his parenthesis, "In all flatt Maps (and I am one)," positioned at the intersection of East and West. He distills his relationship to his own subjectivity and to God acoustically through the echoes and repetitions of "one," "none," and "Resurrection," as if theology and the erasure of self could be contracted into rhyme. The word *occasion* in the title of the *Devotions* plays on the rich condensation of meanings the poem gathers: a chance afforded by a particular event; the sense of an incipient journey westward toward the setting sun; his own movement from life to death through the gateway of his sickness; and the imperative to fashion a new kind of language and interpretation proportionate to a voyage of discovery.

Donne's use of *emergent* activates a similar set of associations. The title's *emergent* registers the emergency of his life-threatening illness, but in the context of the sermon's imagery it also affiliates his crisis with

3. Debora Shuger offers a more theologically inflected etymological interpretation of Donne's title in "The Title of Donne's *Devotions*," *English Language Notes* 22, no. 4 (1985): 39–40. She understands *emergent* as rising, especially from water, and it is thus tied to a pun on resurrection, of rising from "the waters of death" (40). She also probes the root of *occidere* as falling or death, but she does not tie it, as we do, to its geographical connotations and Donne's tropological activation of Occidental exploration and scientific discovery.

4. *OED*, s.v. "occasion," n.1 and n.2.

5. Bal. 453–54 summarizes the dating controversy, arguing strongly for the 1623 dating.

scientific novelty and the geographical exploration that was so radically recasting global relationships. *Emergent* conveys a sense of that newness, chronological futurity, of transition from one state to another, from one well-known world to an as-yet undiscovered realm beyond life as he had known it. His capacity to probe his physical and mental state as he moved toward apparent death drew on his eclectic knowledge of natural philosophy and new medical and anatomical ideas. His image of the hemispheres becomes a kind of biblical typology, ancient knowledge extended into new discoveries. He uses the metaphoric lens of geographical exploration to map the future of innovation in medical, scientific, and natural philosophical arenas, casting his personal history and the world's accumulated knowledge into the web of an unknown occidental future. Donne's title tilts his gaze, and ours, toward the emergent, collateral, and occasional knowledge systems that were vertiginously, often alarmingly, transforming his understanding of the world around him.

Devotions represents, questions, examines, and ultimately manages the impact of these varied changes in and through its intricate structure. The text is split into twenty-three stations, which move from the onset of illness, through its crisis and resolution, to the fear of relapse. These stations are, in turn, subdivided into three parts, each of which works in different ways. First, the meditations describe and lament an emergent occasion in Donne's illness: his confinement in a sickbed, the arrival of his physicians, the use of cordials, the administration of purgatives, and the application of medicinal pigeons. Second, the expostulations wring meaning from these occasions by wrestling with relevant passages from scripture to see how the spots on Donne's skin, say, are so many signs pointing his attention heavenward. Third, the prayers resolve the crisis presented in the meditation by releasing it into God's hands. Repeated in each of the twenty-three stations, this tripartite arrangement of meditation, expostulation, and prayer provides a firm structure capable of containing the baroque energies of the prose that animate the text—an otherwise labyrinthine efflorescence of metaphoric conversion and comparison that is dizzying in its complexity.

Many previous critics have sought to understand *Devotions* by appealing to the meditative and devotional traditions with which it seems naturally affiliated: Augustinian confession, Protestant devotional writing, the Ignatian meditative tradition.[6] Although such studies shape our

6. These approaches include Louis L. Martz, *The Poetry of Meditation: A Study of English Religious Literature of the Seventeenth Century* (New Haven, CT: Yale University Press, 1954); Joan Webber, "The Prose Styles of Donne's *Devotions upon Emer-*

understanding of *Devotions*, we hold that no tradition can account for the radical generic and linguistic innovations of this text. While we draw on doctrinal, devotional, and homiletic antecedents, our analysis foregrounds a different approach: we concentrate on the dense latticework of images, metaphors, and allusions to the scientific, physical, material, natural philosophic, and medical aspects of Donne's encounters with his environment. Donne continually introjects this world, pulling it deep inside his mind and body. The famous funeral bells are not just external sounds: they are anthropomorphized as a "voice," which then becomes a "*pulse*," echoing within Donne's mind and body, beating in his veins (*Dev.* 302; 17.3).[7] Much like these incorporated bells, Donne gathers the many contingent particulars of his world into the depths of his being. This restless internalization provides a key for unlocking Donne's thought.

He continually marvels at the mind's capacity to create an immensity that "bestrides" the sea and land, indeed the sun and firmament, only to have it shrink into a close prison or a handful of dust. His devotions showcase the variety and complexity of his ambient world as it was refracted through what he describes as the "spectacles" of his thought.[8] "Spectacles" are a recurrent figure for Donne; they signal the variable perspectives that time ("old mens Spectacles"), historical belief (the inherited "spectacles" of Aristotle, Galen, Ptolemy), and personal idiosyncrasy confer (*Ser.* 7:260). Just as the migratory soul in Donne's *Metempsychosis* carries the memories of her previous lives with her, so are Donne's habits and ways of thinking gathered into *Devotions*. We read the text as a culmi-

gent Occasions," *Anglia* 79 (1961): 138–52; Janel Mueller, "The Exegesis of Experience: Dean Donne's 'Devotions upon Emergent Occasions'," *JEGP* 67, no. 1 (1968): 1–19; Jonathan Goldberg, "The Understanding of Sickness in Donne's *Devotions*," *Renaissance Quarterly* 24, no. 4 (1971): 507–17; Anthony Raspa, introduction to *Devotions upon Emergent Occasions* (New York and Oxford: Oxford University Press, 1987): xiii–lvi; Mary Papazian, "The Latin 'Stationes' in John Donne's *Devotions upon Emergent Occasions*," *Modern Philology* 89, no. 2 (1991): 196–210; B. Nelson, "Pathopoeia and the Protestant Form of Donne's *Devotions upon Emergent Occasions*," in *John Donne and the Protestant Reformation: New Perspectives*, ed. M. Papazian (Detroit: Wayne State University Press, 2003): 247–72; and Katrin Ettenhuber, *Donne's Augustine: Renaissance Cultures of Interpretation* (Oxford: Oxford University Press, 2011).

7. Elaine Scarry eloquently describes this moment in *Literature and the Body: Essays on Population and Persons* (Baltimore and London: Johns Hopkins University Press, 1988), 93.

8. Our formulation of the relationship between thought and world chimes with recent work in the history of the passions, especially Benedict S. Robinson, *Passions Fictions from Shakespeare to Richardson: Literature and the Sciences of the Soul and Mind* (Oxford: Oxford University Press, 2021).

nating moment in Donne's writing career, a condensation of his lifelong habits of repetitively grappling with ideas, language, and his place in a changing world. Donne survived his illness and went on to expand his extraordinary corpus of sermons (and perhaps write several great poems), but *Devotions* is composed from the vantage point of imminent death. It gazes backward toward Donne's mortal and poetic achievements even as it anticipates the next world. We do not see a rupture between his early poetic career—preoccupied with court, coterie, and erotic relations— and his later spiritual one, recorded in his sermons and religious writing. Rather, *Devotions* sutures together these apparently diverse selves and modalities of thought.[9] Our approach opens *Devotions* to Donne's earlier poetic idiom and to the recursiveness of his intellectual history, the way his past is gathered into his emerging future through the repetition of images, concepts, forms, and intertexts. We see *Devotions* as a window into his thought, an entrance into an unfolding mind poised at what seems to be the end of dying and the beginning of death.

Recreating Donne's thought is an ambitious enterprise.[10] A question Donne poses about "my *thoughtfulness*" in the central station of *Devotions* reveals why: "was I not made to *thinke*?" (*Dev.* 279; 12.1). Donne saw thinking as the telos of human life, as what the human *I* was "made" to do. It is no surprise, then, that he was remarkably reflexive about his cognitive and creative processes, that his writing is dense with vivid depictions of "Thoughts" as "my mindes creatures" (*Son.* 92; 7) or as "starres of soule" (*Sat.* 84; 99). For Donne, thought is dynamic, and his *Second Anniversarie* (1612) offers an instructive meditation on this active quality of thinking. The *Anniversarie* poems furnish a condensed, evocative lament about epistemological change, the inscrutability of the changing world, and the body's mysteries: how kidney stones enter the "bladders Cave," how blood flows from one ventricle in the heart to the other, how "putrid stuffe" accumulates in the lungs (*Ann.* A2:49; 269–74). These poems depict knowledge as either unfathomable or ossified by tradition. The refrain of the *Second Anniversarie*—"Shee, shee is gone; shee's gone"—reiterates loss as the bereavement of a knowledge understood

9. John Carey influentially argued for the powerful continuities that join Donne's early and later writing in *John Donne: Life, Mind and Art* (London: Faber and Faber, 1981).

10. Recent models for this enterprise include Gordon Teskey, *Spenserian Moments* (Cambridge, MA: Harvard University Press, 2019), 285–309; and Gerard Passannante "On Catastrophic Materialism," *Modern Language Quarterly* 78, no. 4 (2017): 443–64. See also Helen Hackett, *The Elizabethan Mind: Searching for the Self in an Age of Uncertainty* (New Haven, CT: Yale University Press, 2022).

to be a stabilizing force: "when thou knowst this, / What fragmentary rubbidge this world is / Thou knowst, and that is not worth a thought" (*Ann.* A2:43; 81–83). If knowledge is extinguished, however, thought is not. This moment is a hinge in the architecture of the poems that sets *knowledge* in relation to *thought*. Thinking as an active process proffers the consolations these elegies seek to provide. In *The Second Anniversarie*, Donne initiates an anaphoric catalog of imperatives that begin with the verb "Thinke," each one an apostrophe to the soul that anticipates topics treated at greater length in *Devotions*: "Thinke then, my soule, that death is but a Groome" (*Ann.* A2:43; 85). These imperatives implicate the reader in imagined scenes. Donne summons the image of a deathbed on which soul and body lie, "loose and slacke." The self is "parch'd with fevers violence," and as the speaker anticipates death, he hears a ringing church bell. The dying self then imagines "Satans Sergeants" gathering to collect their legacies of sin. Weeping friends surround the bed. Donne's apostrophic summoning of this scene interpellates both soul and reader in the moment of death: "Thinke that they close thine eyes," and "shroud thee up" (*Ann.* A2:43–44; 93–113). Donne lingers long enough to notice the burial, vermiculation, and rotting of the body. When death has "enfranchis'd" the soul, it "freely flies," in a metaphor that recalls the Platonic underpinnings of the sparrow episode in *Metempsychosis*: "Thinke thy shell broke, thinke thy Soule hatch'd but now," as it "Dispatches in a minute" toward heaven (*Ann.* A2:46; 179–88).[11]

This extraordinary passage is notable for two reasons. First, it stages with uncanny accuracy the death scenes that Donne imagines during his 1623 illness in *Devotions* and in the final approach to death in 1631 that Izaak Walton reports in his *Lives*. That Donne visualizes a deathbed scene in the *Second Anniversarie* is not all that unusual, especially in early seventeenth-century London. What is striking for our purposes is a second point: the multiple imperatives to "think," a verb that invokes the mind's active engagement in fabricating and vividly inhabiting these events in anticipation of their occurrence. For Donne, thinking—an activity entangled with imagination, memory, and intellection—replaces the decay of knowledge. It becomes a vitalizing activity that draws on the mind's power to create alternate worlds. For many decades and across many genres (elegy, love lyric, progress poem, prose treatise, sermon),

11. For the sparrow episode, see *Sat.* 33–34; 171–90. For a discussion of the Platonic intertext to the sparrow episode, see Elizabeth D. Harvey, "Winged Desire: The Erotics of Ensoulment," in *Eros, Family, and Community*, ed. Yoav Rinon (Hildesheim, Zurich, New York: Olms Weidmann Verlag, 2018), 67–84.

Donne had used his powers of thought to rehearse for death. Donne was, in T. S. Eliot's words, "Expert beyond experience," a poet who sought to know "the anguish of the marrow / The ague of the skeleton."[12] In *Devotions*, Donne invented a generic form and perfected a style adequate to this task.

Mortal Rehearsals

Shortly before his death, Donne commissioned miniatures of the crucified Christ affixed to an anchor. In his *Life of Dr. John Donne* (1640), Izaak Walton, who knew Donne for many years and became close with him toward the end of his life, describes these figures as "Emblem[s] of hope" (Wal. 63). These tiny sculptures were carved in *"Helitropian"* stones (bloodstone) and set in gold.[13] Donne sent the precious objects to his "dearest friends" to be inserted into seals and rings as memorials of him (Wal. 63). The anchor carries obvious nautical connotations, but also stretches etymologically back to the Greek *anachorein*, to retreat or retire. Donne's "Emblem" might also, then, have designated anchorites, the monastic recluses who enclosed themselves in grave-like cells designed for the contemplation of and preparation for death. Donne invokes the anchorites in Meditation 3 of *Devotions*, which describes his confinement to his sickbed. His newly recumbent posture becomes a proleptic grave, which he contrasts with the space and upright bodily posture a prison or an anchorite's cell might afford: "The *Anchorites* that barqu'd themselves up in hollowe trees, and immur'd themselves in hollow walls . . . could stand, or sit, and enjoy some change of posture. A sicke bed, is a grave; and all that the patient saies there, is but a varying of his owne *Epitaph*" (*Dev.* 239; 3.1). Donne nevertheless uses the occasion of taking to his sickbed to offer an anchoritic meditation on dying, imagining that as he lies in bed he is already in his grave, having become his "owne *Ghost*" (*Dev.* 239; 3.1). He remarks on the "Strange fetters to the feete, strange Manacles to the hands," a paradoxical shackling, given that the sinews and ligaments are looser. He compares the grave he foresees, from which

12. T. S. Eliot, "Whispers of Immortality," in *Collected Poems, 1909–1962* (London: Faber & Faber, 2002), 45; 12–14. We are grateful to Richard Strier for directing us to this poem.

13. Helitropian stone, also known as martyr's stone or bloodstone, takes its name from the spots of red iron oxide in the dark green chalcedony, spots that signified its association with the sun. Christian tradition claimed that the red spots were the crucified Christ's blood that had fallen from his side onto the jasper at the foot of the cross.

he might "speak through the stones" in the voice of those friends who cherish his memory, to his apparent silence here in his bed, where he must "practise [his] lying in the grave, by lying still," and "not practise [his] Resurrection, by rising any more" (Dev. 239; 3.1). Unlike Christ, he is confined to what he names an "inhuman posture" (Dev. 239; 3.1), not rising out of an anchor of hope, but rather immured in the uncertainty of his illness and his very human death.

Donne's sense in Devotions that "lying still" in a sickbed is "practice" for the stillness of the grave is an expression of a career-long consideration of threshold states. In his earlier writing, he repeatedly returned to such scenes as the opening moment of "A Valediction: forbidding Mourning," in which a dying man's "sad friends" watch in order to ascertain when the breath stops and the soul departs (Son. 62; 1–4), or the figure of the executed man who continues to gesticulate after his decapitation in The Second Anniversarie, as if he could communicate even after death (Ann. A2:41; 13–17). Metempsychosis, a poem that charts the lives of a migratory soul as it passes in and out of a succession of vegetable and animal bodies through a spiraling rhythm of life and death, begins with an epistle that situates the author at a porch, a threshold to a building. We might note, as such scholars as Ramie Targoff do, that Donne wanted to investigate the ligature that tethered soul to body.[14] What better way to understand it than in its moment of severance, a time of insight heightened by the recognition that thought itself was about to be snuffed out?

But Donne possessed additional motivations that augmented his wish to apprehend the "subtle knot" that knits body to soul (Son. 61; 64). Although Donne acknowledged death's obliterating power and while he sometimes longed to cast off his body so that he could enter heaven, he also clung to awareness and articulation. Donne did no much fear the altered state that death would inevitably bring, as he resisted losing the capacity to think, to observe and record what the passage beyond his earthy existence might be like. His frequent deferrals of that ultimate severance become structuring principles in poems like "The Exstasie," which celebrates the "dialogue of one" and the seamless melding of souls but which nevertheless chooses the vehicle of the body and articulate cognition as instruments of knowing (Son. 61; 74). In "Goodfriday, 1613. Riding Westward," Donne courts God even as he turns away from him, aware that the face-to-face encounter that he most ardently desires will also entail the eradication of his human, sentient mind: "Who sees Gods face, that is

14. Ramie Targoff, John Donne: Body and Soul (Chicago: University of Chicago Press, 2008).

selfe life, must dye" (*Div.* 31; 17). The question standing behind Donne's various rehearsals for death is this: how can he manage to prolong and stretch the feeling of being poised on the threshold of death, or indeed, of incipient life, for as long as possible so that he can peer into and record these mysteries that lie beyond ordinary human apprehension?

As he grew older, Donne moved from a consideration of threshold states in a more general sense to a concentrated series of mortal rehearsals. "Hymne to God My God, in my sicknesse" crystallizes Donne's concern with threshold states. In the "Hymne," Donne describes how, as he approaches the "Holy roome" where he will be made God's music, he pauses to "tune the Instrument here at the dore" (*Div.* 50; 1–4). The poem hovers at this threshold, animated by a heightened awareness of the impending transition between worlds. Folding future into present, Donne imagines "now before" what he "must doe then," a rehearsal for his passage through the "strait" of fever and death, "*Per fretum febris*" (*Div.* 50; 5–10). In *Devotions*, Donne offers a different kind of rehearsal: a sustained autobiographical account, stretched out over the days he spent at this doorway between life and death. *Devotions* is only proleptic of the ultimate translation from one world to the next because Donne survived his illness. Donne's project in *Devotions* is not to watch as an observer the moment the soul detaches from the body but rather to chart that moment from *inside*. He aims to inhabit death. What does it feel like to die? What is the sensory, emotional, and epistemological impact of death as it happens?

Seven years later, Donne publicly enacted his proximity to death in his last sermon. Delivered just a month before his death, it reaches into the future he envisions for himself and his auditors, toward the actual deathbed scene that Izaak Walton later describes. Like "Hymne to God My God, in My sicknesse" and *Devotions*, *Deaths Duell* is a threshold text, an imaginative representation of what it feels like to die. *Deaths Duell* was delivered in the presence of Charles I at Whitehall in February 1631, and it seemed to stage Donne's fervent hope that he might "die in the Pulpit" (*Let.* 243), alive to record his own extinguishing. To his spectators on that February day, he appeared like a figure of death; many believed that he had prophetically preached his own funeral sermon. According to Walton, Donne's cadaverous, spectral appearance made him look as if he had just risen from his own deathbed (Wal. 74–75). He seemed poised at the edge of death, still anchored in a mortal body that enabled his Janus-faced insight into his own human condition and God's divine perception of it. In a contemporary note "To the Reader," the author claims that although all of Donne's sermons were "*excellent*," this one carries the special authority of its almost posthumous articulation: a dying man's words make "*the deepest impression*," poised as he is at life's verge (*Ser.* 10:229).[15] The subtitle of *Deaths Duell, A Consolation to the Soule, against the dying Life, and living Death of the Body* (*Ser.* 10:229), captures this sensibility, suspended between differently inflected iterations of the identity of living and dying.

Intent on actualizing this identity as fully as possible before he slipped into death, Donne famously posed for his own funeral monument, wrapping himself in his shroud, which was knotted at his head and feet (figure 1). Walton tells us that after the "dying Picture"—the portrait that served as the model for his marble funeral monument—was completed, Donne placed the picture by his bedside so that he could gaze upon it (Wal. 80). He faced the shrouded image of himself throughout the last weeks of his life, as if he could transport himself into the afterworld through its contemplation. Donne's confrontation with his effigy disturbs linear time, for the figure of his future dead self is also a memory of a life he has not yet relinquished, a monument that gazes back at the past from the perspective of the future at which he has not yet arrived.

Walton tells us that Donne prepared for his end in stages: first he took leave of his beloved study, and then he retired to his bed chamber, where he conducted farewells with his closest friends and appointed his servants to complete any unfinished business that concerned him. Having disposed of his earthly responsibilities and connections, he awaited death, confident that he was prepared for his dissolution. Incredibly, he then lay for "fifteen days earnestly expecting his hourly change" (Wal. 81). Despite Donne's rehearsals, the final moment was not within his power. He said, according to Walton, "*I were miserable if I might not dye*" (Wal. 81). His speech did not desert him until the last moment. When it did, he gazed toward heaven where, Walton assures us, Donne saw, just as Saint Stephen had, "*the Son of man standing at the right hand of God his Father*" (Wal. 81). Walton's gaze follows Donne's, and when Donne's own language finally deserts him, Walton supplies a ventriloquized account (mediated by scriptural martyrdom) of what he imagines Donne saw in his final moments.

As Donne's "last breath departed from him, he closed his own eyes; and then disposed his hands and body into such a posture as required

---

15. Targoff, 132, argues that *Devotions* was Donne's way of practicing a "brinksmanship" that was "central to his metaphysics," a way of controlling the uncertainty and terror of sickness and death. See also Evelyn M. Simpson, *A Study of the Prose Works of John Donne* (Oxford: Clarendon, 1924), 278.

1. *Deaths Duell* (1632). Frontispiece engraved by Martin Droeshout.
Photograph: Folger Shakespeare Library, Washington, DC.

not the least alteration by those that came to shroud him" (Wal. 81–82). Walton's phrasing suggests that Donne's "clos[ing] his own eyes" entailed not simply lowering his eyelids. Rather, mimicking the action usually performed after death by those around him, he drew "his own" lids down with his hands. That act, as Donne proleptically imagined it in *Devotions*, entailed "the closing of these bodily Eyes here" in order to open "the *Eyes* of my *Soule*, there" (*Dev.* 285; 13.3). The eyes are a metonym for cognitive awareness. Like a gateway that shuts so that it can open, they are a hinge between worlds and states of being. In closing his own eyes and arranging his limbs, Donne signals his volitional embrace of death, which is perhaps in keeping with the gravitational pull toward death that he explored throughout his life, including the voluntary rush into the "secret house of death" in his posthumously published defense of suicide, *Biathanatos*, a text on a "subject" so "misinterpretable" that Donne penned a letter asking his friend Robert Ker to keep it safe from prying eyes (*Let.* 21). Although he argued in this text for the right to use the "keyes" of life's "prison," and even though his final days suggest an acknowledgment that the voluntary act of dying must, finally, surrender to God's will, his last gestures express his agency, his eagerness to assist in his own dying.[16] The elongated approach to death and Donne's agency in assuming the posture of burial dramatizes a relationship with God that restlessly alternated between Donne's articulate agency and his desire to be with God in the afterlife. He continually longed for and resisted the end of his mortal life, the approach of which he imagined many times prior to the closing of his own eyes on his deathbed.

   Devotions, itself a rehearsal for death, describes in vivid detail the confusion that the approach to death through sickness entails:

> O multiplied misery! we die, and cannot enjoy death, because wee die in this torment of sicknes; we are tormented with sicknes, and cannot stay till the torment come, but pre-apprehensions and presages, prophesy those torments, which induce that *death* before either come; and our *dissolution* is conceived in these *first changes, quickened* in the *sicknes* it selfe, and *born* in *death*, which beares date from these first changes. (*Dev.* 232; 1.1)

Death, in other words, is not a singular event, especially if the gateway is illness; the condition brings with it "torment." The affliction of sickness is contaminated with "pre-apprehensions and presages" that summon death long before it arrives. The "*first changes*" in the body predict dissolution, which is "*quickened*" through sickness and "*born*" in death. Physical signs of disease induce fear and engender thoughts of life's precarity. Death occupies thought long before it arrives as an event. Symptoms are enigmatic, but pain and the uncertainty of outcome accentuate the suf-

---

16. John Donne, *Biathanatos a declaration of that paradoxe or thesis, that selfe-homicide is not so naturally sinne* (London: John Dawson, 1644), 18.

fering. More deeply, death is life's companion in Donne's account, for the conditions are, to place a Donnean word in the past tense, intrinsicated: one is born into mortality and becomes cognizant of death's inevitability, but that coupling is also reversible. Donne imagines dying into eternal life. Both life and death are transitional states.

Deaths Duell is organized around a conventional idea that Donne transfigures in various moments of his career: the analogy between dying and being born. This is a familiar idea with an ancient history, evident in Neolithic burial practices, explored in religious imagery, and encapsulated in William Shakespeare's repeated womb-tomb rhymes, but Donne reimagines it viscerally in innovative ways. His last sermon meditates on the line from Psalm 68:20, "AND UNTO GOD THE LORD BELONG THE ISSUES OF DEATH" (*Ser.* 10:230). *Issues* means in the first instance "exit, release, what flows out of," but its secondary definition is offspring or progeny. Donne is concerned with the *"transmigration* wee shall have out of this world,"* whether violent, peaceful, sudden, or "disordered by sicknes," but his assertion that God will furnish a *"deliverance in death"* (*Ser.* 10:230) provides an accumulation of words and images—*"deliver,"* "passage,"* "pregnantly,"* "issue" (*Ser.* 10:231)—that anticipates the central argument of the sermon: that birth and death are interlaced versions of each other.[17] We enter into life from the death of the womb, Donne asserts, a place of captivity, a *"putrid . . . prison"* in which *"wee have eyes and see not, eares and heare not"* (*Ser.* 10:232). Although Donne's wording is borrowed from Psalm 115:6, it also recalls the mandrake root of *Metempsychosis*, which, having forced itself into the earth to grow, stretches out its arms. Like the fetus, "our life of *vegetation"* (*Ser.* 10:233), the mandrake has "A mouth, but dumbe . . . blinde eyes, deafe eares" (*Sat.* 32; 151). The root both forecasts and echoes the developing fetus in Themech's womb at the end of *Metempsychosis*, where we see the growing human infant as if we had sensory access to and visual knowledge of the womb's interior.

Watching the growing fetus from an impossible interior perspective becomes for Donne a physics of inception. In *Deaths Duell*, he peers into the gestating body and into the transitional process of becoming human. He describes the carceral conditions of the uterus, where "deprived of light," we are "taught *cruelty"* because we are *"fed with blood"* and "fitted for *workes of darkenes"* (*Ser.* 10:232). If the child cannot be born because "there is not *strength to bring [it] forth,"* it dies and commits matricide at the same time. The womb, which should be a *"house of life,"* becomes instead an agent of death (*Ser.* 10:232). Donne knew well from perilous

17. *OED*, s.v. "issue," n.

childbirth, stillbirths, and early childhood mortality in his world at large and in his own family how closely death shadowed new life: six of his children died during his lifetime, two of them stillborn; his wife, Ann, died five days after giving birth to a stillborn child. It was her twelfth pregnancy.[18] Coming into the world and exiting from it are coupled in *Deaths Duell* as straddling states, partaking simultaneously of this world and the next, understood both as external observation and as an inner inhabitation of them. As Donne puts it in *Deaths Duell*, "Wee have a winding sheete in our Mothers wombe, which growes with us from our conception, and wee come into the world, wound up in that *winding-sheet*, for wee come to *seeke a grave*" (*Ser.* 10:233). The amnion or caul that becomes a shroud inevitably evokes Donne's death portrait, an image that materializes his reiterated awareness that human beings are born multiple times. In the dedicatory letter to Prince Charles that prefaces *Devotions* Donne announces that he has undergone three births, one natural when he was born, one supernatural when he entered the ministry, and one "preter-naturall" (*Dev.* 230), when he returned to the world from his almost fatal illness.[19]

Just as birth is multiple and perilous, human beings encounter death in complex ways that amplify and repeat that arduous passage. In *Deaths Duell*, Donne describes the continued disintegration of the body after burial: "this *dissolution* after *dissolution*, this *death* of *corruption* and *putrefaction*, of *vermiculation* and *incineration*, of *dissolution* and *dispersion* in and *from* the grave" (*Ser.* 10:238). These insults to the flesh and bodily integrity are properties of Adam's descendants. Christ was mortal, but he chose his suffering and death as an act of personal will: "There was nothing more free, more voluntary, more spontaneous then the death of *Christ*" (*Ser.* 10:244). Even as he acknowledges Christ's embrace of human nature, Donne examines Christ's exceptionalism around questions of necessity (did God decree the necessity of his dying?) and, most compellingly, his exemption from the postmortem, postburial decay that is the fate of human beings. Christ's immunity to disintegration and putrefaction rests, according to Donne, not on the hypostatic union of human and Divine, not in the embalming process (Joseph's gums and spices), and not in Christ's freedom from original sin, but rather on "the *will* and pleasure of *God*": "*God* had *decreed*" that Christ's body should not undergo corruption (*Ser.* 10:236–37).

18. See Bal. 547–56.

19. Jonquil Bevan, "'*Hebdomada Mortium*': The Structure of Donne's Last Sermon," *RES*, n.s., 45 (1994), 185–203, explores the sermon's elaborate tripartite structure, which is then multiplied into nine Passion meditations.

This is a crucial point. Christ shares with human beings the capacity to suffer and die, but the ignominy of what happens to the human body after death is a special and terrible anticipation. This fundamental difference ushers in other ways in which the nature of being human diverges from what the divine underwent through Christ's incarnation. Donne recognizes that we must all endure a "*posthume* death," a "*death* after *death*," a "death after buriall," a "*dissolution* after *dissolution*" (*Ser.* 10:238). Donne's imagination carries him into a future—emphasized by the relentless repetition of "after"—that is populated by the indignities visited on the fleshly body: dilapidation, ruination, and scattering. Human beings are subject to partially understood principles that are explored and recorded in traditional and emergent natural philosophy and physick or medicine. Donne raids the resources of these exploratory discourses, plucking ideas and terms that help him to make sense of his human nature. He compares the physick of animals—how certain creatures seem to possess inborn knowledge of what plants to eat when they are ill—with the impulses that human beings have toward their own health, the way physick borrows healing properties from the plant and animal worlds by observing characteristics and properties that might serve as antidotes and supplements to human deficiency. Human beings are blessed and cursed with self-awareness, the capacity to dream, the felt subjection to time, the depredations of aging, the vulnerability to sickness. Donne explores his human properties in conversation with God, not because he wishes to teach God what God does not know, but because creating a written account mitigates the possibility of solitude and loneliness so central to the human condition. To be in continual conversation with God as he strives to understand his fear and pain and confusion becomes, for Donne, a way of creating order and meaning out of his threatened dissolution.[20] If God employs various translators—sickness, war, age—to effect the transition from life through death to a "better *language*," Donne wants to study the material, sensible nature of that translation (*Dev.* 299; 17.1).

Physics and Physick

The critical tradition has long recognized that the most distinctive features of *Devotions* are its generic characteristics, its intricate structural elements, and the thick metaphoricity of its language. In this last respect, Donne's text bears a closer resemblance to his own poetry and sermons

---

20. Achsah Guibbory, *Returning to John Donne* (London: Routledge, 2015), 7–15, argues that this work of dialogical sense-making is the very core of *Devotions*.

than to the prose meditations of such contemporaries as Joseph Hall or William Drummond. George Puttenham called style the *"mentis character,"* the mark of the mind, claiming that the "inward conceits [are] the mettle of [the writer's] mind, and his manner of utterance the very warp and woof of his conceits" (Put. 233). This formulation helps explain how Donne's habits of language, particularly his use of metaphor, reveal his thought. Readers have always recognized that Donne's metaphors are a defining feature of his work. Janel Mueller, for instance, speaks of Donne's "prodigious sensitivity to metaphor"; Joan Webber argues that Donne uses metaphor to "connect different levels of being"; Mary Papazian in her interpretation of Donne's Latin headnotes reads *Devotions* as "a sustained prose-poem."[21] Puttenham's definition of metaphor as "an inversion of sense by transport" aptly captures Donne's capacity to transpose ideas through figuration (Put. 238). As Donne said of God's figural language in Expostulation 19, *"figures* flowed into *figures,* and poured themselves out into *farther figures"* in a self-generating metaphorical profusion (*Dev.* 310; 19.2). If these are God's habits of thought, they are also Donne's.

Our readings of *Devotions* draw frequently on his poetic corpus. Poems that treat the nature of the linkage—or separation—between body and soul are especially germane. Two earlier poems prefigure Donne's efforts in *Devotions* in specially focused ways. First, as we have already suggested, *Metempsychosis,* the strange, apparently unfinished poem about the journey of a transmigratory soul and its passage between bodies furnishes fresh, often startling insight into how Donne understood his own soul and its passage between worlds. The poem is a series of inhabitations of different bodies, an imaginative occupation of other forms of being. Second, the *Anniversarie* poems, records of elegiac transition, offer a similar repository of thought about separation. Both works are progresses; they stage a movement *through.* This attention to the act of passing through is in keeping with Donne's general habits of thought, for he is a profoundly prepositional thinker: he continually draws attention to those small, apparently inconsequential words that orchestrate spatial directions, temporal movement, location, and place.

In *Devotions,* the elaborately textured nature of Donne's figural analogies and associative choices are rooted not only in devotional and biblical

---

21. Mueller, "The Exegesis of Experience," 19; Joan Webber, "Prose Styles of John Donne's *Devotions,"* *Anglia* 79 (1961): 149; Mary Papazian (Arshagouni), "The Latin 'Stationes' in John Donne's *Devotions upon Emergent Occassions,"* *Modern Philology* 89, no. 2 (1991): 210.

sources, but specifically in the complex materiality of his epistemologically shifting world, which was, as Donne often remarked, at the threshold of cultural and scientific change. Across his corpus, Donne continually drew on images and metaphors derived from natural history, astronomy, medicine, cartography, botany, anatomy, mineralogy, alchemy, chemistry, and physics, as if he could summon that world into the "little roome" of his thought, making it an "every where" (*Son.* 70; 11). He provides a vivid figure for this impulse to assemble metaphors in *The First Anniversarie*, where he describes men fashioning nets to draw the stars down: "For of Meridians, and Parallels, / Man hath weav'd out a net, and this net throwne / Upon the Heavens, and now they are his owne" (*Ann.* A1:30; 278–80). Latitudes and longitudes, the imaginary lines that encircle the globe, were part of an ancient geographical and cartographic technology. New astronomical discovery and voyages of exploration modified that system of coordinates.[22] In Donne's image, meridians and parallels wove a schematic net that allowed cartographers to map the globe and astronomers to capture, "spur," and "raine" the stars (*Ann.* A1:30; 283), as if they were harnessing and domesticating a horse. Scientific curiosity was in Donne's figuration a way of colonizing the heavens, probing its mysteries for human ends.

In his extended metaphors, Donne mimetically enacts his own poetic techniques and most profound habits of thought. Donne's elaborate conceits condense allusions to the changing fabric of the world he inhabited. His metaphor of snaring the stars registers the new knowledge through which astronomers sought to tame the cosmos, just as the extensive erudition he displays in *Devotions, The Anniversaries, Ignatius His Conclave, Essays in Divinity*, or *Pseudo-Martyr* reveals his own fascination with the epistemological expansions that characterized his historical moment.[23]

22. See Ayesha Ramachandran, *The Worldmakers: Global Imagining in Early Modern Europe* (Chicago: University of Chicago Press, 2015); and Klaus A. Vogel and Alisha Rankin, "Cosmography," in *Cambridge History of Science*, vol. 3, *Early Modern Science*, ed. Katharine Park and Lorraine Daston (Cambridge: Cambridge University Press, 2006): 469–96.

23. The foundation for understanding Donne's keen interest in astronomy and the new philosophy was established early on by such scholars as Charles M. Coffin, *John Donne and the New Philosophy* (New York: Columbia University Press, 1937; rpt. New York: Humanities Press, 1958); Marjorie Hope Nicolson, *The Breaking of the Circle: Studies in the Effect of the "New Science" upon Seventeenth-Century Poetry* (Evanston, IL: Northwestern University Press, 1950); and William Empson, "Donne the Space Man," *Essays on Renaissance Literature*, vol. 1, *Donne and the New Philosophy*, ed. John Haffenden (Cambridge University Press, 1993), 78–128. For some recent considerations, see Mary Thomas Crane, "John Donne and the New Science," *The Pal-*

Donne uses language to pull revolutionary innovations of knowledge into his own phenomenological point of view. In *Devotions*, Donne uses these upheavals in knowledge as the metaphoric fabric for an investigatory understanding of his own illness. It is this movement of internalization, this act of pulling the contingent particulars of the world into the mind, that we name in the title of our book: *John Donne's Physics*.

What do we mean by *physics*? For Donne, physics encompassed a wide range of knowledge that included Aristotelian principles of nature (matter and form; natural change or rest; the four causes; relations between the body and the vegetative and animal souls) and "new philosophy" with all its many challenges to how change, motion, and substance were understood across the natural world, from the tiniest corpuscle to the expanse of the universe itself. But physics was not an isolated discourse; it was enmeshed in a wider network. On the one hand, physics fluidly overlapped with metaphysics, which for Donne included within its purview all that existed beyond natural change, including the nature of the rational soul and its ligature with the body.[24] The sciences of the soul spanned physics and metaphysics. On the other hand, as the pun in our title suggests, physics and physick (medicine) were telescoped through their shared etymological root in the Greek *physis*, nature. The medical *techne* for treating disease, physick designated the art and practice of healing the microcosmic human body. Physics was the natural philosophy that strove to understand the principles that regulated the cosmos or macrocosm as well as all things within that macrocosm, including the microcosm. As Dennis Des Chene notes, Aristotelian physics was the study of "corporeal or natural being"; it was inevitably intertwined with medical and anatomical knowledge.[25] The arenas of medical and natural historical learning stand in relation to one another not as simple analogies or mirrors, but as complex, overlapping, entangled systems of exploration and understanding.

D. C. Allen long ago remarked that Donne's curiosity moved naturally in the direction of medicine and the body. Donne was even more inter-

---

grave *Handbook of Early Modern Literature and Science*, ed. Howard Marchitello and Evelyn Tribble (New York: Palgrave Macmillan, 2017), 95–114; Gerard Passannante, "On Catastrophic Materialism," *Modern Language Quarterly* 78, no. 4 (2017): 443–64; and Howard Marchitello, *The Machine in the Text: Science and Literature in the Age of Shakespeare and Galileo* (Oxford: Oxford University Press, 2011).

24. For this point, see, e.g., Dennis Des Chene, *Physiologia: Natural Philosophy in Late Aristotelian and Cartesian Thought* (Ithaca, NY: Cornell University Press, 1996); and Fernando Vidal, *The Sciences of the Soul: The Early Modern Origins of Psychology*, trans. Saskia Brown (Chicago: University of Chicago Press, 2011).

25. Des Chene, *Physiologia*, 1.

ested in physick, "in the intrinsic agonies of his own viscera," Allen suggested, than he was in the innovations in astronomical knowledge that
have so often preoccupied scholars of his poetry.[26] Donne says in Expostulation 22 that the body "*effigiate*[*s*]" his soul to him; it is the material
portrayal of his innermost self (*Dev.* 326; 22.2). Seen as a whole, *Devotions*
might be understood as an effigiation in this sense: the text uses Donne's
sick body to make manifest the operations of his soul. Though he might
ponder the "*occasion*" or cause of his illness, neither a Hippocrates nor a
Galen could reveal the root of disease because that root lies in the "*union*
of the *body* and *soule*" (*Dev.* 325; 22.2). The illness that occasioned *Devotions* occupied an in-between space: neither the realm of the soul nor
that of the physical body; neither the earthly nor the heavenly; neither
Donne's limited human understanding nor God's transcendent knowing.
Devotions is a record of that restless dialogue at the threshold, a colloquy
that employs the languages of metaphysics, physics, and physick to elaborate and enlarge its apprehensions of human nature.

Our emphasis is less on tracing Donne's putative beliefs about the
new philosophy in their historical contexts—what he knew about Ty-
cho Brahe, Johannes Kepler, Galileo Galilei; whether he believed in
the Paracelsian challenges to Galenic medicine—and more about how
he fabricates textual structures and tropes and figures from these allusions. Whereas old and new historicisms typically prioritize the referen-
tial contexts of a literary work and New Critical or more recent formalist
approaches characteristically eschew the specificity of biographical and
historical references, we are interested in the passionate dialogue between the material and metaphoric, the material nature of language and
its figurative flights, the mechanisms and motivations for transmutation
from one register into the other. We have modeled our critical procedures
on Donne's own verbal practices, attempting to make methodologically
reflexive a way of understanding and using language that Donne illuminates in *Devotions*:

> *My God*, my *God*, Thou art a *direct God*, may I not say, a *literall God*, a *God*
> that wouldst bee understood *literally*, and according to the *plaine sense* of
> all that thou saiest? But thou art also . . . a *figurative*, a *metaphoricall God*
> too: A *God* in whose words there is such a height of *figures*, such *voyages*,
> such *peregrinations* to fetch remote and precious *metaphors*, such *exten-
> tions*, such *spreadings*, such *Curtaines* of *Allegories*, such *third Heavens* of

26. D. C. Allen, "John Donne's Knowledge of Renaissance Medicine," *JEGP* 42,
no. 3 (1943): 322.

Hyperboles, so *harmonious eloquutions,* so *retired* and so *reserved expressions,* so *commanding perswasions,* so *perswading commandements,* such *sinewes* even in thy *milke,* and such *things* in thy *words,* as all *prophane Authors* seeme of the seed of the *Serpent,* that *creepes;* thou art the *dove,* that flies. (*Dev.* 309–10; 19.2)

This apostrophe to God comes in an expostulation. The expostulations are crowded with biblical citation (most frequently to the Hebrew Bible, especially the Psalms), setting scriptural language and Donne's debates with God as a bridge between each meditation and prayer. Janel Mueller saw the expostulations as the "crux of the Devotions," for they create a passionate dialogue with God that places human and divine perspectives in conversation.[27] Like the double-sided "Rols" of *The Second Anniversarie* (*Ann.* A2:55; 504), the expostulations are amphibious in their contentious desire to reconcile human, mortal perspectives with God's language. In this passage, Donne borrows God's language as a way of investigating how human and divine nature are intertwined, how literal and figurative language are interlaced.

Donne's distinction between the literal and the figurative rests on Augustine's *De Doctrina Christiana.* Whereas Augustine worked tirelessly to winnow literal from figurative expression, however, Donne repeatedly confounds it. It is as if he is putting into practice Augustine's adages about obscurity: figurative language produces better insight because it requires effort to understand it. The language of the prophets is obscure because of their figurative language, and their use of metaphor enhances their obscurity, which in turn deepens the reader's pleasure when they understand the meaning.[28] Yet Donne never wanted to discard literal underpinnings. His figurative flight stays rooted in a bodily and material nature that seems to supply an endlessly renewed source for metaphoric innovation and conceptual surprise.

In Expostulation 19, Donne first defines God's language as literal, a conformity with the letter, a kind of *"plaine sense."* But language and letters refuse to remain *"plaine"* for Donne: their materiality—as letters, words, punctuation, translation, grammar, pages, books—is transmuted into metaphor throughout *Devotions.* God puts *"things"* in his words, and even his nurturing is metaphorized in a catachrestical figure: "the *sinewes*" of "thy *milke*" (*Dev.* 310; 19.2). Donne's own description of God's

---

27. Mueller, "The Exegesis of Experience," 4.

28. Augustine, *De Doctrina Christiana,* ed. and trans. R. P. H. Green (Oxford: Clarendon Press, 1995), 65, 217.

metaphorical language mimetically reproduces that language, moving quickly into a swelling, increasingly complex praise for its figural and metaphorical aspects. God's "height of *figures,*" "*voyages,*" and "*peregrinations* to fetch remote and precious *metaphors*" (*Dev.* 309; 19.2) all mirror the propensities of Donne's language and methods in this passage and throughout *Devotions*. He continually juxtaposes the literal and material with the metaphorical and figural, creating a dialogue between them that is as vigorous as his debates with God. Donne is, in other words, situated between worlds, secured in his humanity through the insistent physicality of his afflicted body and leaning toward the "straight know[ing] all" of divine understanding in *The Second Anniversarie* (*Ann.* A2:49; 299). If "heaven keepes soules" and the "grave keeps bodies," "Verse hath a middle nature," as he says in *The First Anniversarie* (*Ann.* A1:35; 473–74). Verse mediates between registers, a capacity Donne appropriates in his elaborate devotional prose.

In *Devotions*, Donne uses the middle nature of figural language in two intersecting ways. First, he gathers "remote and precious metaphors" from the changing epistemologies of his seventeenth-century world and uses them to understand the questions about his own human materiality with which he grappled on what might have been his deathbed. What is the nature of the bond between the body and the soul? How do individual human beings participate in communities? How does the human body correspond to the body of the world? Are the principles that govern the sublunar realm and the cosmos the same as the laws that regulate the body? Second, he uses his conversations with God to weave together Aristotelian physics, the new philosophy that sought to revise that inherited knowledge, and the Christian theological tradition.[29] The physicians who visit Donne on his sickbed, including Théodore de Mayerne (James I's personal physician), treated Donne with such remedies as purgatives and a cordial derived from vipers' flesh. Donne writes about the material effects of these treatments even as they take on a metaphorical aspect. He stages an implicit colloquy between the efficacy of his worldly physicians and the remedies that God as divine physician can provide. The structural and linguistic complexity of *Devotions* emerges from the confluence of literal, mate-

29. See Daniel Garber, "Physics and Foundations" for a discussion of the Aristotelian inheritance. *Cambridge History of Science*, vol. 3, *Early Modern Science*, ed. Katharine Park and Lorraine Daston (Cambridge: Cambridge University Press, 2006), 19–69.

rial, figural, and metaphorical language, from the constant interplay between the macrocosmic perspectives and the little world of Donne's body, and from the passionate conversations between Donne's inner self and the God he addresses.

In this book, we follow this movement across six chapters, each of which treats a feature of Donne's *Devotions* in relation to a set of overlapping contexts, ranging from the manifold ways that early modern writers understood genre, textual structure, style, poetry, and rhetoric; through various modes of autobiographical writing, medical case histories, and practices in physick; to the most technical concepts and arguments from physick, physics, metaphysics, and theology, among other discourses. Beginning in chapter 1 with an examination of the insistently first-person voice of *Devotions* in relation to earlier autobiographical experiments, Montaigne in particular, we then turn in chapter 2 to the precondition of that voice: the dynamic between change and time and the instant, as filtered from the technical abstractions of physics into Donne's devotional prose. By considering the structure and genre of *Devotions*, with particular attention to the "progress," in chapter 3 we show how the text attempts to manage the change it represents, only for that work of containment to be undercut by the historicity of the technical diction that Donne makes a hallmark of his style, as we discuss in chapter 4. Throughout the book we treat the intersections of physics, metaphysics, and physick, but in the final two chapters we focus on how Donne transforms his relationship with his three physicians and their learned practices of healing (chapter 5) into a sophisticated conceptual vocabulary for grasping the relationship between body and soul (chapter 6). In the opening chapters we focus on the horizontal axis of *Devotions*, the temporal narrative that unspools from station to station. As the book progresses, we open our analysis to the vertical axis of the book (the dynamic between meditation, expostulation, and prayer) and its reflexive axis (how it folds back in on itself to measure the nature of the change in attitude and disposition it fosters).

Composition

We end this introduction by returning to where our preface began, with the unusual composition process that brought *Devotions* into the world. In a letter describing this process, Donne wrote that he was "barred" from his ordinary practice of reading during his illness. The meditations that he composed on approximately twenty "sheetes" (*Let.* 249) during and shortly after his illness were "exercises" that formed part of his "Physick."[30] Writing and physick were thus linked through the physicality of his suffering. If the backbone of *Devotions* is Donne's falling ill, the development of his symptoms, the interventions of his physicians and his fragile recovery, then the elements of his writing—typography, punctuation, paragraphs, headings, and the importation of Latin phases and scriptural citation, among others—take on a significatory role that imbricates them with his body. To read *Devotions* is to be pulled into a practice of early modern physick that illuminates Donne's mind and body and the world in which he lived. In a letter Donne wrote that accompanied a presentation copy of *Devotions*, he uses the idea of parenthesis as a metaphor for his illness: life "is like a Sentence," he wrote. Lives are shaped in much the same way that literary styles define the writer. Some writers use "open Parentheses, Sentences within Sentences." Typical of Donne's mind, he identifies not with the writer and his style but with the sentence itself: "I am in such a parenthesis now (in a convalescence) when I thought my self verie near my period. God brought me into a low valley, and from thence shewed me high Jerusalem, upon so high a hill, as he thought fit to bid me stay, and gather more breath. This I do, by meditating, by expostulating, by praying."[31] These activities, which form the tripartite structure of each station in *Devotions*, become the exercise of his physick, the record of his sojourn within the parenthesis of his illness, convalescence, and mortal life.

30. Tobie Matthews, ed., *A Collection of Letters, Made by Sr Tobie Mathews Kt.* (London, 1660), 302–3. Mary Ann Lund cites this letter and Donne's composition of *Devotions* as part of his recovery in "Donne's Convalescence," *Renaissance Studies* 31, no. 4 (2016): 532–48.

31. Matthews, *A Collection of Letters*, 302–3.

1

Donne's Experience

Devotions upon Emergent Occasions and Severall Steps in my Sicknes presents a first-person narrative focused on what it is like to live through a debilitating illness. Donne's examination of *"my Sicknes"* (*Dev.* 229) emphasizes the *"propriety"*—that is, the proprietorship—signaled by the first-person possessive (*Dev.* 328; 23.1). Consider this passage from Station 2, *"The strength, and the function of the Senses, and other faculties change and faile"* (*Dev.* 235; 2.1):

> In the same instant that I feele the first attempt of the disease, I feele the victory; In the twinckling of an eye, I can scarce see; instantly the tast is insipid, and fatuous; instantly the appetite is dull and desirelesse; instantly the knees are sinking and strengthlesse; and in an instant, sleepe, which is the picture, the copy of death, is taken away, that the *Originall, Death* it selfe, may succeed, and that so I might have death to the life. (*Dev.* 236; 2.1)

The sentence's compounding clauses, the repetition of the adverb *instantly*, and the accumulating symptoms combine to pull readers into the first-person feel of illness's onset. Vision fades. Taste recedes. The promptings of appetite and desire disappear. The ability to actualize bodily movements, mobility in space, and even sleep is reduced to almost nothing. No longer a distant possibility, death is terrifyingly close.

Although the meditations, expostulations, and prayers of each station invoke explicit or invisible interlocutors, *Devotions* is focalized through Donne's subjective impressions. It is a critical commonplace to refer to this feature of the text as expressing first-person "experience" or as being dedicated to "the experience of illness."[1] Such claims can often imply

---

1. Donne's *experience* is sometimes understood as deriving from a tradition of Protestant meditation practices that took "former experiences" as a basis for con-

that when a given critic has said that *Devotions* represents the "experience of illness," they have revealed what the text is *about*. Although such claims are true in a limited way, they fail to capture what is so radical about *Devotions*. This is because *Devotions* demands nothing less than a rethinking of *experience* as a concept. What did Donne mean by *experience*? What do we mean when we use the term? Neither of these questions is easy to answer.[2] Reading *Devotions* raises with startling insistence the question of what experience might be, and it does so because Donne himself was thinking through and experimenting with this question.

It is well known that the terms *experience* and *experiment* are lexically intertwined through their shared roots in the Latin *experientia* and the Greek *empeiria*. Written in a moment when both terms were undergoing profound changes, *Devotions* examines the power of the *experiment* and the *experimental*.[3] In early seventeenth-century Europe, this power enabled one to test the limits and the truth of phenomena by forcing an encounter with the world, the self, the divine.[4] Donne would have seen

---

templation. See, e.g., Barbara Kiefer Lewalski, *Protestant Poetics and the Seventeenth-Century Religious Lyric* (Princeton, NJ: Princeton University Press, 1979), 158–70. Lewalski follows Mueller, "The Exegesis of Experience." Both were responding to Louis Martz, *Poetry of Meditation: A Study in English Religious Literature of the Seventeenth Century* (New Haven, CT: Yale University Press, 1976); and Helen C. White, *Tudor Books of Private Devotion* (Madison: University of Wisconsin Press, 1951). For the "experience of illness," see, e.g., Gary Kuchar, "Embodiment and Representation in John Donne's *Devotions upon Emergent Occasions*," *Prose Studies* 24, no. 2 (2001): 21; Targoff, *John Donne*, 132; Mary Ann Lund, "Experiencing Pain in John Donne's *Devotions upon Emergent Occasions (1624)*," in *The Sense of Suffering: Constructions of Physical Pain in Early Modern Culture*, ed. Jan Frans van Dijkhuizen (Leiden: Brill, 2009), 333, 339, 340, 343; Guibbory, *Returning to John Donne*, 8; Tabak, "'O Multiplied Misery!': The Disordered Medical Narrative of John Donne's *Devotions*," *JMEMS* 46, no. 1 (2016): 167–68; and Lund, "Donne's Convalescence," 538, 540, 542, 547, 548.

2. The concept is notoriously opaque. Michael Oakeshott, *Experience and Its Modes* (Cambridge: Cambridge University Press, 1933), 9, claims, "Of all the words in the philosophic vocabulary, experience is the most difficult to manage." We are grateful to Ethan Guagliardo for this reference. Oakeshott's view is shared by Hans Georg Gadamer, *Truth and Method*, trans. Joel Weinsheimer and Donald G. Marshall (London: Continuum, 1975), 341, who argues that *experience* is "one of the most obscure [concepts] that we have." For a history of modern attempts to make sense of *experience*, see Martin Jay, *Songs of Experience: Modern American and European Variations on a Universal Theme* (Berkeley: University of California Press, 2005).

3. For this semantic overlap, see, e.g., Charles B. Schmitt, "Experience and Experiment: A Comparison of Zabarella's View with Galileo's in *De motu*," *Studies in the Renaissance* 16 (1969): 80–138.

4. See, e.g., Pamela H. Smith, *The Body of the Artisan: Art and Experience in the Scientific Revolution* (Chicago: University of Chicago Press, 2004).

the power of this experimental mode in the natural philosophical innovations embodied by such figures as Francis Bacon and Galileo Galilei
and in the religious innovations evident in the period's Puritan spiritual
autobiography and experimental theology.[5] We argue that in *Devotions*
he uses the emergent occasions of his own illness as an opportunity to
transform his body into a laboratory, a site of experimentation. The aim
of this experimentation is to encounter the form, contours, limits, and
truth of what we now might call *experience*. In 1624, the English *experience*
could refer to hard-won knowledge or know-how accumulated over time,
describe an encounter with the world sufficient to disprove the claims of
reason or inherited authority, or invoke an experiment. But it was not yet
synonymous with consciousness, in the sense nowadays presupposed by
many thinkers and writers—even if *experience* was in the early stages of
acquiring that semantic force.[6] In *Devotions*, Donne experiments with
this emergent concept. This is not to say that Donne represents consciousness in the later seventeenth-century sense of the term. As we will
see, Donne's use of *experience* and his representation of the phenomenally
available states indexed by that term are revelatory precisely because of
their experimental quality, because of the way that Donne plays with a
concept the meaning of which was unstable, productively destabilized.

German uses two words to cover the semantic territory that English
encompasses with *experience*: *Erfahrung* is experience in the sense of
knowledge or skill gathered over time, and *Erlebnis* is experience in the

5. For the philosophical senses of *experience* and *experiment*, see, e.g., Peter Dear,
Discipline and Experience: The Mathematical Way in the Scientific Revolution (Chicago: University of Chicago Press, 1995); and Marco Sgarbi, *The Aristotelian Tradition and the Rise of British Empiricism: Logic and Epistemology in the British Isles
(1570–1689)* (Dordrecht: Springer, 2013). For the religious senses of these terms, see,
e.g., Owen C. Watkins, *The Puritan Experience* (London: Routledge, 1972); and Peter
Harrison, "Experimental Religion and Experimental Science in Early Modern England," *Intellectual History Review* 21 (2011): 413–33.

6. Galen Strawson, *The Subject of Experience* (Oxford: Oxford University Press,
2017), 3, sees *experience* and *consciousness* as "interchangeable." Here is Alva Noë, *Out
of Our Heads: Why You Are Not Your Brain and Other Lessons from the Biology of
Consciousness* (New York: Hill and Wang, 2009), 8: "I use the term 'consciousness'
to mean, roughly, experience. And I think of experience, broadly, as encompassing
thinking, feeling, and the fact that a world 'shows up' for us in perception." Here is
Christof Koch, *The Feeling of Life Itself: Why Consciousness Is Widespread but Can't
Be Computed* (Cambridge, MA: MIT Press, 2019), 1: "Consciousness is experience.
That's it. Consciousness is any experience." This alignment was achieved in the late
seventeenth century. See Timothy M. Harrison, *Coming To: Consciousness and Natality in Early Modern England* (Chicago: University of Chicago Press, 2020).

sense of a lived encounter, living through a given situation in the present. The former is *diachronically synthetic*, involving the acquisition of experience over time, the process of coming to be experienced. The latter is *synchronically synthetic*, involving the coordination of the aspects of consciousness operative at a given time. Donne plays with the possibilities inherent in both forms of experiential synthesis, tarrying with these possibilities only to reject them so that he can reveal the meaning of "*our Humane Condition*" (*Dev.* 229).

In this chapter, we unfold a conceptual history of experience to explain why Donne wrote a series of meditative devotions organized around a narrative written in the first-person perspective. This was not a choice Donne needed to make. He could have written meditations on the meanings of human createdness and mortality. But *Devotions* instead presents a first-person account of "*my Sicknes*," full of idiosyncratic detail, rich in phenomenal particularity, based on singular events from biographical time. Why did Donne write *Devotions* in this way? Any answer to this question must address how Donne's representations of the first-person perspective are tied up with both human nature and the nature of the world. Every human being is what Donne calls a "peece of the *world*" (*Dev.* 319; 21.1), a part of a larger whole. Although Donne represents events from his own life, *Devotions* is not straightforwardly autobiographical.[7] In addition to the devotional, spiritual, political, and aesthetic work performed by the text, *Devotions* participates in what Dennis Des Chene calls the early modern "philosophy of nature," a discursive "clearing house in which physics, metaphysics, and theology could meet and negotiate their claims."[8] *Devotions* is a first-personal exploration of the philosophy of nature.

To illuminate these claims, in this chapter we compare these features of Donne's *Devotions* with Michel de Montaigne's *Essais* (1580, 1588, 1592), a book that presents a similar view of *experience* by engaging in the experiment of the *essai*. A discursive form initiated by Montaigne, *essai* is best translated as an attempt or even as a taste, a tentative and intelligently probing encounter with some feature of the self and the world. Less a claim about literary influence than a recognition of the traditions shared by both writers, our comparative analysis of Donne and Montaigne explores how, in different ways, both writers experimented

---

7. For the traditions of autobiography in which Donne might be participating, see Frost, *Holy Delight*, 15–38.

8. Dennis Des Chene, *Physiologia: Natural Philosophy in Late Aristotelian and Cartesian Thought* (Ithaca, NY: Cornell University Press, 1996), 3.

with themselves so that they might understand the world. Their parallel experimentation displays a shared desire for the continued questioning of received knowledge, a skeptical orientation toward epistemic frameworks, disparate belief systems, and practices. Just as Donne's treatment of experience resonates with that of Montaigne, so his development of a first-person philosophy of nature is illuminated by Montaigne's *Essais*, a text that examines "l'humaine condition" as well as the surrounding world through the lens of the self. "I study myself more than any other subject," Montaigne claims: "That is my metaphysics, that is my physics" (Mon. 821; 1119). Donne similarly studied physics, metaphysics, and theology by investigating himself. Donne's anatomization of his sickness opens onto a philosophy of nature funneled through the self.

Donne's first-person investigation of nature unsettles the assumed regularities of physics. As Aristotle claims in the *Physics*, nature or *physis* is a "principle or cause of being moved and of being at rest in that to which it belongs primarily, in virtue of itself and not accidentally" (Ar. 1:329; 192b). Unless subject to an accidental occurrence, something natural will be moved and be at rest "in virtue" of something internal to it. For instance, barring something unexpected, a lynx will be born with four limbs, grow up, have some cubs, and then die.[9] Such patterns of movement and rest do not, as Aristotle puts it, "always come to pass in the same way"; they are not necessary. Instead, they "come to pass . . . for the most part," in regular ways (Ar. 1:335; 196b). As he says in *Posterior Analytics*, "Some things come about universally," while others occur "not always, but for the most part"—for instance, "not every male man has hair on his chin, but for the most part they do" (Ar. 1:158–59; 96a). The various species of natural things all change and rest in ways that are, for the most part, predictable. Insofar as a human being is a "peece of the world" (*Dev.* 319; 21.1), a part of nature, this predictability is key to human life. If one brackets ethics and politics (which change in unpredictable ways) and instead sees human beings as belonging to nature, then they become predictable: they are born, they live, they eat, they drink, they sleep, they die.[10] It is this aspect of human species-being that Donne captures in his invocation of the "*Humane Condition*" on the title page of *Devotions* (*Dev.* 229).

9. The lynx example flags our indebtedness to Michael Thompson's thinking with Aristotle, *Life and Action: Elementary Structures of Practice and Practical Thought* (Cambridge, MA: Harvard University Press, 2012).

10. On how kinds of knowledge one can have of ethics and politics differs from the kinds of regularity or certainty available to other topics, see Ar. 2:1735–36; 1098a–b.

Yet whereas the predictable regularity of Donne's participation in the human species is the horizon of *Devotions*, it is not the text's substance. By inhabiting the first-person perspective, Donne showcases how the life of the individual is thoroughly unpredictable. Although all the regularities of human species-being occur, how they take place can be surprising. All human beings die. For the most part, most human beings fall ill. But how and when these events happen is, in terms of the individual, completely unexpected: a given individual might fall ill now in any number of ways, might die now, this moment, in ways that truly surprise.[11] When understood not as a measure of natural regularities (the movements, say, of the sun or stars) but rather as how the events of an individual life unfold, time becomes the medium through which unexpected, unpredictable change becomes suddenly manifest: "In the same instant that I feele the first attempt of the disease, I feele the victory" (*Dev.* 236; 2.1). Donne's first-person physics aims to illuminate what it is like to be an individual human being, existing between birth and death, uncertain how or when the changes to which we are subject will occur.

A Piece of the World

In Station 4, Donne claims that it is "too little to call *Man* a *little world*; Except *God*, man is a *diminutive* to nothing" (*Dev.* 242; 4.1). Dismantling conventional depictions of the microcosm, Donne reshapes an early modern commonplace. "Man consistes of more pieces, more parts, than the world; than the world doth, nay than the world is": the human creature exceeds the world, for if the human body were "extended, and stretched out"—its veins rivers, its muscles hills, its bones quarries—then it would dwarf the world and "the *aire* would be too little for this *Orbe* of Man to move in" (*Dev.* 242; 4.1). Spread out so that its inner extension expands past planetary proportions, this gigantic, anatomized body is more com-

---

11. Jonathan Lear, *Wisdom Won from Illness: Essays in Philosophy and Psychoanalysis* (Cambridge, MA: Harvard University Press, 2017), 11–12, writes: "For living organisms, Aristotle thought that what they are shows up in conditions of health. From this perspective, wisdom is essentially about health and well-being. Pathology is a falling away from health, and there are indefinitely many ways in which that might happen. Such multiplicity and falling short is not the stuff of wisdom—at least, so Aristotle thought." By contrast, for Lear, "wisdom can be won from illness—and not simply in the sense that pathology lends insight into health, but in that it gives us direct and immediate insight into who and what we are." *Devotions* is a manifestation of this argument.

plex than the world, for human existence contains "many pieces, of which the whole world hath no representation" (*Dev.* 243; 4.1).

This passage is characteristic of *Devotions*, a text that pulsates, following a logic of dilation and contraction.[12] Alone, aging, ill, trapped in a sickbed, and radically diminished, Donne's shrunken human body suddenly expands outward so that it exceeds the world of which it is a "peece." This rapid inversion of microcosm and macrocosm is facilitated by an anatomical impulse.[13] If one pays proper attention to the human body's folds and compressed energies, then one can see how the immensity of the world is in fact distributed throughout long-suffering flesh. It is as if Donne uses early modernity's new optical technologies to explore his own condition: the lens-powered enlargement of veins and sinews renders the human body massive.[14] Zooming in to examine a given part, the anatomical imagination alters the whole to which that part belongs. But Donne's self-anatomization is not carried out on a dead body, like those examined by Andreas Vesalius or Helkiah Crooke. Instead, Donne treats a dying body, a mortal body living through what, in the *Confessiones*, Augustine calls a "dying life" (*vitam mortalem*) or a "living death" (*mortem vitalem*) (Aug. 6; 1.6.7)—a phrasing that Donne picks up on in the subtitle for his final sermon, *Deaths Duell*, which discusses the *Dying Life, and Living Death of the Body*.[15] *Devotions* provides an anatomy of this mortal existence in which living is isomorphic with dying. Performing dilations and contractions—from the macro to the micro and then back

12. In Harvey and Harrison, "Embodied Resonances," we argued that this coupling of expansion and contraction is one of Donne's most characteristic ways of thinking.

13. Our argument here resonates with Gerard Passannante, *Catastrophizing Catastrophizing: Materialism and the Making of Disaster* (Chicago: University of Chicago Press, 2019), 1–26 and 79–113, which examines how materialist analogy falls back into itself and also makes the point that Donne's materialism should be understood most importantly as a style of thought.

14. The telescopic discoveries recorded by Galileo Galilei in the *Sidereus Nuncius* (1610) were in Donne's hands the same year they were published, while the microscopic lenses of Cornelius Drebbel were generating amazement in London in the early 1620s. For Donne's knowledge and use of Galileo, see Piers Brown, "Donne and the *Sidereus Nuncius*: Astronomy, Method and Metaphor in 1611," PhD diss. (University of Toronto, 2009). For Drebbel, see Edward G. Ruestow, *The Microscope in the Dutch Republic: The Shaping of Discovery* (Cambridge: Cambridge University Press, 2004), 6–9. Our claims here are inspired by Joanna Picciotto's arguments about the relationship between literary texts and optical technologies in *Labors of Innocence* (Cambridge, MA: Harvard University Press, 2007).

15. We thank Ryan Campagna for the connection between Donne's subtitle and Augustine.

again—*Devotions* formally mimics the pulse of the living body. As Donne makes clear, the pulse in question is both bodily ("one hand askes the other by the pulse . . . how we do" [*Dev.* 232; 1.2]) and spiritual (God "hast imprinted a *pulse* in our *Soule*" [*Dev.* 234; 1.1]). Donne uses the events of sickness to manifest the various pulsating, moving, metabolizing changes soul and body undergo together in a human being's dying life.

Writing about the recently deceased Elizabeth Drury in the *Second Anniversarie*, Donne claims: "her pure and eloquent blood / Spoke in her cheekes, and so distinctly wrought, / That one might almost say, her bodie thought" (*Ann.* A1:48; 244–46). Donne does not hold that the body itself thinks; corpses do not think. But during human life, the body and the soul are so closely intertwined that it is as if the "bodie thought." This is why Donne figures the array of "representation[s]" that generate first-person mental life as among the "peece[s]" human beings contain such that they exceed the world—the "peece[s]" that, when gathered, conspire to make "*Man*" the "*great world.*" "Inlarge this Meditation upon this *great world, Man,* so farr, as to consider the immensity of the creatures this world produces," Donne commands his readers as he transitions to human thought:

> our *creatures* are our *thoughts*; *creatures* that are born *Gyants*; that reach from *East* to *West*, from *earth* to *Heaven*; that doe not onely bestride all the *Sea*, and *Land*, but span the *Sunn* and *Firmament* at once; My thoughts reach all, comprehend all. Inexplicable mistery; I their *Creator* am in a close prison, in a sicke bed, any where, and any one of my *Creatures*, my *thoughts*, is with the *Sunne*, and beyond the *Sunne*, overtakes the *Sunne*, and overgoes the *Sunne* in one pace, one steppe, every where. (*Dev.* 243; 4.1)

The microcosm exceeds the macrocosm not only because the human body could be extended past the circumference of the physical world but also because the human mind produces thoughts that leap past the world, striving to encompass "all" and be "every where." Insofar as thought belongs to human beings, it is "too little to call *Man* a *little World.*"

"Inexplicable mistery": this phrase positions Donne's rethinking of microcosm and macrocosm as a response to an ancient tradition that sees the self as all but impossible to understand. Here we see the telltale trace of Augustine's *Confessiones*, a text that left an indelible mark on Donne.[16]

---

16. For Donne and the *Confessiones*, see Ettenhuber, *Donne's Augustine*. For a more general reception history of the *Confessiones*, see, e.g., Pierre Courcelle, *Les Confessions de Saint Augustin dans la tradition littéraire* (Paris: Institut d'Etudes Augustiniennes,

Donne did not agree with all that Augustine said; he pushed back strenu-
ously on Augustine's privileging of soul or mind over body. By resisting
this aspect of Augustinian thought, Donne adopted a position analogous to that of Montaigne. Although it seems likely that Montaigne read
the *Confessiones* and that Donne read the *Essais*, there is no absolutely
clinching philological evidence tying Montaigne to Augustine or Donne
to Montaigne.[17] But both Donne and Montaigne were part of a larger
Augustinian tradition of self-examination, which included such thinkers
as Francesco Petrarca. Although we cannot demonstrate that the *Essais*
exerted a direct influence on Donne, Montaigne nevertheless provides an
illuminating model: he reworked aspects of the Augustinian tradition in a
manner analogous to Donne.

Augustine was perhaps the most influential theorist of Donne's "Inexplicable mistery." In the *Confessiones*, Augustine represents the human
condition as a puzzle: "I had become to myself a vast problem [*factus
eram ipse mihi magna quaestio*]" (Aug. 57; 4.4.9). The enigmas of his nature are an ongoing issue. Speaking of his memory, which is so extensive that it (somehow) contains even what he has forgotten, Augustine
writes: "This power of memory is great [*magna*], very great, my God. It is
a vast and infinite profundity. Who has plumbed its bottom? This power
is that of my mind and is a natural endowment, but I myself cannot grasp
the totality of what I am [*nec ego ipse capio totum, quod sum*]" (Aug. 187;
10.8.15). The mind exceeds itself, moves beyond its own limitations toward "infinite profundity." This quality makes mind more incredible than
world. "People are moved to wonder by mountain peaks, by vast waves
of the sea, by broad waterfalls on rivers, by the all-embracing extent of
the ocean, by the revolutions of the stars," he claims before adding: "But
in themselves they are uninterested" (Aug. 187; 10.8.15). This impulse to
elevate mind over world was adopted by Petrarch.[18] In a letter from his
Epistolae familiares (printed in 1492), Petrarch describes his ascent of

---

1963); Brian Stock, *After Augustine: The Meditative Reader and the Text* (Philadelphia:
University of Pennsylvania Press, 2001); Arnaud S. Q. Visser, *Reading Augustine in
the Reformation: The Flexibility of Intellectual Authority in Europe, 1500–1620* (Oxford:
Oxford University Press, 2011); and Willemien Otten, ed. *The Oxford Guide to the Historical Reception of Augustine*, 3 vols. (Oxford: Oxford University Press, 2013).

17. For Montaigne and Donne, see Louis I. Bredvold, "The Naturalism of Donne
in Relation to Some Renaissance Traditions," *Journal of English and Germanic Philology* 22, no. 4 (1923): 471–502; and Robert Ornstein, "Donne, Montaigne, and Natural
Law," *Journal of English and Germanic Philology* 55, no. 2 (1956): 213–29.

18. For Petrarch's relation to Augustine's *Confessiones*, see Courcelle, *Les Confessions de Saint Augustin*, 329–51; and Stock, *After Augustine*, 71–85.

Mount Ventoux in 1336. At the peak, Petrarch attempts to raise his mind "after the example of my body." He opens his copy of *Confessiones* to the passage we have just quoted. "I was angry with myself," Petrarch recalls, "that even now I was still marveling at earthly things, although I should have learned a long time since from the gentile philosophers that nothing is marvelous except the spirit, which being great counts nothing else as great."[19] Following Augustine's lead, Petrarch claims that the "shows" of the world are insignificant when compared with the mind.

A reader of Petrarch's *Epistolae familiares* and perhaps of Augustine's *Confessiones*, Montaigne alters this ancient trope.[20] To be sure, the *Essais* focus on self rather than world. In contrast to those who are interested in such issues as how the world is governed, how the moon operates, where the winds come from, and by what means the clouds come to be laden with water, Montaigne focuses on himself, turning such study into his metaphysics and his physics (Mon. 821; 1119). Montaigne studies the "shapeless subject" of his own "cogitation," noting that it is a "thorny undertaking . . . to follow a movement so wandering as that of our mind, to penetrate the opaque depths of its innermost folds [*penetrer les profondeurs opaques de ses replis internes*], to pick out and immobilize the innumerable flutterings that agitate it [*de choisir et arrester tant de menus airs de ses agitations*]" (Mon. 273–74; 396). Montaigne presents the mind in language resonant with Augustine's depths and folds and innumerable movements.[21] The Platonic impulse that subtends the *Confessiones* is visible when Montaigne asks: "What does Socrates treat of more fully than himself? To what does he lead his disciples conversation more often than to talk about themselves, not about the lesson of their book, but about

19. Francesco Petrarch, *Selected Letters*, 2 vols., trans. Elaine Fantham (Cambridge, MA: Harvard University Press, 2017), 1:56–59.

20. For Montaigne as inheritor of Petrarch's *Familiares*, see Kathy Eden, *The Renaissance Rediscovery of Intimacy* (Chicago: University of Chicago Press, 2012), 96–118. There is no direct evidence that Montaigne read the *Confessiones*. Unlike such texts as *De civitate Dei*, Montaigne nowhere cites the *Confessiones*.

21. Balsamo, Magnien, and Magnien-Simonin claim that this passage from "De l'exertication" in fact translates Augustine: "Traduit de saint Augustin, *Confessions*" (1522, 396n3). But the textual evidence they marshal in support of this claim is based on an error of transcription. They claim that Montaigne's *penetrer les profundeurs opaques de ses replis internes* translates Augustine's *penetrare amplum et infinitum* from *Confessiones* 10.8.15. If they had quoted Augustine's Latin correctly, this might be evidence sufficient to suggest that Montaigne did in fact read the *Confessiones*, thereby contradicting note 17 above. But so far as we know, Augustine does not in fact write the verb *penetrare* (to penetrate) but rather the noun *penetrale* (the inner part of a place). Montaigne is not, so far as we can tell, translating Augustine here.

the essence and movement of their soul?" (Mon. 273; 397). It might seem that the self about which Montaigne writes is aligned with mind or soul and that, like Augustine and Petrarch before him, when Montaigne elevates self over world he focuses only on the mind. Yet such an account neglects the aspect of the *Essais* that most chimes with Donne's writings: the importance Montaigne came to assign to the human body as an essential part of the self. For Montaigne, the elevation of self over world came to mean turning not only to the wonders of the mind, to what Augustine calls the "inner man," but to one's embodied being.[22]

When Montaigne defends his project of writing about himself in "De l'exercitation," he does so with reference to anatomy. "I expose myself entire," he writes, using an untranslated Greek word, *skeletos* (a dried body, a mummy), to emphasize the unusual nature of his undertaking: "my portrait is a cadaver [*skeletos*] on which the veins, the muscles, and the tendons appear at a glance, each part in its place. One part of what I am was produced by a cough, another by a pallor or a palpitation of the heart—in any case dubiously. It is not my deeds that I write down; it is myself, it is my essence [*c'est moy, c'est mon essence*]" (Mon. 274; 398). Montaigne seems to depict himself as an anatomist of the mind. But the meaning of anatomy shifts. If Montaigne writes not of his deeds but his "essence" and if aspects of this essence are revealed through a cough, a pallor, a palpitation, then the essence about which he writes must include the body.[23] Like Donne, Montaigne anatomizes not a cadaver but a living human being: heart beating, throat itching, cheeks blushing, hands shaking. When Montaigne advocates self-study, he rejects the elevation of mind over body. Modifying the line of thought presented by Augustine and Petrarch, Montaigne claims that human beings "seek other conditions because we do not understand the use of our own, and go outside of ourselves [*sortons hors de nous*] because we do not know what it is like inside" (Mon. 857; 1166). But knowledge of what is within is not limited to the mind: "Yet there is no use our mounting on stilts," Montaigne adds, "for on stilts we must still walk on our own legs. And on the loftiest throne in the world we are still sitting only on our own rump" (Mon. 857; 1166). The *Essais* propound a knowledge of minded, embodied human life.

22. On Augustine's "inner man," see, e.g., Brian Stock, *Augustine's Inner Dialogue: The Philosophical Soliloquy in Late Antiquity* (Cambridge: Cambridge University Press, 2010); and Philip Cary, *Augustine's Invention of the Inner Self: The Legacy of a Christian Platonist* (Oxford: Oxford University Press, 2003).

23. On Montaigne and the body, see esp. Jean Starobinski, *Montaigne in Motion*, trans. Arthur Goldhammer (Chicago: University of Chicago Press, 1985), 138–84.

Donne shares this orientation. Across his career, Donne returned obsessively to the body, the soul, and what binds them together.[24] Consider this passage from a sermon about the general resurrection preached in 1620 at Lincoln's Inn, just a few years before he wrote *Devotions*: "*Ego,* I, I the same body, and the same soul, shall be recompact again, and be identically, numerically, individually the same man. The same integrity of body, and soul, and the same integrity in the Organs of my body, and in the faculties of my soul too; I shall be all there, my body, and my soul, and all my body, and all my soul" (*Ser.* 3:109–10).[25] Donne defines the "ego" or "I" as a combination of body and soul, the union of which makes the whole person.[26] In the sermon, he repeats this definition: "*Ego,* I am here; I, body and soul; I, soul and faculties . . . *Ego,* I, body and soul, soul and faculties, shall say to Christ Jesus, *Ego sum,* Lord, it is I . . . *Ego,* I, the same person" (*Ser.* 3:110). To live as a human being is to live as an ego, an irreducible combination of body and soul, a whole person.

Donne also articulates this view in *Devotions*. The "I" of the text's speaker is part body and part soul. "I am more than *dust and ashes,*" Donne asserts, suggesting that he is not simply a body: "I am my best part, I am my *soule*" (*Dev.* 233; 1.2). Donne presents the ego as the tension that holds these parts together: "*Earth* is the *center* of my *body, Heaven* is the *center* of my *Soule*; these two are the naturall places of those two; but those goe not to these two, in an equall pace: My *body* falls down without pushing, my *Soule* does not go up without pulling: *Ascension* is my *Soules* pace and measure, but *precipitation* my *bodyes*" (*Dev.* 236; 2.1). Tugged upward by the soul and downward by the body, the "I" is pulled taut between heaven and earth, stretched into the consistency requisite for life in the first person. The intricate tangles of what, in "The Exstasie," Donne describes as the "subtile knot, which makes us man" (*Son.* 61; 64) are here performed by a syntax that shifts from heavenly pole to earthly pole across the thresholds of punctuation.

Donne refuses to elevate the mind or the soul at the expense of the body.[27] In reversing the traditional hierarchy of macrocosm and micro-

24. See, e.g., Targoff, *John Donne*.

25. For an extended analysis of this passage, see David Marno, *Death Be Not Proud: The Art of Holy Attention* (Chicago: University of Chicago Press, 2016), 206–11.

26. For Montaigne's *homo totus*, see Harrison, "Personhood and Impersonal Feeling in Montaigne's 'De l'exercitation.'" See also Richard Strier, *The Unrepentant Renaissance: From Petrarch to Shakespeare to Milton* (Chicago: University of Chicago Press, 2001), 225–29.

27. For different articulations of this point, see Elaine Scarry, "'But Yet the Body Is His Booke,'" in *Literature and the Body: Essays on Populations and Persons* (Baltimore: Johns Hopkins University Press, 1988), 70–105.

cosm, he resembles Montaigne; the elevation of the human over the world is not limited to mind. If the complexity of the body were unfurled—its veins, sinews, muscles, and bones extended—then microcosm would out-strip macrocosm. But Donne does not just reverse the usual microcosm and macrocosm hierarchy along an axis of resemblance. He also tracks the strands of contiguity that bind each human both to the species and to the world.[28] "*All mankinde* is of one *Author*, and is one *volume*," writes Donne, and this fact means that "when one *Man* dies, one *Chapter* is not *torne* out of the *booke*, but *translated* into a better *language*; and every *Chapter* must be so *translated*; *God* emploies severall *translators*; some peeces are trans-lated by *Age*, some by *sicknesse*, some by *warre*, some by *justice*; but *Gods* hand is in every *translation*" (*Dev.* 299; 17.1). Each human being is a piece of humankind, a participant in our collective species-being. Although this passage is religiously and denominationally motivated, Donne claims that each individual human is wrapped up in the life of the species, "involved in *Mankinde*": "No Man is an *Iland*, intire of it selfe; every man is a peece of the *Continent*, a part of the *maine*" (*Dev.* 299; 17.1).[29] This is what Donne means when, on the frontispiece, he claims that *Devotions* includes "MED-ITATIONS *upon our Humane Condition*" (*Dev.* 229). Examining himself, he examines a "peece" of the "*Humane Condition*," thereby shedding light not only on himself, but also on the species in which he is "involved."[30]

Donne embeds an investigation of "*Mankinde*" in an account of his own illness organized around what Joan Webber calls a "generalized *I*,"

28. Our treatment of Donne's intertwining of resemblance and contiguity is based on Elizabeth D. Harvey and Timothy M. Harrison, "Embodied Resonances: Early Modern Science and Tropologies of Connection in Donne's *Anniversaries*," *ELH* 80 (2013): 981–1008.

29. For the confessional leanings of this passage, see Richard Strier, "The Politics of Devotion"; and Brooke Conti, *Confessions of Faith in Early Modern England* (Phila-delphia: University of Pennsylvania Press, 2014), 65–67.

30. It is worth pointing out that the shift from singular to plural is characteristic of Donne's thought. Consider a sermon preached at Lincoln's Inn in 1618, when Donne moves from a discussion of David, a particular human being, to a discussion of the human race as a whole: "All these particulars will best arise to us in our second con-sideration, when wee consider, *Humanitatem*, not *Hominem*, our humane condition, as we are all kneaded up in *Adam*, and not this one person *David*" (*Ser.* 2:76). The oscillation between *I* and *we* in *Devotions* performs this shift from *homo* to *humani-tas*, from "*my Sickness*" to "*our Humane Condition*," which is, as he writes in 1618, "all kneaded up in *Adam*." It is significant, however, that instead of beginning with the general condition of humanity or with an exemplary individual like David, in *Devo-tions* Donne begins with his own sickness, moving from the first-person singular to the first-person plural that stands in for humanity.

which we have described as the predictable horizon of species-being against which the individual encounter with unexpected events take place.[31] Here we see another shared affinity with Montaigne, a writer who explores the contours of humankind within the idiosyncrasies of the particular.[32] "*C'est moy que je peins*," "it is myself that I portray" (Mon. 2; 27), Montaigne declares in "Au lecteur," the prefatory note to a book that discusses its author's singular dietary, sexual, medical, affective, and intellectual proclivities. Montaigne "portray[s] a particular [man], very ill formed," as he puts it in "Du repentir," but this depiction of an individual approaches the generality of what Donne calls "*Mankinde*," for "Every man bears the entire form of the human condition" (*Chaque homme porte la forme entiere de l'humaine condition*). In portraying his own "universal being" (*mon estre universel*), Montaigne writes about every human being (Mon. 610–11; 845).[33] Crafting a text about "*my Sicknes*" that meditates on "*our Humane Condition*," Donne leverages his own relation to himself to disclose the shape of "*Mankinde*" as it appears through the first-person perspective. As a "peece" of "*Mankinde*," Donne has privileged access to what it is like to be that "peece." This access grants him insight into the whole of which he is a part.

But Donne's ambitions in *Devotions* go further, for he is also "a peece of the *world*" (*Dev.* 319; 21.1). Human beings are part of the cosmic whole to which they belong. Each human has a nature, and that nature shares in the principles that organize the cosmos. This means that the first-person perspective affords a view, *from within*, not only of the human species but also of nature as such. In relating events from "*my Sicknes*," Donne adopts a first-person view on that nature, seen or felt from within. He develops a version of Montaigne's idea that self-study can be "my metaphysics" and "my physics," an insight on which Montaigne elaborates by describing his approach to "the world": "I ignorantly and negligently let myself be guided

31. Joan Webber, *The Eloquent I: Style and Self in Seventeenth-Century Prose* (Madison: University of Wisconsin Press, 1968), 34. See also Goldberg, "The Meaning of Sickness," 507.

32. Where we see affinities with Montaigne, others have argued that this feature of the text is indebted to traditions of devotional soliloquy and occasional meditation. See, e.g., Kate Narveson, "The Devotion," in *The Oxford Handbook of John Donne*, ed Jeanne Shami, Dennis Flynne, and M. Thomas Hester (Oxford: Oxford University Press, 2011).

33. For treatments of this topic, see, e.g., Jean-Luc Marion, "Qui suis-je pour ne pas dire *ego sum, ego existo*," in *Montaigne: Scepticisme, métaphysique, théologie*, ed. Vincent Carraud and Jean-Luc Marion (Paris: Presses Universitaires de France, 2004), 229–66.; and Strier, *Unrepentant Renaissance*, 221–29.

by the general law of the world. I shall know it well enough when I feel it [*Je la sçauray assez, quand je la sentiray*]" (Mon. 821, 1120). One can study metaphysics and physics by studying only oneself, but only if one understands that human life participates in nature, governed by rules according to which the world itself is ordered.[34] To approach metaphysics or physics from the vantage of the self is to operate from a privileged perspective, for insofar as one is a part of the natural order one gains insight into that order by the access that embodied thought permits. Of the "general law of the world," as Montaigne puts it, "I shall know [it] sufficiently when I feel it." Every human life is lived through the first-person perspective, a perspective that enables a unique point of view on the world and the living body, a perspective within which, Donne suggests, the natural regularities of the "general law of the world" are encountered as irregular emergent occasions.

This is why, in *Devotions*, Donne frames his elevation of human life over the world by intertwining relations of resemblance (the microcosm is like the macrocosm) with relations of contiguity (the microcosm is part of the macrocosm). Human veins, sinews, muscles, and bones are *like* rivers, "*vaines of Mines*," hills, and "*Quarries* of stones" (*Dev.* 242; 4.1), but they are also made of the same materials. They are contiguous because no distance separates them. Donne makes this point throughout *Devotions*, but with extreme precision in the opening of Station 2:

> The *Heavens* are not the less constant, because they move continually, because they move continually one and the same way. The *Earth* is not the more constant, because it lyes stil continually, because continually it changes, and melts in al the parts thereof. *Man*, who is the noblest part of the *Earth*, melts so away, as if he were a *statue*, not of *Earth*, but of *Snowe*. We see his own *Envie* melts him, hee growes leane with that; he will say, anothers *beautie* melts him; but he feeles that a *Fever* doth not melt him like *snow*, but pour him out like lead, like yron, like brasse melted in a furnace: It doth not only *melt* him, but *Calcine* him, reduce him to *Atomes*, and to *ashes*; not to *water*, but to *lime*. (*Dev.* 235; 2.1)

As "the noblest part of the *Earth*," a human being is subject to the continual changes that rive the earth. Human beings are melted by a terrible fever just like lead or iron or brass is melted by a furnace. But although the comparison to metal is based on resemblance, there is more at stake, for in

---

34. For insights into this aspect of Montaigne's thought, see George Hoffman, "The Investigation of Nature," in *Cambridge Companion to Montaigne*, ed. Ullrich Langer (Cambridge: Cambridge University Press, 2005), 170–71.

sickness human beings are subject to the processes and reactions that affect other bodies, other "part[s] of the *Earth*." A fever can "melt" a human being. It can also "*Calcine* him"—burn him away such that he is reduced to quicklime, as an alchemist would do with minerals or metals—or "reduce him to *Atomes*, and to *ashes*."[35] A fever does to human bodies what extreme heat does to all other material bodies. As "part of the earth," human beings undergo the same processes of change that rule the natural world.

There is, however, a significant difference between "the noblest part of the *Earth*" and its other parts: human beings can access what it is like to undergo such processes, and they can attempt to translate such feelings into language. A human being who is in the grip of sickness "feeles that a *Fever* doth not melt him like *snow*, but pour him out like lead." This first-person difference grants a quality of "*propriety*" to the changes that continually alter human existence (*Dev.* 328; 23.1). Drawing on the natural law tradition inaugurated by such texts as Cicero's *De finibus*, Donne understands "*propriety*" to index what is most one's "*owne*" (*Dev.* 274; 11.1); he focuses on his feelings. Human beings feel natural change from within: "In the same instant that I feele the first attempt of the disease, I feele the victory" (*Dev.* 236; 2.1). This is Donne's devastating version of Montaigne's claim that "I ignorantly and negligently let myself be guided by the general law of the world. I shall know it well enough when I feel it" (Mon. 821, 1120). In Donne's work, a topic handled with nonchalance in the *Essais* is instead treated with an insistence on the suffering that comes with being a creature able to think sublime thoughts but subject to the same changes undergone by all other earthly bodies, even minerals and metals.[36] Montaigne proposes a physics of the self that opens onto nature insofar as nature is something one feels. Donne's *Devotions* present a similar undertaking. But unlike Montaigne's optimistic view of *l'humaine condition*, Donne begins his treatment of "*our Humane Condition*" with a sentence that aligns change and suffering: "Variable, and therefore miserable condition of Man" (*Dev.* 232; 1.1).

What Does Experience *Mean?*

Donne's account of "*my Sicknes*" represents change as something through which one lives. A serious illness is a potentially illuminating instance of the changes to which human beings and all earthly creatures are subject.

35. See *OED*, s.v. "calcine," v. 1a.

36. For Montaigne and nonchalance, see David Carroll Simon, *Light without Heat: The Observational Mood from Bacon to Milton* (Ithaca, NY: Cornell University Press, 2018), 35–79.

The quality of "*propriety*" that Donne flags in Station 23 stresses our special access to these natural changes in a way that reveals his attention to
what we might now call *experience* in each of the preceding twenty-two
stations. Looking back over the illness he has just endured, forward to the
uncertainty of his immediate future, and outward toward the community
into which he will be reintegrated, in the final station Donne meditates
on the "feare of a *relapse*" (*Dev.* 328; 23.1). Even after recovery, one might
be forced to live through illness again, to suffer once more from symptoms and pains the potential iterability of which makes them even more
dreadful. At the end of *Devotions*, Donne returns the reader to the territory covered in Station 1. He once more suffers from being "pre-afflicted,
super-afflicted with these jelousies and suspitions, and apprehensions of
Sicknes, before we can cal it a sicknes" (*Dev.* 232; 1.1)—but with a difference. This time, the future-oriented fear is also directed to the past, for
to anticipate relapse is to look forward to a repetition of something that
has already happened. Importantly, this condition of backward-oriented
futurity requires that the sufferer already be first-personally acquainted
with the "*bodily paines*" the repetition of which they fear:

> in a fit of the *stone*, the patient wonders why any man should call the *Gout*
> a *paine*: And hee that hath felt neither, but the *tooth-ach*, is as much afraid
> of a fit of that, as either of the other, of either of the other. *Diseases*, which
> we never *felt* in ourselves, come but to a *compassion* of others that have
> endured them; Nay, *compassion* it selfe, comes to no great *degree*, if wee
> have not *felt*, in some *proportion*, in *our selves*, that which wee lament and
> condole in another. But when wee have had those torments in their *exal-
> tation*, *our selves*, wee tremble at a *relapse*. (*Dev.* 328; 23.1)

In Donne's view, we might feel "*compassion*" for someone who suffers
from a disease we have never "*felt* in ourselves," but we cannot fear those
diseases. Unable to relive "those torments in their *exaltation*," we cannot
"tremble at a *relapse*." If one has suffered from a toothache, one fears the
relapse of that condition but cannot feel the same way about gout, kidney
stones, or another condition from which one has not suffered. Compassion (feeling alongside another) is not as strong as the anticipation that
we might again feel something that we have already felt.

It is in this context that Donne uses the word *experience*: "Even in
pleasures, and in *paines*, there is a *propriety*, a *Meum et Tuum*; and a man
is most affected with that *pleasure* which is *his*, *his* by former enjoying
and experience, and most intimidated with those *paines* which are *his*,
his by a wofull sense of them, in former afflictions" (*Dev.* 328; 23.1). Our

pleasures or pains have a *"propriety."* They belong to us. When we think about or observe pleasures and pains, each of us is affected differently. If, in the past, one has suffered from an asthma attack, when one considers this condition one will be affected otherwise than someone who has no relationship of *"propriety"* to it. Using the term "a man" in the quasi-pronominal sense akin to how modern English speakers might use the indefinite *one* to refer to "any person of undefined identity,"[37] Donne claims that "a man is most affected with that *pleasure* which is *his, his* by former enjoying and experience," just as he is "most intimidated" by those pains that he can relive "by a wofull sense of them, in former afflictions."

Embedded in a complex network of related terms—pleasure, pain, affect, enjoyment, intimidation, sense, affliction—all of which describe a *"propriety"* between self and stimulus, *experience* requires interpretation. What does Donne mean here? The gist of the issue seems to be that just as "a man" is "most affected" by the "former enjoying and experience" of previous pleasures, so, in the same way, he is "most intimidated" by the "wofull sense of" pains from which we have suffered in "former afflictions." But although this parallelism might seem thoroughgoing, it is asymmetrical.[38] Whereas the pleasures that affect "a man" are "his" by virtue of "former enjoying and experience" that took place in the past, the pains that intimidate "a man" are "his" by a "wofull sense"—grounded in the present—of those pains "in former afflictions." Donne's use of "former" is instructive: although the "enjoying and experience" of previous pleasures are modified by "former" and therefore have taken place "earlier in time," only the "afflictions" associated with pain are modified in this way.[39] Pain differs from pleasure insofar as the "wofull sense" of pain stretches from "former afflictions" into the present moment while the "former enjoying and experience" of pleasure are no longer sensed but are available through memory.

This asymmetry opens onto another temporal difficulty. According to Donne, "a man" is "affected" by the pleasure and "intimidated" by the pains that he feels in the present but has already felt in the past. Likewise, the "former enjoying" of pleasure and "former afflictions" of pain were states that had, in previous moments, taken place in the present. However, experience seems to inhabit a different temporality. Recall the passage's nearly complete parallelism: "a man is most affected with that

37. *OED*, s.v., "man," V 17a; *OED*, s.v., "one," VI 17a.

38. On Donne's use of asymmetrical parallelism in *Devotions* (along with other rhetorical strategies), see Joan Webber, *Eloquent I*, 144–47.

39. *OED*, s.v., "former," adj. 1a.

pleasure which is *his, his* by former enjoying and experience, and most intimidated with those *paines* which are *his, his* by a wofull sense of them, in former afflictions." One is affected by pleasure and intimidated by pain because one has a relationship of *"propriety"* with one's previous pleasures and pains, one's "former enjoying" and "former afflictions." Here the parallelism is perfect. But if the "wofull sense" through which one feels pain is not modified by the adjective "former," the term *experience* still hangs in its shadow, bound to the past through the conjunction *and*: "*his* by former enjoying and experience." Experience is tethered to the past in a way that "sense" is not. In Donne's hands, the term is not, then, fully assimilable to the modern notion of *experience* as equivalent to *consciousness*, a synchronic unity of all possible modalities of thought (sensation, imagination, passion, desire, memory, intellection, intuition, and so on) mingling and jostling in the present moment. If *experience* does not, for Donne, mean something like consciousness in the synchronically synthetic sense, what, then, does it mean?

The pastness of experience is key to how Donne understands the concept. He uses the term in twenty-nine of his sermons. In each of these instances, he frames experience as something one has already acquired. Human beings learn, Donne tells the attendees of a wedding in 1620, from what "experience hath taught us" (*Ser.* 1:340), while in a sermon dedicated to Psalm 6:1 we are told that the Jewish people "had learnt by experience of daily tribulation" (*Ser.* 5:328). According to a sermon preached at White Hall in 1618, when we "consider" God's mercies in themselves, we must do so "in our thankfulness, and experience, as truths already performed unto us" (*Ser.* 1:270). In a 1622 sermon, Donne describes how "the tongue of bad Angels who know damnation by a lamentable experience, is able to expresse it" (*Ser.* 5:265). Experience is consistently rooted in the past; it is not something one possesses in the present.

Donne uses two models in his discussions of experience, both oriented toward the past. First, he draws on the legacies of Aristotle's discussions of *empeiria* in the *Posterior Analytics* and *Metaphysics*, a paradigm at the heart of how logic was taught in sixteenth- and seventeenth-century English universities. For Aristotle, all knowledge of universals begins in sensations, which are collected, as he puts in the *Metaphysics*, into "many memories of the same thing" until these accumulated memories become robust enough to form "a single experience [*empeiria*]," which is, in turn, the condition enabling the transition toward universals (Ar. 2:1552; 980b–981a). Aristotle uses medicine to illuminate how his theory works. If one remembers that a medicine helped Calias, Socrates, and others when they suffered from a given illness, this is a "matter of experience" (Ar.

2:1552; 981a). Experience is a synthesis of memories that enables one to combine past cases and recognize when, say, a given medicine should be administered to an individual here and now. Having experience does not yet mean that one has knowledge, since knowledge comes from science (*epistēmē*) or art (*technē*), both of which require the use of universals and the understanding of causes: "*knowledge* and *understanding* belong to art rather than experience" for the simple reason that "men of experience know that the thing is so, but do not know why, while the others know the 'why' and the cause" (Ar. 2:1553; 981a). Experience can act as a step toward knowledge.

Donne often draws on this theory. In a sermon preached at White Hall in 1620, he claims that "a man" receives the "riches" of the nutritive soul involuntarily from parents, but that "a man" must acquire the "riches" of the sensitive soul "by his owne acquisition, and experience, and conversation" (*Ser.* 3:85–86). This use of *experience* points to a strand in the reception history of Aristotle's *empeiria* that transformed the philosopher's account of how humans acquire knowledge in the arts and sciences into a story about how humans acquire the world as infants and children. Following the contours of this variation on Aristotle's model, Donne suggests that the repeated encounters with the world synthesized by "acquisition, and experience" enable the sensitive soul to gather the "riches" disclosed by its encounters with the world. Donne draws on Aristotle's theory of experience in a sermon preached in 1618. Writing about the metaphorical link between spiritual and physical health, Donne considers the figure of the physician:

> because we are in the consideration of *health*, and consequently of *phys-ick*, (for the true and proper use of physick is, to *preserve* health, and, but by accident to restore it) we embrace that Rule, *Medicorum theoria experientia est, Practice is a Physicians study*; and he concludes out of events, for, says he, He that professes himself a Physician, without experience, *Chronica de future scribit*, He undertakes to write a Chronicle of things before they are done, which is an irregular, and a perverse way. (*Ser.* 2:76)

Donne casts experience in the diachronically synthetic sense of Aristotelian *empeiria*. *Medicorum theoria experientia est*: the accumulated experience that comes from practicing medicine simply *is* the implicit theory according to which physicians work. We will return to this topic, showing how Donne reworks the relationship between experience and medicine as articulated by Hippocrates, Aristotle, and Galen and then refracted by Paracelsus and Vesalius, among others. For now, it suffices to point out that one cannot be a physician "without experience," without a synthesis derived from previously sensed events.

But although Donne sometimes uses this diachronically synthetic sense of *experience*, he more often uses the term in a non-synthetic but past-oriented way. In a sermon preached at King's Cross in 1622, just months before he fell ill, Donne discusses the importance of catechism, recalling how an "Arificer of this Citie brought his Childe to mee, to admire . . . the capacitie, the memory, especially of the child." The small girl could continue quoting almost any scriptural verse that Donne began to recite. But despite her ability to remember the Bible, she was not properly catechized, and she "understood nothing of the *Trinity*." Donne introduces this singular story, positioned amidst a wealth of detail, by asking some hypothesized Calvinist members of his audience to give "mee leave to tell them that of which I had the experience" (*Ser.* 4:203–4). In this sermon, experience refers to a singular event that happened once; it is not synthetic. Similar uses occur in other sermons. For instance, he informs his listeners about the "experience" of opening a vault, closed for many centuries, only to find a candle within it, still burning (*Ser.* 3:357). In such examples, experience refers not to the accumulation of remembered events, but to singular events that occurred once in the past.

The valences of *experience* that Donne presents in *Devotions* registers, once again, an affinity with the *Essais*. Montaigne opens "De l'experience" by attacking the synthetic qualities necessary for Aristotle's *empeiria* to work:[40]

There is no desire more natural than the desire for knowledge. We try all the ways that can lead us to it. When reason fails us, we use experience—

Per uarios usus artem experientia fecit:
Exemplo monstrante uiam

[Experience, by example led,
By varied trials art has bred]

—which is a weaker and less dignified means. But truth is so great a thing that we must not disdain any medium that will lead us to it. Reason has so many shapes that we know not which to lay hold of; experience has no fewer. The inference that we try to draw from the resemblance of events

40. On the centrality of experience for Montaigne, see, e.g., Timothy Hampton, "Putting Experience First," *Republic of Letters* 1, no. 2 (2010): 61–66.

is uncertain, because they are always dissimilar [*La consequence que nous voulons tirer de la conference des evenemens, est mal seure, d'autant qu'ils sont tousjours dissemblables*]: there is no quality so universal in this aspect of things as diversity and variety. (Mon. 815; 1111)

Paraphrasing the opening lines of the *Metaphysics* ("All men by nature desire to know"), Montaigne inserts a Latin translation of Aristotle's claim that *empeiria* leads to *technē*, that experience makes art: *artem experientia fecit*, a phrase taken from Manilius's *Astronomica*, which in turn translates a passage from Aristotle's *Metaphysics*.[41]

Although Montaigne reaffirms Aristotle's epistemological hierarchy by stressing both that experience is a knowledge-directed "medium" and that it is "weaker and less dignified" than reason, "De l'Experience" undermines Aristotle's understanding of *empeiria* by refusing its synthetic powers. Whereas Aristotle's *experience* brings many memories of past events together, Montaigne stresses that such an operation is "uncertain," since it relies on an "inference" about the "resemblance" of various memories. Since each event is dissimilar, there is no true resemblance on which experience, understood as *empeiria*, can draw. Experience remains, in Montaigne's account, confined to particulars, full of "diversity and variety." Montaigne's experience cannot act as the bridge to the universal required for Aristotle's theory of knowledge.[42] "As no event and no shape is entirely like another, so none is entirely different from another," writes Montaigne, "All things hold together by some similarity; every example is lame, and the comparison that is drawn from experience is always faulty and imperfect" (Mon. 819; 1116). Since everything is related equivocally, there exists no true similarity from which experience might begin to do its work. Without this synthetic property, experience remains idiosyncratic. Variety upends synthesis.

Donne thinks similarly about *experience* in *Devotions*. When he writes that the pleasures "a man" has encountered in the past remain "*his, his* by former enjoying and experience," *experience* refers not to the synthetic properties of Aristotelian *empeiria* but to an experience that is as singular as the moments in which pleasure was formerly enjoyed. In

41. Manilius, *Astronomica*, 1.61. Polus's "experience made art" stems from Aristotle's *Metaphysics* (2:1552; 981a).

42. See Kathryn Murphy, "The Anxiety of Variety: Knowledge and Experience in Montaigne, Burton, and Bacon," in *Fictions of Knowledge: Fact, Evidence, Doubt*, ed. Yota Batsaki, Subha Mukherji, and Jan-Melissa Schramm (Basingstoke: Palgrave, 2011).

"De l'Experience," Montaigne claims that "at the present moment, when I have passed through virtually every sort of experience, if some grave stroke threatens me, by glancing through these little notes, disconnected like the Sibyl's leaves, I never fail to find grounds for comfort in some favorable prognostic from my past experience" (Mon. 838; 1141). Responding to the same tradition, though less optimistically, Donne arrives at a similar conclusion. The *experience* presented in *Devotions* indexes a singular event that one has "passed through" in the "past," an event that remains available to one in "the present moment" and is so particular that it is "disconnected" from all others. When Donne describes the "former enjoying and experience" by which pleasures from the past continue to affect us in the present, he tells readers what experience in *Devotions* means: a singular event that one has lived through and that one can now recall in the present.

Living Through

Experience in *Devotions* is not synthetic in the diachronic, Aristotelian sense of being derived from memories of sensed events that have accumulated over time. And it is not synthetic in the modern synchronic sense of a consciousness that binds all conscious appearances into a unified phenomenal field. Donne's disconnected sense of experience impresses the extent to which "*our Humane Condition*" is, in a view indebted to Augustine, scattered, riddled with absences, distracted, and fractured, unable to be synthesized as a diachronic line stretching from past toward future or as a synchronic horizon unifying the various aspects of the present moment.[43]

This is the burden carried by Donne's elaborate sentences, the byzantine chains of inference, the leaps from topic to topic that structure each station in *Devotions*. Although the central twelfth station is entitled "*They apply Pidgeons, to draw the vapors from the Head*" (*Dev.* 278; 12.1), it is only in the final sentence of the meditation that the pigeon appears. The meditation begins with a consideration of how vapors, which are generated within one's own body, can halt the life of that body, before moving past Pliny and Mount Etna, the idea of fortune, communal strife, melancholy, the many instruments of death—"a pin, a comb, a hair pulled" (*Dev.* 279; 12.1)—only to settle on the analogy between bodily vapors and gossip

43. We draw here on Marno, *Death Be Not Proud*, 124–43; and Andrea Nightingale, *Once Out of Nature: Augustine on Time and the Body* (Chicago: University of Chicago Press, 2011). We also extend the argument made in Tabak, "'O Multiplied Misery!'"

within the political state, then dally with international relations, before ending, several breathless pages later, with a pigeon finally put to a medical use but still carrying associations with poison and political gossip. Here is the meditation's closing sentence:

> For, as they that write of *Poysons*, and of creatures naturally disposed to the ruine of Man, do as well mention the *Flea*, as the *Viper*, because the *Flea*, though hee kill none, hee does all the harme hee can, so even these libellous and licentious *Jesters* [who speak rumors dangerous to the state], utter the *venim* they have: though sometimes *vertue*, and alwaies *power*, be a good *Pigeon* to draw this *vapor* from the *Head*, and from doing any deadly harme there. (*Dev.* 280; 12.1)

The meditation is grounded in the first-person present. "I have don nothing, wilfully," Donne laments, thinking of the self-produced vapors that might kill him, "yet must suffer in it, die by it" (*Dev.* 279; 12.1). But the event the station explores is presented primarily through its mention in the title, appearing only as a metaphor for the *"vertue"* and *"power"* that can act like a medicinal pigeon and "draw this *vapor*" of rumor from the head of state before it does "deadly harme." The meditation scatters. To exist in the present, to live or pass "through" the *now* when change might or might not take place, is, in Donne's view, to fail at being present, even when one's situation (say, a severe illness) forces one into stillness and solitude. Returning to the theme of Station 4, recall how Donne laments his confinement "in a close prison, in a sicke bed, any where, and any one of my *Creatures*, my *thoughts*, is with the *Sunne*, and beyond the *Sunne*, overtakes the *Sunne*, and overgoes the *Sunne* in one pace, one steppe, every where" (*Dev.* 243; 4.1). Confined in one place, Donne finds himself scattered, never truly here but always in the midst of the vast, unrealized potentiality of "every where."

Thus, even as Donne sidles up to the sense of *experience* as *consciousness* through his representational practices, he resists the urge to unite, to synthesize. Looking back, one can, in Donne's view, recover the "experience" of what happened. But these experiences are what Montaigne calls "little notes, disconnected like the Sibyl's leaves," the traces of having lived through and been scattered into a past event. This explains why *Devotions* is structured as it is: station after station, each disconnected from the others. When the reader reaches the second station, the events described in the first have been transformed into an experience, confined to the past but reaching into the present, separated from what has happened before or what will happen in the future. Each station becomes a singular experience as it recedes into the reader's past. *Devotions* does not even attempt to achieve a diachronic narrative synthesis. Jumping across longer or shorter distances of time, each station is isolated from its peers, trapped in a present moment that must be lived through but cannot bring the event it is supposed to describe fully into focus.

Here Donne again reveals his debt to Augustine. To live through the present moment is, as Augustine theorizes in the *Confessiones*, to be cut off from that present in two ways: first, one is extended backward into the past and forward into the future, diachronically stretched away from the present; and second, one is synchronically scattered into the competing spheres of perception, imagination, and desire. This double Augustinian movement, both diachronic and synchronic, blocks access to the real presence that subtends every moment of human life: bodily presence. One's own body always exists in an abiding present that is unavailable, obstructed by the *distentio animi* that, during mortal embodied life (after the Fall and before the resurrection of the body), prevents one from ever fully attending to one's body.[44] The act of *living through* that Donne captures in each station is an asynthetic performance of Augustine's theories of fallen human life.

The concerns about relapse that Donne examines in Station 23 emphasize what we call the *throughness* that characterizes human life as it is represented in *Devotions*:

> When wee must *pant* through all those *fierie heats*, and *saile* through all those *overflowing sweats*, when wee must *watch* through all those long *nights*, and *mourne* through all those long *daies*, (*daies* and *nights*, so *long*, as that *Nature* her selfe shall seeme to be *perverted*, and to have put the *longest day*, and the *longest night*, which should bee *six moneths* asunder, into one *naturall, unnaturall day*) when wee must stand at the same *barre*, expect the return of the *Physitians* from their *consultations*, and not bee sure of the same *verdict*, in any good *Indications*, when we must goe the same *way* over againe, and not see the same *issue*, this is a *state*, a *condition*, a *calamitie*, in respect of which, any other *sickenesse* were a *convalescence*, and any *greater, lesse*. (*Dev.* 328; 23.1)

The speaker anticipates relapse. In the present inscribed by Station 23, he anticipates a future in which he will once more suffer as he has just finished suffering in the recent past. Yet despite the familiarity of what might be coming his way, Donne's speaker knows that the future need

---

44. See Nightingale, *Once Out of Nature*, 23–54.

not resemble the past. Although a relapse might mean "stand[ing] at the same *barre*" and going "the same *way* over again," these similarities do not mean that he will hear the "same *verdict*" or "see the same *issue*." Each event is singular, disconnected from those that have preceded it. The iterability encoded in the prefix *re* carries the threat and opportunity of difference coiled within it.[45] What remains the same is only the quality of through-ness that pervades each present moment, a structural sameness always populated with content that is different no matter how similar it may seem. Donne points toward this feature of what Edmund Husserl calls the "standing-streaming" nature of the "living present"—always the same, always different—by varying his verbs and keeping his preposition constant: the speaker will, he anticipates, "*pant* through" a high fever, "*saile* through" terrible sweats, "*watch* through" the long nights, and "*mourne* through" the never-ending days.[46] Each previous station in *Devotions* has captured some aspect of this throughness, in all of its miserable dispersal and inevitable self-scattering.

Donne's use of *through* in this passage reflects the extent to which he is a poet of prepositions. Prepositions of location (*above, behind, inside*), time (*during, before, after*), and movement (*against, toward, from*) are the grammatical medium through which Donne articulates the physics that implicitly structures his understanding of the world and his place within it. The use of *through* in *Devotions* is an extension of a sustained, career-long experiment with the affordances of prepositions. "License my roving hands," he writes in "To his Mistris Going to Bed," transforming an erotic encounter into a testing ground for the rhetorical power of prepositions, "and let them goe / Behind, before, above, between, below" (*Son.* 15; 25–26). Prepositions of location are integral to Donne's sense of bodies in space; in *Devotions* he is particularly fascinated by *through*, a preposition of time that evokes the crossing of thresholds.

Across his corpus, Donne returns to the word *through*, using it to express what it means to be a minded being that feels and thinks and knows. Consider the "Epistle" to *Metempsychosis*, in which Donne claims that although other authors "at the Porches and entries of their Buildings set their Armes; I, my picture; if any colours can deliver a minde so plaine,

45. This observation draws on Jacques Derrida, "Signature, Event, Context," trans. Alan Bass, in *Limited Inc.*, ed. Gerald Graff (Evanston, IL: Northwestern University Press, 1988), 1–24.

46. For Husserl on the "living now," see Evan Thompson, *Mind in Life: Biology, Phenomenology, and the Sciences of Mind* (Cambridge, MA: Harvard University Press, 2007), 326.

and flat, and through light as mine" (*Sat.* 25). There is no fancy coat of arms, but only the representation of a speaking ego ("I, my picture"), depicted not visually but through poetry, which Philip Sidney calls "a speaking picture."[47] But this picture is conditional; it will work only if colors can "deliver," or make manifest, "a minde so . . . through light" as Donne's. The phrase "through light" was relatively uncommon in the late sixteenth and early seventeenth century. To take the most relevant example, in *A Worthy Treatise of the Eyes* (1587), Jacques Guillemeau writes that although much of the eye is "darke and verie thick & grosse," the iris is "bright, & hath a through light, that so colours might have the better passage and entertainment."[48] The iris contains a "through light" for the "passage" of colors; similarly, Donne's mind is "through light," enabling not the passage of colors from the outside in but rather the external "deliver[y]" of a "picture" of a plain and flat mind through the colors of poetic language. Here, at the "porch and entry" of *Metempsychosis*, Donne presents his mind as "through light," as transparent enough to afford a passage from inside out.

A similar use of *through* appears in "A Valediction: of My Name in the Window." Meditating on his name, etched in the glass of a window that he imagines reflecting the image of his beloved, in the poem's second stanza Donne writes:

> 'Tis much that Glasse should bee
> As all confessing, as through-shine as I,
>   'Tis more, that it shewes thee to thee,
>   And cleare reflects thee to thine eye.
> But all such rules, loves magique can undoe,
> Here you see mee, and I am you. (*Son.* 64; 7–12)

Contemporary writers understood windows, just like the eyes, to be "through light." In Sir Edward Monings's 1596 account of a diplomatic visit to Germany, he describes the interior of a building as featuring "the through light of fower faire windowes."[49] In the "Epistle" to *Metempsychosis*, Donne describes his mind as "through light"; here he compares his

---

47. Philip Sidney, *Defence of Poesie*, in *Miscellaneous Prose of Sir Philip Sidney*, ed. Katherine Duncan-Jones and Jan van Dorsten (Oxford: Oxford University Press, 1973), 80.

48. Jacques Guillemeau, *A Worthy Treatise of the Eyes*, trans. W. Bailey (London, 1587), 6v.

49. Edward Monings, *The Landgrave of Hessen his princelie receiuing of her Maiesties embassador* (London, 1596), 12.

ego to a window that is "as through-shine as I." The speaker of this vale-dictory poem is "all confessing," eagerly and transparently taking what is inside into the outside. The I is "through-shine," like the window. But the window is also a reflective surface, mirroring the beloved, showing "thee to thee," so that it "cleare reflects thee to thine eye." The conceit of the stanza collapses two properties of glass—transparency, a property shared with the confessing *I*; and the ability to reflect the beloved's image—so that the speaker's name, engraved in the glass, unites first and second person: "Here you see mee, and I am you." Seeing *through* the engraved window, the beloved finds herself there, having passed through the boundary separating *I* from *you*.

In both of these texts, the preposition implies motion across or change in time: light passing through a window, the secrets of the speaking *I* passing into the outside world through confession, the interiority of the ego passing through the mind into poetic representation. The same sense of temporal passage through a medium is at work in *Devotions*, in Donne's anticipation of a relapse in which "we must *pant* through," "*saile* through," "*watch* through," and "*mourne* through" the various states of illness. Much like *Metempsychosis* and "A Valediction: of my Name in the Window," here *through* captures the life of the ego. The preposition *through* captures embodiment itself, the medium through which the life of the ego unfolds, held in tension between body and soul. If we listen closely, we might hear once more an affinity with Montaigne, who, in "Du repentir" describes his subject and his method in ways that resonate with Donne's *Devotions*:

> Others form man; I tell of him, and portray a particular one [*un partic-ulier*], very ill-formed. . . . I cannot keep my subject still. It goes along befuddled and staggering, with a natural drunkenness. I take it in this condition, just as it is, at the moment I amuse myself with it [*Je le prens en ce poinct, comme il est, en l'instant que je m'amuse à luy*]. I do not por-tray being: I portray passing [*Je ne peinds pas l'estre, je peinds le passage*]. Not the passing of one age to another, or, as the people say, from seven years to seven years, but from day to day, from minute to minute. My his-tory [*histoire*] needs to be adapted to the moment. (Mon. 610–11; 844–45, translation modified)

Donne shares Montaigne's topic. In *Devotions*, Donne invents a new way to "portray passing"—not through the relatively unstructured medita-tions of Montaigne's *Essais*, but rather through the highly structured rep-etition of stations designed to capture a personal *histoire* grounded in the change that unfolds in a human body that is "part of the *Earth*" (*Dev.* 235;

2.1) and a "peece of the *world*" (*Dev.* 319; 21.1). Focusing on the movement through the "*Severall Steps of My Sicknes*," Donne presents readers with a portrait of *passage*, minute to minute, that is scattered in the present and disconnected from the past and the future. As we will see more fully in chapter 3, Donne structures *Devotions* as a series of passages through embodied time that is, station after station, always different but always repeating. This passage through a present riddled with absence structures what it is like to be human and, at the same time, what it is like to be a natural body, a part of the world. Donne's approach to physics emerges from a sophisticated first-person perspective on natural change as it unfolds in time.

2

The Time of the Body

Devotions represents the activity of living through change. In this chapter, we examine the distinctive habits of thought that enable this representational practice. We argue that Donne phenomenalizes concepts taken from the physics of time. From Aristotle onward, time had been integral to physics. "The concept of time belongs to physics, not metaphysics," as James Conant puts it, for time "presupposes the concepts of motion and change as well as that of substances susceptible to alteration."[1] Physics is dedicated to nature, which is subject to change both by definition and by etymology; the Greek *physis* refers to that which is born, grows, and decays. Time is central to physics because through it change is measured and perhaps in it change occurs. Donne borrows from various traditions of physics a complex network of technical concepts for thinking change, time, and the relation that obtains among them: the instantaneous, the successive, substantial change, accidental change, alteration, generation, corruption, creation, and annihilation, as well as others. His borrowings from the technical apparatus of physics achieve an astonishing literary effect. This network of concepts scaffolds Donne's imaginative attempts to slow time down so that he can observe the mechanisms of change from within, as dilated, elongated, felt events.

Donne splits time into at least three categories: the cosmic time measured in planetary movements and lunar orbits and astral light; the calendrical, social time of seasons and harvests and holidays; and the felt time that, in his view, belongs to bodily life, to what, in chapter 1, we called the activity of *living through*. In this chapter, we argue that Donne sees the latter as fundamental, as the basis for both social, calendrical time and any apprehension of cosmic time. Seen in one way, there is nothing

---

1. James Conant, *The Logical Alien: Conant and His Critics*, ed. Sofia Miguens (Cambridge, MA: Harvard University Press, 2020), 381.

new here. Aristotle's definition in *Physics*—"Time is a measure of motion" (Ar. 1:374; 220b)—had been similarly challenged centuries earlier. Augustine's *Confessiones* grounds time in the felt extension of the human soul, stretching back to the past through remembrance and forward to the future through anticipation.[2]

Yet although Donne is indebted to Aristotle, Augustine, and the debates they inspired, when he distinguishes between felt time and time as a measure of motion, he is in fact doing something new.[3] For Augustine, the feeling of time passing belongs to a soul distinct from a body. Donne holds instead that felt time is a property of the living body.[4] Across his corpus, Donne takes concepts from the study of how time intersects with changing natural bodies, understood as objects in the world, and represents those concepts as they might be felt in the first-person perspective.[5] He translates time from an abstraction into a structural feature of the phenomenal field through which he lives. In doing so, however, Donne maintains that this time belongs irreducibly to the body. He attempts to represent what we call the *time of the body*, a first-person physics of time. Donne's idiosyncratic physics of time is central to *Devotions*, inflecting everything from its organization to its style.[6] In this chapter,

2. According to Jean-Luc Marion, *In the Self's Place: The Approach of Saint Augustine*, trans. Jeffrey L. Koskey (Stanford, CA: Stanford University Press, 2012), 206, Augustine's stress on the feeling of time passing is the only "step forward" that he takes in relation to Aristotle's understanding in the *Physics*. As Ettenhuber, *Donne's Augustine*, 230, argues, Donne drew on the *Confessiones* "more frequently than any other Augustinian text."

3. Although we see Donne's position as novel, there are also analogous early modern stances. See, e.g., Walter Pagel, "J. B. van Helmont, *De Tempore*, and Biological Time," *Osiris* 8 (1948): 346–417.

4. See Tabak, "'O Multiplied Misery!,'" 167–68, for the claim that *Devotions* attempts to communicate "affectively" the temporality of illness by expressing the *distentio animi* that Augustine describes in the *Confessiones*. For approaches to Donne's treatment of embodiment and time, see, e.g., Felecia Wright McDuffie, *To Our Bodies Turn We Then: Body as Word and Sacrament in the Works of John Donne* (New York: Continuum, 2005); and Robert Watson, *The Rest Is Silence: Death as Annihilation in the English Renaissance* (Berkeley: University of California Press, 1994), 156–252.

5. For earlier examinations of Donne and time, see, e.g., G. F. Waller, "John Donne's Changing Attitudes to Time," *SEL* 14, no. 1 (1974): 79–89; Jonathan Z. Kamholtz, "Immanence and Eminence in Donne," *Journal of English and Germanic Philology* 81 (1982): 480–91; Theresa M. DiPasquale, "Donne's Naked Time," *John Donne Journal* 29 (2010): 33–44; and Hilary Binda, "'My Name Engrav'd Herein': John Donne's Sacramental Temporality," *Exemplaria* 23 (2013): 390–414.

6. For time in *Devotions*, see, e.g., Frost, *Holy Delight*, 106–66; and Tabak, "'O Multiplied Misery!'"

we argue that Donne's approach to felt time underpins his understanding of change, a topic central to the entirety of his career that receives its most brilliant treatment in his representation of sickness as a series of emergent occasions.[7] We trace Donne's engagement with the physics of time across his career in order to reveal the unnoticed conceptual motor that, as we will argue in chapters 3 and 4, powers Donne's generic and stylistic innovations in *Devotions*.

Time and Change

In Station 14 of *Devotions*, Donne stresses that whatever "*Happinesses*" we have while we live in the world "have their *times*, and their *seasons*, and their *Critical days*, and they are *Judged*, and *Denominated* according to the times, when they befall us" (*Dev.* 286; 14.1). The good things in life are all relative to the time or the season when they occur. For instance, "We rejoyce in the Comfort of *fire*," but not during the heat of "*Midsomer*." Likewise, "Wee are glad of the freshnesse, and coolenes of a *Vault*," but no one will "keepe his *Christmas* there" (*Dev.* 287; 14.1). Since the pleasures of spring are not "acceptable" in autumn, this means that "happinesse be in the *season*, or in the *Clymate*," relative to the context in which it is felt, and not something in its own right (*Dev.* 287; 14.1). Donne makes a similar point in Meditation 19: "we cannot," he writes, "awake the *July-flowers* in *Januarie*, nor retard the *flowers* of the *spring* to *Autumne*. We cannot bid the *fruits* come in *May*, nor the *leaves* to stick on in *December*" (*Dev.* 308; 19.1). Human life is hostage to the rhythms of nature, to planetary movement, to the structures of the cosmos. Happiness is thus impermanent, both because it depends on these broader temporal shifts and because it is itself temporal (and therefore temporary), caught up in changes and motions that split both its psychosomatic substance and the forces by which it is environed. Framing the possibilities of happiness in terms of the seasons and their attendant climates as well as the social, ritual, and agricultural activities that correspond to the movement of the calendrical year, he presents human life in terms of socially and seasonally attuned rhythms.[8]

---

7. For change, see Carey, *John Donne*, 167: "[Donne] did not regard mutability just as an implacable external force. He saw, rather, that it was a part of himself, and that to talk about himself (as he repeatedly tried to do in the poems) was to talk about change, and to change as he talked." See also, e.g., Guibbory, *Returning to John Donne*, 19–48.

8. For social time, see Richard J. Quinones, *The Renaissance Discovery of Time* (Cambridge, MA: Harvard University Press, 1972); and Cathy Yandell, *Carpe*

In *Devotions*, Donne excavates the conditions that underpin such happiness and sorrow, particularly the relationship between change and time, concepts shared by physick and physics:

> Variable, and therfore miserable condition of Man; this minute I was well, and am ill, this minute. I am surpriz'd with a sodaine change, and alteration to worse, and can impute it to no cause, nor call it by any name. We study *Health*, and we deliberate upon our *meats*, and *drink*, and *Ayre*, and *exercises*, and we hew, and wee polish every stone, that goes to that building; and so our *Health* is a long and a regular work; But in a minute a Cannon batters all, overthrowes all, demolishes all; a *Sicknes* unprevented for all our diligence, unsuspected for all our curiositie; nay, undeserved, if we consider only *disorder*, summons us, seizes us, possesses us, destroyes us in an instant. (*Dev.* 232; 1.1)

Donne yokes physick—the study of illness and health and the various practices of "*meats*, and *drink*, and *Ayre*, and *exercises*" that might prevent the onset of sickness in specific cases—with physics, with its concerns for the general conditions of change and time. He highlights this intertwining in the opening sentences of *Devotions*, which dwell on various forms of change (variability, alteration, demolition, destruction) and simultaneously flag the time in which such changes occur: "this minute," "this minute," "a minute," "an instant."[9]

By 1623, Donne had been writing about change for decades. In the elegy "Change," Donne claims that "Change is the nursery / Of musicke, joy, life, and eternity" (*Son.* 20; 35–36). These lines weave the philosophy of change into the conclusion of a poem that pleads for sexual freedom, much like the opening of the elegy "Variety": "The heavens rejoyce in motion, why should I / Abjure my so much lov'd variety, / And not with many youth and love divide?" (*Son.* 104; 1–3). The Ovidian promiscuity of Donne's desire is isomorphic with a change that extends as far as the mind can reach: even eternity comes of age in change's "nursery." Donne also explores the annihilating change that comes with loss in "Nocturnall upon S. Lucies Day," where love ruins him and he is "re-begot / Of absence, darknesse, death; things which are not" (*Son.* 85; 17–18). Human

Corpus: Time and Gender in Early Modern France (Newark: University of Delaware Press, 2000).

9. On Donne's stylistic habit of repeating words or phrases to build unity across his rhetorical periods, see Joan Webber, *Contrary Music: The Prose Style of John Donne* (Madison: University of Wisconsin Press, 1963), 51–52, 67–69.

beings change as quickly as the world, a fact highlighted in *The Second Anniversarie*, where lovers are rivers: "she" and "thou," who "did begin to love, are neither now. / You are both fluid, chang'd since yesterday . . . So flowes her face, and thine eies" (*Ann.* A2:52; 391–97). Heraclitus is dressed in Petrarchan garb: you never kiss the same lover twice. In *Devotions*, Donne deepens such speculation, revealing a poetic dialogue with the physics of time. In Station 10, he claims that it is only the "light of *God*" that "bends not to this *Center*, to *Ruine*," for "that which was not made of *Nothing*, is not threatned with this annihilation. All other things are; even *Angels*, even our *soules*; they move upon the same *poles*, they bend to the same *Center*; and if they were not made immortall by *preservation*, their *Nature* could not keepe them from sinking to this *center*, *Annihilation*" (*Dev.* 269; 10.1). Just as God alone is capable of creation, so only God can annihilate or reduce something to nothing. Yet every created thing is haunted by an originary nothingness that makes change inevitable.[10] All created things move and bend in an ongoing process of change indelibly marked by the *nihil* from which God first created.

Annihilation was a technical term that Donne borrowed from scholastic philosophy, which provided the conceptual space within which he represents change.[11] This is not to say that Donne held scholastic views on the nature of change. He treated the topic according to multiple models, including the various frameworks propounded by what he calls "new philosophy." But if Donne was not committed to scholastic thought, he nevertheless relied on an Aristotelian conceptual matrix because its treatment of change was fine-grained and nuanced. As Aristotle says in *Physics*, "there are as many types of motion or change as there are of being" (Ar. 1:343; 201a). According to Thomas Aquinas, "change means that the same thing should be different now from what it was previously."[12] This

10. In a sermon preached at the funeral of Sir William Cokayne in 1626, Donne puts it this way: "in temporall [things], there is nothing Permanent . . . nothing upon Earth is permanent" (*Ser.* 7:271).

11. On scholastic understandings of change, see Des Chene, *Physiologia*, 21–52; and Robert Pasnau, *Metaphysical Themes, 1274–1671* (Oxford: Clarendon Press, 2011). For an earlier treatment of Donne and scholastic thought, see Theresa M. DiPasquale, "From Here to Aeviternity: Donne's Atemporal Clocks," *Modern Philology* 110, no. 2 (2012): 226–52. For Donne's *annihilation* in relation to *kenosis*, see Ross Lerner, *Unknowing Fanaticism: Reformation Literatures of Self-Annihilation* (New York: Fordham University Press, 2019), 59–82.

12. Thomas Aquinas, *Summa theologica*, 5 vols., trans. Fathers of the English Dominican Providence (South Bend, IN: Christian Classics, 1948), 1:234 (P1.Q45.A2). Subsequent quotations cited parenthetically.

emphasis on the "same thing" is why Aquinas insists that demonstrations of divine power—creation and annihilation—are distinct from ordinary forms of change. Since creation brings something out of nothing and annihilation brings something back to nothing, it is impossible for the "same thing" to persist.[13]

In the Aristotelian framework on which Donne drew, there are two types of change, an English word used to translate the Latin *motus*, which, like the Greek *kinesis*, refers to both change and motion. First, *substantial change* affects prime matter. Substantial change takes place when a substance (a combination of matter and form like a human being, cat, rose, or rock) comes into being from some other substance or substances through prime matter (*generation*) or ceases to be and returns to some other substance or substances through prime matter (*corruption*). Second, *accidental change* affects individual substances. This category of change includes how a given substance moves, how its quantity increases or decreases, and how its qualities—color, temperature, health, sickness—change. Both substantial and accidental changes were understood to be ordinary kinds of change, "the actualization of what is potentially, qua potential" (Ar. 1:343; 201a). Such changes involve the actualization of a potentiality, for *kinesis* "occurs just when the actualization itself occurs, and neither before nor after" (Ar. 1:343; 201b). Change involves the actualization of a potential both in what acts (the agent) and in what is acted upon (the patient). But this relationship is asymmetrical insofar as "motion [or change] is in the movable" (Ar. 1:344; 202a). To use scholastic terms, *motus* inheres in the patient. If one becomes ill, then that change marks the actualization of a potential through an agent (a disease) acting on a patient (the bodily life affected) so that change inheres in that patient.

In a philosophical context, the phrase "the patient suffers" refers to something that passively receives an act such that some feature of its own potentiality becomes actualized and change inheres within it. Beyond this philosophical context, the phrase also refers to someone suffering from illness. *Devotions* unfolds the implications of this semantic overlap. Donne uses his own sickness as an occasion to articulate a first-person philosophy of change. The suffering patient becomes a patient who suffers. In the title of the first station, Donne positions his sickness within this framework: "Insultus Morbi Primus; *The first alteration, The first grudging of the sicknesse*" (Dev. 232; 1.1). This invocation of *alteratio* is carried into text's first sentences: "Variable, and therfore miserable condi-

13. As Aquinas puts it, "*Creatio non est mutatio,*" creation is not substantial change (1:234; P1.Q45.A2).

tion of Man; this minute I was well, and am ill, this minute. I am surpriz'd
with a sodaine change, and alteration to worse, and can impute it to no
cause, nor call it by any name" (*Dev.* 232; 1.1). The speaker's substance
suffers an unexpected alteration, a qualitative change so sudden that it
causes surprise, obscures its cause, and resists the act of naming.

This passage reworks a 1618 sermon in which Donne quotes from
Aquinas, who, in *Summa theologica*, claims that Adam was subject only to
positive alterations. In the sermon, Donne asks,

> Had there been no sicknesse, if there had been no sinne? *Secundum pas-*
> *siones perfectivas*, we acknowledge in the School, man was passible before:
> Every *alteration* is in a degree a *passion*, a *suffering*; and so, in those things
> which conduced to [Adam's] *well-being*, *eating*, and *sleeping*, and other
> such, man was *passible*: that is, subject to *alteration*; But, *Secundum pas-*
> *siones destructivas*, to such sufferings, as might frustrate the end for which
> he was made, which was *Immortality*, he was not subject, and so, not to
> sicknesse. Now he is; and put all the miseries, that man is subject to, to-
> gether, *sicknesse* is more than all. (*Ser.* 2:79)[14]

Drawing on Aristotle's definition of *kinesis* and scholastic debates about
motus, Donne casts alteration as "a degree a *passion*," the actualization
of a potential that brings about qualitative change. Whereas Adam was
subject only to alterations that "conduced to his *well-being*," his descendants are also subject to negative alterations like sickness, which lead
to corruption, the loss of substance that progresses, in the words of the
sixteenth-century Jesuit scholastic Pedro da Fonseca, "from the perfect to
the imperfect and in all ways toward nonbeing."[15] Reframing this insight
in *Devotions*, Donne positions the onset of his own sickness as an "alteration to worse" that is a consequence of Adam's "first sinne" (*Dev.* 232; 1.1).

Devotions represents the accidental changes that affect Donne in what,
as he suffered from severe illness, he thought were the moments leading
up to the substantial change introduced by death. "*Mortalitas Mutabili-*
tas," Donne writes in a 1617 sermon: "even this, That we must die, is a continual change" (*Ser.* 1:231). But death is not just any change. It is a corruption, a substantial change. Since the term *change* applies only to the "same
thing," when a human substance dies it can no longer change. After death,
one's human substance no longer exists. To put it in more technical terms,

---

14. The Latin in this passage is quoted from Aquinas, *Summa theologica*, 1:490
(P1.Q97.A2).

15. Quoted in Des Chene, *Physiologia*, 33.

since, in Aquinas's words, "the generation of one thing is the corruption of another [*generatio unius est corruptio alterius*]," the moment of death is a substantial change in which a living human substance is corrupted and a corpse is generated (1:352; P1.Q72.A1). Change continues to affect the generated corpse. "There is," as Donne puts it in *The Second Anniversarie*, describing twitching corpses, "motion in corruption" (*Ann.* A2:41; 22), a phrase that playfully suggests that change bubbles even in *corruptio*. But if, in Donne's revision of Lucretius, the body of a "beheaded man" still moves—"His eies will twinckle, and his tongue will roll"; "He graspes his hands, and he puls up his feet" (*Ann.* A2:41; 13–15)[16]—it is no longer possible for the human being to change, for that substance is gone, at least until the general resurrection.

In *Deaths Duell*, Donne dwells on what will happen after "the *final dissolution* of body and soule, the end of all," asking: "But then is that the end of all? Is that dissolution of body and soule, the last death that the body shall suffer? (for of spirituall death wee speake not now). It is not. . . . [There is still] an *entrance* into the *death of corruption and putrefaction* and *vermiculation* and *incineration,* and *dispersion* in and from the *grave*" (*Ser.* 10:235–36). That is, after the corruption of a given human substance, there remains the process of decomposition in which the substance of the corpse is repeatedly corrupted, in turn generating new and smaller substances while "my *mouth* shall be *filled* with *dust,* and the *worme* shall *feed,* and *feed sweetely* upon me" (*Ser.* 10:238).[17] Attached to his own body as *his,* Donne describes the rotting body in first-person terms. But his use of *corruption* suggests that he understands decomposition as substantial change. Death corrupts an individual human substance such that it ceases to exist. Whereas substantial change happens only at the beginning and end of human life, the duration of that life, poised between generation and corruption, is characterized by alteration and other forms of accidental change. *Devotions* chronicles the many accidental changes that propel Donne's speaker—the verbal representation of a human substance— toward (but not quite into) the climactic instant when it will suffer the substantial change wrought by death.

Donne attempts to represent this ultimate change as well. He attempts, that is, to phenomenalize corruption, the substantial change we call death.

16. See Lucretius, *The Nature of Things,* trans. A. E. Stallings (London: Penguin Classics, 2007), 91 (3:654–66).

17. For an especially compelling reading of this passage, see Kimberly Johnson, *Made Flesh: Sacrament and Poetics in Post-Reformation England* (Philadelphia: University of Pennsylvania Press, 2014), 91–94.

This phenomenal representation of substantial change was daring, a literary experiment that inverted long-established ideas from the physics of time. As Arnold Brooks has shown, there was a centuries-old debate over the time in which accidental and substantial changes were thought to take place, a topic about which Aristotle was himself perhaps divided.[18] Was all change continuous, unfolding in time? Or were some changes instantaneous? Various commentators took up differing stances on this issue, but a gradual consensus took hold. In *Kitāb al-shifā'*, Ibn Sina (known in the Latin west as Avicenna) argues that substantial change is always instantaneous.[19] Following his lead, thinkers writing in Arabic and Latin adopted similar views.[20] Donne thus inherited a long line of arguments in which such substantial changes as the corruption of death were held to be necessarily instantaneous. However, when Donne imagines his way inside the substantial change known as death, he represents an event thought to be instantaneous as though it were successive.

The Physics of Time

We turn now to focus on how Donne understood and represented instantaneous change. Sometimes called "the instant of change," a canonical framing of the difficulty in conceptualizing the relation between change and the instant is this: if a body changes from rest to movement, it is unclear at what point in time that change took place, since it did not occur when the body was resting and it has already occurred when the body is moving.[21] Donne phenomenalizes this abstract relation between change

18. Arnold Brooks, "A Fault Line in Aristotle's *Physics*," *Ancient Philosophy* 39 (2019): 335–61.

19. See, e.g., Avicenna, *The Physics of the Healing*, 2 vols., trans. Jon McGinnis (Provo, UT: Brigham Young University Press, 2009), 1:109–10 (2.1.3). See also Jon McGinnis, *Avicenna* (Oxford: University of Oxford Press, 2010), 84: "Unlike accidental changes, which always take a period of time to occur, substantial changes, according to Avicenna, do not take any time, but occur all at once. In other words, when a substance of kind A becomes a substance of kind B, then that change must occur at an instant."

20. See Brooks, "A Fault Line," who discusses the commentators on Aristotle's physics of time, noting a lineage of thinkers reading substantial change as instantaneous from Ibn Bajja to Aquinas.

21. For the instant of change, see Richard Sorabji and Norman Kretzman. "Aristotle on the Instant of Change," *Proceedings of the Aristotelian Society, Supplementary Volumes* 50 (1976): 69–114. The Donne scholar who comes closest to the instant of change is Julia J. Smith, "Moments of Being and Not-Being in Donne's *Sermons*," *Prose Studies: History, Theory, Criticism* 8 (1985): 3, who references Donne's fascina-

and time, thereby developing a representational strategy adequate to absolute velocity. Across his career, he experiments with such a strategy, a way of transforming language into a temporal technology for slowing time down, for rendering the instantaneous successive. Such scholars as Robert Ellrodt have argued that although Donne's focus "on the here and now" has some precedents in Roman elegy, in Petrarch, and in Sidney, "Donne's arresting of the present tenuous instant is peculiar," something deeper than "a mere characteristic of his art."[22] We argue that Donne's focus on the "present tenuous instant" is underpinned by two overlapping techniques that took him decades to develop: first, the phenomenalization of abstractions like the "instant of change," which he repurposed from the physics of time; and second, the poetic deceleration of such phenomenalized concepts. Reconstructing how Donne thought his way inside changes too swift for human beings to perceive, we move from abstraction to sensation, following one of the paths by which Donne came, in T. S. Eliot's words, to feel his thought.[23]

The earliest evidence of Donne's engagement with the instant of change is in a flourish at the end of a 1608 letter, written in the midst of what Bald has described as "the most disturbed and anxious years" of his life (Bal. 235). During this period Donne underwent a spiritual crisis, made faltering attempts to right his capsized career, struggled to provide for an expanding family, and lived in unwanted solitude at Mitcham (outside of London). In the letter, Donne reflects on the loss of his career in the aftermath of a marriage that has brought him "wretched fortune" and a "melancholy" mood he must hide from his family (Let. 137–38). "I am the worst present man in the world," he tells Sir Henry Goodyer before rallying his creative energy in the letter's final sentence: "yet the instant, though it be nothing, joynes times together, and therefore this unprofitableness, since I have been, and will still indevour to be so, shall not interrupt me now from being / Your servant and lover, J. Donne" (Let. 139). Donne views the isolation of Mitcham as a state of suspension that

---

tion with an "instant which spans two adjacent times." Targoff, John Donne, 150, references "Donne's preoccupation with capturing the exact instant of change," but does not bring to light the technical meanings of the term or invoke its history.

22. Robert Ellrodt, Seven Metaphysical Poets: A Structural Study of the Unchanging Self (Oxford: Oxford University Press, 2000), 111. We agree with Ellrodt, 320–30, that Donne opened "new perceptions of time," but we differ on what is new.

23. See T. S. Eliot, "The Metaphysical Poets," TLS 1031 (1921): 669: "Tennyson and Browning are poets and they think; but they do not feel their thoughts as immediately as the odour of a rose. A thought to Donne was an experience; it modified his sensibility."

has decelerated time; he could dissolve into "unprofitableness" were it not for his relationship with Goodyer.

The dark emotional charge of this sentence is conveyed through a conception of time at odds with itself: Donne positions the instant as part of time (a synonym for the present moment) and as outside of time (a joint separate from but nevertheless connecting points of time). On the one hand, he aligns the "instant" with the present moment or now. Since the instant is "nothing" but only "joynes times together," the "unprofitableness" in which Donne finds himself cannot "interrupt" his role as Goodyer's "servant and lover." Donne's status as "the worst present man in the world" is reduced to an instantaneous nothing that connects what Donne has "been" in the past to what he "will still endeavor to be" in the future. He can say that he is "now" Goodyer's "servant and lover" because the instant is nothing. But such a reading contradicts the premise that makes it possible: namely, that the present moment, the now, is an instant. Donne provides continuity between past, present, and future iterations of himself by claiming that his "present" condition is a nothing, a pure form of mediation, an instant joining points of time. For the sentence to work, the present moment needs to be both a part of time (the "now" in which Donne is Goodyer's servant) and outside of time (an "instant" that is "nothing" and joins times together). Donne folds the central crux of the instant of change—"Is the instant part of time or outside of time?"—into an epistolary valediction.

Derived ultimately from the paradoxes of Zeno of Elea, perhaps the most influential treatment of this question is found in Plato's *Parmenides*: "the instant [*exaiphnes*] seems to signify something such that change proceeds from it into either state. There is no change from rest while resting, nor from motion while moving; but this instant [*exaiphnes*], a strange nature [*physis atopos*], is something inserted between motion and rest, and it is no time at all."[24] In the 1590 edition of Plato's *Opera omnia* that Donne consulted during the 1614 composition of his *Essays in Divinity*, Marsilio Ficino flags this passage in a printed marginal note: "*inuenitur momentum & instans*," the invention or discovery of the moment and instant.[25] For Plato, the instant is a "strange nature" because it facilitates

24. Plato, *Complete Works*, ed. John M. Cooper (Indianapolis: Hackett, 1997), 388 (*Parmenides*, 156d–e). For Zeno's treatment of the instant, see W. C. Salmon, *Zeno's Paradoxes*, 2nd ed. (Indianapolis: Hackett), 2001.

25. Plato, *Opera omnia*, ed. and trans. Marsilio Ficino (Frankfurt, 1590), F iiij. For Donne's familiarity with this edition, see Donne, *Essayes in Divinity*, ed. Anthony Raspa (Montreal: McGill-Queen's University Press, 2001), 176.

change in time but remains, in Ficino's translation, "*nullo prorsus in tempore est*," outside of time.[26] Here is the source for Donne's claim that the instant is a "nothing" that "joynes" parts of time.

The other half of Donne's valedictory flourish—the instant is coterminous with the present "now"—stems from Aristotle. In the *Physics*, Aristotle defines *exaiphnes* as "what has departed from its former condition in a time imperceptible because of its smallness" (Ar. 1:376; 222b). The *exaiphnes* occurs not outside of time but in time, and it is therefore of a piece with Aristotle's notion of the now or *to nun*, which is "indivisible and is inherent in all time" (Ar. 1:395; 233b). Since it reaches indivisibility by being a limit of both future and past, *to nun* shares in the nonbeing of past and future. This means that *to nun* cannot be part of time: "But of time some parts have been, while others are going to be, and no part of it *is*, though it is divisible. For the 'now' [*to nun*] is not a part; a part is a measure of the whole, which must be made up of parts. Time, on the other hand, is not held to be made up of 'nows'" (Ar. 1:370; 218a). *To nun* is difficult to parse because, as Richard Sorabji argues, Aristotle uses the term in two ways, sometimes as a static period (which Sorabji calls the "instant") and sometimes as "the flowing notion of presentness."[27] The ambiguity of Aristotle's *to nun* engendered disagreement among early modern commentators, who differed on whether the now is part of time. In *De communibus omnium rerum* (1576), Benedictus Pereirius glosses Aristotle as claiming that "no part of time exists, since the past does not exist but was, and moreover the future does not exist but will be, and moreover the present is nothing other than the indivisible now [*nunc*], which cannot be a part of time."[28] Adopting another view, in his *Commentaria on the Physics* (1573), Franciscus Toletus argues that although time is unlike "other permanent existences," which present all of their "parts" at once, it nevertheless possesses "real existence" through the "instant [*instans*]."[29]

---

26. Plato, *Opera omnia*, F iiij.

27. Richard Sorabji, *Time, Creation, and Continuum: Theories in Antiquity and the Early Middle Ages* (Ithaca, NY: Cornell University Press, 1983), 48.

28. Quoted in Michael Edwards, *Time and the Science of the Soul in Early Modern Philosophy* (Leiden: Brill, 2013), 26–27. For Donne's knowledge of Pereira, see Donne, *Essayes in Divinity*, 117.

29. Quoted in Edwards, *Time and the Science of the Soul*, 24–26. For Donne's knowledge of Toletus, see Donne, *Pseudo-Martyr*, ed. Anthony Raspa (Montreal: McGill-Queen's University Press, 1993), 102. If, as Ettenhuber, *Donne's Augustine*, demonstrates, Donne read Augustine through a tapestry of sources, the same is true of Aristotle. For the plurality of "Renaissance Aristotelianisms," see Charles B. Schmitt, *Aristotle in the Renaissance* (Cambridge: Harvard University Press, 1983), 10–33.

Is the instant of change part of time or outside of time? Plato places it outside. Aristotle folds it into time's flow, but claims that *to nun* is not, strictly speaking, part of time. The Latin through which Donne read this debate would have muddied his understanding. Ficino translates Plato's *exaiphnes* as *momentum*, but he synonymizes the term with *instans*. The numerous translations of and commentaries on Aristotle render *to nun* in different ways, often as *nunc* but also as *momentum* or *instans*, the very terms Ficino uses for Plato's *exaiphnes*. The difficulty of parsing this question is manifest in the slippage in Donne's 1608 letter between the instant as a "nothing" that joins points of time and the instant as the present moment itself.

The longevity of Donne's interest in this question is registered in a sermon delivered a decade later. Preaching on June 16, 1619, Donne places the present moment at the center of Christian belief: "There is not a more comprehensive, a more embracing word in all Religion, than *Now.*" The word *Now* speaks to the transformations at the heart of Christianity—incarnation, conversion, resurrection—denoting "an Advent, a new coming, a new operation, otherwise than it was before." This transformative power raises a question: what is the now that enables these religious possibilities? "It is an extensive word, *Now*," Donne claims, passing from semantics to physics through the instant of change: "for though we dispute whether this *Now*, that is, whether an instant be any part of time or no, yet in truth it is all time; for whatsoever is past, was, and whatsoever is future, shall be an instant; and did and shall fall within this *Now*" (*Ser.* 2:250). Donne here conjures the instant of change. Is this instant when things become "otherwise than [they were] before" part of time's flow? Or is it outside of time?

The solution Donne offers in this sermon—that the instant is synonymous with the present moment, that the instant is not only in time but "is all time"—suggests how far his 1619 view departs from that of 1608. No longer associated with a "nothing" that joins points of time, the instant is here the constitutive unit of all time. This movement from nothingness (the instant as an empty form of mediation) toward plenitude (the instant as the very stuff of time) is based on the "new Advent" of Christ's *parousia*, the second coming when time will be redeemed and, as Donne puts it, "death shall be no more" (*Div.* 9; 6.14).[30] The sermon presents a vision in which the radical plenitude of Christ's resurrection and reincarnation will triumph over death. It is worth stressing that Donne articu-

30. This quotation comes from Donne's "Death Be Not Proud." The most sophisticated treatment of Donne's relationship to the second coming is David Marno, *Death Be Not Proud: The Art of Holy Attention* (Chicago: University of Chicago Press, 2016).

lates this theological point through the language of physics. The instant of change is the scaffold upon which Donne explains Christian doctrine.

Inside the Instant

Sometime before the summer of 1609, Donne began to use the instant of change as a conceptual model from which to explore what it is like to live through change in time:[31]

> This is my playes last scene, here heavens appoint
> My pilgrimages last mile; and my race
> Idly, yet quickly runne, hath this last pace,
> My spans last inch, my minutes last point,
> And gluttonous death will instantly unjoynt
> My body,' and soule, and I shall sleepe a space,
> But my'ever-waking part shall see that face,
> Whose feare already shakes my every joynt:
> Then, as my soule, to'heav'n her first seate, takes flight,
> And earth-borne body, in the earth shall dwell,
> So, fall my sinnes, that all may have their right,
> To where they'are bred, and would presse me, to hell.
> Impute me righteous, thus purg'd of evill,
> For thus I leave the world, the flesh, and devill. (*Div.* 7; 3.1–14)[32]

The sonnet begins with deictic phrases that blur space into time. As the speaker proposes and abandons commonplaces that figure human life as a temporal movement through space (a play, a pilgrimage, a race), each deictic marker ("This," "here") moves closer to the "last" event of a life reduced from mile, to span, to inch. This condensation triggers a turn to time, as minute falls into "point."[33] Donne's conceit is that the poem is

---

31. In Donne, *The Variorum Edition of the Poetry of John Donne*, ed. Gary A. Stringer and Paul A. Parish (Bloomington: University of Indiana Press, 2005), 7.1:lxxxviii–ci, Stringer and Parrish challenge the dating of 1608–10 put forward by Helen Gardner, ed., *The Divine Poems*, 2nd ed. (Oxford: Clarendon, 1978). According to Stringer and Parish, c–ci, the evidence only enables one to say that the "Group-III sequence antedates the summer of 1609."

32. In the manuscripts for this poem, here is a significant variant in line 7: "Or presently (I knowe not) see that face."

33. For Donne and deixis, see Heather Dubrow, *Deixis in the Early Modern English Lyric: Unsettling Spatial Anchors like "Here," "This," "Come"* (New York: Palgrave, 2015), 93–110.

uttered from this precipice. Stalled on the last "point" of a living present, the speaker anticipates a future in which death "will instantly unjoynt" soul from body. Much of the poem is uttered in expectation: death
"will" separate the speaker's body and soul, his I "shall sleepe a space," his
soul "shall see that face," and "Then, as" his soul "takes flight"—a phrase
uttered in the present but pitched toward the future—his body "shall
dwell" in the earth. The events signaled by these future-oriented phrases
are staved off. Time stops and a "point" swells to include a theologically
vexed prayer for God to "Impute [the speaker] righteous" so that he can
"leave the world" "purg'd of evill."[34] In this soteriological fantasy, Donne
stalls time both to represent an anticipated instant of change and to provide his speaker with an impossible pause from which a plea for grace can
be expressed.[35]

"This is my playes last scene" reworks Augustine's handling of the instant of change in *De civitate Dei* (426 CE). In Augustine's view, one cannot locate the exact "moment of time when the soul is separated from the
body": before death comes, one is alive and the soul is in the body, but
when death has come, the soul has departed and one has already died.[36]
Donne imagines this moment by organizing his sonnet around a temporal pause that enables lyric speech to emerge from a precipice overlook-
ing the instant of change when life gives way to death.[37] Note how Donne
coordinates the noun *point* and the adverb *instantly*. In *Essays in Divinity*,
Donne claims that the beginning described in Genesis entered existence
alongside time itself and then "instantly vanished," for "being but the
first point of time, [this beginning] died as soon as it was made, flowing
into the next point."[38] If a temporal point is evanescent, it remains a thing
best articulated by a noun (*point*); an adverb (*instantly*) can only modify

34. Richard Strier, "John Donne Awry and Squint: The 'Holy Sonnets,' 1608–
1610," *Modern Philology* 86 (1989): 357–84, argues that Donne's struggles to accept
Calvinism are registered in poems that refuse theological coherence.

35. This plays out similarly in "At the round earths imagin'd corners," in which the
general resurrection is conjured and held off: "But let them sleepe, Lord, and mee
mourne a space, / For if above all these, my sinnes abound, / 'Tis late to aske abundance of thy grace" (*Div.* 8; 4.9–11).

36. Augustine, *City of God against the Pagans*, trans. R. W. Dyson (Cambridge:
Cambridge University Press, 1998), 549–50 (*De civitate Dei*, 13.9). In all quotations
of Augustine, we have made reference to J. P. Migne, ed., *Patralogia cursus completus,
series Latina*, 221 vols. (Paris, 1844–65).

37. For a different way of understanding this issue, see Thomas Docherty, *John
Donne, Undone* (London: Methuen, 1986), 95–96.

38. John Donne, *Essays in Divinity*, ed. Evelyn M. Simpson. (Oxford: Clarendon,
1952), 17.

an action.[39] In "This is my playes last scene," Donne stresses the difference between time-bound action and tenuous entity through a rhyme based on polyptoton ("appoint" with "point") that grammatically stalls temporal movement by translating a verb into the noun from which it is etymologically derived. The status of *point* is emphasized by the term's derivation from Euclidian geometry, a heritage Donne invokes by allowing the temporal point to emerge from spatial images ("My pilgrimages last mile," "My spans last inch") and lead to a spatialization of time ("I shall sleepe a space") further encouraged by how the term *space*, like the Latin *spatium*, has both spatial and temporal connotations.[40]

The model of time presupposed in "This is my playes last scene" is similar to that envisioned in Donne's 1608 letter to Goodyer: the instant is the "nothing" that "joynes" points of time, facilitates temporal flow, and accompanies change. As a non-thing, its function is best expressed adverbially: "And gluttonous Death will instantly unjoynt / My Bodie, and Soule." This adverb has two temporal meanings. First, at the moment of death the soul will be "instantly" unjointed from the body "at this very moment," "at once."[41] And second, the onset of death will occur "instantly," as soon as the speaker's impossibly stalled "last point" expires, "in a moment" or "forthwith."[42] "This is my playes last scene" probes the distinction between point and instant: the poem is uttered from a temporal point stalled at the brink of an instant that will not join the speaker's "last point" to another but will instead open onto the unjointing of lived time. Distinguishing point from instant, Donne gives readers an indivisible unit of time that can be paused and inhabited, a stable unit from which anticipation of the coming instant is possible. "This is . . . my minutes last point": the pronoun marks the "point" as belonging to the speaker, something of which he is aware. Donne takes the instant of change as a conceptual model from which to represent what it is like to live through change. Here his poetic invention begins to translate abstraction (the instant of change) into the terms of life as it is lived.[43]

39. For Donne's grammatical play, see Brian Cummings, *The Literary Culture of the Reformation: Grammar and Grace* (Oxford: Oxford University Press, 2002), 366–77.

40. In *The Second Anniversarie*, Donne toys with this geometrical meaning: "though all doe know, that quantities / Are made of lines, and lines from Points arise, / None can these lines or quantities unjoynt / And say this is a line, or this a point" (*Ann.* A2:44–45; 131–34).

41. *OED*, s.v. "instantly," adv. 2.

42. *OED*, s.v. "instantly," adv. 3a.

43. Donne draws on a long tradition dedicated to the phenomenality of time's passage. In *De sensu*, Aristotle argues that it is not "conceivable that any portion of time

What does this sonnet's stalled "last point" allow Donne to disclose? The sonnet shoots off in contradictory directions, sketching what
Richard Strier describes as a theologically strained "fantasy of material
purification."[44] Between the speaker's invocation of his "last point" and
the poem's concluding prayer, a parade of terms and personifications takes
the stage: after "gluttonous Death" unjoints body from soul, the speaker's
"I" will go to sleep, his soul will fly to heaven and receive a beatific vision,
and his body will return to earth, while his sins will fall into Hell. Each
shares the temporal modality of expectation. This futurity is signaled by
the phrases "will instantly unjoynt" and "shall sleepe a space." The immediacy of this future is heightened by Donne's use of the future-oriented
but grammatically present demonstrative adverb *then*, which, with a
quick sleight of hand, positions an imminent future event as already here,
thereby making the expected future seem inevitable, already here: "Then
as my soule, to heav'n her first seat, takes flight / And earth-borne body,
in the earth shall dwell, / Soe fall my sinnes." In this funny temporality, featuring a future that falls back ambiguously into the present, the
speaker's utterance is nevertheless framed as spoken in the absolute present inscribed in "my minute's last point." The speaker's anticipation of a
vision of the divine causes an embodied response here and now—the
"feare" of God's face "already shakes my every joynt"—and he concludes
by returning to the present: "For thus I leave the world." What Donne's
paused temporal point discloses is the simultaneous jumble of human
perception ("This is . . . my minute's last point"), emotion ("feare"), and

---

should be imperceptible, or that any should be unnoticeable; the truth being that it
is possible to perceive every instant of time." Even the tiniest portions of time must
be available to perception because if there were "a time so small as to be absolutely
imperceptible, then it is clear that a person would, during such a time, be unaware of
his own existence, as well as of his seeing and perceiving" (Ar. 1:711; 448a). Augustine
made temporal perception central to *Confessiones*: "Human soul, let us see whether
present time can be long. To you the power is granted to feel [*sentire*] intervals of
time, and to measure them" (Aug. 231–32, translation modified; 11.15.19). Augustine's
redefinition of the future as the "present of things to come"—the future exists only
as a modality of "expectation" (Aug. 235; 11.19.26)—is registered in "This is my playes
last scene" insofar as the final moment of the speaker's life is shaped by expectation.
The closest predecessor is the anonymous author of the *Cloud of Unknowing* (late
fourteenth century). *Cloud* argues that the atom is the "leest partie of tyme," so "litil"
that it is indivisible and almost "incomphrensible." These atoms correspond to the
workings of the will, such that exactly "so many willinges or desiringes" may be felt in
one hour as "aren athomus in one oure" (Anonymous, *The Cloud of Unknowing*, ed.
Phyllis Hodgson [Salzburg: Institut für Anglistik, 1982], 10).
    44. Strier, "Awry and Squint," 373.

bodily reaction (shaking "joynt[s]") that share the stage with an array of contradictory expectations. The poem evokes the complex states of mind that precede the moment of death, bringing literary representation to the edge of a change the first-personal qualities of which seem impossible to depict.

Dilating the Instant

By phenomenalizing the conceptual model of time referenced in the 1608 letter, "This is my playes last scene" develops a poetic decorum answerable to the state of mind that precedes imminent substantial change. But in this sonnet the contents of the instant of change remain elusive. To imagine his way inside this change, Donne needed to think the instant not as an empty form of mediation but as a successive process. Perhaps in response to this issue, in the second decade of the seventeenth century, Donne worked his way inside instantaneous change.

Take the "Obsequyes upon the Lord Harrington" (1614) as an example. Harrington died in 1614 at the age of twenty-one. One of the poem's conceits is that a short lifespan does not limit virtue. Donne writes that if Harrington had lived longer, "Wee might have seene, and said, that now he is / Witty, now wise, now temperate, now just" (*Ann.* 69; 72–73). Harrington's early demise does not permit such elaboration: forced to be "his owne epitomee," Harrington exhibited as many virtues "As all the long breath'd Chronicles can touch" in so "few yeares" that verse cannot accommodate these virtues (*Ann.* 69; 78–80). But this does not mean that these virtues were not there. Donne explains:

> As when an Angell downe from heav'n doth flye,
> Our quick thought cannot keepe him company,
> Wee cannot thinke, now hee is at the Sunne,
> Now through the Moon, now he through th'aire doth run,
> Yet, when he's come, we knowe he did repaire
> To all twixt Heav'n, and Earth, Sunne, Moone, and Aire;
> And as this Angell in an instant, knows,
> And yet wee know, this sodaine knowledge growes
> By quick amassing severall formes of things,
> Which he successively to order brings;
> When they, whose slow-pac'd lame thoughts cannot goe
> So fast as hee, thinke that he doth not so;
> Just as a perfect reader doth not dwell,
> On every syllable, nor stay to spell,

Yet without doubt, hee doth distinctly see
And lay together every A, and B;
So, in short liv'd good men, is'not understood
Each severall vertue, but the compound, good
For, they all vertues paths in that pace tread,
As Angells goe, and know, and as men reade. (*Ann.* 69; 81–100)

Donne uses three similes to explore the idea that what seems to occur instantly is in fact comprised of parts.

In the first, an angel descends, passing sun, moon, and air. But this trip happens too quickly for us to perceive; we can piece it together only after the event. And yet, angelic flight takes place in time: "Wee cannot thinke, now hee is at the Sunne, / Now through the Moon, now he through the'aire doth run." The angel moves past these places sequentially, but not in human time, for he accomplishes this motion faster than we can think three "now[s]." Donne draws selectively from Aquinas, who, in *Summa theologica*, describes two modes of angelic locomotion. In the first, "as a body, successively, and not all at once, quits the place in which it was before, and thence arises continuity in its local movement; so likewise an angel can successively quit the divisible place it was before" (1:270; P1.Q 53.A1). This means that "every movement, even of an angel, is in time"—although it is important to stress that this time is not that "whereby all corporeal things are measured" but of a more subtle variety. In the second mode, an angel can "all at once quit the whole place, and in the same instant apply himself to the whole of another place, and thus his movement will not be continuous" (1:272; P1.Q 53.A3). Donne articulates Aquinas's notion of successive angelic movement, but jettisons the noncontinuous, instantaneous movement on which Aquinas insists.[45] Donne performs a similar operation in his claim that although it seems to our "slow-pac'd lame thoughts" that an angel "in an instant, knowes," this instantaneousness is illusory because the angel actually shapes his thought, bringing the "severall formes of things" "successively to order." This claim departs from Aquinas, who argues that angelic knowledge is neither discursive nor tied up in composition or division, for angels "at once behold all things whatsoever that can be known to them" (1:289–90; P1.Q 58.A3–4).

<hr>

45. See Robert Ellrodt, "Angels and the Poetic Imagination from Donne to Traherne," in *English Renaissance Studies Presented to Dame Helen Gardner in Honor of Her Seventieth Birthday*, ed. John Carey (Oxford: Oxford University Press, 1980). For successive angelic movement, see also *Ser.* 7:409.

The third simile moves from abstraction to phenomenality. Donne appeals to the phenomenological evidence at hand: the first-person activities of the reader, who apprehends the temporal structure in question. A "perfect reader" is someone who no longer needs to fumble syllable by syllable, letter by letter; this reader looks at a word and instantly sees what it is. But this speed, known by everyone "perfect" enough to read Donne's poems, is underwritten by the skill of the eyes, which "distinctly see / And lay together every A, and B," even if this process goes unnoticed. This simile asks the reader to attend to the act of reading, to "see" oneself seeing the letters one takes for granted when one mentally grasps a word in what seems to be an instant. In performing this simple task, the reader perceives the successive assembly of letters that subtends the capacity to grasp words, and the reader does this by slowing down a process that should take only an instant. Donne asks his reader to perform an act of temporal deceleration that discloses parts of the phenomenal world that are usually ignored.

Embodying the Instant

Developed haltingly in "Obsequyes," this intertwining of felt temporality and the physics of time is perfected a decade later in *Devotions*, the first sentence of which invokes the instant of change: "[T]his minute I was well, and am ill, this minute" (*Dev.* 232; 1.1). In the same instant of change—its immediacy flagged by a repeated deictic "this"—Donne falls from health into sickness, from "was" to "am." But if Donne moves from health to illness in one and the same "minute," this means that he cannot isolate when he became sick. The centrality of this problem is signaled by the station's title, "Insultus Morbi Primus; *The first alteration, The first grudging of the sicknesse.*" There must be a moment when Donne's health "*first*" began to alter, when the sickness "*first*" grudged (that is, both seized and bore ill will toward) his body.[46] Before we become ill, Donne writes, we are "pre-afflicted, super-afflicted with these jelousies and suspitions, and apprehensions of *Sicknes*, befor we can cal it a sicknes; we are not sure we are ill; one hand askes the other by the pulse, and our eye askes our own urine, how we do" (*Dev.* 232; 1.1). Prior to the onset of illness, we are "not sure we are ill"; we examine ourselves. But even if we see signs of health, we can never be certain because in the same moment we feel a healthy pulse we could be "surpriz'd" with a "sodaine change, and alteration to worse." We cannot isolate the *primus insultus* because sickness "destroyes us in an instant" (*Dev.* 232; 1.1). Human existence is subject to

46. *OED*, s.v. "grudge," v. 5a, 1a, 2a.

emergent occasions, to events that arise instantly and "unexpectedly," to the brute fact of "happening."[47] It is for this reason that *Devotions* ends much as it begins, with uncertainty, with a fear of relapse.

Station 1 presents the instant of change as an ontologically urgent but phenomenally distant problem, an event of "discomposition" undisclosed to awareness (*Dev.* 233; 1.1). In a single instant we fall from health to illness, but we only register this fall later, when we feel the illness's effects as we live through them. The second station shifts from the event of the *primus insultus* to the moment when this event is phenomenally registered. When describing how, in the words of the second station's title, "*The strength, and the function of the Senses, and other faculties change and faile*," Donne situates this series of felt changes in the instant: "In the same instant that I feele the first attempt of the disease, I feele the victory; In the twinckling of an eye, I can scarce see; instantly the tast is insipid, and fatuous; instantly the appetite is dull and desirelesse; instantly the knees are sinking and strengthlesse" (*Dev.* 236; 2.1). Whereas the sudden change of illness has struck his body in the first station, here the disease manifests as a felt diminution of bodily powers. When Donne claims that he "can scarce see," he depicts the felt capacities of his lived body confronting the contracted limits of an unresponsive physical body. He situates these changes in felt time; he feels the "first attempt" and the "victory" of the disease in the "same instant" of change. Donne situates abstract problems from the physics of time within a phenomenal field capable of discerning the slightest bodily change. Like Augustine, Donne invokes the feeling of time passing. Instead of singing a hymn, as Augustine does in *Confessiones*, he finds the feeling of temporal change in the bodily manifestations of sickness.

This translation of Augustine's understanding of time from the soul to the body is reinforced by Donne's explicit engagement with *Confessiones* 11:

> All things are done in *time* too; but if we consider *Tyme* to be but the *Measure of Motion*, and howsoever it may seeme to have three *stations*, *past*, *present*, and *future*, yet the *first* and *last* of these *are* not (one is not, now, and the other is not yet) And that which you call *present*, is not *now* the same that it was, when you began to call it so in this *Line*, (before you found that word, *present*, or the *Monosyllable*, *now*, the present, and the *Now* is past,) if this *Imaginary halfe-nothing*, *Tyme*, be of the essence of our *Happinesses*, how can they be thought *durable*? (*Dev.* 286; 14.1)

---

47. *OED*, s.v. "emergent," adj. 5a; *OED*, s.v. "occasion," n. II 6a.

Donne responds here to Augustine's account of the difficulties we have in measuring the "intervals" of time to which we are "sensible" (Aug. 233, translation modified; 11.16.21). But he does not simply "evoke Augustine's example."[48] He replaces Augustine's recitation of Saint Ambrose's hymn with a printed line of words on a page. Donne assigns the reader the impossible task of locating the now in the sound of the "*Monosyllable, now.*" But by directing the reader's gaze to those words "in this *Line*" of printed text, he embodies the instant in a way that Augustine rejects by insisting that "the present occupies no space" (Aug. 232; 11.15.20).

The allusion to Saint Paul in Donne's discussion of illness' onset illuminates the alignment of the body with a feeling of time that was, for Augustine, the prerogative of the soul: "In the same instant that I feele the first attempt of the disease, I feele the victory; In the twinckling of an eye, I can scarce see" (*Dev.* 236; 2.1).[49] This sentence structures the fall into illness as an echo of Paul's description in 1 Corinthians 15:51–52 of what will happen to those still alive during the general resurrection: "Behold I show you a mystery, We shall not all sleep, but we shall all be changed, In a moment, in the twinkling of an eye, at the last trump: for the trumpet shall sound, and the dead shall be raised incorruptible, and we shall be changed." Donne's movement from the "instant" to the "twinckling of an eye" invokes Paul's "in a moment, in the twinkling of an eye," an English translation of the Greek *en atomo, en rhipe ophthalmou*, which the Vulgate's Latin renders *in momento, in ictu oculi.*[50] Donne had Paul in mind.[51] A few sentences earlier, he claims that a fever "doth not only *melt* [man], but *Calcine* him, reduce him to *Atomes* . . . And how quickly? Sooner than thou canst receive an answer, sooner than thou canst conceive the question" (*Dev.* 235–36; 2.1). Paul's *atomo* signifies an indivisible unit of time—a "brief moment, which leaves no room to divide it," in

48. Tabak, "'O Multiplied Misery!,'" 173. See also Targoff, *John Donne*, 145.

49. Donne may have discovered his sense of embodied time in Augustine, since, as Nightingale, *Once Out of Nature*, 56–57, argues, Augustine roots his grasp of "psychic time" in "earthly time": "The human mind always stretches away from the present moment, but this is not a random or abstract present. Rather, a person's mind distends from the present of his or her own body."

50. For Donne's bibles, see Donne, *Sermons Preached at the Court of Charles I*, The Oxford Edition of the Sermons of John Donne, 12 vols., ed. David Colclough (Oxford: Oxford University Press, 2013), 3:xlii–xliii.

51. For Donne's use of Paul's twinkling in relation to materialism, see Passannante, *Catastrophizing*, 111–13.

Augustine's words.[52] Using the trick developed in such poems as "Obsequyes," Donne inserts succession into the instant conjured by Paul's *in
ictu oculi*: "In the same instant that I feele the first attempt of the disease, I feele the victory" (*Dev.* 236; 2.1). Two feelings (the disease's first
attempt, its victory) jostle in "the same" instant. Donne draws on Paul's
terms for the resurrection's velocity to pause the instant of change and
reveal its phenomenal contents. This use of 1 Corinthians is in keeping
with Donne's most extensive interpretation of the passage. He discovered
in 1 Corinthians a precedent linking the successive contents of the instant
with the felt time of the body.

Exegesis of the Instant

In sermons delivered between 1619 and 1622, Donne phenomenalizes and
embodies the instant of change in readings of this passage from 1 Corinthians. His understanding of Paul inspires his representation of bodily
time in *Devotions*. Donne treats the passage in a 1619 sermon on Psalm
89: "*What man lives, and shall not see death?*" Although it is likely that
everyone must die, there may be some who do not: those invoked in 1
Corinthians, "whom Christ shal find upon the earth alive, at his returne
to Judge the World." It is clear that they "shall have a present and sudden dissolution, and a present and sudden re-union of body and soul
again" (*Ser.* 2:204). But it is unclear if this dissolution constitutes death.
Paul is enigmatic: "Behold, I shew you a mystery; We shall not all sleep,
but we shall all be changed." If, Donne argues, "sleep" is death, then Paul
means that those who are alive "shall not die," for in them "the coming
of Christ shall change the course of Nature." But if Paul's "sleep" is not
equivalent with death and signifies instead "a rest in the grave," then there
will be "An instant and sudden dis-union, and re-union of body and soul,
which is death." Donne cannot decide: "who can tell?" He has combed
exegetical history and found the interpreters divided: patristic writers argue one way, scholastics another; Donne's contemporaries—"later men"
like Luther and Calvin—are in conflict. What is "certain" is that both the
quick and the dead will undergo judgment and that whatever happens to
those still living during the resurrection will be instantaneous: "This is
certain, this all S. *Pauls* places collineate to, this all the Fathers, and all the
Schoole, all the *Cajetans*, and all the *Catharins*, and all the *Luthers*, and all
the *Calvins* agree in, *A judgement must be*, and it must be *In ictu oculi, In*

52. Augustine, *Sermon* 362.20, in *The Works of Saint Augustine*, 41 vols. (New York:
New City, 1995), 3.10:256.

the twinkling of an eye" (*Ser.* 2:205–6). Although the question of death is undecidable, the question of time is "certain"—it will occur *in ictu oculi.* What does this mean?

Donne provides an answer in a sermon delivered on Easter 1622, a few months after he became dean of Saint Paul's and about a year before *Devotions* was composed in 1623:

> In that change then, which we who are then alive, shall receive, (for though we shall not all sleep, we shall all be changed) we shall have a present dissolution of body and soul, and that is truly a death, and a present redintegration of the same body and the same soul, and that is truly a Resurrection; we shall die, and be alive again, before another could consider that we were dead; but yet this shall not be done in an absolute instant; some succession of time, though indiscernible there is. It shall be done *In raptu,* in a rapture; but even in a rapture there is a motion, a transition from one to another place. It shall be done, sayes he, *In ictu oculi, In the twinkling of an eye;* But even in the twinkling of an eie, there is a shutting of the eie-lids, and an opening of them again; Neither of these is done in an absolute instant, but requires some succession of time. (*Ser.* 4:75)

Some features of this interpretation are standard.[53] Less usual is Donne's insistence that the event "shall not be done in an absolute instant" but must take place in "some succession of time, though indiscernible," a view he shared with Aquinas.[54] Donne is alone in his reading of Paul's *in*

53. It was standard to claim that those alive at the end will die and be resurrected again along with the dead. In making this decision, Donne sided with Augustine, who argued for this view in *De civitate Dei* (1012–13; 20.20). This view was reiterated by Luther, who in Donne's 1619 summary understood Paul to mean that "all shall die, though all shall not be buried" (*Ser.* 2:205). See also Martin Luther, *Commentary on 1 Corinthians 15,* in *Luther's Works,* 55 vols., ed. Hilton C. Oswald (St. Louis: Concordia, 1973), 28:199–201.

54. Aquinas holds that the events in question will involve "some succession of time." If the resurrection will involve multiple "actions following another"—the "gathering of ashes, the refashioning of the body"—then it cannot be instantaneous since, as Aristotle says, "no local movement can be sudden." But this argument cannot withstand the authority of Paul's *in momento, in ictu oculi;* the "resurrection will be sudden." Yet Aquinas introduces a fine-grained distinction that preserves the bond between change and time while remaining true to 1 Corinthians: angels will reconstitute the body and God will re-fuse body and soul. What is "done by the ministry of angels, will not be instantaneous [*non erit in instant*], if by instant we mean an indivisible point of time [*si instans dicat indivisibile temporis*], but will be instantaneous if by instant we mean an imperceptible time [*erit tamen instans si instans accipiatur*]

momento, in ictu oculi. "But even in the twinkling of an eie, there is a shutting of the eie-lids, and an opening of them again," Donne writes, "Neither of these is done in an absolute instant, but requires some succession of time" (*Ser.* 4:75). His stress on the "succession of time" required for the movement of eyelids militates against an interpretive consensus about the parallelism of *in momento* and *in ictu oculi.* Gregory of Nyssa showcases how this relation was construed: "an instant will suffice to transform the creation and the twinkling of an eye expresses an indivisible instant, a limit of time with no part or extension."[55] Whereas tradition insisted that the twinkling eye rearticulates the speed implied by Paul's *atomo,* Donne separates these clauses: the "succession of time" required for "shutting the eyelids and opening them again" enables the suggestion that the transformation of the living "shall not be done in an absolute instant." Since there is hardly a better translation of Paul's *atomo* than "an absolute instant," Donne pits Paul against himself, prying *in momento* apart from *in ictu oculi.* This strategy was shaped by the physics of time. If the living must die during the resurrection, they must undergo a substantial change in which soul is separated from body before their "redintegration." The instant of change shapes Donne's scriptural interpretation: the motion from life to death and back to life requires passage through two instants of change. Such change requires time's passing, and so Paul's *in ictu oculi* cannot mean an "absolute instant."

There is also a deeper impulse at work here: the question of embodiment, the felt time Donne intuits in Paul's language and that enables the suggestion that even the end of time can be seen. Donne reads Paul's *ictu* as the movement of flesh. Avoiding the primary sense of the English *twinkling* as the "action of shining," Donne uses the term in its secondary sense, blinking.[56] He draws on the etymological claim that *oculi* stems from the verb *occludo,* that the Latin term for eyes arises because "they are covered

---

pro tempore imperceptibili]. But that which will be done immediately by God's power will happen suddenly [*subito*]" (5:2873; P3sup.Q77. A4).

55. Quoted in Ellrodt, *Seven Metaphysical Poets,* 325. Augustine makes a similar argument. See, e.g., Augustine, *Works,* 2.3:383 (*Epistle* 205.2.14). Luther similarly equates the *Augenblick* with the *atomo* that precedes it. See Luther, *Works,* 28:199–200. Likewise, Calvin claims that the second clause is an attempt to "convey [in different words] the idea of a moment" signaled in the first clause. See Jean Calvin, *Commentary on First Corinthians,* trans. John W. Fraser (Grand Rapids, MI: Eerdmans, 1996), 49.

56. *OED,* s.v. "twinkling," n. 1, 1 and 2.

and hidden with their Liddes."[57] In connecting this etymology to scriptural exegesis, Donne suggests that there is a difference between the abstraction of an absolute instant and things that seem to occur instantaneously. The blinking of an eye only seems to take place in an instant: it requires the temporal duration necessary for bodily movement, and this duration is, in principle, phenomenologically available. Donne attempts to inhabit the phenomenal thickness of what, in the human body, seems instantaneous.

Donne produces an interpretation of Paul that is pitched against Augustine. Consider Augustine's discussion of 1 Corinthians in a late sermon: "Rightly did the apostle Paul compare the ease of the resurrection with this speed, when he said, *in ictu oculi*. The twinkling of an eye does not consist in closing and opening the eyelids, because this is done more slowly than seeing. You bat an eyelid more slowly than you direct a ray [of vision]. Your ray gets to the sky more quickly than the batted eyelids reach the eyebrow."[58] Augustine stresses the phenomenal valences of Paul's image, situating a second-person addressee in the scene of vision. Paul's *ictu* must refer not to a blinking eyelid (a slow-moving body) but to the act of seeing itself, an act accomplished while the eyelids are still opening. Augustine's interpretation of *in ictu oculi* draws out the phenomenality of the image but preserves its velocity and maintains the parallelism. Donne reverses these priorities and insists on the embodiment of Paul's *ictu*, an interpretive move that enables him to render the instant of change embodied, successive. Even if the "succession of time" required for blinking may be "indiscernible," a "shutting of the eyelids and an opening of them again" remains an embodied action, phenomenally available in a way the abstraction of an "absolute instant" could never be. Donne's interpretation of *in ictu oculi* inserts felt embodied life into a conceptual space that had presupposed its absence.

Feeling Time, Feeling Change

In *Devotions*, Donne projects his reading of 1 Corinthians onto his illness. The disease acts on Donne's body in a way that changes how the world normally acts upon it (food, for instance, no longer elicits appetite) and

57. Helkiah Crooke, *Mikrokosmographia* (London, 1615), 535. Bede refers to this etymology in relation to Paul's *in ictu oculi*, "that tiniest interval of time in which the lids of our eyes move when a blow is launched against them, and which cannot be divided or distributed" (Bede, *The Reckoning of Time*, trans. Faith Wallis [Liverpool: Liverpool University Press, 1999], 16). Bede is the only figure we have found who reads Paul's twinkling eye as the closing of eyelids, and he maintains that this bodily movement "cannot be divided or distributed."

58. Augustine, *Works*, 3.8:39 (*Sermon* 277.11).

how it acts upon the world. When Donne claims "in the twinckling of an eye, I can scarce see," the adverb *scarce* invokes the relationship between the disclosure of the world and the bodily ability that makes such disclosure possible (*Dev.* 236; 2.1). Just as Donne feels the "first attempt" and the "victory" of the disease in the same instant, so he registers an alteration in visual capacity and the appearance of the world in the "twinckling of an eye" (*Dev.* 236; 2.1). The language of instantaneousness remains, but the passage works only because the instant is successive; it has slowed down so that the change in time at the heart of *Devotions* can be represented as something through which one lives. Donne holds that the sentient body is disclosed to attention when normal relations between self and world break down.

As he did in his 1622 sermon, in *Devotions* Donne enlists Augustine's Sermon 277 to conceive the relationship between illness and bodily life. Attempting to illuminate what the health of the resurrected body will be like, Augustine tries to "infer" how the glorious body will feel by appealing to the "sort [of health] that we do know." "What is health?" Augustine asks, and his answer is illuminating: "Sensing, feeling nothing." But health "isn't just not to feel, as a stone doesn't feel, as a tree doesn't feel, as a corpse doesn't feel; but to live in the body and to feel nothing of its being a burden [*sed vivere in corpore, et nihil ex eius onere sentire*], that's what being healthy is."[59] When Donne describes how "instantly the knees are sinking and strengthlesse" (*Dev.* 236; 2.1), he articulates what it is like to live through an illness, to "live in the body and to feel . . . its being a burden."

Devotions meditates on the relationship between two aspects of the body discerned by Augustine: first, the phenomenal feel of "liv[ing] in the body"; and second, the body as burden. The disease attacks the processes at work within Donne's body in unfelt ways; but he feels the disease's effects in the body through which he engages the world. "*Man,* who is the noblest part of the *Earth,* melts so away, as if he were a *statue,* not of *Earth,* but of *Snowe,*" Donne claims, before correcting himself: "[man] feeles that a *Fever* doth not melt him like *snow,* but pour him out like lead, like yron, like brasse melted in a furnace: It doth not only *melt* him, but *Calcine* him, reduce him to *Atomes,* and to *ashes*" (*Dev.* 235; 2.1). Illness changes the body as though it were in an alchemical experiment. Donne's sick body behaves like any aggregate of particles would behave under adverse conditions: it melts and calcines; it is reduced to atoms and ashes, the constitutive parts of all bodies. Yet, as Donne claims in the first station, he is "more than *dust and ashes*" (*Dev.* 233;

59. Augustine, 3.8:36–37 (*Sermon* 277.6).

1.2), for he possesses a proprietary relationship to his body. His body undergoes the material transformations associated with sickness, but he also "feeles" these processes (*Dev.* 235; 2.1). When Donne claims that at the onset of his sickness he "can scarce see" (*Dev.* 236; 2.1), he depicts the felt capacities of his lived body pushing up against the instantly contracted limits of an unresponsive and burdensome physical body.

Donne isolates the felt time of the body. Consider his cosmic account of rising from bed in Station 21: "I am *up*, and I seeme to *stand*, and I goe *round*, and I am a *new Argument* of the *new Philosophie*, That the *Earth* moves round; why may I not beleeve, that the *whole earth* moves in a *round motion*, though that seeme to mee to *stand*, when as I seeme to *stand* to my *Company*, and yet am carried, in a giddy, and *circular motion*, as I *stand*?" (*Dev.* 319–20; 21.1). This passage highlights the difference between being and seeming: standing, Donne seems to stand. He introduces a disjunction between the external and internal success conditions for standing. In the eyes of his "*Company*," his body stands, yet he feels that he is "carried, in a giddy, and *circular motion*." His inability to feel balanced denies him the right to claim that he stands, but he maintains the appearance of standing. Illness calls attention to how the felt phenomenality of life is distinct from the world in the same way that "the *new Philosophie*" uncouples the subjective perception of cosmic motion from the actual movements of the earth through the cosmos. Although Donne's body is, as we saw in chapter 1, a "peece of the *world*" (*Dev.* 319; 21.1) and is governed by the principles that organize the cosmos, the time that accompanies the changes of the universe is distinct from the lived temporality accessible from the first-person perspective. For Donne, illness emphasizes how felt time is separate from the objective time of the world. The "long *nights*" and "long *daies*" of sickness are "so *long*, as that *Nature* her selfe shall seeme to be *perverted*, and to have put the *longest day*, and the *longest night*, which should bee *six moneths* asunder, into one *natural, unnaturall day*" (*Dev.* 328; 23.1).

Donne brings the time of the body into view through his transition from the "minute" (*Dev.* 232; 1.1) in which his health changes in Station 1 to the "instant" in Station 2 when he "feele[s] the victory" "of the disease" (*Dev.* 236; 2.1). The smallest particles of time expand so that Donne can imagine the felt diminution of his bodily powers in one and the same instant. This account of felt bodily time may be a fantasy, but it enables Donne to imagine from within the impossible phenomenal scene he anticipates in "This is my playes last scene." "Only be thou ever present to me, O *my God*," he writes in *Devotions*, "and this *bed-chamber*, and thy bed-chamber shal be all one roome, and the closing of these bodily *Eyes* here, and the opening of the *Eyes* of my *Soule*, there, all one *Act*" (*Dev.* 285; 13.3).

3

Changing Genres

Donne often bends and reshapes existing literary forms, especially genres—a term we use to mean the organization of a text according to a pattern that exceeds that text either through inheritance or by virtue of being primed for iterability.[1] Donne delights in calling attention to his simultaneous acceptance and refusal of this repetition, the iterability that is the backbone of literary tradition and the heart of humanist *imitatio*.[2] Consider some familiar examples taken from Donne's poetry. His verse about love and sex, the *Songs and Sonnets*, is full of nonce stanzas—uneven lines, rough rhythms—that had not existed before he put pen to paper. This collection of poems famously contains only two near sonnets, stacked one atop the other in "Aire and Angels." Instead, he reserves the sonnet form for unusual ends: meditations on religious despair, theological riddles. He transforms the Ovidian epic into *Metempsychosis*, a highly structured, deeply bitter satire about a serially reincarnating Pythagorean soul. The *Anniversarie* poems are so formally unfamiliar that Barbara Lewalski dedicates a monograph to the various genres on which they draw.[3] Donne's poetry swerves from the normative constraints of formal and generic expectation.

The same holds for his prose. Much scholarly energy has been spent attempting to determine the generic prototype against which *Devotions* should be judged. As already noted, many candidates have been proposed.[4] In this chapter, we will add the lyric poem, the epistle, and the

---

1. This formulation is indebted to Julie Orlemanski, "Genre," in *A Handbook of Middle English Studies*, ed. Marion Turner (Wiley-Blackwell, 2013), 207–21.

2. See, e.g., Thomas M. Greene, *The Light in Troy: Imitation and Discovery in Renaissance Poetry* (New Haven, CT: Yale University Press, 1982).

3. Barbara Kiefer Lewalski, *Donne's Anniversaries and the Poetry of Praise: The Creation of a Symbolic Mode* (Princeton, NJ: Princeton University Press, 1973).

4. For these candidates, see the introduction. For other scholarly accounts of the genre of *Devotions*, see Frost, *Holy Delight*; Goldberg, "Understanding of Sickness";

progress; in chapter 5, we consider the Hippocratic medical case history. However, in contrast to other scholars, who often propose a generic antecedent and then use the proposed genre to explain how *Devotions* works, we argue that no single antecedent can explain the role of genre in *Devotions*. For us, what matters is less the matrix of genres from which Donne drew than the fact that he makes what might be called a structural spectacle out of these generic forms. He repurposes elements from previously existing genres to craft a work that carefully and elaborately displays its artifactuality. As we will see in chapter 4, this tendency is intertwined with Donne's use of diction. Just as he strives to showcase the substantiality of the words he uses (a substantiality sometimes in excess of the things or ideas to which they refer), so Donne emphasizes the substantiality of the generic forms he employs.

Donne often substantializes the structural features of his poetry and prose through architectural metaphors. In *Metempsychosis*, he compares his text to a building with "porches" that announce the entrance. Where other authors "set their arms" at the door, he hangs his "portrait" (*Sat.* 25), a proclamation not of lineage and family heritage but of individual identity and poetic innovation. One of Donne's distinctive procedures as a writer is to complicate metaphors, to multiply the associations of a comparison. It is not just that a book is like a building, but a house is also like a body. *Metempsychosis* frequently refers to its varied bodies as buildings: the soul "left her house the fish, and vapour'd forth" (*Sat.* 36; 244); when she enters a whale, "in a roomfull house this Soule doth float" (*Sat.* 39; 333); when her host ape is killed, "This house thus batter'd down, the Soule possest a new" (*Sat.* 45; 490); and when the mouse enters the elephant's body, it "Walk'd" through and "surveid the roomes of this vast house," including the "braine, the soules bedchamber" (*Sat.* 41; 392–93). Donne folds buildings, texts, and bodies into this rich semantic field. Each metaphor accrues associations and interlaced connections with the others. This metaphoric constellation allows Donne to convert the properties of texts, bodies, and architectural structures into one another, exchanging them in order to extend his poetic range.

Donne responds to architectural elements, to poetic structure, and to such traditional tropes as Seneca's *hospitium*, the body as a temporary

---

Mueller, "Exegesis of Experience"; Kate Narveson, "Piety and the Genre of the *Devotions*," *John Donne Journal* 17 (1998): 107–36; and Brent Nelson, "*Pathopoeia* and the Protestant Form of Donne's *Devotions upon Emergent Occasions*," in *John Donne and the Protestant Reformation: New Perspectives*, ed. M. Papazian (Detroit: Wayne State University Press, 2003), 247–72.

inn for the soul.[5] *The Second Anniversarie* elaborates this idea of the soul "fowly" dwelling in "their first-built cels," coming eventually to acknowledge that human being are housed in "a poore Inne, / A Province Pack'd up in two yards of skinne" (*Ann.* A2:46, 172–76). Edmund Spenser's Castle of Alma presents a different intertextual opportunity for Donne in two ways. First, rather than simply describing the edifice of the human body, the knights in Spenser's *Faerie Queene* enter it and come to know it intimately from the inside, its teeth, digestive processes, and passions that inhabit the parlor of the heart. The different bodily hosts in *Metempsychosis* are infiltrated and occupied by the soul, and both soul and host are changed through their brief union. Second, the Castle of Alma becomes a structuring trope in Helkiah Crooke's *Mikrokosmographia*. In this text, the anatomist is portrayed as a knight who ventures inside its walls of slime and also an explorer and recorder of its inner working. Donne's anatomical structure in *The First Anniversarie* is in dialogue with all of these antecedents. Similarly, when the mouse in *Metempsychosis* walks into the elephant's brain or bedchamber, it shares with the anatomist a curiosity to know and the capacity to kill or be powerfully associated with death.

Donne repeatedly plays with this semantic field. In "A Funeral Elegie" (1612), Donne laments the death of Elizabeth Drury in terms of a building ("shee's demolish'd"). The poem's speaker worries that Drury—who, while she lived, embodied Paul's equation between the human body and a "Tabernacle"—will not now "stoope to bee / In paper wrap't": why, "when she would not lie / In such a house," would she consent to "dwell in an Elegie?" (*Ann.* 35–36; 9–18).[6] Both poem and human body are portrayed as buildings, a connection that Donne works to a different effect in "Valediction: of My Name in the Window." In that poem, he asks his lover, who he imagines gazing at his name inscribed in her window, to "think this ragged bony name to bee / My ruinous Anatomie" (*Son.* 65; 23–24). If his lover can think of etched letters as resembling the bones, then, since the speaker's soul is already hers, "The rafters of my body, bone / Being still with you, the Muscle, Sinew, and Veine, / Which tile this house, will come againe" (*Son.* 65; 28–30). Metaphorized as a building, the human body is easier to anatomize. Its bloody, beating, messy seams and joints acquire increased visibility as they transform into "rafters" and "tile."

5. Seneca, *Epistles*, trans. Richard M. Gummere, Loeb Classical Library (Cambridge, MA: Harvard University Press, 1925), 120:90–91.

6. For the connection between these verses and Paul's "tabernacle of the Holy Ghost" in 2 Corinthians 5:4 and 6:16, see Mueller, *John Donne*, 430.

The same holds true for texts. In *Deaths Duell*, Donne says: "Buildings stand by the benefit of their *foundations* that susteine and *support* them, and of their *butteresses* that comprehend and *embrace* them, and of their *contignations* that knit and *unite* them: The *foundations* suffer them not to *sinke*, the *butteresses* suffer them not to *swerve*, and the *contignation* and knitting suffers them not to *cleave*" (*Ser.* 10:230).[7] His sermon is a building organized just like any other, Donne tells his congregants. Referring to the selection from Psalm 68:20 on which *Deaths Duell* is based, he says, "But of this building, the *foundation*, the *butteresses*, the *contignations*, are in this part of the *verse*, which constitutes *our text*" (*Ser.* 10:230). Donne erects the building of his sermon about the death of the body on and out of the "body" of a biblical verse.

In *Devotions*, Donne figures the semantic field of building, body, and text in newly complex ways. We examine how the foundations, buttresses, and contignations—the "joining or framing together of beams or boards"[8]—of this text are "knit" while also offering an account of why Donne structured *Devotions* in such an elaborate manner. The metaphorical cluster of building, body, and text is central to *Devotions*:

> We study *Health*, and we deliberate upon our *meats*, and *drink*, and *Ayre*, and *exercises*, and we hew, and wee polish every stone, that goes to that building; and so our *Health* is a long and a regular work; But in a minute a Cannon batters all, overthrowes all, demolishes all; a *Sicknes* unprevented for all our diligence, unsuspected for all our curiositie; nay, undeserved, if we consider only *disorder*, summons us, seizes us, possesses us, destroyes us in an instant. (*Dev.* 232; 1.1)

Here the "building" of human health is painstakingly constructed through the moderation of such Galenic nonnaturals as "*meats*, and *drink*, and *Ayre*, and *exercises*," the polished "stone[s]" out of which the "building" of health is made. Like a cannon ball crashing through a wall, sickness destroys health "in an instant." This sudden change is the foundation for the building that is *Devotions*.[9] In chapters 1 and 2, we argued that *Devotions* represents what it is like to live through dramatic bodily change

7. Donne makes frequent recourse to such architectural metaphors in his sermons. See, e.g., *Ser.* 7:302: "I know no figurative speech so often iterated in the Scriptures as the name of a *House*."

8. *OED*, s.v. "contignation," n. 1.

9. Whereas Donne's sermons are founded on a given biblical "verse which constitutes our text," *Devotions* is, as Mueller has argued, an "exegesis" of events through which Donne has lived. See Mueller, "Exegesis of Experience."

as it unfolds in and through the first-person perspective. In this chapter, we examine the intersection of change and structure—the organizational principles according to which the text's disparate topics are "knit" and ordered.

Such a shift in focus also requires an altered interpretive practice. In this chapter, we show how Donne's treatment of change in time is managed by the text's structure such that these earthly changes in time undergo a profound change and thereby acquire new meanings. *Devotions* is exactingly structured, framed by the intersection of three axes. The first, horizontal axis is the sequential narrative of Donne's illness, which unfolds across twenty-three stations, moving from the first alteration of the sickness to the fear of relapse after recovery. This structural feature progresses across earthly time, moving from present moment to present moment, across multiple instants of change, in an attempt both to trace the development and effects of the disease and to investigate the contours and meaning of each successive stage. For the second, vertical axis, each station is "Digested" (*Dev.* 229), as the frontispiece puts it, into three discursive modes: a meditation on "*our Humane Condition*" (*Dev.* 229) that is invariably grounded in a specific manifestation of variability, the changes that cleave all earthly creatures; an expostulation that wrestles with the topic of the meditation, refocusing it through the lens of scripture, working to reframe how the problem should be understood; and finally a prayer, which extends the insights gleaned from the expostulation by releasing the meditation's initial problem into God's care, by apostrophizing God directly and appealing to him in intimate ways. Whereas the station-by-station narrative tracks the involuntary effects of a disease that wracks Donne's bodily life with terrible changes, the organization within each station nurtures a voluntary movement upward, from earthly problems toward divine resolution through a carefully cultivated and scripturally mediated change in orientation or attitude. Along the third, reflexive axis, the text can also be seen to fold back on itself, pivoting on the central twelfth station, which divides *Devotions* in two. This feature—which has not, so far as we know, previously been noticed—enables the generation of reverberated meaning. Individual stations echo each other in an intricately orchestrated reflexive sequence.

In chapters 1 and 2, we focused how *Devotions* represents change in time along the horizontal axis. In this chapter and for the rest of the book, we integrate this examination of the text's horizontal extension across time with its vertical and reflexive impulses. We trace how the structure of *Devotions* responds to the *Emergent Occasions* it represents, arguing that Donne erects this complicated structure to analyze and manage the

fact of change so vividly represented in the text's prose. This tension between change and structure animates *Devotions*, a text that showcases an
efflorescence of content—winding sentences, intricate strategies of quotation and intertextual interpretation, complex networks of allusion, an
overabundance of rhetorical energy, an almost unmanageable fecundity
of metaphor often on the verge of catachresis—pressing up against rigid
formal limits: the twenty-three stations, the repeated meditation, expostulation, and prayer. *Devotions* pulsates, constantly struggling to exceed
its own self-imposed boundaries. This tension between emphatically displayed structure and what threatens to overwhelm that structure generates a text that repeatedly performs the spilling of vitality past the mortal
casing of the body and into the unknown beyond. Donne erects a textual
building that displays its structural joints, that delights in showcasing
its buttresses and contignations—not as an end in itself, but rather as a
way of managing the dialectical relationship between the endless flux of
earthly change and the unchanging stability of the God who created the
world and its creatures.[10]

The Iterable Present

Devotions is written in the present tense. This present tense is at odds with
the time that had passed between Donne's sickness and the publication of
Devotions. In the epistle to Prince Charles that opens *Devotions*, Donne
emphasizes the pastness of the illness relative to the moment of writing
by comparing his own project on that of Hezekiah, who *"writt the* Meditations *of his* Sickness, *after his* Sicknesse" (*Dev.* 230).[11] But Donne does
not present the events of *"my Sicknes"* (*Dev.* 229) as though they were
written "after." He does not write in the retrospective mode of such texts
as Augustine's *Confessiones*, which looks back to a past recorded in the
past tense. To be sure, the *Confessiones* is presented as a prayer uttered in
the present. "The house of my soul is too small for you to come to it," Au-

10. In this regard, *Devotions* is similar to other early modern English texts, especially the "Mutabilitie Cantos" that end Edmund Spenser's *Faerie Queene*. See,
e.g., Angus Fletcher, "Complexity and the Spenserian Myth of Mutability," *Literary
Imagination* 6, no. 1 (2004): 1–22.

11. Izaak Walton claimed that Donne "writ on his sick-bed; herein imitating the
holy Patriarchs, who were wont to build their altars in that place, where they had
received their blessings." Tying Donne's Hezekiah together with Walton's remarks,
Mary Ann Lund, "Convalescence," 540, draws attention to Walton's *on*. "Although it
can certainly imply that he was still *in* bed," she writes, "the comparison to building
an altar, however, suggests an act of commemoration and consecration *on top of* it."

gustine tells God early in Book I, before making a request: "May it be enlarged by you. It is in ruins: restore it" (Aug. 6; 1.5.6). But when the present tense of Augustine's ongoing confession ceases to focus on "what I am now" and instead looks back to "what I was" (Aug. 181; 10.4.6), the text moves into the past tense: "I was welcomed by the consolations of human milk" (Aug. 6; 1.6.7).[12] In contrast to such normal ways of describing "what I was," Donne expresses past events as though they were present.

Each station of *Devotions* is advertised, in its Latin and English chapter headings, as taking place in the present: "Decubitus sequitur tandem / *The Patient takes his bed*" (*Dev.* 238; 3), "Ex Rex ipse suum mittit / *The King sends his owne Phisician*" (*Dev.* 260; 8), or "Intereà insomnes noctes Ego duco, Diesque / *I sleepe not day nor night*" (*Dev.* 291; 15). Each station in *Devotions*, from the "*first alteration*" of the sickness (*Dev.* 232; 1.1) to the final warning about the "*feareful danger of relapsing*" (*Dev.* 328; 23.1), takes place in a newly established present. Between the prefatory letter to Prince Charles and the first meditation, Donne places a metrically composed Latin text—"Stationes, *sive* Periodi *in* Morbo, / *ad quas referuntur* Meditationes sequentes" (*Dev.* 230)—that serves as a table of contents and provides an epitome of the text's overarching structure, thereby managing and imposing order on the radical dispersal of experience discussed in chapter 1.[13] Each numbered phrase is then abstracted from its initial context and scattered throughout the text, appearing as part of the title for the station it summarizes. The text plays out from present moment to present moment, working through each of the emergent occasions named in metrically composed Latin.

This focalization of Donne's unfolding sickness in and through the present moment is related to many possible generic antecedents—Jesuit spiritual exercises, Protestant traditions of occasional meditations, and the sermon foremost among them.[14] But a clue to a deeper influence is Donne's repetition of the phrase "My God, my God" in each of the book's twenty-three expostulations. As Achsah Guibbory points out, this phrase echoes not only Christ's questioning of God during the crucifixion, re-

12. For how the *Confessiones* is organized around the distinction between "what I am" and "what I was," see Robin Lane Fox, *Augustine: Conversions to Confessions* (New York: Basic, 2015).

13. The best analysis of these Latin stations remains Papazian (Arshagouni), "The Latin 'Stationes.'"

14. For Donne and Jesuit spiritual exercises, see, e.g., Martz, *Poetry of Meditation*; Anthony Raspa, ed. *Devotions upon Emergent Occasions*, xix–xl; Thomas F. Van Laan, "John Donne's *Devotions* and the Jesuit Spiritual Exercises," *Studies in Philology* 60 (1963): 191–202; and Frost, *Holy Delight*, 7–11, 85–86.

corded in both Matthew 27:46 and Mark 15:34, but also its ultimate source in the opening line of Psalm 22: "My God, my God, why hast thou forsaken me?"[15] The Psalms are central to Donne's thinking, across his career and in *Devotions*.[16] In a sermon delivered on the penitential Psalms, Donne claims that David's "example is so comprehensive, so generall, that as a well made, and well placed Picture in a Gallery looks upon all that stand in severall places of the Gallery, in severall lines, in severall angles, so doth Davids history concerne and embrace all." Like Adam and Christ, David is a figure who contains everyone: "David's case is our case" (*Ser.* 5:299).[17]

But the influence of the Psalms is even more pervasive than this, for in early modern England the Psalms were widely understood to be an archetype for lyric poetry. The Psalms were, in the words of Sir Philip Sidney, "a divine poem," a claim that Donne strengthens in a sermon that figures the Psalms as "Metricall Compositions" and each Psalm as a "Poem" (*Ser.* 6:41).[18] One of the central ways in which the Psalms shaped later lyric poetry was through their insistent use of the present tense. Psalm 22 begins with the question, "My God, my God, why hast thou forsaken me?" and then goes on to articulate how the terror of the present differs from the stability of a past invoked with nostalgic longing: "you have brought me out of the womb; you made me trust in you even at my mother's breast. From birth I was cast upon you; from my mother's womb you have been my God" (22:9–10). God provided succor in the past, but in the now of lyric utterance he seems to have abandoned the psalmist. "I am poured out like water, and all my bones are out of joint," the psalmist laments, "My heart has turned to wax; it has melted away within me.... [Y]ou lay me in the dust of death" (22:14–15).

Donne reworks the language of Psalm 22 in *Devotions*, maintaining the psalmist's use of the present tense but folding all humanity into Da-

---

15. Guibbory, *Returning to John Donne*, 8.

16. For Donne and the Psalms, see, e.g., Mueller, "Exegesis of Experience"; Gary Kuchar, "Ecstatic Donne: Conscience, Sin, and Surprise in the 'Sermons' and Mitcham Letters," *Criticism* 50, no. 4 (2008): 631–54; Hannibal Hamlin, *Psalm Culture and Early Modern Literature* (Cambridge: Cambridge University Press, 2004); and Jeanne Shami, "John Donne," in *The Blackwell Companion to the Bible in English Literature*, ed. Rebecca Lemon, Emma Mason, Jonathan Roberts, and Christopher Rowland (Wiley-Blackwell, 2012), 239–53.

17. For a fuller treatment of this topic, see Guibbory, *Returning to Donne*, 33.

18. Sir Philip Sidney, *Defence of Poesy*, in *Sidney's "The Defence of Poesy" and Selected Renaissance Literary Criticism*, ed. Gavin Alexander (New York: Penguin, 2004), 7. For the Psalms in relation to early modern English poetry, see esp. Hamlin, *Psalm Culture*.

vid's lament: "*Man*, who is the noblest part of the *Earth*, melts so away," Donne writes in the second station. Donne intensifies the language of the Psalms. Whereas David is "poured out like water" and his heart "has melted away," Donne notes that "he feeles that a *Fever* doth not melt him like *snow*, but pour him out like lead, like yron, like brasse melted in a furnace" (*Dev.* 235; 2.1). Mingling the psalmist's melting with pouring, Donne brings those suffering from fevers toward what David calls "the dust of death" by claiming that sickness "reduce[s] him to *Atomes*, and to *ashes*" (*Dev.* 235; 2.1).[19] To borrow an observation about Donne's style made by Joan Webber, we might say that in using the Psalms it is not so much that Donne "speaks Bible" but rather that "he makes it speak Donne."[20]

Donne's use of the first person and the present tense in *Devotions* draws on the resources of lyric poetry. Grounded in the first-person here and now, in the immediacy of repeated deictics like *this* and *here*, Donne manufactures a rich and complex present tense in which readers are brought into a present moment that is thick with other temporal resonances. In doing so, he intensifies a variety of techniques used by much lyric poetry and in many of the Psalms, a set of practices we call *modes of presencing*. Lyric poetry frequently transforms an event that happened before or might happen in the future or might happen only in the imagination into a present tense that indexes the now in which the act of reading or speaking or hearing the poem's words takes place. Jonathan Culler argues that the predominance of the present tense in lyric poetry makes visible the fact that the events invoked or described in such poems "happen now, in time, but in an iterable *now* of lyric enunciation, rather than in a now of linear time." For Culler, the present tense of the lyric is a "floating now" that is "repeated each time the poem is read [in the] present of enunciation."[21] As we have already seen, "This is my playes last scene" emerges from Donne's transformation of an imagined future into the present tense, the substitution of a *then* and *that* for a *now* and *this* that remain entangled with other temporal horizons but are situated in the

---

19. The violence of this psalmic language was on Donne's mind around this time. In a sermon delivered on Easter 1623, he writes: "And therefore when our bodies are dissolved and liquefied in the Sea, putrified in the earth, resolv'd to ashes in the fire, macerated in the ayre, *Velut in vasa sua transfunditur caro nostra*, make account that all the world is Gods cabinet, and water, and earth, and fire, and ayre, are the proper boxes, in which God laies up our bodies, for the Resurrection" (*Ser.* 4:359).

20. Webber, *Contrary Music*, 24.

21. Jonathan Culler, *Theory of the Lyric* (Cambridge, MA: Harvard University Press, 2015), 289, 294.

present. The poem makes present a future in which the speaker perceives an instant that is yet to come from the perspective of "my minutes last point." But this "minutes last point" is not the time of writing; it is the "iterable *now* of lyric enunciation," a present moment repeated each time a reader or listener encounters the poem.

Many of Donne's lyrics perform similar acts of presencing. "The Sunne Rising" invites the reader to be present with the lovers, watching them "here in one bed" while the sun "Shine[s] here to us" (*Son*. 73; 20, 29). In "The Canonization," the present tense of the speaker's opening imperative ("For Godsake hold your tongue, and let me love") shifts subtly, over the course of the poem, to the reader who "shall approve" the speaker and his lover "*Canoniz'd* for Love" and then "invoke us" in the present tense of poem's closing prayer (*Son*. 73–74; 1, 35–37). "Aire and Angels" asks readers to engage with the now of enunciation, a now they are excluded from but nevertheless privy to:

> Twice or thrice had I lov'd thee,
> Before I knew thy face or name;
> So in a voice, so in a shapelesse flame,
> *Angells* affect us oft, and worship'd bee;
>   Still when, to where thou wert, I came,
> Some lovely glorious nothing I did see.
>   But since my soule, whose child love is,
> Takes limmes of flesh, and else could nothing doe,
>   More subtile then the parent is,
> Love must not be, but take a body too,
>   And therefore what thou wert, and who,
>   I bid Love aske, and now
> That it assume thy body, I allow,
> And fixe it selfe in thy lip, eye, and brow. (*Son*. 75; 1–14)

The poem begins with past events. Opening with the two or three times in the relatively distant past in which the speaker "lov'd thee / Before I knew thy face or name," the poem flashes forward to a more recent past in which the speaker "came" to "where thou wert" and "did see." This moment, when the speaker "bid Love aske" "what" and "who" "thou wert," paves the way for the present moment of lyric utterance, the "now" when love "assume thy body" and the speaker "allow[s]"—that is, "receive[s] with favor and approval"[22]—how love "fixe[s] it selfe in thy lip, eye, and

22. *OED*, s.v. "allow," v. I 1a.

brow." The "now" when love "assume thy body" is tied to the present of the poem's utterance, which reaches out to encompass its readers: "So in a voice, so in a shapelesse flame, / *Angells* affect us oft, and worship'd bee." That angels "affect us" often is a possibility that readers are invited to entertain here and now.

By focusing with such intensity on the fleeting *now*, Donne brings to a fever pitch a tendency in Renaissance lyric that Ullrich Langer calls the "effect of singularity."[23] This phrase refers to verbal effects couched in the "pointing, intending function of language" that were used by Petrarch and subsequent poets in order to conjure "a designation of self, and a designation of another, as something radically singular, that is, as something or someone beyond or simply not encompassed by categories, by attributes shared" (1–2). The verbal summoning of such an "existential singular" (6) is visible everywhere in Donne's lyric poetry. In "Aire and Angels," the speaking "I," entangled in the evanescent "now," gazes back to what once was and anticipates what might be while addressing a profoundly singular "thee" and finding love "in thy lip, eye, and brow." If Donne's use of the present moment conjures the Psalms, it also draws on Petrarch, a poet who, in Langer's words, "foreground[s] the moment or instant, the *punto* or less frequently, the *momento*" at which the lover first sees the beloved (34).

Donne repurposes in the prose of *Devotions* the verbal effects of singularity he perfected in his poetry. Here is the sixth station's depiction of an interaction with a physician:

> I observe the *Phisician*, with the same diligence, as hee the *disease*; I see hee *feares*, and I feare with him: I overtake him, I overrun him in his fear, and I go the faster, because he makes his pace slow; I feare the more, because he disguises his fear, and I see it with the more sharpnesse, because hee would not have me see it. (*Dev.* 250–51; 6.1)

The intimacy of this description startles, in part because the scenario draws on dynamics from Donne's earlier erotic verse, in which a speaker doubts his ability to know what the beloved is feeling or doing behind his back: "Although thy hand and faith, and good workes too, / Have seal'd thy love which nothing should undoe," Donne writes in "Elegy 3," "yet much, much I feare thee" (*Son.* 19; 1–4). Just as the beloved's state of mind and intentions are unknown and therefore to be feared, so, in *Devotions*, is

---

23. Ullrich Langer, *Lyric in the Renaissance: From Petrarch to Montaigne* (Cambridge: Cambridge University Press, 2015), 2. Subsequent quotations cited parenthetically.

the physician's knowledge of the speaker's condition unknown and therefore to be feared. The fact of the physician's own fear only intensifies the
situation. The speaker observes the physician and, seeing the latter's fear,
begins to fear more, an acceleration that causes the physician to hide his
own fear, which, in turn, causes the speaker to perceive that fear more
acutely. The dance between *I* and *he* generates an effect of singularity, isolating the intersubjective complexity of a fleeting encounter. The same
holds for Station 18's meditation on tolling bells, a marker of temporal
passing. "The *Bell* rings out; the *pulse* thereof is changed," Donne writes,
"the *tolling* was a *faint*, and *intermitting pulse*, upon one side; this *stronger*, and argues *more* and *better life*" (*Dev.* 302; 18.1). Earlier in Station 17,
the bell had rung faintly. In the *now* manufactured by Station 18's drive
to presence, the bell rings out in a "*stronger*" way, which "argues" that the
"*soule*" of the person for whom the bells tolls has now "gone out" (*Dev.*
302; 18.1).

Through deictics, first-person pronouns, the present tense, and other
verbal features, Donne crafts fictions of presence by manipulating the effects of singularity he inherited from and used in lyric poetry. This is not
to say that the singularity crafted in *Devotions* is absolute, for, as we argued
in chapter 1, Donne blends *I* with *we*, "*my Sicknes*" with "*our Humane Condition*"; Station 18 is titled "*The bell rings out, and tells me in him, that I am
dead*" (*Dev.* 302; 18). Rather, we argue that Donne uses the techniques
of lyric poetry as a way of organizing his prose. In doing so, he deploys a
strategy also used by Montaigne, whose *Essais* treats the relationship of
the particular and the universal in what Langer calls a "dialectical" way,
so that "the particular is linked to the universal, and the universal always
is reminded of the insistent particular" (129). Montaigne follows the lead
of such poets as Petrarch in using "the deictic as a technique of rendering 'present' an object" (146)—recall, for instance, "*C'est icy un Livre de
bonne foy, Lecteur*" (Mon. 2; 27)—in such a way that, as Langer puts it,
"the distinct preference for effect over meaning leads to a privilege ac-
corded to the singular, the existential, as opposed to universal finality"
(147). Donne intensifies Montaigne's translation of lyric effects of singularity into prose, for *Devotions* is structured by the station-by-station
repetition of the present moment.

Donne pursues a strategy akin to what Samuel Richardson would
later call "writing to the moment," a technique Richardson develops in
his epistolary novels *Pamela* (1740) and *Clarissa* (1747).[24] These novels,

24. From Ian Watt, *The Rise of the Novel: Studies in Defoe, Richardson, and Fielding* (London: Chatto, 1957), to Thomas Pavel, *The Lives of the Novel: A History*

grounded in the first-person perspective, feature characters who write letters at a given moment, from within a particular set of (one might say) emergent occasions. The plot advances in the time that passes between the composition of each letter, which reconstructs the events that have taken place during that interval. The characters remain ignorant of what the future will bring. *Devotions* operates according to a similar principle. Donne represents a present state of affairs while portraying himself as ignorant of the changes that lie in store when future emergent occasions will emerge.

As both a writer and a theorist of the letter, Donne had intimate knowledge of the epistle's temporality, the peculiar way this mode of writing roots the past and the future in a fixed but fleeting present.[25] In a letter written in 1608 to Goodyer, Donne invokes the difference between present and past occasions: "I Write not to you out of my poor Library, where to cast mine eye upon good Authors kindles or refreshes sometimes meditations not unfit to communicate to near friends; nor from the high way, where I am contracted, and inverted into my self; which are the ordinary forges of Letters to you. But I write from the fire side in my Parler, and in the noise of three gamesome children" (*Let.* 137). Donne sits with his children and his wife, whom he has "transplanted into a wretched fortune" such that he feels the need to "disguise" this fact through constant conversation; "all the time which I give this Letter" is, Donne says, time that "I steal from her" (*Let.* 137–38).[26] Set in a vivid present, which captures both the spatial and temporal dislocation of Donne's fall from professional grace, this letter invokes both a sense of the past and the blank screen of future circumstances: "If I have been good in hope, or can promise any little offices in the future probably, it is comfortable, for I am the worst present man in the world" (*Let.* 139).

(Princeton, NJ: Princeton University Press, 2013), Richardson's "writing to the moment" has played a prominent role in the historiography of the novel.

25. For Donne as a theorist of the letter, see, e.g., Targoff, *John Donne*, 25–48. See also Brian Cummings, "Donne's Passions: Emotions, Agency and Passions," in *Passions and Subjectivity in Early Modern Culture*, ed. Brian Cummings and Freya Sierhuis (Farnham, Surrey: Ashgate, 2013): 51–71. This feature of epistolary form was common to humanist prose, stretching back to Petrarch's letters written during the Black Death, in which the poet reflects on the fact that he does not know whether the intended recipient of his letter is alive or dead. See Gerard Passannante, *The Lucretian Renaissance: Philology and the Afterlife of Tradition* (Chicago: University of Chicago Press, 2011), 20–21.

26. For a compelling account of letter writing in relation to these biographical circumstances, see Piers Brown, "Donne's Hawkings," *SEL* 49, no. 1 (2009): 67–86.

Donne frequently appeals to this aspect of futurity, the unknowability of what, in a 1615 letter that anticipates *Devotions,* he calls "future emergent occasions" (*Let.* 219). Written in a present in which he cannot know what will emerge, letters intensify the presence of the present.

In *Devotions,* Donne borrows the temporality of epistolary correspondence and embeds it within a series of stations, each of which looks with "pre-apprehensions and presages" (*Dev.* 232; 1.1) at the changes that will be wrought by the occasions lurking beyond the temporal horizon. This structure enables Donne to write toward death in each station. The *alteratio* each station describes might, for all the speaker knows, lead, in the very next moment, to the dissolution of his being, to *corruptio,* the substantial change brought about by death. Grounding the text in a repeated present, Donne gathers within every sentence the fundamental surprise toward which each individual human life is oriented. By "writing to the moment" in this iterative way, Donne maintains the primacy of lyric effects of singularity in a narrative that moves forward in time. He traces the progress of his suffering.

Stationary Progress

Progress: this term names a generic antecedent that Donne uses to shape *Devotions.* Understood in general terms, a progress performs "advancement through a process, a sequence of events, a period of time."[27] In Donne's lifetime, the word most often referred to the "act of journeying or moving onward in space," usually in relation to the royal progresses of monarchs touring their territories, stopping in various locations to exhibit their magnificence before moving to the next stop.[28] Donne saw many such progresses in his life, and during the summer he took orders and joined the Church of England, accompanied King Charles, who was, as Izaak Walton informs us, "going his Progress" (Wal. 50). In *Metempsychosis,* Donne describes a scene from such a progress to illustrate how a mandrake root, newly "abled" by the migrating soul, stretched into the surrounding soil and "to it selfe did force / A place, where no place was":

> His spungie confines gave him place to grow:
> Just as in our streets, when the people stay
> To see the Prince, and have so fill'd the way
> That weesels scarce could passe, when she comes nere

27. *OED*, s.v. "progress," n. I 1a.
28. *OED*, s.v. "progress," n. II, II 5a.

They throng and cleave up, and a passage clear,
As if, for that time, their round bodies flatned were. (*Sat.* 32; 131–40)

Donne's simile of the mandrake's urgent, forceful rooting is anachronistic, evoking Queen Elizabeth's theatrical circuits with their lavish spectacles of power. The image he conjures is focalized from the thronged
crowd's perspective, as if a seventeenth-century London street has been
inserted into the poem's precivilized landscape. His anachronistic folding
of time literalizes the ceremonial roots of the progress even as he mobi-
lizes its generic potential for his poem. Dedicated to describing one stop
or station of a progress made by a "Prince," this stanza performs a generic
meta-gesture; the stanza is one station in the progress of the poem.

Another title for *Metempsychosis* is *The Progresse of the Soule* (*Sat.* 27), and
the poem opens by declaring: "I sing the progresse of a deathlesse soule"
(*Sat.* 27; 1). Like the royal progresses it invokes, *Metempsychosis* is a progress
poem that traces the progress of a soul through its host bodies. The poem is
structured according to fifty-two numbered stanzas, each of which is a box:
ten lines, nine containing five metrical feet, the final a six-foot alexandrine.
As Donne knew, the English *stanza* traces its etymology back to the Italian *stanza*, which meant a "stopping place" or a "room."[29] Donne plays with
the latter meaning in "The Canonization," when he declares, "We'll build in
sonnets pretty roomes" (*Son.* 74; 32). In *Metempsychosis*, the little "roomes"
figured on the page—stanza rolling into stanza—are linked to the houses
of the host bodies the soul serially enters. Donne drives the point home as
the poem's narrative begins at the transition between stanzas 7 and 8. In the
last line of 7, he claims that the soul "Had first in paradise, a low, but fatall
roome," before, in the first line of 8, clarifying that it was "no low roome"
(*Sat.* 29; 70–71). Insofar as the soul's first host body is an apple it is a "low"
room. But insofar as this apple belongs to the fateful tree in paradise, which
would become the site of Christ's crucifixion, it is "no low roome."

The progress of the poem represents the progress of the soul, thereby
performing another of the etymological cognates of *stanza*: a "stopping
place." Just as each town on the monarch's progress marks a stopping place
in that journey, so does each successive embodiment marks a stopping
place for the soul. Between bodies, the soul moves. This is how Donne
describes what happens when the paradisal apple is plucked:

Just in that instant when the serpents gripe,
Broke the slight veines, and tender conduit-pipe,

---

29. *OED*, s.v. "stanza," n.

Through which this soule from the trees root did draw
Life, and growth to this apple, fled away
This loose soule, old, one and another day.
As lightning, which one scarce dares say, he saw,
'Tis so soone gone, (and better proofe the law
Of sense, then faith requires) swiftly she flew
T'a darke and foggie Plot; Her, her fate threw
There through th'earth's pores, and in a Plant hous'd her anew.
　　　(*Sat.* 31; 121–30)

The soul flies from apple to mandrake in an "instant," like "lightning" that flashes so quickly one cannot be sure one has seen it. When the mandrake dies and the soul travels to a baby bird, this language continues: "To an unfetterd soules quick nimble hast / Are falling stars, and hearts thoughts, but slow pac'd: / Thinner than burnt aire flies this soule" (*Sat.* 33; 171–73). This pattern shapes the poem, with bodily stopping places connecting the soul's motion.

Donne enhances his design in his second progress poem, *The Second Anniversarie*, the title of which, *Of the Progresse of the Soule*, is nearly identical to that of *Metempsychosis*. Published just over a decade after Donne's first *Progresse of the Soule*, the *Second Anniversarie* expands a metaphor with which Donne begins *The First Anniversarie* or *Anatomy of the World*. In that poem, he likens the recently deceased Elizabeth Drury to Queen Elizabeth, who had died in 1603: "When that Queene [Elizabeth Drury] ended here her progresse time, / And, as t'her standing house, to heaven did clymbe . . . This world, in that great earth-quake languished" (*Ann.* A1:22; 7–11). The recently deceased girl has ended her earthly "progresse" and returned to her final station, her "standing house" in heaven. This metaphor is the seed for the *Second Anniversarie*, which tracks the double movement of Elizabeth Drury's soul and that of the poem's speaker. The latter soul will, the speaker declares in "*The Harbinger to the Progres*," a kind of poetic porch to the poem, aim to follow the former as it ascends heavenward: "*So while thou mak'st her soules Hy progresse knowne / Thou mak'st a noble progresse of thine owne*," a progress he plans to repeat at every anniversary of her death, vowing he will "*every yeare / Mask'st a new progresse, while thou wandrest here*" on earth (*Ann.* A2:40; 27–28, 33–34).

A progress moves through time, from stopping place to stopping place. Whereas Donne had experimented with the progress in the transition from body to body in *Metempsychosis*, in *The Second Anniversarie* he works out the minute underpinnings of this logic, noting that although "quantities / Are made of lines, and lines from Points arise / None can these lines or quantities unjoynt, / And say this is a line, or this a point" (*Ann.* A2:44–45; 131–34). The lines that generate figures or shapes are made up of points, and yet it is impossible to distinguish points from lines. The lines of flight along which motion (or a progress) travels must also function according to similar rules. It is for this reason that Donne's imagined progress slows down the progress made by Elizabeth Drury's soul:

> But ere shee can consider how shee went,
> At once is at, and through the Firmament.
> And as these stars were but so many beades
> Strunge on one string, speed undistinguish'd leades
> Her through those spheares, as through the beades, a stringe,
> Whose quicke succession makes it still one thing:
> As doth the Pith, which, least our Bodies slacke,
> Strings fast the little bones of necke, and backe;
> So by the soule doth death string Heaven and Earth. (*Ann.*
>   A2:47; 205–13)

The progress of Elizabeth Drury's soul through the "spheares" is like a "stringe" threaded through "beades."[30] Transforming spheres into the beads of a rosary or necklace, Donne puns on "quicke," a word that refers to both speed and life. He inflects the meaning of "still," summoning both motionlessness and the stability of an enduring entity that remains "still one thing" over time. This initial simile is then intertwined with an anatomical analogy in which Donne likens the necklace of stars to the "little bones of necke, and backe" that the "Pith" "strings fast." Astral beads are like the vertebrae of the spine connected by the pith or spinal cord. The force of the comparison not only describes a double threading (beads, bones), but it also joins these similes in a second ligature: the spinal vertebrae are linked by their similitude with the beaded stars. The soul's movement up in a line that crosses spheres as though they were beads or vertebrae provides an image of how Donne's poetry works to distinguish or "unjoynt" point from line. Like the square stanzas and bodily houses in *Metempsychosis*, these articulations showcase the buttresses and contignations that structure the building of the poem, the arc of a progress moving forward from stop to stop, station to station.

30. The following analysis of this passage is based on Harvey and Harrison, "Embodied Resonances."

Donne composed three progresses in his career, written about a decade apart from each other. *Progress of the Soul* (1601) was succeeded by *Of the Progress of the Soul* (1612), which was, in turn, succeeded by *Devotions upon Emergent Occasions* (1624), a text that turns a new variation on Donne's idiosyncratic progress genre. *Devotions* traces the progress of a sickness by moving across the twenty-three "stopping places," separated by a gap of time across which movement has implicitly taken place, symbolized by the white space separating the stations. Like the etymology of *stanza*, which traces its way back through Italian to the Latin *stare* (to stand), the English *station* also stretches back to the Latin *stare* by way of the Anglo-Norman *statiun* (a pause, a stop) and the Latin *statio*, which means a "state of standing still," a "halting-place," or the "apparent stationary position of a planet."[31] Stations are stopping places along a progress route. They are also stanzas, textual units from which the speaker's first-person voice expresses itself in the floating time of the lyric now.

Critics have missed this fact about the genre of *Devotions*—the text is, among other things, a progress—because Donne's religious and devotional work is usually (although not always) kept separate from his earlier more secular, often satirical work. The claim that the generic form of *Devotions* is indebted to Donne's early, ostensibly unfinished experimental satire, *Metempsychosis*, might seem unreasonable. But, as we will see in chapter 4, *Devotions* draws much of its stylistic energy from his earlier progress poems. And it is through the generic opportunities of the progress genre that Donne develops the resources to maintain tension between the stability articulated through the text's repeating structure and the change that is so vividly represented from station to station.

Managing Change

In this chapter's final section, we show how the discursive shifts within each station work to stabilize the problems of emergent accidental changes and an anticipated substantial change posed in the initial meditation of each station. In *the Second Anniversarie's* prefatory *"Harbinger to the Progres,"* Donne says that he aims to help both himself and his readers *"mak[e] a noble progresse"* from "this worlds carcasse" up to "that pure life of Immortalitie" (*Ann.* 40; 28–30). In *Devotions*, Donne has a similar aim, and it is the structure of text that enables this transformation. The frontispiece claims that *Devotions* will be *"Digested"*—"dispose[d] methodi-

cally according to a system" or "reduce[d] into a systematic form."³² The
unwieldiness of a life disorganized by illness will be organized, the events
of *"my Sickness" "Digested into"* three modes of writing: first, "MEDITA-
TIONS *upon our Humane Condition"*; second, "EXPOSTULATIONS, *and
Debatements with God"*; and third, "PRAYERS, *upon the several occasions, to
him."* These involve distinct modes of address. The meditations speak to
the natural state of human embodied life. In the expostulations, Donne
apostrophizes God through the medium of scripture. The prayers speak
to God directly. The movement from meditation, through expostulation
to prayer traces a change in mental posture or attitude, a different way
of understanding the sufferings wrought by sickness and followed from
station to station. Each station grapples with a different aspect of human
life to better understand it. The text's structure, then, involves two kinds
of change. The sequential narrative of unfolding illness, developed across
the stations, describes the involuntary change from which all human life
suffers. The repeated shift in discursive registers and apostrophe submits
the involuntary changes of sickness to a spiritual discipline that enacts a
voluntary change in attitude toward the phenomenon addressed by the
meditation. In station after station, Donne struggles to submit alteration
and the fear of substantial change to spiritual and scriptural exercises that
redefine the meaning of change itself.

Let us take, as an example, Station 3, which examines what happens
when, in the words of the title, *"The Patient takes his bed"* (*Dev.* 238; 3).
In the meditation of Station 2, Donne invokes the speed of this sickness,
which affects his bodily abilities, making it difficult to do the things he
once did with ease: "In the twinckling of an eye, I can scarce see" (*Dev.*
236; 2.1). When Donne uses the modal verb of ability to claim that at
the onset of his sickness he "can scarce see," he depicts his felt capacities
pushing up against the newly contracted limits of an unresponsive body.
In Meditation 3, this loss of ability expands, and the speaker cannot do
very much. Sickness upends this natural honor, for "a fever can fillip [a
man] downe, a fever can depose him; a fever can bring that head, which
yesterday carried a *crown* of gold, five foot towards a *crown* of glory, as low
as his own foot, today" (*Dev.* 239; 3.1). The modal verb of ability (*can*)
applies to the illness, which acts; the patient is passive, suffering from
alteration.

Station 2 is dedicated to the felt features of *alteratio*: qualitative changes
such as being scarcely able to see, losing one's sense of taste and appetite, losing one's ability to sleep, and feeling the knees to be "sinking and

32. *OED*, s.v. "digest," v.2.

strengthlesse" (*Dev.* 236; 2.1). Station 3 focuses on *latio*: the disease strips Donne of his erect posture, and he is no longer capable of moving his body in space. In his limited range of movement, he is like the anchorites who confined themselves within hollow trees or walls. But Donne's case is worse, for such ascetics "could stand, or sit, and enjoy some change of posture" (*Dev.* 239; 3.1). Donne cannot move at all: "Strange fetters to the feete, strange Manacles to the hands, when the feete, and hands are bound so much the faster, by how much the cords are slacker; So much the lesse able to doe their Offices, by how much more the Sinewes and Ligaments are the looser" (*Dev.* 239; 3.1). Voluntary local motion rests on the capacity of the body to respond to the will. This response relies upon a tautness that illness has undone. The problem laid out in Meditation 3, then, is the inability to move no matter how much effort one exerts. Even one's most basic powers—the ability to move or to see—are subtended by a fundamental powerlessness over those powers.[33] The modal verb of ability is the tool through which Donne makes this phenomenological truth both legible and viscerally present: human life is subject to all kinds of natural change; what we take the body or the mind to be capable of doing are little more than assumptions that can, at any moment, be proven false.

In Expostulation 3, Donne tries to understand this disappearance of abilities. He does so by shifting his address from the human "we" to Christ as mediated by scripture:

My *God*, and my *Jesus*, my *Lord*, and *my Christ, my Strength*, and *my Salvation*, I heare thee, and I hearken to thee, when thou rebukest thy *Disciples*, for rebuking them, who brought children to thee; *Suffer little children to come to mee*, saiest thou. Is there a verier child than I am now? I cannot say with thy servant *Jeremy, Lord, I am a child, and cannot speake*; but, *O Lord*, I am a sucking childe, and cannot eat, a creeping childe, and cannot goe; how shall I come to thee? Whither shall I come to thee? To this bed? I have this weake, and childish frowardnes too, I cannot sit up. (*Dev.* 239–40; 3.2)

In Matthew 19:14, Jesus tells his disciples to let the children to "*come to me*." In his sickness, Donne has become childlike. He has lost most of his physical abilities. He "cannot eat." He "cannot goe." He "cannot" even

---

33. This formulation is indebted to Michel Henry, *I Am the Truth: Toward a Philosophy of Christianity*, trans. Susan Emanuel (Stanford, CA: Stanford University Press, 2002).

explain his inability ("I cannot say," he tells his readers, that "*I . . . cannot speake*"). How, having lost all ability to change position, can he "come" to Christ? Even if Christ were sitting on his bedside, Donne would be unable to "come," for he "cannot sit up." He begins to shift responsibility for his changed condition from the disease to God: "How shal they come to thee, whom thou hast nayled to their bed?" (*Dev.* 240; 3.2).

Donne's first attempt to answer this question conflates the act of coming to God with physical movement to the church, where God's presence is most intensely felt. After all, "Thou art in the *Congregation*, and I in a solitude" (*Dev.* 240; 3.2).[34] Even if one cannot move oneself, one might be moved by others. Donne finds examples from scripture: in Matthew 8:17, the centurion's servant "lay sicke at home, his *Master* was faine to come to Christ" when "the sicke man could not"; in Matthew 9:2, the "four charitable men" brought their friend, "sicke of the *Palsey*," to Christ when the sick man "could not come" (*Dev.* 240; 3.2). But being carried to church is not a solution—not because Donne "would not" go, but because, due to fears of contagion, he "must not" (*Dev.* 240; 3.2). Donne then switches gears and begins to interpret Christ's imperative to "*Suffer little children to come to mee*" in a mental register: "I lye here and say, *Blessed are they, that dwell in thy house*; but I cannot say, *I will come into thy house*; I may say, *In thy feare will I worship towards thy holy Temple*; but I cannot say in thy holy *Temple*" (*Dev.* 240; 3.2). Mixing quotations from Psalm 84 and Psalm 5 with his own imagined speech, Donne reinterprets the act of coming "*into thy house*" as an intentional act. Although he cannot be "in thy holy *Temple*," he can direct his thoughts "*towards thy holy Temple*." Even if Donne's body cannot move, his mind can still intend, is still capable of bending its attention toward distant intentional objects.

In the expostulations, Donne tries to make sense of his current condition through God's word. He grapples with scripture so that it produces a semantic framework within which the negative change described in the meditation—here, the inability to move—is understood in a new way, seen as a positive development. The prayers take this new, hard-won understanding and open it toward a resolution via direct apostrophe to God. "O most mightie and most merciful *God*," begins the prayer of the third station:

who though thou have taken me off of my feet, hast not taken me off of my foundation, which is *thy selfe*, who though thou have removed me

34. For the religious polemic that lies behind this point, see Strier, "Politics of Devotion."

from that upright forme, in which I could stand, and see thy throne, the *Heavens*, yet hast not removed from mee that light, by which I can lie and see thy selfe, who, though thou have weakened my bodily knees, that they cannot bow to thee, hast yet left mee the knees of my heart, which are bowed unto thee evermore. . . . I come unto thee, *O God, my God*, I come unto thee, (so as I can come, I come to thee, by imbracing thy I to me) I come in the confidence, and in the application of thy servant *Davids* promise, *That thou wilt make all my bed in my sicknesse; All my bedd;* That which way soever I turne, I may turne to thee. (*Dev.* 241; 3.3)

The changes that Donne had described in natural terms are here reinscribed in terms of divinity. In Meditation 3, human beings are as "naturally built, and disposed to the contemplation of *Heaven*," for "*Man* in his naturall forme, is carried to the contemplation of that place, which is his *home, Heaven*" (*Dev.* 239; 3.1). In Prayer 3, Donne realizes that his ability to stand was not predicated upon the skill of his feet. His "foundation" has always been God. And it was not, as he claimed in the meditation, a "fever" that "fillip[ed]" or "depos[ed]" him, but rather God Himself who has "taken me off of my feet." Now that he is flat upon his back, this foundation remains the same, for it is God upon whom Donne's entire existence is grounded. This means that even when confined to his sickbed he "can lie and see" God. Although he cannot bow his "bodily knees" to God, he can "bow" the "knees of my heart." Locomotion is not needed to "come to" God, but only an altered state of mind. Even while trapped in his bed, Donne can indeed "come unto thee, O God," for this act requires coming "as I can come, I come to thee, by imbracing thy comming to me." Since God is always present, coming to God involves a change in attitude, a reframing of passive receptivity in active terms, not as suffering but as "imbracing."

Each station's meditation presents a natural change through which Donne, as patient, must suffer. The work of each expostulation and prayer is to change his orientation toward this change, to show how these changes are not, in fact, problems (or at least not all-consuming problems)—so long as they are understood in the right way. The tripartite structure of each station manages the speaker's relation to change. This principle of resolution, internal to each station's movement from meditation to expostulation to prayer, is complemented by another structural feature that folds *Devotions* in half so that each station echoes a partner in such a way that the deleterious changes of the earlier stations resonate in reparative

ways with the later stations.[35] The text pivots on the central twelfth station, which figures an attempt by the physicians to "*apply Pidgeons, to
draw the vapors from the Head*" (*Dev.* 278; 12).[36] Placed on Donne's feet,
these medicinal pigeons are supposed to attract dangerous vapors from
the top of the body to the bottom. The initiation of this motion from
head to feet serves as a structural joint, a key contignation in the text's
architecture:

1	2	3	4	5	6	7	8	9	10	11	
											12
23	22	21	20	19	18	17	16	15	14	13	

As an illustration of this structural principle, consider how the opening sentence of the meditation in the first station mirrors a sentence in
the prayer of the final twenty-third station. The text's first sentence—
"Variable, and therefore miserable condition of Man; this minute I was
well, and am ill, this minute" (*Dev.* 232; 1.1)—is echoed near the end
of the final station, which repeats the epanalepsis "this minute . . . this
minute" to suggest the shift in attitude initiated through the course of
Donne's illness: "Since therefore thy *Correction* hath brought mee to such
a *participation of thy selfe* (*thy selfe*, O my *God*, cannot bee *parted*), to such
an *intire possession* of thee, as that I durst deliver my selfe over to thee this
Minute, If this *Minute* thou wouldst accept my *dissolution, preserve* me,
O my *God*" (*Dev.* 332; 23.3). This repetition shows the extent to which
Donne's relationship with both accidental and substantial change has altered over the course of the disease's progress. Whereas, in the opening
line of *Devotions*, Donne bemoans the fact that health can shift into illness "this minute," in the final prayer, Donne claims he will "deliver my
selfe" to God "this *Minute*" on the condition that God would accept his
"*dissolution*" in "this *Minute*." Donne arranges these two passages so that
they resonate numerically and structurally across the book and, as a re-

35. Much like Dante's *Commedia*—which can be read horizontally (following the
Pilgrim as he moves, say, from Canto 2 to 3 in *Inferno*) and vertically (following the
Pilgrim from, for example, *Inferno* 3, through *Purgatorio* 3, to *Paradiso* 3)—Donne's
Devotions are also designed to be read in multiple directions.

36. Many critics have noted the centrality of Station 12, but no one, so far as
we know, has articulated the architectonic force of the station's position. The critic
whose view is closest to ours is Judith H. Anderson, *Translating Investments: Metaphor and the Dynamic of Cultural Change in Tudor-Stuart England* (New York: Fordham University Press, 2005), 75, in which she claims that in Station 12 "Donne openly
transacts the shift into another register."

sult, suggest the full extent of his altered disposition. The speaker's fear of change has, over the course of *Devotions*, been recontextualized so that even if that fear remains, it is no longer as debilitating as it once was.

The formal complexity of this mirroring operates across the entire text, but it snaps into focus in the echoic relations between Station 3 (*"The Patient takes his bed"* [*Dev.* 238], when the possibility of locomotion vanishes) and Station 21 (*"God prospers their practise, and he by them calls Lazarus out of his tombe, mee out of my bed"* [*Dev.* 318], when the possibility returns). Whereas the state of becoming bedridden was undertaken alone and was initially felt as a loss of individual ability, Donne's emergence from his bed is framed as a collective effort. In Station 21, ability is dependent not only on divine assistance but also on sociality and intersubjectivity. Donne roots his meditation in an acknowledgment of human frailty: "O what a *Giant* is Man, when hee fights against himselfe, and what a *dwarfe*, when hee *needs*, or *exercises* his own assistance for himselfe?" (*Dev.* 319; 21.1). Here, human beings are only giants when they sin or work to destroy themselves—a far cry from Donne's claim in Station 4 that it is "too little to call Man a *little World*" (*Dev.* 242; 4.1). By this point in his illness, Donne has incorporated the knowledge he purported to possess at its onset, namely, that unlike animals "Man hath not that *innate instinct*, to apply those naturall medicines to his present danger, as those inferiour creatures have" (*Dev.* 243; 4.1). Now he truly knows that human beings do not have the ability to help themselves or make themselves better.

As Donne's treatment of *can* and *cannot* in Station 3 suggests, every human ability relies on powers they do not control. In Station 21, he renders that implicit lesson explicit:

> I cannot *rise* out of my bed, till the *Physitian enable* mee, nay I cannot tel, that I am able to rise, till *hee tell* me so. I *doe* nothing, I *know* nothing of my selfe: how little, and how impotent a peece of the *world*, is any *Man* alone? and how much lesse a peece of *himselfe* is *that Man*? So little, as that when it falls out, (as it falls out in some cases) that more *misery*, and more *oppression*, would bee an *ease* to a *man*, he cannot give himselfe that *miserable addition*, of *more misery*; A *man* that is *pressed to death*, and might be eased by more *weights*, cannot lay those more *weights* upon himselfe; Hee can sinne *alone*, and suffer *alone*, but not *repent*, not be *absolved*, without *another. Another tels mee, I* may rise; *and I* doe so. (*Dev.* 319; 21.1)

In this passage that invokes the horrors of torture by pressing, Donne reverses the strategy he developed in the third station by pairing the modal verb of disability (*cannot*) with the recovery of his abilities. He begins by formulating the relationship in an unsatisfactory way—he "cannot" leave his bed until the physician has "*enable[d]*" him—and then corrects this view with an even deeper sense of his dependency: "I cannot tel, that I am able to rise, till *hee tell* me so." In the first expression, the physician "*enable[s]*" Donne; in the second, he can rise but is not aware of his own ability. The repetition of *tell* brings home the nature of this intersubjective debt. Donne can only "tel" (recognize or distinguish) his recuperated ability once he has heard the physician "*tell*" him (reveal through verbal communication) that he is in fact "able to rise."

He cannot, "of [him] selfe," do or know anything, for by himself a man is not only an "impotent peece of the *world*," but even more dramatically, a "*Man* alone" is "lesse a peece of *himselfe*." When alone, a given human being is a helpless "peece of the *world*," a physical body among physical bodies, prone to the vicissitudes of natural change, to illness, degeneration, corruption. At the same time, the isolated human being is even "lesse a peece of *himselfe*" than he is a piece of the world. If truly alone, one is "lesse a peece" of oneself because such a state of aloneness is a refusal of one's intersubjective makeup, a failure to see that one is already social through and through. Here, Donne puts into practice the lessons learned in his encounter with ringing bells in Station 17. Who, he asks, can "remove" his ear "from that *bell*, which is passing a *peece of himselfe* out of this *world*?" (*Dev.* 299; 17.1). The death of another Christian, signified by tolling bells, is always a diminishment of self: "No Man is an *Iland*, intire of it selfe; every man is a peece of the *Continent*, a part of the *maine*; if a *Clod* bee washed away by the *Sea*, *Europe* is the lesse, as well as if a *Promontorie* were . . . Any Mans *death* diminishes *me*, because I am involved in *Mankinde*" (*Dev.* 299; 17.1). The repetition of "peece of *himselfe*" in Station 21 suggests that to be "less a peece of *himselfe*" than one is a "peece of the *world*" is to engage in self-deception, to believe in a false ontology in which the word *alone* possesses significance when applied to a human being.

In Donne's view, nothing worth doing can be done alone. To illustrate this point, he argues in Station 21 that a given man "cannot give himselfe that *miserable addition*, of *more misery*," and provides an evocative example: "A *man* that is *pressed to death*, and might be eased by more *weights*, cannot lay those more *weights* upon himselfe" (*Dev.* 319; 21.1). Evoking the "thin sheets" like "yron dores" (*Dev.* 240; 3.2) that imprisoned and pressed upon him when he first took his sickbed in Station 3, Donne conjures the image of a man tortured and pinned in place, unable to add the weights that would end his suffering and his life. This extreme example clarifies the existential *I cannot* that lies at the base of human endeavor, for although we are able to "sinne *alone*, and suffer *alone*" we cannot "*repent*" or "be *absolved*, without *another*" (*Dev.* 319; 21.1). Emerging from his illness, Donne has realized that there is no meaningful connection between *I* and *can*, that any worthwhile ability is thoroughly intersubjective. "*Another tels mee*, I may rise; *and I* doe *so*" (*Dev.* 319; 21.1): the doing is here dependent on the telling, and the sense of permission conveyed in "may" suggests the social element that, for Donne, permeates any and every *can*.

Donne uses the structure of *Devotions* to manage the very change he represents in the illness's station-by-station progress. In the ameliorative discursive and apostrophic shifts from meditation to expostulation to prayer, Donne transforms what initially seem like the horrors of alteration on the cusp of corruption into a way of coming closer to God's benevolent and changeless eternity. Moving through twenty-three stations, each of which repeats this movement from terror to consolation, *Devotions* folds back on itself so that the stations communicate across the gap of time separating the earlier stages of the illness from the later stages. Donne manages change through these echoes, using them to measure his own progress by placing the emergent occasions of his illness in their proper context. The panicked "I cannot" of Station 3 and the measured "I cannot" (ameliorated by a "we can") of Station 21 are separated by distance greater than the onset of and recovery from a severe illness. This distance represents an achievement in the ability to respond to a human condition the meaning of which is not reducible to earthly life.

4

The History of Words

Donne uses structure and generic affiliation to manage the changes he represents in his depiction of living through illness. As we saw in chapter 3, in *Devotions* Donne develops a complex textual whole in which the hypervisibility of its parts enables a transformation of change's meanings across the horizontal axis of the text's narrative throughline, the vertical axis of its movement from earthly event through scripture toward God, and the reflexive axis of its inward echoes. And yet even as Donne seeks to manage the most deleterious effects of change through genre and textual structure, he simultaneously widens the scope of his reflection on change through what Quintilian calls the most basic element of style, which exists "in individual words and in words taken together."[1] The diction of *Devotions* disrupts its containing structures. Donne holds that human knowledge is subject to change, that many or even most truths come and go, that they vary according to culture and to historical time. For this reason, the words, images, and concepts that Donne uses both to represent and manage change are drawn from discourses that were themselves caught up in profound historical flux: physics, metaphysics, physick, astronomy, cartography, and alchemy, among others. In a world where even the distinction between substantial change and accidental change was disappearing, Donne's poetry and prose metabolize the features of an intellectual climate that was redrawing the conceptual and discursive boundaries within which change was thought, understood, and represented.

Donne's view of intellectual change shares much with that of Montaigne. "The sky and the stars have been moving for three thousand years;

---

1. Quintilian, *Institutio Oratoria (The Orator's Education)*, Books 6–8, ed. and trans. Donald A. Russell (Cambridge, MA: Harvard University Press, 2001), 324–25 (8.1). The classic study of early modern English poetic diction is Josephine Miles, *The Continuity of Poetic Language* (Berkeley: University of California Press, 1965).

everybody had so believed," writes Montaigne, "until it occurred to Cleanthes of Samos, or (according to Theophrastus) to Nicetas of Syracuse, to maintain that it was the earth that moved, through the oblique circle of the Zodiac, turning about its axis; and in our day Copernicus has grounded this doctrine so well that he uses it very systematically for all astronomical deductions." But it is not as though Copernicus is correct: "And who knows whether a third opinion, a thousand years from now, will not overthrow the preceding two?" (Mon. 429; 604). As both Montaigne and Donne knew, Copernicus's innovations were part of a centuries-old debate, stretching at least to Cleanthes. The true innovation lay not in the declaration that the earth was mobile, but in how Copernicus used the epistemological possibilities opened by the new role played by mixed mathematics in physics. Like Montaigne, Donne understood intellectual innovation as a product of shifting epistemic frameworks. For Donne, Copernicus was emblematic of the epistemic upheaval of his time. In *Ignatius His Conclave* (1611), Donne offers a satirical treatment of great contemporary "Innovators"—Ignatius, Paracelsus, Machiavelli, Galileo, and others, including Copernicus, he who has "raised" the earth "up into the Heavens." Others may have "innovated in small matters" but Donne's Copernicus has, he claims, "turned the whole frame of the world, and am thereby almost a new Creator [*pene novo Creatori*]" (*Con.* 14–15). This aggrandized claim for the import of epistemological shifts satirizes the quest for novelty that Donne thought characterized his age.

Although the massive changes in astronomy across early modernity are sometimes treated as paradigmatically revelatory of this view, what we might call (following Lorraine Daston and Arnold Davidson) the period's inchoate historical epistemological practices had a much broader scope.[2] When Donne coins the phrase "new Philosophy" to suggest that it calls "all in doubt," he means "all" quite literally (*Ann.* A1:27; 205)—everything from the earth's stability to the existence of the elements.[3] It is the deep awareness of and engagement with this intellectual upheaval that the image of Donne as the "late Copernicus of poetry," as he was described by an anonymous contemporary, captures with such

2. See, e.g., Lorraine Daston, "Historical Epistemology," in *Questions of Evidence: Proof, Practice, and Persuasion across the Disciplines*, ed. James Chandler, Arnold I. Davidson, and Harry D. Harootunian (Chicago: University of Chicago Press, 1994), 282–89; Arnold Davidson, *The Emergence of Sexuality: Historical Epistemology and the Formation of Concepts* (Cambridge, MA: Harvard University Press, 2004); and Lorraine Daston and Peter Gallison, *Objectivity* (Cambridge, MA: Zone Books, 2007).

3. An Early English Books Online search suggests that Donne was the first to put the phrase "new philosophy" into print.

brilliance: the words, images, and concepts out of which Donne's poetry and prose are built are themselves borrowed from discourses entangled in epistemological revolution.[4] From the beginning of his career, this relationship between diction and intellectual innovation had been central to what made Donne's work innovative. In *Devotions*, this feature of his style achieves mature expression.

Physick and the De-Metaphysicization of Physics

To grasp Donne's sense of the historicity of epistemological systems, in this section we examine words in *Devotions* that Donne took from metaphysics, physics, and physick. Although such language is everywhere in the text, it is clearly displayed in Station 22, where Donne reflects on his physicians' consideration of "*the root and occasion, the embers, and coales, and fuell of the disease*" (*Dev.* 323; 22). In the meditation, he laments that the root occasion is not "some *violent* and dangerous *accident* of a disease*" that one could pluck like a "*weed*" (*Dev.* 324; 22.1). Instead, it is the "whole *soile*" of the "*body*, out of which without any other *disorder, diseases* will grow" (*Dev.* 324; 22.1). In the expostulation, Donne intensifies his diagnosis: it is not the body that causes disease, but sin—both original sin, which corrupted subsequent human life, and the everyday sins we commit. Asking about "the *root*, the *fuell*, the *occasion*" of his sickness, Donne deflates his physicians' pretensions: "What *Hippocrates*, what *Galen*, could shew mee that in my *body*?" (*Dev.* 325; 22.2). It is likewise impossible for an "*Anatomist*" to find such a cause "by dissecting a *body*" (*Dev.* 326; 22.2), for it "lies deeper" than the body (*Dev.* 325; 22.2). After all, we "consider the *body*, before the *soule* came, before *inanimation*, to bee *without sinne*; and the *soule* before it come to the *body*, before that *infection*, to be *without sinne*" (*Dev.* 325; 2.2). Since sin is the cause of illness and since sin does not belong to body alone or soul alone, then the root of illness lies "in *both together*; It is the *union* of the *body* and the *soule*; and, O my *God*, could I *prevent* that, or can I *dissolve* that? The *root*, and the *fuell* of my *sicknesse*, is my *sinne*, my *actuall sinne*; but even that *sinne* hath another *root*, another *fuell*, *originall sinne*" (*Dev.* 325; 2.2). As we saw in chapter 1, Donne thinks that the *I* simply *is* the union of body and soul. No *I* can "*prevent*" its own coming to be; no human can help being the cause of disease. This is why, as Donne claims in Prayer 22, the only

4. Quoted from Bodleian Library Malone MS 14, 38, in W. Milgate, "The Early References to John Donne," *Notes and Queries* 195 (1950): 292. See also Carey, *John Donne*, 9.

solution lies in "true *repentance*," which involves a transfer of sin from the sinner to the "*Sonne*," who offers mercy and forgiveness (*Dev.* 327; 22.3).

Donne uses diction borrowed from metaphysics, physics, and physick to make this argument. Physick is integral to this etiological consideration: there is nothing in one's own body that works "by way of *Physicke*" on itself (*Dev.* 325; 22.1); all physick comes from other bodies, whether plant, animal, or human bodies (*Dev.* 324; 22.1). But as Donne's attempt to link disease and "*accident*" suggests (*Dev.* 324; 22.1), physick is interwoven with physics and metaphysics. Consider Donne's treatment here of what he elsewhere calls the "long and regular work" of maintaining "*Health*" (*Dev.* 232; 1.1):

> I undertooke to make such a thing *wholsome*, as was not *poison* by any manifest quality, *intense heat*, or *cold*, but *poison* in the *whole substance*, and in the *specifique forme* of it. To cure the *sharpe accidents* of *diseases*, is a great worke; to cure the *disease it selfe*, is a greater; but to cure the *body*, the *roote*, the *occasion* of *diseases*, is a worke reserved for the great *Physitian*, which he doth never any other way, but by *glorifying* these *bodies* in the next world. (*Dev.* 325; 22.1)

Substance, species, form, accident, quality: the language of metaphysics dominates this passage. In trying to make "such a thing" as the body "*wholsome*," Donne neglected to account for how the poison is not an accident (a "manifest quality") inhering in his substance but *is* his "*whole substance*." It is hard to cure the "*accidents*" of disease, but human beings cannot cure their very substance, particularly since the disease is not simply "in" the "*whole substance*" of an individual human being but is also "in" the "*specific forme*" of that substance—the very form of the species in which that substance participates. The presence of such metaphysical language is not accidental.

Donne uses these words with full knowledge of what Dmitri Levitin calls the "de-metaphysicization of natural philosophy," the historical process by which natural philosophy came to all but exclude metaphysics.[5] In 1610, the lexicographer Edmund Bolton defined "PHYSICKS" as

5. Dmitri Levitin, *The Kingdom of Darkness: Bayle, Newton, and the Emancipation of the European Mind from Philosophy* (Cambridge: Cambridge University Press, 2022), 46. Our argument also intersects with Wendy Beth Hyman, "Physics, Metaphysics, and Religion in Lyric Poetry," in *Blackwell Companion to British Literature*, vol. 2, ed. Robert DeMaria Jr., Heesock Chang, and Samantha Zacher (West Sussex: Blackwell, 2014), 197–212, who focuses on the role of physics in metaphysical poetry. We agree with Hyman that such poets as Donne "were often as intrigued by

"Naturall Philosophy" or "those speculations which concern the works of nature."[6] This sense of the term extended across the period: Thomas Elyot's *Dictionary* (1538) defines "Physica" as "warkes treatynge of the nature of things, or the operacion of nature," a definition repeated more than a century later in Thomas Blount's *Glossographia* (1656), which casts "Physics (physica)" as "books treating of Physick or natural phylosophy."[7] *Physics* encompassed all of natural philosophy. This makes etymological sense, since the term derives from the Greek *physikê*, an elaboration of *physis* or nature. Physics focused on substances in motion, coming into existence (generation), undergoing qualitative change (alteration), going out of existence (corruption), moving according to the dictates of various natural forces. By contrast, metaphysics, understood in the simplest terms, referred to what was beyond or alongside nature (*meta + physis*).[8] Although early modern thinkers grasped the distinction between physics and metaphysics in a variety of ways, we focus on two: first, the difference between physical and metaphysical *objects*; and second, the difference between physical and metaphysical *concepts*.

Aristotle's *Metaphysics* were often read as providing a theory of metaphysical objects. Aristotle isolates "first philosophy" or the inquiry into "being qua being" as the "theoretical science" elevated over the other theoretical sciences, physics and mathematics (Ar. 2:1619; 1025b).[9] Physics studies objects that are "moveable" (that change in time) and that are "inseparable from matter." Mathematics studies objects that are "immovable" (the angles of a triangle do not change in time) and "separable from matter" (the relations of these angles may possess an ideal form). Metaphysics surpasses these sciences because it concerns "something which is eternal and immovable and separable," that which does not change in time and exists independently (Ar. 2:1620; 1026a).[10] This is the back-

---

physics—the nature of matter and its motion in space and time—as they were by 'metaphysics,' those spiritual domains ostensibly outside of material concern" (207).

6. Edmund Bolton, *The Elements of Armories* (London, 1610).

7. Thomas Blount, *Glossographia* (London, 1656).

8. As the title of Aristotle's *Metaphysics* was probably meant to indicate, *after*— the book that came after the *Physics*.

9. See Gordon Teskey, "The Metaphysics of the Metaphysicals," in *John Donne in Context*, ed. Michael Schoenfeldt (Cambridge: Cambridge University Press, 2019), 239, for a similar overview.

10. For a history of the early modern reception of Aristotle's double definition of metaphysics, see Dmitri Levitin, *Ancient Wisdom in the Age of New Science: Histories of Philosophy in England, c. 1640–1700* (Cambridge: Cambridge University Press, 2015), 242–52.

ground for the Latin distinction between *naturalia* from *supernaturalia* captured by the English translation of the French philosopher Pierre de La Primaudaye's *L'academie Française* (1577): "Physicke" is the "studie of naturall things" while "Metaphysicke" is the study of "supernaturall things."[11]

The presence or absence of change is what separates objects of physics from those of metaphysics. Sublunary things (earthly bodies) were thought to be subject to change; they belonged to physics.[12] By contrast, superlunary things (the heavens, celestial spheres, angels) were not subject to change; they belonged to metaphysics. Donne is indebted to this framework.[13] In *Essays on Divinity*, he distinguishes "Morall Divinity" (a topic that "becomes us all") from "Naturall Divinity, and Metaphysick Divinity" (topics that "almost all may spare").[14] Donne distinguishes metaphysics from nature, the realm of *physis*, a move he repeats in *Paradoxes and Problems*, where he defines "Metaphysique" in terms of the "supernaturall."[15] As Gordon Teskey argues, Donne's poetry is metaphysical because it uses metaphysical objects, drawing "things that are free of change and have independent being" into his verse:[16] "So thy love may be my loves spheare" (*Son.* 76; 25), he writes in "Aire and Angels," using the supernatural spheres of the Ptolemaic cosmos as a way of distinguishing his relationship with his beloved from what, in "A Valediction: forbidding Mourning," he calls "Dull sublunary lovers love" (*Son.* 63; 13).

Donne also uses metaphysical *concepts*, which were thought to apply

11. Pierre de La Primaudaye, *The French Academie*, translated by T. B. (London, 1586), 76. This text was republished in 1589, 1594, 1601, 1602, 1605, and 1614. For an earlier discussion of the nested relationship between physics and metaphysics, see Elizabeth D. Harvey, "'Mutual Elements': Irigaray's Donne," in *Luce Irigaray and Premodern Culture: Thresholds of History*, ed. Elizabeth D. Harvey and Theresa Krier (London: Routledge, 2004), 66–87.

12. Aquinas puts it this way in a commentary on Boethius, in *Selected Philosophical Writings*, ed. Timothy McDermott (Oxford: Oxford University Press, 1993), 13–14: "all creatures are changeable and only God, as Augustine says, unchanging. . . . [N]atural science studies natural things, things with an interior tendency to move and change. But, as Aristotle says, wherever there is change there must be material change. So natural science is concerned with material, changing things."

13. He references Aristotle's *Metaphysics* in his sermons, using the fact that *"Aristotles Metaphysicks* were condemned for Heresie" as proof of the "extreme ignorance that damp'd the *Roman* Church" (*Ser.* 10:149).

14. John Donne, *Essays in Divinity*, ed. Evelyn M. Simpson (Oxford: Clarendon Press, 1952), 88.

15. John Donne, *Paradoxes and Problems*, ed. Helen Peters (Oxford: Clarendon Press, 1980), 8. .

16. Teskey, "Metaphysics of the Metaphysicals," 240–41.

to everything. The concepts central to Aristotle's *Metaphysics*—matter, form, substance, actuality, potentiality, necessity, and so on—were important for understanding not just things free of change but also the natural world. Metaphysics is the science of "being qua being," a phrase parsed by many to mean that it must be about the basic properties of being—what, in *Disputationes metaphysicae* (1597), Francisco Suárez called "transcendentals."[17] Johannes Clauberg's definition of metaphysics from his *Elementa philosophiae* (1647) summarizes the tradition familiar to Donne: "There is a certain science that investigates being qua being, that is, being understood as having a common nature or a degree of nature which is, in its own way, in both corporeal and incorporeal things, God and creatures, and including all particulars. This science is generally called metaphysics."[18] The study of the transcendentals—concepts that pertain to angels, the cosmos, the earth, and the many creatures living and nonliving that come into and out of existence—is metaphysical because these transcendentals explain being. The transcendentals are necessary for understanding the natural world; they are metaphysical but applicable to physics.

Although Donne was educated to think that physics was contained within metaphysics, he knew that this relationship was changing. New astronomical ideas, the work of Bacon and his followers, the spread of corpuscular theories of various sorts, and many other intellectual dynamics conspired to disarticulate physics from metaphysics. An important vector of this change involved the shift from one set of concepts to another, what Robert Pasnau describes as the substitution of "integral parts" for "metaphysical parts." A given substance—a dog, say—has many *integral parts*: heart, lungs, brain, limbs, eyes, blood, cells, molecules, atoms. These are, as Pasnau puts it, "parts of bodies that are also bodies." By contrast, *metaphysical parts* are "not bodies but are instead ingredients of bodies."[19] An Aristotelian would claim that, in addition to integral parts, a dog is composed of metaphysical parts like matter and form. According to Pasnau, the "new philosophy" intensified a tendency, already present in thinkers like William of Ockham, to understand nature in corpuscular terms that reject metaphysical parts in two ways:

17. See, e.g., Francisco Suárez, *Metaphysical Disputation I: On the Nature of First Philosophy or Metaphysics*, trans. Shane Duarte (Washington, DC: Catholic University of America Press, 2022), 67.

18. Quoted in Jean-Christophe Bardout, "Johannes Clauberg," in *A Companion to Early Modern Philosophy*, ed. Steven Nadler (Malden, MA: Blackwell, 2002), 131.

19. Pasnau, *Metaphysical Themes*, 7. Subsequent quotations cited parenthetically.

first, bodies were increasingly thought to be composed only of integral parts; and second, bodily movement and change were thought to be governed only by local motion produced through contact between bodies, one body moving another (7–9). Consider prime matter, the "enduring substratum of change" that precedes and survives the generation and corruption of any substantial form. For Aquinas and others, prime matter was "pure potential," undetermined in every way (35–40). For René Descartes and many other "corpuscular" thinkers, bodily extension was the defining feature of matter. In Pasnau's words, "in the seventeenth century, matter becomes body, and body becomes the object of natural science" (76).

Donne was writing when new theories that explained things in terms of integral parts were supplanting forms of explanation that had for centuries been organized by metaphysical parts. Before Donne was born, physics tended to be explained in metaphysical terms.[20] When Donne began to write, physics was coming to be understood in the absence of the accompanying conceptual apparatus of form, the four elements, and so on.[21] The replacement of metaphysical parts with integral parts meant that the concepts of physics began to extend into territory that had been metaphysical, pushing aside matter, form, and other concepts that had subtended the explanation of natural things. This expansion also pushed *up* into the superlunary, the preserve of metaphysical objects: new discoveries about planetary orbits, new stars, and the infinity of the universe began to destabilize the very existence of unchanging metaphysical objects.[22] Perhaps physical objects were the *only* objects. Donne plays with this development when he invokes "new philosophy," the newness of which is grounded in historically situated changes to how the natural world was understood to work: the Copernican cosmos inverted the Ptolemaic vision; Paracelsus's mercury, sulfur, and salt reoriented understandings of bodies away from the four elements as understood by Aristotle, Avicenna, and Galen.

---

20. As Levitin, *Kingdom of Darkness*, 26, puts it: natural philosophy could "be characterized as a 'metaphysical physics,' the primary purpose of which was to explain the underlying principles of natural bodies by exploring the nature and the interrelationship of the various metaphysical parts that were said to constitute them."

21. This observation describes a tendency, not an absolute rule. Metaphysics and physics continued to be entangled. See, e.g., Daniel Garber, *Descartes's Metaphysical Physics* (Chicago: University of Chicago Press, 1992).

22. For a related account, see Mary Thomas Crane, *Losing Touch with Nature: Literature and the New Science in Sixteenth-Century England* (Baltimore: Johns Hopkins University Press, 2014).

But Donne does not subscribe to epistemological supersession. He reveals why this is the case in a sermon preached at the funeral of Sir William Cockayne in 1626, two years after *Devotions* was published: "I need not call in new Philosophy, that denies a settlednesse, an acquiescence in the very body of the Earth, but makes the Earth to move in that place, where we thought the Sunne had moved; I need not that helpe, that the Earth it selfe is in Motion, to prove this, That nothing upon Earth is permanent" (*Ser.* 7:271). New philosophy "makes" the earth move, replacing what "we thought" to be the case. Shattering as such ideas might be, they do not dislodge traditional ways of thinking. Donne makes this point earlier in the same sermon: "Young men mend not their sight by using old mens Spectacles; and yet we looke upon Nature, but with *Aristotles* Spectacles, and upon the body of man, but with *Galens*, and upon the frame of the world, but with *Ptolemies* Spectacles. Almost all knowledge is rather like a child that is embalmed to make Mummy, then that is nursed to make a Man" (*Ser.* 7:260).[23] The striking image of an embalmed child epitomizes Donne's critique of the arrested development that he believes characterizes most learning; it either petrifies inherited knowledge paradigms or, conversely, seeks revolutionary new ideas. Rejecting both options, Donne enjoins a gradual integration of new ideas as an "emproving, an advancing, a multiplying of former inceptions" (*Ser.* 7:260).[24] Buried here is a deeper point about how human understanding works—not by looking at the new but by drawing from the past, by see-

23. Spectacles are Donne's favored image for thinking about the relationship between old and new knowledge. Consider the spectacles that enable the narrator of *Ignatius* to see the souls of the dead innovators in dialogue with Satan. The narrator's eyeglasses are, he hypothesizes, like the ones Gregory the Great and Bede wore, which allowed them to recognize the souls of their friends once they had been "discharged" from their bodies (*Con.* 7). Note Donne's joke: the soul's capacity to see the cosmos, to glimpse the souls of the dead, and to observe Lucifer's infernal court as he judges religious, political, medical, and scientific innovators is enabled by a recent technological invention: eyeglasses. Although the identity of their creator is unknown, spectacles were thought to be a late thirteenth-century Pisan invention. As Vincent Ilardi, *Renaissance Vision from Spectacles to Telescopes* (Philadelphia: American Philosophical Society, 2007), has shown, the artisanal manufacture and distribution of eyeglasses was initiated by Friar Alessandro della Spina (who may have known the inventor) and expanded quickly in fourteenth-century Italy, drawing on the skills of glassmakers, jewelers, and goldsmiths.

24. In a sermon, Donne writes: "God loves not innovations; Old doctrines, old disciplines, old words and formes of speech in his service, God loves best. But it is a Renovation, though not an Innovation, and Renovations are always acceptable to God" (*Ser.* 2:305). For a related discussion of innovation, see Rundell, *Super-Infinite*, 239–42.

ing through ancient concepts. The generation of knowledge proceeds by encasing new within old.[25] Even the discovery by "new philosophy" that "the Earth it selfe is in Motion" works by seeing this new idea through ancient ideas about change and how it works. Epistemic frameworks shift slowly, and although Donne thought Copernicus correct, he could not help but "looke upon Nature, but with *Aristotles* Spectacles," orienting himself within established metaphysical terms—substance, accident, matter, form—and within a network of terms for change: *motus, mutatio, generatio, corruptio, alteratio,* and *latio,* among others.

Donne understood knowledge to be historically contingent. And he thought this contingency to be felt, a phenomenon through which one lives. These features of how Donne grasps epistemological change are visible in his earlier uses of the phrase "new philosophy." Donne famously positions the *First Anniversarie* in the epistemological upheaval of the early seventeenth century: "And new Philosophy cals all in doubt, / The Element of fire is quite put out; / The Sunne is lost, and th'earth, and no mans wit / Can well direct him, where to looke for it" (*Ann.* A1:27–28; 205–8). Donne draws on philosophical developments to showcase the historicity of the intellectual tools human beings use to understand change. He mentions the Aristotelian "Element of fire" and the "Atomis" of Epicurus and Lucretius (*Ann.* A1:28; 212), but he also meditates on the rejection or new use of these tools by "new Philosophy." This phrase recurs in *Devotions.* Describing how, when he emerges from his sickbed in Meditation 21, he stands up but suffers from a vertigo that makes him feel like he is spinning, Donne appeals to the historicity of knowledge: "I am *up,* and I seeme to *stand,* and I goe *round*; and I am a *new Argument* of the *new Philosophie,* That the *Earth* moves round" (*Dev.* 319; 21.1). In the eyes of his attending physicians, Donne seems to stand, but he is in fact "carried, in a giddy, and *circular motion,* as I *stand*" (*Dev.* 319–20; 21.1). He depicts his own embodied existence as a *"new Argument"* for "the *new Philosophie*": the intersection of standing and spinning showcases how the earth seems to stand still but in fact spins, as Copernicus proved, around the sun. Donne imports an emergent form of physics into his own first-person perspective, folding an account of how the cosmos works into his embodied condition as it is lived and felt and known.

25. Herbert Grierson puts this dynamic well in the introduction to his *Metaphysical Lyrics and Poems of the Seventeenth Century: From Donne to Butler* (Oxford: Clarendon, 1921), xxi: Donne's writing drew on "the same scholastic learning . . . as controlled Dante's thought, jostling already with the new learning of Copernicus and Paracelsus."

This passage offers a vivid example of what, in chapter 1, we described as a first-person philosophy of nature. By calling himself a *"new Argument"* for "the *new Philosophie*," Donne transforms his own bodily feeling of standing, balancing, and inhabiting space into a laboratory for understanding what "the *new Philosophie*" has done to the cosmos. It has simultaneously destabilized the earth and begun to turn superlunary metaphysical objects into little more than fictions. Donne claims that "in the *Heavens*, there are but a few *Circles*, that goe about the whole world, but many *Epicycles*, and other lesser *Circles*" (*Dev.* 320; 21.1). This phrase captures the end of the Ptolemaic cosmos; its fixed, metaphysical spheres ("*Circles*, that goe about the whole world") are in the process of being replaced by the "*Epicycles*" and "lesser *Circles*" required to save the phenomena.[26] Donne describes the corruption of the Ptolemaic world system by appealing to alterations in bodily feeling. This scene captures Donne's sense of the historical epistemological shifts though which he lived; it represents change through words ("*Epicycles*," "lesser *Circles*") taken from the terrain of a physics that had expanded into that of metaphysics. It also aligns these words, borrowed from shifting technical discourses, with embodied feeling so that readers are ushered inside change as it unfolds.

Donne uses physick to frame his representation of natural change. In doing so, he adopts a language of substance and change that was itself caught up in the de-metaphysicization of physics. Station 22 positions its discussion of substances, accidents, forms, qualities, and species between a discussion of the "*Physicke*" of Hippocrates or Galen, the "*Physicke*" of medicines taken from other bodies, and God, the "great *Physitian*" who will heal us at the end of time (*Dev.* 324–25; 22.1–22.2). This is not accidental. As Levitin has argued and as Donne and many of his contemporaries knew, the uncoupling of metaphysics from physics was partly orchestrated by the increased importance of physick relative to natural philosophy.[27] In what remains of this section, we examine his use of physick, showing how he treats both Paracelsus and Paracelsian concepts as emblematic of shifting regimes of knowledge.

26. See Mueller, *John Donne*, 597n21.

27. Levitin, *Kingdom of Darkness*, 43–45: "by the time we come to the early seventeenth century we can speak without any great fear of anachronism of a programme of medical experimental research that clashed with the traditional philosophical conception of what it was to explain natural phenomena. . . . The physicians played a crucial role in two moves that went hand in hand: a shift towards an emphasis on experience, experiment, the importance of natural history, etc.; and an anti-scholastic programme of ontological minimization directed above all against substantial forms."

Donne offers a portrait of Paracelsus in *Ignatius*. The hilarity of the initial encounter between Paracelsus and Lucifer in this text captures the derision, admiration, and fear that attended the European reception of Paracelsian medicine. When Lucifer asks for Paracelsus's identity, the physician intones his extravagant name: "Philippus Aureolus Theophrastus Paracelsus Bombast of Hohenheim." Lucifer recoils as if he were hearing the incantation of an exorcism found in "*Welsh*, or *Irish Bibles*" (*Con.* 19), but when he realizes that the words are Paracelsus's name, he responds with a similarly florid concatenation of his own titles. Donne's depiction satirizes Paracelsus's violent attacks on Galen and academic medicine in general, his outrageous behavior, his idiosyncratic methods, and especially his ostentatious account of his achievements, but his medical achievements remain uncontested.[28] Paracelsus claims to have challenged all "*Methodicall*" physicians and their beliefs so effectively that he destroyed this traditional medicine (*Con.* 21). The Methodic school to which Donne refers was inaugurated by Asclepiades, a Greek physician who practiced in Rome, incorporated atomism into a theory of disease, challenged the principles of Hippocratic medicine, and resisted anatomical discovery.[29] Paracelsus's use of the term, however, also targets the prevailing hegemony of Galenic medicine. As Donne has Paracelsus put it in *Ignatius*, his physick runs counter to certainty and "fixed rules" (*Con.* 21, 9). His "uncertain, ragged, and unperfect experiments" and "dangerously drawne" remedies have, he says, necessitated "triall[s]" that have turned men into "carkases" (*Con.* 21, 5–15). As Donne's Paracelsus describes the various "minerals" and "fires" of his alchemical cures, Ignatius observes that a "tempest" has risen in Lucifer's countenance, since Ignatius was of "the same temper" as Lucifer and therefore "suffered" with him and "felt al his alterations" (*Con.* 21, 23–30.). The joke is that this moment of passional connection at Paracelsus's long-winded account rests on multiple medical theories. On the one hand, the "temper" that Ignatius and Lucifer share relies on a theory of temperament and the passions rooted in Hippocratic and Galenic humoral medicine. But the linkage Ignatius feels with Lucifer is also forged by sympathy, the concept that Donne saw as central to Paracelsian physick.[30]

28. For this point about Donne, see Coffin, *Donne and the New Philosophy*, 209. See also Weeks's edition of *Paragranum*, 8off. (in *Paracelsus: Essential Theoretical Writings*, ed. Andrew Weeks [Leiden; Boston: Brill, 2008]).

29. See Healy's notes in *Con.* 21, l.6.

30. In a letter to Sir Henry Goodyer, Donne provides a capsule history of changing medical beliefs in which he characterizes Paracelsian physick as a doctrine of "antipathy and sympathy" (*Let.* 15). For a general account of sympathy in Paracelsus, see Walter

In *Ignatius,* Donne satirizes Paracelsus's style and arrogance. Yet the technical diction of these writings furnished Donne with some of his most evocative images.[31] Consider Donne's elaboration of the Paracelsian human-cosmic correspondence in *Devotions.* As a *"little world,"* "Man" experiences *"earthquakes* in him selfe, sodaine shakings; these *lightnings,* sodaine flashes; these *thunders,* sodaine noises; these *Eclypses,* sodain obfuscations, and darknings of his senses; these *blazing* stars, sodaine fiery exhalations; these *rivers of blood,* sodaine red waters" (*Dev.* 232–33; 1.1). Donne's lines echo Paracelsus's explication in *Paragranum* of the first pillar of his fourfold foundation of medicine: philosophy. Paracelsus defines philosophy as "invisible nature," arguing that the role of the physician is to be a student of nature and to intuit the unseen correspondences between the cosmos and the human body. He proclaims that the physician is a student of nature. Proper understanding of humans rests on knowing the heavens and the earth: "the pulse can be comprehended from the firmament; [or] physiognomy in the stars; chiromancy in *mineralia;* breath in *Eurus* and *Zephyrus;* the fevers in earthquakes; and so on with the one thing based on the other."[32] Donne likewise adopted the Paracelsian belief in balm as a quintessence or spirit of life that informed body and world.[33] Donne refers to *"Balsamum"* as the body's *"Spirits"* in a sermon of 1618, since like the spirits of Galenic theory, balm has inherent life-giving properties (*Ser.* 2:81). Physicians, following Paracelsus, describe this *"Naturale Balsamum"* as possessing intrinsic healing properties to cure wounds and hurts, an idea central to *The First Anniversarie.* The poem describes how Elizabeth Drury's death deprived the sick world of that "preservative," its "intrinsique Balm," exposing its fundamentally corrupt and mortal nature (*Ann.* A1:23; 57). Donne enlarges his Paracelsian ideas about balsam to include original sin as disease. As we have seen, Station 22 of *Devotions* argues that original sin entered the mortal body as a natural "Poyson" that countered its inherent healing balm. In a sermon of 1624, Donne rebukes those who have "attributed to the power

Pagel, *Paracelsus: An Introduction to Philosophical Medicine in the Era of the Renaissance* (New York: Karger, 1982), and for his note on sympathy and antipathy, see 336.

31. See the accounts of Donne's relationship with Paracelsian medicine in Charles M. Coffin, *Donne and the New Philosophy* (New York: Humanities Press, 1958), 93, 209; and W. A. Murray, "Donne and Paracelsus: An Essay in Interpretation," *Review of English Studies* 25 (1949): 115–23.

32. Paracelsus, *The Book Paragranum,* in *Paracelsus: Essential Theoretical Writings,* ed. Andrew Weeks (Leiden; Boston: Brill, 2008), 62–295, esp. 129.

33. Paracelsus, *The Archidoxies of Theophrastus Paracelsus,* in *The Hermetic and Alchemical Writings,* ed. Arthur Edward Waite (London: James Elliott, 1894), 2:22–23.

of nature, more than a naturall man can doe," who "over-valu[e]" nature's power, however, for as he asserts, it is only with Christ as the physician and through God's grace that we can be preserved and recovered (*Ser.* 6:116–19).[34] Paracelsus's understanding of correspondence structures Donne's imagination and theological beliefs.

In a letter to Sir Henry Goodyer, Donne provides a brief overview of the history of physick in which Hippocrates was supplanted by Galen, who was in turn displaced by Paracelsus (*Let.* 14–15).[35] But as we just saw in relation to the de-metaphysicization of physics, Donne does not sub-scribe to successionist accounts of intellectual change. Paracelsian medi-cine coexisted awkwardly, even contentiously, with Hippocratic and Ga-lenic theory and practice both for Donne and, as we will see in chapter 5, for the physicians who treated him—some of whom were self-professed Paracelsians.[36] Although the novelty of Paracelsus's methods and his re-bellion against the authority of Galen and Avicenna provoked censure by the medical establishment, Paracelsian physick was anchored in the ancient doctrines of Hermetic medicine. Paracelsian medicine appealed to Donne because it combined classical erudition, Hermetic philosophy, and alchemical practice with bold new experimentation. Poised between old and new in the way Donne thinks the search for knowledge ought to proceed, Paracelsus's approach explores uncharted territory through ancient spectacles.

34. For a discussion of these passages as aspects of Calvinist and Lutheran theol-ogy, see Mary Anne Lund, "Experiencing Pain in John Donne's *Devotions upon Emer-gent Occasions* (1624)," 333–35.

35. See Bald's discussion (Bal. 162n2) and Hester's attribution of this letter (*Let.* xvii). In the same letter, Donne suggests that established theories of physick arose from a desire for "certain Canons and Rules," but the practical consequence of this longing was that competitive, destructive arguments about theoretical models of medical knowledge overshadowed the primary purpose of physic: "plain curing" (*Let.* 13). Theoretical controversy about the right methods "distempered" physick as a system of knowledge. According to Donne's dark view of the profession, people preferred the "lazie wearinesse" of doctrinal opinion to the "painfull inquisition" of knowledge (*Let.* 13). We might read this letter as Donne's indictment of medicine as an epistemological system of competing doctrines. It is also a condemnation of ossified ideas.

36. Paracelsian ideas informed both the medical treatments Donne received from his physicians, who were almost certainly versed in these practices, most likely through the mediating influence of the Danish physician Severinus, and the under-standing of his illness and of the human body that he portrays in *Devotions*. We dis-cuss Donne's physicians in chapter 5. For a superbly detailed account of competing medical knowledge systems in early seventeenth-century Europe and England, see Trevor-Roper, *Europe's Physician*.

Like the many strands of thinking about physics and metaphysics, schools of physick in seventeenth-century Europe overlapped in complex relationships of antagonism and influence. Donne's attraction to Paracelsian teachings was above all a symptom of his fascination with the controversies that accompanied changing regimes of knowledge. Like the speaker of "Satire III," Donne eschews established belief systems in favor of a searching self-exploration that examines and adjusts doctrine, making it plastic, adaptable, capable of fitting his own idiosyncratic circumstances. Donne has a "temperamental unwillingness," as he puts it in *Pseudo-Martyr*, "to betroth or enthral my selfe, to any one science, which should possesse or denominate me."[37]

The question for us is not, then, whether Donne was a Paracelsian. We should instead ask how such bodies of learning furnished Donne with a storehouse of metaphorical opportunity. Donne's references to theories of physick are not fundamentally medical. Although physick provides him with important insight into the workings of the natural world and the human body, more importantly it provided a set of words and concepts (like that of physics and metaphysics) upon which his poetic imagination could work. Donne converts Paracelsus's diction through metaphoric transformation, distilling physick into poetic images. Donne does with Paracelsus what he does with so much of his reading: he absorbs it, digests it (to borrow Ben Jonson's formulation), and makes it his own.[38] In *Devotions*, we can track Paracelsus's influence in words like "*Calcine*" (*Dev.* 235; 2.1), a rare term in the seventeenth century that had an alchemical resonance.[39] The transmutation that incessantly refashions human and cosmic matter does not just burn and melt. Instead, Donne remarks, his disease threatens to calcinate him, to change his body into quicklime (*Dev.* 235; 2.1), a reduction that Paracelsus's *Paragranum* calls an alchemical process.[40] "If a physician is to understand the requisite things," declares Paracelsus, "He needs to know what calcinating and sublimating are." This technical dis-

---

37. John Donne, *Pseudo-Martyr* (London, 1610), B2r. Richard Strier quotes this passage in "Radical Donne: Satire III," *ELH* 60, no. 2 (1993): 284. Strier makes the case for Donne as a truly radical thinker. We have tried to expand on this vision in our book.

38. See, e.g., Ben Jonson, *Discoveries*, in *The Complete Poems*, ed. George Parfitt (New Haven, CT: Yale University Press, 1982), 448: "The third requisite in our poet, or maker, is . . . to be able to convert the substance . . . to his own use . . ." "to concoct, divide, and turn all into nourishment."

39. *OED*, s.v. "calcine," v. 1a; For a fuller account of Paracelsian resonance in Donne's *Anniversaries*, see Harvey and Harrison, "Embodied Resonances."

40. Paracelsus, *The Book Paragranum*, 223.

course shapes *Devotions* through the Paracelsian idea that antidotes and poisons or disease are linked, indeed, versions of one another. As Donne says in Meditation 7, "There is scarce any thing, that hath not killed some body; a *haire*, a *feather* hath done it; Nay, that which is our best *Antidote* against it, hath donn it; the best *Cordiall* hath bene *deadly poyson*" (*Dev.* 256; 7.1).[41] It is this principle of convertibility between the literal and the metaphorical, the somatic and the spiritual, between disease and cure that appealed to Donne. And it is his borrowing of technical words from physics, metaphysics, and physick that powers his thinking.

Technical Diction and Poetic Thinking

In Station 18 of *Devotions*, Donne uses metaphysical words to reflect on how the soul's departure relates to its entrance. Denying the validity of arguments that claim the soul is not a "*seperable substance*, that over-lives the *body*" (*Dev.* 303; 18.1), Donne ponders a question central to *psychologia*, the study of the soul, a topic perched between physics and metaphysics. The language of substance continues. If Donne were to ask "*Philosopicall Divines*" about "*how* the *soule*, being a *separate substance*, enters into *Man*," then:

> I shall finde some that will tell me, that it is by *generation*, and *procreation* from *parents*, because they thinke it hard, to charge the *soule* with the guiltinesse of *Originall* sinne, if the *soule* were infused into a *body*, in which it must necessarily grow *foule*, and contract *originall sinne*, whether it *will* or *no*; and I shall finde some that will tell me, that it is by *immediate infusion from God*, because they think it hard, to maintaine an *immortality* in such a *soule*, as should be begotten, and derived with the *body* from *Mortall parents*. (*Dev.* 303; 18.1)

If one takes the traducian position that the soul comes from natural generation, then one can explain the transmission of original sin but have trouble with the soul's immortality. If one argues, along with the infusionists, that the soul comes from God's immediate action, then one can explain the soul's immortality but struggle with the transmission of original sin. Donne was agnostic about how soul enters body.[42] In Meditation 18, he

41. Paracelsus, *Archidoxies of Theophrastus Paracelsus*, Book II, *The Hermetic and Alchemical Writings of Paracelsus*, ed. Arthur Edward Waite (London: James Elliot, 1894), 2:10n. See also Allen, "John Donne's Knowledge of Renaissance Medicine," 325–26.
42. See, e.g., Targoff, *John Donne*.

quips that "It is the *going out*, more than the *comming in*, that concernes us" (*Dev.* 303; 18.1). Yet despite this agnosticism, Donne cannot help but return to this scene throughout his career. In this section, we compare Donne's handling of the issue in *Devotions* with his inhabitation of the scene of ensoulment in *Metempsychosis*, a scene the basic form of which he derives from Dante's *Commedia*. Donne's repurposing of Dante sheds light on his views about the relationship between poetic making and shifting epistemological systems. The representation of fetal ensoulment in *Metempsychosis* and the meditation on this topic in *Devotions* show us how Donne explores the history of words and stylistic novelty, as well as how his poetic thinking relates to physics, metaphysics, and physick. In approaching the diction of *Devotions* from this unusual angle—through Donne's reworking of Dante in *Metempsychosis*—we aim to show the extent to which the repurposing of technical language, a central feature of Donne's writing practice, was a self-conscious strategy designed to both perform and explicitly reflect upon his place in European literary history.

At the conclusion of *Metempsychosis*, when the Pythagorean soul ends its life as an ape, it enters its next host at the exact moment that "*Adam and Eve* had mingled bloods" (*Sat.* 45; 493). It then animates a developing human embryo in Eve's womb, and the poem follows the embryo until it becomes human.[43] After the growth of heart and liver, the brain begins to develop:

> Another part became the well of sense,
> The tender well-arm'd feeling braine, from whence,
> Those sinowie strings which do our bodies tie,
> Are raveld out; and fast there by one end,
> Did this Soule limbes, these limbes a soul attend;
> And now they joyn'd. (*Sat.* 45–46; 501–6)

43. Donne was fixated on embryological development throughout his career. Recall, for instance, the striking images of fetuses wound in burial shrouds in *Deaths Duell.* In "our first life, our life of *vegetation*," we "are so dead, so, as *Davids Idols* are dead" for "wee have *eyes and see not, eares and heare not*," Donne writes, before hammering home the awful implications of this seeming death in the womb in his description of birth: "this deliverance *from* that *death,* the death of the *wombe,* is an *entrance,* a delivering over to *another death,* the manifold deathes of this *world.* Wee have a winding sheete in our Mothers wombe, which grows with us from our conception, and wee come into the world, wound up in that *winding sheet,* for wee come to *seeke a grave*" (*Ser.* 10:233). Such images pervade *Devotions* as well, a text that is framed in terms of "three births" in Donne's prefatory letter to Prince Charles (*Dev.* 230). Across his career, Donne uses fetal development and birth to capture change.

Once the brain has been strung together with the rest of the body, the fetus acquires a name: "*Themech* she is now" (*Sat.* 46; 509). Donne's account borrows from a lecture delivered by Statius in Dante's *Purgatorio*. Despite the extent of Donne's engagement with Dante—Donne owned a copy of the *Commedia* and was one of the few early modern English writers to have read Dante in Italian—this connection has, so far as we know, gone unnoticed by previous scholars.[44] To see the depth of Donne's borrowing, note how Donne structures the embryo's development through the strategic repetition of *now* (*Sat.* 45–46; 493, 506, 509). Donne borrows this structural principle from Dante's repetition of *si* in *Purgatorio* (558–61; 55, 58, 82). Dante's *si* and Donne's *now* demarcate distinct developmental stages. Donne also reworks Dante's comparison of the embryo's limited powers of movement and feeling to those of a "sea-sponge" (*spungo marino*) (558–59; 25.56): in *Metempsychosis*, Themech's liver is "spungie" (*Sat.* 45; 496). This debt to *Purgatorio* is visible, yet in a letter written in 1600—just before he stopped working on *Metempsychosis*— Donne advances claims about his own novelty by declaring his independence from literary authority. He jokes that he has "flung away Dante the Italian" because of how Pope Celestine V is treated in *Inferno*.[45] Around 1600, then, Donne modeled the final scene of *Metempsychosis* on the *Commedia* while also claiming to have flung the *Commedia* away. This tension can be reconciled insofar as *Metempsychosis* pits Dante against Dante.

Donne fashions Themech as a reflexive image of his own place in literary history—a sign of his novelty and his indebtedness to tradition. In this he borrows a strategy from Dante's *Purgatorio*. Statius's lecture occurs

44. For an earlier account of Donne's borrowings from Dante, see Harrison, *Coming To*, 163–67. Donne's copy of the *Commedia* is currently housed at the Princeton University Library: Dante Alighieri, *Dante con l'espositione di M. Bernardino Daniello da Lvcca, sopra la sua Comedia dell'Inferno, del Purgatorio, & del Paradiso* (Venice: Pietro da Fino, 1568). For the unusualness of Donne's reading Dante in Italian, see, e.g., Carey, *John Donne*, 18. It is worth pointing out that Donne's borrowing from Dante is analogous to his more well-known borrowings from Chaucer—at least insofar as both poets considered the "fathers" of their respective vernacular literary traditions. For Donne and Chaucer, see, e.g. Rebecca M. Rush, *The Fetters of Rhyme: Liberty and Poetic Form in Early Modern England* (Princeton, NJ: Princeton University Press, 2021), 57–83.

45. Donne, *The Complete Poetry and Selected Prose*, ed. Charles M. Coffin (New York: Random House, 2001), 379. Donne is here referencing Dante, *Inferno* 3.59–60: "I saw and knew the shade of him / who, through cowardice, made the great refusal" (translated by Robert Hollander and Jean Hollander [New York: Anchor, 2000], 50–51). These lines were thought by contemporaries to reference Celestine V, who abdicated after four months.

in Canto 25, nested between the two cantos in which Dante meets his immediate literary predecessors: Bonagiunta of Luca in Canto 24, Guido
Guinizelli in Canto 26. Dante situates a novel representation of embryonic development—the perfect image for the emergence of the new—
between Bonagiunta (a poet whose outdatedness Dante criticized) and
Guinizelli (a poet who inspired Dante). In Canto 24, Bonagiunta asks
Dante if he composed such "new rhymes" (*nove rime*) as "Donne ch'evete
intelletto d'amore" (24.50–51). Dante confirms. Bonagiunta responds:

> "O my brother," he said, "now I understand the knot [*nodo*]
> that kept the Notary, Guittone, and me
> on this side of the sweet new style [*dolce stil novo*] I hear.
>
> "I clearly understand that your pens follow
> faithfully whatever Love may dictate,
> which, to be sure, was not the case with ours." (24.55–60)

Bonagiunta concedes that his poetry remained on the far side of a "knot"
separating them from the *dolce stil novo*, a loosely affiliated school of poetry written by Dante's contemporaries and exemplified in *Vita nuova*.
Dante explains this "knot" in *De vulgari eloquentia* (ca. 1302). He focuses
on Bonagiunta's use of "foul jargon," his "mental intoxication" with a language fitted more for "city council" than "court." Bonagiunta failed to "understand the excellence of the vernacular."[46] In Canto 26 of the *Purgatorio*,
Dante implies that the *dolce stil novo* was made possible by Guinizelli, a
poet Bonagiunta condemned for writing about love using philosophical
and theological diction. Bonagiunta claims that Guinizelli "changed the
style [*mutata la mainera*] / Of pleasing love lyrics [*ditti de l'amore*] / From
the essential form they once had." Worse, he has debased love poetry by being "preeminent in subtlety" so that "no man can be found to explain / Your
language, so obscure [*iscura*] is it," muddied with "learning."[47] Whereas
Bonagiunta was dismayed by this incorporation of technical language into
poetry, Dante approved, claiming in *De vulgari* that "the great Guido Guinizelli" had "fully understood the nature of the vernacular."[48] In Canto 26,

46. Dante, *De vulgari eloquentia*, 8; 1.13.

47. Bonagiunta da Lucca, "Voi, Ch'avette mutata la mainera," in *The Poetry of
Guido Guinizelli*, ed. and trans. Robert Edwards (New York: Garland, 1987), 58–59.

48. Dante, *De vulgari eloquentia*, 9; 1.15. This is related to *Convivio* (ca. 1304–7),
in which Dante supports his own views on nobility by citing "Al cor gentil rempaira
sempre amore," a Guinizelli poem that employs words taken from minerology, astrol-

Dante claims that the older poet "had been / father to me and to others, my betters, / who always used love's sweet and graceful rhymes [rime d'amor usar dolci e leggiardre]" (26.97–99). Guinizelli could teach "sweet" rhymes because he wrote what Dante calls "sweet verses" (dolci detti) (26.112).

But while Guinizelli's verse is sweet, it is not novo. The difference between dolci detti and the dolce stil novo can be found in Dante's theologizing of poetry. The sweet novelty that Dante inaugurated in "Donne ch'avete" continues into the Commedia—a work that draws on the innovations of the dolce stil novo but extends them. This is why Bonagiunta claims that "now I understand [issa vegg' io]" what kept "me / on this side of the sweet new style I hear [ch'i' odo]" (24.55–57). Bonagiunta hears the dolce stil novo in the present tense, now. He has been hearing it around town, as it were, in the work of various poets, but this phrasing also suggests that he hears echoes of this style in Dante's speech. Bonagiunta can only use issa—an old-fashioned word—to make this point.[49] By contrast, Dante speaks beyond even the sweet new style, in a language shaped by the innovations of the Commedia, which draws on all kinds of language.

Statius's embryological lecture allows Dante to declare the novelty of his own style by describing two separate entrances into being. First, Statius discusses the moment when "perfect blood" is transformed into seed and then "drops into the natural vessel of another's blood" where it is "mingled with the other, / one fitted to be passive and the other active" (25.37, 45–47). The product of this mingling then "begins to function" (comincia ad operare), coagulating and quickening until this "active force" (virtute attiva) becomes a soul (anima) akin to that of a plant (qual d'una pianta) (25.49–53). But whereas a plant would, by this point, have "come to shore," the embryo continues to acquire functions, "moving now and feeling, / like a sea sponge" (move e sente, / come spungo marino), at which point it becomes an animal soul, actualizing the "force" (virtù) of spirit transmitted through the father's seed (25.54–56). Here the processes of nature cease, for to see "how from animal [the embryo] turns to human" (come d'animal divegna fante) is to see how God is involved in the generation of each new human substance (sustanzia) (25.61, 74). Dante moves from embryology to theology:

> "Open your heart to the truth that follows
> and know that, once the brain's articulation
> in the embryo [al feto] arrives at perfection,

ogy, astronomy, and theology. See Guinizelli, "Al cor gentil rempaira sempre amore," in Poetry of Guido Guinizelli, 20–23.

49. We are indebted to Justin Steinberg for this point.

"the First Mover turns to it, rejoicing
in such handiwork of nature [*arte di natura*], and breathes [*spira*]
into it a new spirit [*spirito novo*], full of power

"which then draws into its substance [*sustanzia*]
all it there finds active and becomes a single soul [*alma sola*]
that lives, and feels, and reflects upon itself [*che vive e sente e sé in
sé rigira*]." (25.67–75)

Creating a *spirito novo*, God breathes (*spira*) into nature's work of art.
The fetus transforms from animal into human, *fante*, a word choice that
suggests the degree to which the capacity for speech is bound up with human existence—even while the embryo remains *infans*, without speech.
Rejecting the traducian view, Dante favors infusionism. When God in-
fuses the rational soul, this *spirito novo* "draws" the already ensouled body
"into its substance," becoming a "single soul" capable of living, feeling,
and reflecting in a unified way. At this point, Statius shifts to a second
substantial change: the generation of a "shade" that follows from the corruption of human substance, a "new form" (*forma novella*) crafted out of
the air such that it is capable of "imitat[ing] the spirit" (*spirito*) in a manner analogous to how the human fetus initially came into being (25.85–
99). Statius uses a familiar, embryological account of how something new
emerges so that he can explain a second form of novelty. His lecture tog-
gles between the *spirito novo* of a fetal human being and the *forma novella*
of an embryonic shade.

What is new about this episode? Most notably, Dante intensifies
the use of technical language that Bonagiunta considered "obscure" in
Guinizelli.[50] After dwelling on Aristotelian embryology and deploying
its technical vocabulary—"formative virtue" (*virtute informativa*), the
opposition between passivity and activity, coagulation, quickening, organs, faculties, the various sorts of souls, and even the example of the
zoophyte (the "sea-sponge")—Statius then prepares for his discussion
of how the "First Mover" breathes the *spirito novo* into the fetus by wad-
ing into one of the thorniest philosophical and theological debates of
the Middle Ages. Dante advances an infusionist over a traducian position, but he also takes the time to reject the understanding of the "possible intellect" articulated by Ibn Rushd (known in the Latin West as
Averroës)—a "wiser man," Statius insists, but one who has neverthe-

---

50. Bonagiunta, "Voi, ch'avete mutata la mainera," in Guinizelli, *Poetry of Guido
Guinizelli*, 58–59 (11).

less "stumbled" by "teaching" that the "possible intellect" is separate from the "soul" (25.63–65). Averroës's view was considered dangerous because it erased the individual immortality of the human soul. Dante rebuts this view, arguing that the "possible intellect" *is* the rational soul, infused by God. Poetry is suited for the highest, most abstract ideas. It can arbitrate among technical discourses like philosophy and theology. It can deliver truth.

Donne reworks Dante's image as a declaration of his own novelty. Donne has "flung away" his Italian predecessor, demonstrating a refusal of poetic influence through an appropriation of Statius's lecture that satirically skewers Dante's style. Although Donne maintains the structure of Statius's lecture, he eliminates the activities performed by the soul. Whereas the soul is Statius's protagonist, in *Metempsychosis* embryonic growth is physical. Adam and Eve "mingled bloods" (*Sat.* 45; 493). Eve's "temperate wombe" then "stew'd and form'd" the tiny new being ("it") through a process like "Chimiques equall fires" (*Sat.* 45; 494–95). This physical stewing leads to the generation of many body "part[s]" (*Sat.* 45; 495, 498, 499, 501), a word the repetition of which maintains focus on the body even as it is transformed into the verb "impart" (*Sat.* 45; 500). First, a "part did become / A spungie liver" able to maintain "Life-keeping moisture" to every other "part" through physical forces like those that enable "a free conduit" on a "high hils brow" to manage the flow of rainwater (*Sat.* 45; 495–98). Second, another "Part hardned it selfe to a thicker heart, / Whose busie furnaces lifes spirits do impart" (*Sat.* 45; 499–500). Hardening and thickening through physical processes, the heart is likened to a furnace whose job it is to "impart" "spirits" throughout the body to maintain its life. Dante uses *spirito* to describe the substantial change of the sensitive soul into the rational soul through a divine infusion of *spirito novo*. Donne physicalizes this term, using "spirits" in the early modern medical sense: they are the subtle physical fluids that race through the body.

This physicalizing process crescendos in Donne's account of how "Another part became the well of sense, / The tender well-arm'd feeling braine, from whence, / Those sinowie strings which do our bodies tie, / Are raveld out" (*Sat.* 45–46; 501–4). For Dante, it is not a body "part" that acts as the "well of sense," but the "soul" (*Anima*) (25.52–55). Donne treats the source of sense as a "part" of the body. The brain is capable of "feeling" because it sprouts "sinowie strings"—channels through which the vital and animal spirits flow. *Metempsychosis* translates a process that Dante understood in terms of metaphysical parts (matter, form, substance) into a process that unfolds only through the arrangement of what Pasnau calls integral parts, parts of a body that are themselves bodies. In *Metempsychosis*, the principle of bodily coherence is not the soul but a body "part" that "ravel[s] out" a physical principle of connection ("strings"), which echo the "strings" at the "ends" of the mandrake root's "arme[s]" earlier in the poem (*Sat.* 32; 141–43).

Donne's appeal to integral parts at the expense of metaphysical parts grounds his depiction of Themech in the physics of "new philosophy." He similarly refuses metaphysics in his description of when and how Themech becomes human. In the premodern "sciences of the soul," drawn from *De anima* and the Aristotelian tradition, the study of the nutritive and sensitive souls belonged to the discourse of physics, the study of nature, while the rational, immortal, properly human soul belonged to metaphysics.[51] Whereas Statius's lecture in *Purgatorio* moves from the physics of embryonic development into the metaphysics and theology of rational ensoulment, Donne's narrative stops at the brink of hominization, just as "it" (the embryo) becomes "she" (the human being that will be named Themech). Dante takes a position on the metaphysics of the rational soul: in *Purgatorio*, it is only when, thanks to the powers of the sensitive soul, "the brain's articulation / in the embryo arrives at its perfection" (25.68–69) that God turns to this tiny, already-ensouled body and "breathes into it a spirit, new and full of power," one capable of transforming animal into human (25.71–72). Whereas Dante provides an infusionist explanation for how the rational soul enters the embryonic body, in *Metempsychosis*, soul seems to emerge from body: once the brain has done its work, and "ravelled" its "strings" throughout the body, then "fast there by one end, / Did this soul limbs, these limbs a soul attend, / And now they joined" (193; 503–6). When a bodily host is ready, the soul "attend[s]" to this body's limbs in the now obsolete causal sense: "attend" means to "conjoin," for one thing to "associate" with another.[52] Donne eliminates the metaphysics from his source, accounting for hominization in physical terms. We have here a declaration of stylistic novelty grounded in a historically informed use of technical language.

Diction and Epistemological Change

This interaction with Dante reveals the extent to which Donne, first, considered the place of technical diction within poetic thinking and, second, reflected on what the history of the discourses from which that diction is borrowed says about what and how words mean. Implicitly critiquing

51. Vidal, *Sciences of the Soul*, 24–25.
52. *OED*, s.v. "attend," v. II 11.

Bonagiunta's dismissal of Guinizelli's poetic use of technical words, in the *Commedia* Dante uses words drawn from every conceivable discourse, no matter how low or how learned. Donne followed Dante in this regard. But Donne puts his technical diction into historical motion. He writes about change using words taken from discourses—metaphysics, physics, physick, and others—that were themselves undergoing revolutions. Many of Donne's contemporaries responded to Donne in precisely the way Bonagiunta responded to Guinizelli, critiquing him for being "obscure" or, in the words of John Dryden, for "affect[ing] the Metaphysicks."[53] From the seventeenth century to the twenty-first, Donne has often been associated with what Dryden calls "Metaphysicks." We have shown how flat-footed the epithet "metaphysical" is when applied to Donne, a writer who took inspiration from and even participated in what Levitin calls the "demetaphysicization" of natural philosophy. We now examine seventeenth-century critics who associated Donne with metaphysics, showing what both their negative and their positive valuations of Donne's work teach us about the diction of *Devotions*.

William Drummond, the author of *Cypress Grove*, offers the most illuminating negative response. In a letter written around 1630 that refers to a wider poetic movement of which Donne was certainly a part, if not the leader, Drummond claims that "some men of late (Transformers of every thing) consulted upon her [poetry's] Reformation, and endeavoured to abstract her to *Metaphysical Ideas*, and *Scolastical Quiddities*, denuding her of her own habits, and those Ornaments with which she hath amused the world some thousand years."[54] Whereas the Protestant Reformation was anti-scholastic, the efforts of Donne and his fellow "Transformers" to reform poetry drag it back into an overly intellectual focus on "*Quiddities*," away from Elizabethan humanism, which had restored to poetry the "Ornaments" of Greco-Roman antiquity.[55] Style was often metaphorized as a garment, and this "Reformation" has stripped poetry "of her

53. For contemporary accounts of Donne's obscurity, see Arnold Stein, "Donne's Obscurity and the Elizabethan Tradition," *ELH* 13, no. 2 (1946): 98–118. For Dryden, see "To the Right Honourable Charles, Earl of Dorset and Middlesex," in *The Satires of Decimus Juvenalis*, trans. John Dryden (London, 1693), iii. The most famous critique of Donne's style appears in Samuel Johnson, "Life of Cowley," in *The Lives of the Most Eminent English Poets*, ed. Roger Lonsdale, 4 vols. (Oxford: Clarendon, 2006), 1:200–201.

54. William Drummond, "To his much honoured friend M. A. J. Physitian to the KING," in *The History of Scotland* (London, 1655), 256.

55. We owe this insight to Richard Strier.

own habits," her garments.[56] In so removing the clothing of poetry's style, Donne has, Drummond claims, "abstracted her to *Metaphysical Ideas*, and *Scolastical Quiddities.*" Drummond's phrasing recalls "Elegy 19," in which Donne asks his mistress to disrobe and finds under her clothing not the expected images of seduction poems, but rather images taken from astronomy, theology, cartography.

Whereas Drummond and others recoiled from Donne's technical diction, others embraced it. In "An Elegie upon the death of the Deane of Pauls, Dr. John Donne" (1633), the poet Thomas Carew differentiates Donne from older poets, who possessed a "Mimique fury" and modeled poems on the work of Pindar and other ancients.[57] "The Muses garden, with Pedantique weedes / O'rspred, was purg'd by thee," Carew writes of Donne, "The lazie seeds / Of servile imitation throwne away, / And fresh invention planted" (72; 25–28). Once dominated by outdated forms of expression—emblematized by the Greco-Roman "traine / Of gods and goddesses" (73; 63–64)—English poetry was transformed by Donne's "fresh invention." According to Thomas Wilson's *Art of Rhetorique, invention* is "the finding out of apt matter," the argument or idea or intellectual substance behind or underneath the language through which it is conveyed.[58] The rhetorical tradition holds that invention, the discovery of an argument or underlying idea for one's writing or speech, is primary in the composition process, and English poets usually agreed.[59] Donne rewrote the rules about what sorts of invention were available.

56. As Desiderius Erasmus, puts it in *De Copia* (1512), in *Collected Works of Erasmus*, 24:306, "style [*elocutio*] is to thought as clothes are to the body." On the connection between style and garment, see Kathy Eden, *Rhetorical Renaissance: The Mistress Art and Her Masterworks* (Chicago: University of Chicago Press, 2022), 125–27; and Rosamund Tuve, *Elizabethan and Metaphysical Imagery: Renaissance Poetic and Twentieth-Century Critics* (Chicago: University of Chicago Press, 1947), 61–78.

57. Thomas Carew, "An Elegie upon the death of the Dean of Pauls, Dr. John Donne," in *The Poems of Thomas Carew*, ed. Rhodes Dunlap (Oxford: Clarendon, 1949), 72; 31. Subsequent quotations are cited parenthetically by page and line numbers. On Carew as critic, see Michael Murrin, "Poetry as Literary Criticism," *Modern Philology* 65, no. 3 (1968), 202–7.

58. Thomas Wilson, *The Art of Rhetorique* (London, 1585), A3v. For *invention*, see Roland Greene, *Five Words: Critical Semantics in the Age of Shakespeare and Cervantes* (Chicago: University of Chicago Press, 2013), 15–40.

59. Following Horace, George Gascoigne, "Certayne Notes of Instruction Concerning the Making of Verse or Ryme in English," in *The Posies of George Gascoigne Esquire* (London, 1575), 291r, recommends that writers "grounde" their work "upon some fine invention." Philip Sidney, *Apologie for Poetrie* (London, 1595), C2r, argues that the "skil of the Artificer standeth in the *Idea* or foreconceite of the work." These passages are also quoted side by side in Arnold Stein, "Donne and the Couplet,"

He did so by altering the first three stages of composition taught in the rhetorical tradition stretching from Aristotle, Cicero, and Quintilian, through to the Italian humanists and the Elizabethan textbooks like those of Wilson and John Hoskyns.[60] Known as the *officia* or canons of rhetoric, these stages include *inventio* or invention, *dispositio* or arrangement, and *elocutio* or style.[61] Donne challenged their governing norms. As we saw in chapter 3, he generated novel forms of *dispositio*, organizing his texts in unexpected ways. And as have seen in this chapter, Donne took diction, the basic building block of style, and used it to scramble the relationship between invention and style. Donne borrows words taken from such technical discourses as metaphysics, physics, and physick, and he then uses them to express his thoughts without those words being themselves thoughts. He does not, as Drummond suggests, remove the style of traditional poetry and replace it with the abstractions of philosophy. Rather, he uses those abstractions as the building blocks for his own distinctive style. Kimberly Johnson argues that Donne refuses to subordinate "manner beneath matter": "Donne does not seek a 'stile conformable to his subject,'" as Puttenham puts it in *The Art of English Poesy*, "but instead makes style a subject in its own right. Rather than imagining language as ever in service to the matter of content, he redirects interpretive attention to the *matter* of language."[62] Whatever the shortcomings of Drummond's critique, then, in isolating an asymmetry between invention and

---

PMLA 57 (1942), 689; and Kimberly Jonson, "Donne's Poetics of Obstruction," in *John Donne in Context*, ed. Michael Schoenfeldt (Cambridge: Cambridge University Press, 2019), 52. Wesley Trimpi, *The Poetry of Ben Jonson: A Study of the Plain Style* (Stanford, CA: Stanford University Press, 1962), 28, argues that although Renaissance writers often associated Cicero's style with those who "seemed more concerned with words than subject matter," in fact "Cicero continually stressed the complete command of the subject matter as the first prerequisite for a writer." As Jeff Dolven, *Senses of Style: Poetry before Interpretation* (Chicago: Chicago University Press, 2017), 44, puts it, style is "after the idea, after the substance and its arrangement; after *inventio* and *dispositio*; something added on to something that existed before it."

60. For the Englishing of the rhetorical tradition, see, e.g., Peter Mack, *Elizabethan Rhetoric: Theory and Practice* (Cambridge: Cambridge University Press, 2002); and Catherine Nicholson, *Uncommon Tongues: Eloquence and Eccentricity in the English Renaissance* (Philadelphia: University of Pennsylvania Press, 2014).

61. The other two *officia* were *memoria* (memory) and *pronunciatio* (delivery). For an overview of the stages of composition, see, e.g., Brian Vickers, *In Defence of Rhetoric* (Oxford: Clarendon, 1998), 62–67.

62. Johnson, "Donne's Poetics of Obstruction," 55–56. Johnson here quotes Put. 35. See also Colleen Ruth Rosenfeld, *Indecorous Thinking: Figures of Speech in Early Modern Poetics* (New York: Fordham University Press, 2018).

style he gets something profoundly right: Donne elevates style so that it subsumes invention.

Donne is not the first writer to trouble the priority of invention over style.[63] As Kathy Eden argues, Renaissance theorists of rhetoric sometimes elevated style so that it included all of composition.[64] Consider Erasmus's preface to his edition of Saint Jerome's works: "the term style [*stilus*] comprehends all at once a multiplicity of things," including "manner in language and diction, . . . thought and judgment, line of argumentation, control of material, emotion, and what the Greeks call *Ethos*," each of these categories existing in a "profusion of shadings, no fewer, to be sure, than the differences in talent, which are as numerous as men themselves."[65] Style includes not only the "manner" of verbal utterance, but also invention and even *Ethos* or character. Style is geared to the individual talent. Donne subscribes to this view. In a passage coated with a patina of the unbelievable, taken from a letter written around 1600, he writes: "I am no great voyager in other men's works, no swallower nor devourer of volumes nor pursuant of authors. Perchance it is because I find born in myself knowledge or apprehension enough."[66] This position echoes Puttenham's definition of style: a way of speaking or writing that extends in a "constant and continual" way across a work and is often "natural to the writer," showing "the matter and disposition of the writer's mind more than one or few words or sentences can show." This is why style is called "the image of man, *mentis character* [the mark of the mind], for man is but his mind, and as his mind is tempered and qualified, so are his speeches and language at large, and his inward conceits be the mettle of his mind, and his manner of utterance the very warp and woof of his conceits" (Put. 233). Style is what makes one's speech one's own.[67] One needs this context to understand the opening claim of the

63. It was never the case that invention could be distinguished, in any absolute way, from style. In *De copia*, Erasmus states the obvious when he claims that the various *officia* "interact so closely that any distinction between them belongs to theory rather than practice" and that separating the *officia* was helpful mainly as "a teaching procedure" (Erasmus, *De copia*, in *Collected Works*, 24:301; quoted in Dolven, *Senses of Style*, 43).

64. See Eden, *Rhetorical Renaissance*, 12–13, 125–72. See also Kathy Eden, *The Renaissance Rediscovery of Intimacy* (Chicago: University of Chicago Press, 2012).

65. Erasmus, *Collected Works*, 61:78; quoted in Eden, *Rhetorical Renaissance*, 12.

66. John Donne, *Selected Prose*, ed. Evelyn Simpson, Helen Gardner, and T. S. Healy (Oxford: Oxford University Press, 1967), 109.

67. Croll, *Style, Rhetoric, Rhythm*, 89, argues that such writers as Muret, Lipsius, Montaigne, and Bacon developed a style "appropriate to the mind of the speaker," one that "portrays the process of acquiring the truth rather than secure possession

"Epistle" to Donne's *Metempsychosis*: "Others at the Porches and entries of their Buildings set their [coats of] Armes; I, my picture; if any colours can deliver a minde so plain, and flat, and through light as mine" (*Sat.* 25). A portrait of Donne's mind adorns his poem's entrance. The work is written in a style that is fully his own, that imitates only himself—he has, he insists in the same epistle, "no purpose to come into any mans debt" (*Sat.* 26). This is as true of Donne's prose as it is of his verse. Donne understands his style in terms of self-expression.[68]

As we have seen throughout this book, Donne thinks of himself as a "peece of the *world*" (*Dev.* 319; 21.1), connected to the larger whole to which he belongs. This means that even if he saw his style as expressing himself, he also understood it as related to the world in and through which he lived. In this respect, he was aligned with theorists of rhetoric, who emphasized not only the relationship between style and person but also the circumstances that condition any individuated style—regional location and historical time foremost among them. From Aristotle's *Rhetoric* onward, style was understood as a principle rendering speech or writing adequate to the circumstances of its utterance or composition.[69] As Cicero argues in *Brutus* and as subsequent Roman writers and Renaissance humanists also claimed, style changes in time; a decorous style responds to its moment. If it is impossible for Cato to write in the Ciceronian style, it is indecorous for Cicero to write in the style of Cato. As Erasmus and others argued, it would be un-Ciceronian for a sixteenth-century humanist to rigorously copy Cicero's way of writing. In Eden's words, "style requires not only a history but a historicizing attitude to be adequately understood."[70] Donne radicalizes this idea. For Donne, it is not just that style is a marker of individual minds and historical circumstances. Since Donne understood his own historical moment as one of epistemological, social, political, and religious flux, a style adequate to this moment must, in his view, fold historical change into itself. Producing work decorous to his historical moment, Donne borrowed technical diction from discourses undergoing profound

---

of it" and that "owes its persuasive power to a vivid and acute portrayal of individual experience rather than to the histrionic and sensuous expression of general ideas."

68. According to Stein, "Donne and the Couplet," 696, Donne, "[l]ike the writers of anti-Ciceronian prose, he is trying to convey the energetic spontaneous flow of ideas in corresponding rhythms and music."

69. This is a throughline in Eden's work. See Eden, *Poetic and Legal Fiction in the Aristotelian Tradition* (Princeton, NJ: Princeton University Press, 1986); Eden, *The Renaissance Rediscovery of Intimacy*; Eden, *Rhetorical Renaissance*.

70. Eden, *Rhetorical Renaissance*, 145.

change. Paradoxically, this attempt to be decorous to the exigencies of the moment produced a writing that struck his contemporaries as profoundly indecorous, either in positive ways (Carew) or in negative ways (Drummond).

In *Devotions*, Donne continues the practice of subsuming invention into style through the privileged and careful use of technical diction, a practice he began perfecting in *Metempsychosis*. He adheres to this practice throughout his career, and it is on full display in *Devotions*. In Meditation 17, Donne reflects on the bells tolling for the death of a neighbor, noting that it is a mistake to ask "for whom the *Bell* tolls" (*Dev.* 298; 17.1), since every Christian is "engraftt into that *body*, whereof I am a *member*" (*Dev.* 299; 17.1). It is at this point that Donne alludes to Dante. He reworks the *Paradiso* in a manner analogous to how *Metempsychosis* reworks the *Purgatorio*:

> *All mankinde* is of one *Author*, and is one *volume*; when one Man dies, one *Chapter* is not *torne* out of the *booke*, but *translated* into a better *language*; and every *Chapter* must be so *translated*; *God* emploies severall *translators*; some peeces are translated by *Age*, some by *sicknesse*, some by *warre*, some by *justice*; but *Gods* hand is in every *translation*; and his hand shall binde up all our scattered leaves againe, for that *Librarie* where every *booke* shall lie open to one another (*Dev.* 299; 17.1).

Donne's use of translation as a metaphor for death figures each human life as a "*Chapter*" of a single "*volume*" written by God. No matter the manner of death (whether it be caused by old age or disease or violence), at death, "*Gods* hand is in" the translation from the mortal, earthly language in which each of these chapters was initially written into a "better" but unspecified "*language*." At some future time, God's "hand shall binde up all our scattered leaves againe," adding them to that "*Librarie* where every *booke* shall lie open to one another." In this future state, at the end of time, the human lives that have been lived, scattered, and dispersed since creation and the advent of temporality will once "againe" be bound together.

This vision is tangled in a complex intertextual web. Perhaps most obviously, Donne here echoes the famous closing canto of Dante's *Commedia*, *Paradiso* 33, which features the pinnacle of Dante's vision, the "limit" of what he is capable of feeling and apprehending, the "Eternal light" itself (33.43–47). What Dante saw "exceeded" the powers of speech and even that of memory (33.55–57), the traces of which are akin to "the Sibyl's oracles, [which] on weightless leaves, / lifted by the wind, were swept away" (33.65–66). Asking for divine assistance, Dante is able at least to metaphorize his vision of the "eternal Light" (33.83):

> In its depth I saw contained,
> by love into a single volume [*un volume*] bound,
> the pages scattered [*squanderna*] through the universe:
>
> substances, accidents [*sustanze e accidenti*], and the interplay
>   between them
> as though they were conflated in such ways
> that what I tell is but a simple light.
>
> I believe I understood the universal form [*forma universal*]
> of this dense knot [*nodo*] because I feel my joy expand,
> rejoicing as I speak of it. (33.85–93)

Dante's vision of the unity that underpins creation is articulated through the metaphor of a book, a single volume that binds together what, in the temporal world, seems distinct, particular, divided.[71] This vision is metaphysical. The image of the volume unites in a *forma universal* the metaphysical categories that apply to every created thing that has ever existed—all substances, all accidents, all dispositions. Dante's book is an attempt to grasp the totality of all things brought together in a single "knot." The eternal "volume" binds the Sibyl's "leaves" blown by the wind: creation is not a multiplicity of diverse and transient things; it is unified.

   Donne's invocation of this image alters Dante's vision. Dante's volume indexes the metaphysical unity of all things, all substances, all metaphysical parts. Although Donne eschews Dante's absolute metaphysical totality, he begins his meditation with a nod to Dante, replacing a totality of all things with a human totality: "*All mankinde* is of one *Author*, and is one *volume*" (*Dev.* 299; 17.1). Each of us is a "*Chapter*" in that great book (*Dev.* 299; 17.1). But as the passage proceeds, the workings of the metaphor change.[72] After each human life has been translated by death, God's

---

71. This is, famously, an image of the *liber naturae*, a long tradition carefully reconstructed in such works of scholarship as Ernst Robert Curtius, *European Literature and the Latin Middle Ages*, trans. Willard D. Trask (Princeton, NJ: Princeton University Press, 1953), 302–47.

72. The following analysis is indebted to the astute and generous observations of Joshua Scodel.

"hand shall," Donne tells us, "binde up all our scattered leaves againe, for that *Librarie* where every *booke* shall lie open to one another" (*Dev.* 299; 17.1). In this new iteration of the metaphor, humankind is no longer one book. Instead, each human being belongs to the same "*Librarie*," each a book of their own, in relation to the others—"every *booke* shall lie open to one another"—but fundamentally distinct, individual. The erasure of boundaries and distinctions for which Dante longs is recast, in Donne's vision, as a preservation of precisely those boundaries and distinctions. Donne reworks Dante so that he can foreground his hope that at the end of time it is the individual who will be preserved, for, as we have seen throughout this book, although Donne was fascinated by death, he was also terrified of losing his own unique, idiosyncratic individuality. This is what the metaphor of the heavenly library enables Donne to privilege. He does so by using an image from Revelation 20:12: "And I saw the dead, small and great, stand before God; and the books were opened; and another book was opened, which is the book of life: and the dead were judged out of those things which were written in books, according to their works." Scripture presents two books: first, the "book of life," which includes all of humanity; and second, the books of each respective human life. In *De civitate Dei*, Augustine puzzles over this passage, eventually arguing that John refers not to many books but to only a single one. In the most straightforward reading of the passage, "there will be not one book containing all lives, but a separate book for every life." But Augustine disagrees: "our passage requires us to think of one only."[73] In *Devotions*, Donne argues against Augustine's reading of this biblical passage. Donne's divine "*Librarie*" is full of many books, as many books as human lives. It is here that "all our scattered leaves" will be bound up once again, into many books not open only to God but open to each other. Donne's library is a scene of utopian sociality.

One might think here of the composition of *Devotions* in ways that tie the "scattered leaves" of Donne's heavenly "*Librarie*" with the longer literary tradition of such leaves, a tradition in which the "pages scattered" of Dante's *Paradiso* plays such a prominent role. In a letter to Sir Robert Ker written shortly after he had finished writing the book but before it was printed and bound, Donne describes it as a series of "meditations" that "arise to so many sheetes (perchance 20.)" (*Let.* 249). Whereas the "leaves" Donne invokes and the "sheetes" on which they are inscribed by his pen are separate, particular, unbound (and described as such), Dante uses the term "leaves" (*foglie*) only in reference to his memories,

73. Augustine, *City of God*, 294; *De civitate Dei*, 20.14.

which scatter like the Sibyl's oracles. He metaphorizes whatever he saw in the "Eternal light" as a "single volume" and does not even mention its separate pages. It is only our world in which everything seems to be "scattered"; Dante's divine vision is one of absolute unity. By contrast, Donne invokes the Sibyl's "scattered leaves" even in his depiction of the multiple books into which God will bind all human lives.

Donne use of "scattered leaves" is calculated. It invokes the long tradition that Dante's "single volume"—with its emphasis on the act of binding, not the disparate pieces being bound—attempts to repair. In *Inferno*, Dante invokes scattered leaves to describe the souls waiting to be ferried across the river Acheron into Hell:

> As, in the autumn, leaves detach themselves,
> first one and then the other, till the bough
> sees all its fallen garments on the ground,
> similarly, the evil seed of Adam
> descended from the shoreline one by one (3.112–16).

Dante stresses particularity. Each human being approaches the river "one by one," like falling leaves "first one and then the other."[74] The particularity of individuated substances is precisely what Dante seeks to undo in the *forma universal* of the single volume. As numerous critics have noted, Dante derives the image—humans descending toward Acheron like autumn leaves—from Virgil's *Aeneid* and its account of souls arriving at the Styx.[75] "And here a multitude was rushing, swarming / shoreward," Virgil writes, "thick as the leaves that with the early frost / of autumn drop and fall within the forest" (6.401–7). Dante's and Virgil's images of souls in the underworld are ultimately derived from Homer's *Iliad*: "As is the generation of leaves, so is that of humanity. / The wind scatters the leaves on the ground, but the live timber / burgeons with leaves again in the season of spring returning. / So one generation of men will grow

74. For a powerful reading of the particularity in Dante's vision, see Robert Pogue Harrison, *The Dominion of the Dead* (Chicago: University of Chicago Press, 2003), 131–33.

75. For scholarship on the simile (human lives like falling leaves) from Homer to Milton and beyond, see, e.g., C. M. Bowra, *From Virgil to Milton* (London: MacMillan, 1963), 240–41; Neil Harris, "The Vallombrosa Simile and the Image of the Poet in *Paradise Lost*," in *Milton and Italy: Contexts, Images, Contradictions* (Binghamton, NY: Medieval & Renaissance Texts & Studies, 1991), 71–94; and Harrison, *Dominion of the Dead*, 124–43.

while another dies" (4.145–49).[76] Although Donne claims that, at some future moment, God will bind each fallen human life into a series of open books, his image of human lives as "scattered leaves" reaches back past Dante's divine volume in *Paradiso*, through the fallen leaflike souls in the *Inferno* and the *Aeneid*, to Homer's vision of humanity, scattered like so many "leaves on the ground." To be sure, the translation Donne invokes is divine, but he emphasizes the leaves themselves, individual-ized through their manner of dying, much like the human "leaves" in the *Aeneid*, which, Virgil writes, lost their lives in many ways and at a variety of life stages: "men and mothers, bodies of / high-hearted heroes stripped of life, and boys / and unwed girls, and young men set upon / the pyre of death before their father's eyes" (6.402–5). Likewise, Donne's focus is on the time-bound process of human translation (through age or sickness or war or the violence perpetrated by the state), the change that accompanies death as opposed to the vague "better language" into which those lives will be translated. This is why even in his account of divine binding, Donne emphasizes the "scattered leaves" of these lost human lives, still resolutely particular, even at the end of time. Donne translates Dante's vision of metaphysical unity into an eschatological scene that remains caught up in the time-bound particularity that phys-ics aims to explore. Put otherwise, Donne's deflationary repurposing of Dante is not confined to *Metempsychosis*; *Devotions* continues what the 1601 satire began.

   Donne's evocation of "scattered leaves" in *Devotions* makes this point with extraordinary brilliance, for it works not only through Dante, Virgil, and Homer but also through Horace's repurposing of this image in his *Ars Poetica*, which describes the historical mutability of poetic diction in terms of so many scattered leaves:

It has ever been, and ever will be, permitted to issue words stamped with the mint-mark of the day. As forests change their leaves [*foliis*] with each year's decline, and the earliest drop off so with words the old race dies, and, like the young of human kind, the new-born bloom and thrive. We are doomed to death—we and all things ours . . . all mortal things shall perish, much less shall the glory and glamour of speech endure and live. Many terms that have fallen out of use shall be born again, and those

---

76. For a meditation on Homer's simile and the "seriality of finite beings," see Guido Mazzoni, *Theory of the Novel* (Cambridge, MA: Harvard University Press, 2017), 20–25.

shall fall that are now in repute, if Usage so will it, in whose hands lies the judgement, the right and the rule of speech.[77]

Like Horace, Donne knows the history of words, those "mortal works" of beings "destined for death," caught in the eddies and winds that batter and shape all human language. The leaves in Station 18 of *Devotions* are thus the bibliographical pages, fleeting human lives, and the historically grounded words that humans write on the surfaces of books, the words the meaning and power of which change with historical time, as concepts and ways of life come into being, fade, and emerge anew. Even when the matter of Donne's invention is the pinnacle of theological speculation—what God will do after the end of time—Donne's diction (and his style as a whole) remain grounded in the earthy, sweaty, messy, decomposing, putrefying embodiment of human life and human death.

We conclude by returning to the flickers of *Metempsychosis* in Station 18 of *Devotions*. Considering how, after death, the "*body* hath lost the *name* of a *dwelling house*, because none dwels in it," Donne suggests that this body "is making hast to lose the name of a *body*, and dissolve to *putrefaction*" (*Dev.* 304; 18.1). Drawing on the technical words of physick, Donne takes a stance on when and where putrefaction takes place. Galen had argued that a fever is the result of the putrefaction of the humors. Such scholars as Jean Fernel and Daniel Sennert argued instead that putrefaction was a process bodies underwent after death.[78] By placing putrefaction after the moment of death, Donne once more draws on technical language undergoing historical change—just as he does earlier in Meditation 18 with his use of "*generation*," "*seperable substance*," "*separate substance*," and so on (*Dev.* 303; 18.1). Such words are not necessary to his lament about the fact of an unknown neighbor's death, announced by a ringing bell: "the *pulse* thereof is changed" (*Dev.* 302; 18.1). The station's topic is the death of this man and its import for Donne's own condition: "*The bell rings out, and tells me in him, that I am dead*" (*Dev.* 302). But most words in the meditation are dedicated to recondite technical issues from "meere *Philosophers*" (is the soul "nothing, but the *temperament* and *harmony*, and *just and equall composition of the Elements in the body*"?)

77. Horace, *Ars Poetica*, lines 58–72 (trans. H. Rushton Fairclough, Loeb Classical Library [Cambridge, MA: Harvard University Press, 1929], 455–57).

78. For arguments about putrefaction and its relation to fevers, see Iain M. Lonie, "Fever Pathology in the Sixteenth Century: Tradition and Innovation," *Medical History*, Supplement 1 (1981): 19–44.

or "*Philosophicall Divines*" (how is it that the "*soule*, being a *separate substance*, enters into *Man*"?) (*Dev.* 303; 18.1).

In meditating on death, putrefaction, and the body's "hast to lose the name of a *body*" (*Dev.* 304; 18.1), Donne recalls the language of integral parts he used in his account of Themech's generation in *Metempsychosis*: "*Now* all the parts built up, and knit by a lovely *soule*, *now* but a *statue* of *clay*, and *now*, these limbs melted off, as if that *clay* were but *snow*; and now, the whole *house* is but a *handfull of sand*, so much *dust*, and but a *pecke of Rubbidge*, so much *bone*" (*Dev.* 304; 18.1). Donne's thought about the connection between *generatio* and *corruptio* ties this meditation back to Statius's lecture in *Purgatorio* 25, with its insistence that the only way to understand the existence of the soul after death is to grasp how the soul knits the embryonic body in the womb. "Man before hee hath his *immortall soule*, hath a *soule of sense*, and a *soule of vegetation* before that," Donne writes, recalling Status's account of how the soul develops with the body *in utero*, before continuing: "when this *soule* departs, it carries all with it; no more *vegetation*, no more *sense*" (*Dev.* 304; 18.1). But if Dante's embryology haunts this passage, Donne has again reduced it to bodily terms. Just as in *Metempsychosis*, where his play with "part" and "impart" helped to ground his new style firmly in the terrain of physics, so in the *Devotions* it is the soul that has "built up" "all the parts" of the body only to destroy all when it "departs," taking all sensitive and vegetative life with it. Reduced from "a *statue* of *clay*" to "so much *dust*," the living body disappears as it undergoes "*putrefaction*" and decomposition, until "our *dust* [is] blowne away with *prophane dust*, with every wind" (*Dev.* 304; 18.1).

This thinking with bodies is not confined to the meditation. In Prayer 18, Donne praises God for providing "a new occasion of *prayer to thee*, from the *ringing* of this *bell*" (*Dev.* 306; 18.3). In speaking to Donne through the ringing of the bells, God is in fact serving as a "*Physitian*, that presents health":

Thou presentest me *death* as the *cure* of my *disease*, not as the *exaltation* of it; if I mistake thy voice herein, if I over-runne thy pace, and prevent thy hand, and imagine *death* more instant upon mee than thou has bid him bee, yet the voice belongs to me; *I am dead*, I was *born dead*, and from the first laying of these *mud-walls* in my *conception*, they have *moldered* away, and the whole course of *life* is but an *active death*. Whether this *voice instruct* mee, that I am a *dead man now*, or *remember* me, that I have been a *dead man* all this while, I humbly thanke thee for speaking in this *voice* [the bell] to my *soule*. (*Dev.* 307; 18.3)

Whatever the "I" is, it is dead and has always been dead, even while the parts of its body were knit together "in my *conception.*" Life is but the moldering away of the body, nothing but an "*active death.*" The "health" presented by God the physician is the truth of the speaking "I": the activity of living through is isomorphic with the activity of dying. If the comfort of this passage derives from the voice of God, working through the bells, to "my *soule,*" the message carried by that voice remains the great lesson that must apply to all time-bound bodies: they change, and that change leads ineluctably to death. Donne translates the hard truths of mortality into hard-won consolation.

* 5 *

The Physician Calls

In a sermon delivered at Saint Paul's Cross in 1616, Donne divides medical treatment for the sick into two branches: "bodily, and Ghostly Physick" (*Ser.* 1:197). He defines "ghostly" physick as care that concerns itself with the soul. It depends on the familiar Christian, often fervently Calvinist, interpretation of illness as sin: bodily afflictions are God's corrective rod, and expiating sin is an essential counterpart to effecting a cure in the physical body.[1] Donne warns his congregation against taking both bodily and ghostly physick on one's deathbed—the "Apothecary and the Physician do well together; the Apothecary and the Priest not so well"— for the simple reason that cultivating spiritual health before bodily health must become a habit long before death approaches (*Ser.* 1:197).[2] He amplifies these ideas in another undated sermon delivered on Candlemas Day. His text for that sermon is Matthew 9:2, which describes Christ's forgiveness and cure of a paralyzed man. The "first cause of death, and sicknesse, and all infirmities upon mankinde in generall, was sin," Donne proclaims, but if "wee begin with the Physitian, Physick is a curse." If we do not attend first to "the supernaturall Physick," we are lost. This was the case for Asa, the biblical King of Judah, who in his old age suffered from a foot disease. Because he refused to seek help from God, prefer-

---

1. The strength of Donne's Calvinism in the sermons is a matter of debate. See Carey, *John Donne*, 240–42; and Debora Shuger, *Habits of Thought in the English Renaissance: Religion, Politics, and the Dominant Culture* (Berkeley: University of California Press, 1990), 176–80, who argues both for the strength of, and Donne's nuanced resistance to, Calvinist ideas. See also Kuchar, "Ecstatic Donne." For a consideration of illness as curative of the soul, see Targoff, *John Donne*, 133–37, who discusses Thomas Becon's *Sick Man's Salve*, Lancelot Andrewes' *Manual of Direction for the Sick*, and Jeremy Taylor's *Rule and Exercise of Holy Dying*.

2. The colloquialism "to give up the ghost" registers the long currency of this belief: *OED*, P1.a.

ring to consult earthly physicians instead, he perished (*Ser.* 10:79–81).[3] This account of illness and healing rests on a stark dichotomy between body and soul, a dualism that, we argue in this chapter, is first undercut by Donne's philosophical speculations about the soul's nature and then expanded through the fiercely observed inhabitation of the illness that he chronicles in *Devotions*.

Identifying sin as the root of bodily disease relies on a specific definition of the soul: only the intellective soul, the immortal principle that survives the physical body, is capable of being healed or condemned to everlasting punishment (*Ser.* 10:79).[4] Yet both Donne's philosophical and lived understanding of the soul includes its organic parts, the vegetative and sensible. He refers to the organic soul frequently, remarking in an Easter sermon of 1628 on Augustine's praise of the sense of sight, which allows for the assimilation of vegetative and sensible souls into the reasonable soul (*Ser.* 8:221).[5] In his meditation on the soul in *Devotions*, he watches with melancholy regret as the souls of vegetation and sense are shuffled off when the intellective soul leaves the body (*Dev.* 304; 18.1). Aristotelian faculty psychology recognized that the soul itself could be known only through its operations, its movement through bodily faculties. Donne registers this idea in *Devotions* when he says that God shows his soul to him through his more "*discernible*" body (*Dev.* 326; 22.2). Bodily disease implicates the vegetative soul because illness inevitably affects the nutritive and generative faculties of the body: the ability to eat, to excrete, to regulate temperature, to copulate, to rest. Sickness likewise alters and compromises the sensible soul's capability for movement, sensation, and the passions: the ability to stand or walk, the unfolding variety of painful sensations sickness inflicts, the affective destabilizations of fear and hope. Donne anatomizes the indignities and suffering that illness visits on his body as a way of coming to know "*originall sinne*" (*Dev.* 325; 2.2), which is lodged within and expressed in physically specific, often painful ways through the organic soul.

Material illness reveals bodily faculties most clearly through their

---

3. See 2 Chronicles 16:4.

4. Even though his focus is on spiritual healing, his catalog of physical afflictions is striking in its vividness and variety: "palsie," "slack and dissolv'd sinews," "Cramps, and Coliques, and Convulsions in my joynts and sinewes," "putrefaction of a wound," thorne in the foot, arrow in the flesh, fever, pestilence, gout (*Ser.* 10:79–80).

5. See also his 1621 sermon preached at Whitehall: "bodies inanimated with one soule: one vegetative soule, head and members must grow together, one sensitive soule, all must be sensible and compassionate of one anothers others miserie; and especially one Immortall soule, one supreame soule" (*Ser.* 4:47).

deficits, as Donne discovers in *Devotions* when he can no longer stand or sleep. In his Candlemas sermon on the paralyzed man, he graphically exposes the organic soul in negatively etched outlines: "First, this para- lytique man in our Text, who is *Sarcina sibi*, overloaded with himself, he cannot stand under his own burden, he is *cadaver animatum*; It is true, he hath a soule, but a soule in a sack, it hath no Lims, no Organs to move, this Paralytique, this living dead man, this dead and buryed man, buryed in himselfe, is instantly cured, and recovered" (*Ser.* 10:69). It is a disturb- ingly vivid portrayal of "palsie," of a man burdened by his own body, im- prisoned in his own "sack" of skin because his "*soule of sense*," with its various motive and perceptive powers, is damaged or dysfunctional (*Dev.* 304; 18.1). Although alive, the paralyzed man is "buryed in himselfe," a phrase that echoes the mandrake root in *Metempsychosis*, that "living bur- ied man" who "A mouth, but dumbe, he hath; blinde eyes, deafe ears," a vegetative figure of complete sensory incapacity and deprivation (*Sat.* 32; 151–60). Donne seizes Matthew's laconically abbreviated account of the paralyzed man ("the sick of the palsie") and imaginatively enters it in an act of sympathetic medical *copia*. Donne's elaborated account of palsy reveals its kinship with his extensive poetic exploration of the organic soul in *Metempsychosis*, where diverse plants, animal, and human bodies are the materially specific instruments for expressing the soul's psychic nature. In *Devotions*, his own sick body is the subject for that investiga- tion. When his illness causes him to feel pain, to fear, and to imagine, he explores these faculties of his organic soul in conversation with his intellective soul's reflexive capacity to anatomize these bodily alterations.

In this chapter, we explore Donne's historical physicians and the mate- rial physic they administer in *Devotions* through the refracted lenses of these ghostly and bodily categories. Even if illness is a spiritual conse- quence of sin, surviving a critical sickness implicates the felt body and engages the province of physick. We argue that Donne never subsumes the material, bodily nature of his crisis into a theologically predictable register of Christian understanding. Rather, he sets the spiritual and physiological in fractious dialogue with one another, continually insist- ing on the enabling capacities—now often compromised by illness—of the body he inhabits. He watches the weakening powers of his organic soul even as they remain the instruments of his observing, sensing self. As we argue in this chapter, Donne makes material physick—the remedies and treatments his physicians provide—into a part of his imaginative and philosophical speculation. The physick they prescribe is drawn primarily from a Paracelsian and iatrochemical pharmacopeia that includes miner- als, plants, and animal parts. Ingesting those remedies literalizes and incorporates a philosophy of soul in the moment when Donne anticipates shedding his own soul's vegetative and animal powers.

Donne's physicians themselves occupy a puzzling, nebulous presence in *Devotions*. Although Donne never names or describes them, we can identify them as specific seventeenth-century practitioners who carried the ferment of debate about natural philosophy and medicine into Donne's sick chamber. Throughout *Devotions*, Donne converts these historical figures into instantiations of the *Deus medicus* (God the physician), and his continual conversations with God as divine physician shape the book. But Donne nevertheless subverts the straightforward division between ghostly and bodily physicians in two ways: first, through his overt reference to the material interventions of his earthly physicians; and second, through his internalization of their diagnosing and prescribing functions into his own deliberations about his ailing body. *Devotions* is shaped by the amphibiously diverse nature both of physick and the physician. While Donne continually transmutes the material nature of physick and its purveyors into their spiritual counterparts, they remain resolutely anchored in the sensible world revealed by his organic soul.

Ghostly Physicians

"Ghostly physick" is Donne's term for the spiritual medicine best administered by God and his ministers. "Ghostly" is also an apt term for the obscure presence of Donne's three physicians in *Devotions*; they are present, but unnamed and usually unseen.[6] They remain spectral presences, most visible in the station headings, where they punctuate the course of Donne's illness:

The Phisician is sent for (Dev. 242; 4); *The Phisician comes* (Dev. 247; 5); *The Phisician is afraid* (Dev. 250; 6); *The Phisician desires to have others joyned with him* (Dev. 255; 7); *The King sends his owne Phisician* (Dev. 260; 8); *Upon their Consultation, they prescribe* (Dev. 264; 9); *They find the Disease to steale on insensibly ...* (Dev. 269; 10); *They use Cordials, to keep the venim and Malignitie of the disease from the Heart* (Dev. 273; 11); *They apply Pidgeons, to draw the vapors from the Head* (Dev. 278; 12); *The Phisicians observe these accidents to have fallen upon the criticall days* (Dev. 286; 14); *At last, the Physitians, after*

6. *OED*, s.v. "Ghost," n. I.1. and III.8a. Donne often uses "ghost" in the senses of nebulous presence senses, as, for instance, in *The First Anniversarie* to describe the vestigial presence of Elizabeth Drury (*Ann.* A1:24; 70) and to portray an empty world that is haunted by her absence.

*a long and stormie voyage, see land . . . (Dev. 308; 19); Upon these Indications of
digested matter, they proceed to purge (Dev. 314; 20); God prospers their practise, and he by them calls Lazarus out his tombe, mee out of my bed (Dev. 318;
21); The Phisitians consider the root and occasion . . . (Dev. 323; 22); They warne
mee of the feareful danger of relapsing (Dev. 328; 23).*

It is an extraordinary list. *Devotions* is architected by the summoning, arrival, and interventions of Donne's worldly physician and his colleagues:
nineteen of the twenty-three stations allude to these attending physicians, the only other human beings present in *Devotions*. The physician
who is called in Station 4 and whose silent entrance we witness in Station
5 brings healing and companionship, initiating an implicit conversation
that shapes the physical, emotional, and spiritual dimensions of Donne's treatment.[7] *Devotions* is scaffolded by the patient-physician bond,
which facilitates a complex dialogic dimension to Donne's representation
of his sickness that gestures simultaneously to the human medical figures treating him and to their symbolic filiation with his divine physicians, the *Deus medicus* and *Christus medicus*.[8] He establishes a circuit
of reciprocal influence in which the physick he receives from his earthly
consultants is converted from affective and visceral detail into its spiritual
counterpart in a continual process of mutual transubstantiation. Donne's symptoms—pain, vertigo, fear, maculation, insomnia, weakness—
furnish the material for transmission between bodily and spiritual registers, but the physicality of his metaphors continually resists assimilation
into a realm devoid of bodily sensation.

In a 1627 sermon, Donne alludes to the complexities of this relationship
in his use of two rhetorical terms, "ingemination" and "conduplication":

As God expresses the bitterness of death, in an ingemination, *morte mori-
etur*, in a conduplication of deaths, he shall die, and die, die twice over;

7. Most scholars assume that Donne's primary physician was Simeon Fox, who,
as Izaak Walton details, also cared for Donne in his final illness. In Station 8, alarm
over Donne's condition prompts the king to send his own physician, who was almost
certainly the polymath Sir Théodore de Mayerne to attend Donne. A third physician
arrives in Station 7, probably William Clement, to make up the "trinitie" that consults
about Donne's case.

8. See Rudolph Arbesmann, "The Concept of 'Christus Medicus' in St. Augustine," *Traditio* 10 (1954): 1–28, for a study of this concept in Saint Augustine that
illuminates Donne's evocation of the tradition. Although he does not cite him explicitly, Donne's figuration of his own relationship with the divine physician echoes the
Augustinian model.

So *ægrotando ægrotabit*, in sicknesse he shall be sick, twice sick, body-sick and soul-sick too, sense-sick and conscience-sick together; when, as the sinnes of his body have cast sicknesses and death upon his Soule, so the inordinate sadnesse of his Soule, shall aggravate and actuate the sicknesse of his body. His Physitian ministers, and wonders it works not; He im- putes that to flegme, and ministers against that, and wonders again that it works not: He goes over all the humors, and all his Medicines, and noth- ing works, for there lies at his Patients heart a dampe that hinders the concurrence of all his faculties, to the intention of the Physitian, or the virtue of the Physick. (*Ser.* 8:188)

Donne's language—"he shall die, and die, die twice over"—enacts the rhetorical sense of his terms, the close repetition of adjacent words. George Puttenham notes that the Greeks called this lexical doubling *epizeuxis*, the Latins *subjunction*. Puttenham calls it "the Underlay" for the fastening or "yoking under" that those terms imply (Put. 285). Donne uses "ingemination" in its root sense of twinning (from the Latin *geminus*) to describe the doubling of body and soul in sickness. To be sick is to be "twice sick, body-sick and soul-sick." The sins of the body cast sickness onto the soul, which creates "sadness" in the soul that in turn aggravates the bodily illness. The circuit is not a simple re- flection of body and soul, but a mutual implicatedness. The complex- ity of symptoms engendered by this yoking augments diagnostic dif- ficulty and challenges the physician's medical knowledge. Lodged in the patient's heart is a "dampe" that hinders his faculties and precludes healing.[9]

Donne lived in a transitional historical moment for physick, a moment in which the relative stability of the Hippocratic and Galenic corpus was continually challenged by novel theories and practices, most obviously by Paracelsian medicine and Vesalian anatomy. Donne's stepfather was John Syminges, a prominent physician and several time president of the College of Physicians, which suggests that Donne would have been liber- ally exposed to the profession of physick from an early age.[10] Izaak Wal- ton says in his "*Elegie upon Dr. Donne*" that Donne knew the "grounds and

9. Consider Donne's poem "The Dampe," in which the speaker imagines his own death from causes his doctors cannot discover. When his friends' curiosity demands an autopsy, he fantasizes that they will find a picture of his lover in his heart and that the "sudden damp of love" will be as fatal to them as it was to him.

10. Baird W. Whitlock, "The Heredity and Childhood of John Donne," *Notes and Queries* 6, no. 9 (1959): 348–53.

use of *Physicke*; but because / T'was mercenary wav'd it."[11] Presumably he meant that Donne was intellectually drawn to theories of physick and healing, but found distasteful the financial pressures and potential ethical compromises inherent in the rapidly changing professional practice of physick. While Donne subordinates medical knowledge to poetic purpose, D. C. Allen notes, "[m]edical data, anatomical terminology, physiological theory, apothecary's 'drug tongue,' and physician's jargon elbow from the pages of his poetry and sermons the classical allusions so popular with his contemporaries."[12] As we began to see in chapter 4, Donne actively internalizes the epistemological innovations that were reshaping physick, and his implicated knowledge of these changes permeates *Devotions*. In other words, Donne employs emergent vocabularies and concepts to interpret and, with his physicians, to chart the progress of his condition. His writing showcases how remarkably conversant with and precociously learned about medical controversies he was. Donne's texts consistently internalize his knowledge of physick to track the inscrutable workings of his own physiology.

Donne's eclectic depiction of medicine encompasses Asclepiadic, Galenic, and Hippocratic theories. It also draws on the discoveries of Vesalian anatomical dissection, Paracelsian innovation, and William Harvey's experimentation on the heart.[13] Paracelsian ideas informed both the medical treatments Donne received from his physicians (who were versed in these practices, most likely through the mediating influence of the Danish physician Severinus) and the understanding of his illness and of the human body that he portrays in *Devotions*.[14] This suggests that his conception of physick was intrinsically expansive in its capacity to integrate tradition and new discoveries. Here, in the register of physick, we see a version of the general point we made in chapter 4: he is doctrinally promiscuous and medically heterodox; he refuses to adhere to the truth of one system over another. The question, then, is not whether Donne was a Paracelsian, whether he was a Galenic, whether he adhered to Vesalian principles, or whether he assimilated the significance of Harvey's experiments. Discovering Donne's hidden allegiances in religion, medi-

11. *Donne: Poetical Works*, ed. Herbert J. C. Grierson (Oxford: Oxford University Press, 1971), 345; 46–47.

12. D. C. Allen, "Donne's Knowledge of Medicine," 322.

13. For an instructive account of the affinities between their innovative ideas and far-reaching influence, see Walter Pagel and Pyarali Rattansi, "Vesalius and Paracelsus," *Medical History* 8, no. 4 (1964), 309–28.

14. For a superbly detailed account of competing medical knowledge systems in early seventeenth-century Europe and England, see Trevor-Roper *Europe's Physician*.

cine, or philosophy does not illuminate how he thought—a task that is at the heart of this book. We ask instead how these bodies of learning equipped Donne with a storehouse of metaphorical opportunity and how they allowed him to *imagine* his body and its relationship to the ambient cosmos.[15] In his satirical portrayal of Paracelsus in *Ignatius His Conclave*, for example, Donne mentions homeopathic remedies—the hallmark of the iatrochemical treatments that defined Paracelsian innovations—as removing the "trecherous" qualities of medicines and enabling them to "performe their office as strongly" (*Con.* 21, 20–25). Donne alludes to these homeopathic principles in *Devotions*, where he marvels at God's ability to imprint "medicinall vertues" in all creatures, even the flesh of vipers, which provides the matter for his heart cordial (*Dev.* 277; 11.3). But he is equally struck by the reversibility of innate qualities: "There is scarce any thing, that hath not killed some body; a *haire*, a *feather* hath done it; Nay, that which is our best *Antidote* against it, hath donn it; the best *Cordiall* hath bene *deadly poyson*" (*Dev.* 256; 7.1). For Donne, nothing is intrinsically medicinal or poisonous. The skill of the physician, and the art of the poet, is to perceive the hidden virtue or danger and use it to achieve a particular end.

In *The Advancement of Learning* (1605), Francis Bacon laments the state into which medicine as a science has fallen. He suggests that rather than moving forward in its consideration of the causes for disease and their cures, medicine's progression has been circular, consisting of "much iteration, but small addition." More "professed than laboured, and yet more laboured than advanced," he pronounces medical practices and theories deficient.[16] The first serious fault, according to Bacon, was the discontinuation of a central practice of Hippocratic medicine: the habit physicians had of creating a "narrative of the special cases of his patients." Bacon advocates reviving the case history as a way to understand the unique aspects of patients and diseases: "many things are new in the manner, which are not new in the kind; and if men will intend to observe, they shall

15. The intersection between physics, especially Lucretian physics, and innovation in Vesalian anatomy in evident in Donne's puns on "atomies," a word that gestures both to atomism and anatomy in *The First Anniversarie* (*Ann.* A1; 213). See David A. Hedrick Hirsch, "Donne's Atomies and Anatomies: Deconstructed Bodies and the Resurrection of Atomic Theory," *Studies in English Literature, 1500–1900* 31, no. 1 (1991), 69–94.

16. Francis Bacon, *The Proficience and Advancement of Learning, Human and Divine*, Book 2, ed. James Spedding, in *The Philosophical Works of Francis Bacon*, ed. John M. Robertson (London: Routledge, 2011), 105.

find much worthy to observe."[17] In fact, starting in the fifteenth century, European physicians began to incorporate narrative and examples, particularly in vernacular treatises. Renaissance Hippocratism, nourished by the enlarged body of translations and editions of Hippocratic works that became available through the sixteenth century, accentuated the interest in narrative and medical histories.[18] Of particular significance to the trend was the discovery of *Epidemics* and *Of Air, Water, and Places*, two Hippocratic texts with plentiful cases about the progress of disease in individuals.[19] The medical case history as a genre was supported by the humanist explosion in autobiographical and biographical writing in many areas. Donne had multiple generic influences for the *Devotions*, many of which we explored in previous chapters. We suggest here that the medical case history furnished yet another generic model. One of Donne's attending physicians during his 1623 illness was King James I's personal physician, the Belgian polymath and Paracelsian Sir Théodore de Mayerne, who wrote copious case histories of his patients.[20] His case records provide new insight into how Donne wrote about the progress of his own illness.[21]

In *Devotions*, Donne provides an observational counterpart to the accounts that his attending physicians were concurrently writing. Donne registers this mirroring with exquisite attention in Station 6, "*The Phisician is afraid*," where he observes the physician "with the same diligence,

---

17. Bacon, *Advancement of Learning*, 105. Shakespeare's son-in-law, John Hall, kept detailed case notes of his patients, which were translated from Latin by James Cooke and published as *Select observations on English Bodies: or, cures both empericall and historicall performed upon very eminent persons in desperate diseases*, London, 1657. See Greg Wells, *John Hall, Master of Physicke: A Casebook from Shakespeare's Stratford* (Manchester: Manchester University Press, 2020). William Harvey's treatise on parturition moves back and forth between considering the knowledge he acquired from his teacher in Padua, Fabricius, and his observations of the patients he attended: "On Parturition," in *The Works of William Harvey*, intro. by Arthur C. Guyton (Philadelphia: University of Pennsylvania Press, 1989).

18. For a fuller contextualization of Renaissance Hippocratism and medical narrative, see Nancy Siraisi, *History, Medicine, and the Traditions of Medical Learning* (Ann Arbor: University of Michigan Press, 2007), 63–105.

19. Siraisi, 73.

20. For Mayerne as Donne's physician, see Bal. 452. Brian K. Nance provides a detailed account of Mayerne's casebooks, "Determining the Patient's Temperament: An Excursion into Seventeenth-Century Medical Semeiology," *Bulletin of the History of Medicine* 67 no. 3 (1993): 417–38.

21. For an example of Mayerne's voluminous casebooks, see *Medicinal Councels or Advices, Written Originally in French by Dr. Theodor Turquet De Mayerne, Kt., Englished by Tho. Sherley* (London, 1677).

as *hee* the *disease*" (*Dev.* 250; 6.1). In a complex circle of monitoring, Donne occupies the position of suffering patient, the object of scrutiny, at the same time as he mimics the role of physician, diagnosing his fear as a new pathology: "As the ill affections of the *spleene*, complicate, and mingle themselvs with every infirmitie of the body, so doth *feare* insinuat it self in every *action*, or *passion* of the *mind*: and as *wind* in the body will counterfet any disease, and seem the *Stone*, and seem the *Gout*, so *feare* will counterfet any disease of the *Mind*" (*Dev.* 251; 6.1). Borrowing the language of physiology as analogy for his passional state, he diagnoses his own condition. His fluency with medical terms demonstrates his conversancy with diagnosis and treatment, even as he defers to his physicians and transposes his symptoms into speculation about his emotional state.

The ninth station provides a revealing portrait of Donne's medical observations. Whereas his physicians have seen and heard him and "receiv'd the *evidence*," Donne has "cut up mine own *Anatomy*, dissected my selfe," and his physicians are "gon to *read* upon me" (*Dev.* 264–65; 9.1). He records his physicians' evaluation of his state of health, their diagnosis, and the prescription for physick that they will offer at the end of their consultation. He inserts himself into their role, as if he were imitating their deliberations, envisioning numbers of sicknesses so vast that they can scarcely be counted, let alone named (*Dev.* 265; 9.1). He then categorizes some of these illnesses, starting with those that designate the areas of the body they affect ("*Plurisie*"), moving to the effects they produce ("*falling sicknes*"), what the sickness resembles (the wolf, the canker), and eventually concluding that the limitless number of sicknesses far exceeds the labels that could classify them. He then narrows his scope, concentrating instead on fevers as a smaller category of disease, but even as he does so, he implicitly commiserates with the difficulty his physicians face in deciding which fever afflicts him, what its course will be, and how to "countermind" it (*Dev.* 265; 9.1).

As he watches his physicians conferring, however, he derives great comfort from the fact that they are consulting at all: "where there is room for *consultation*, things are not desperate. They *consult*; so there is nothing *rashly, inconsideratly* done; and then they *prescribe*, they *write*, so there is nothing *covertly, disguisedly, unavowedly* done" (*Dev.* 265; 9.1). Donne reminds himself that with some physical illnesses, "as soon as the *Phisicians* foote is in the chamber, his *knife* is in the patients arme" (*Dev.* 266; 9.1). Donne's use of synecdoche, which Puttenham calls the "quick conceit" (Put. 270), registers his alarm at this ill-considered medical haste: the speed of the physician's arrival is contracted to his foot, and invasive, precipitous treatment—barely slowed by the insertion of the comma—is condensed to the knife in the arm. Donne is acutely aware that the dangers of his illness can be exacerbated by an injudicious diagnosis or a risky course of treatment. His relief at his physicians' conversation registers his own participation in their diagnostic deliberations and the judiciousness of their procedures, which involves writing both on his part and theirs: he writes, "I am glad they know (I have hid nothing from them) glad they consult (they hide nothing from one another) glad they write (they hide nothing from the world) glad that they write and prescribe *Physick*, that there are remedies for the present case" (*Dev.* 266; 9.1). Donne enacts in parenthetical asides his own contributions to the physicians' knowledge, their conversations with each other, and their dilated decision-making process. He slows down and interrupts time through his parenthetical inclusions, demonstrating by way of temporal deceleration the uneasy suspension of awaiting an impending diagnosis.

In Station 8, we learn that the *"King sends his owne Phisician"* (*Dev.* 260), who many scholars, beginning with Bald, identify as Théodore de Mayerne. A learned and well-known physician, Mayerne was closely involved with the court and had treated James since 1611. James called him to attend his son on the fifteenth day of Henry's fatal illness because the prince's high fever was escalating, he was tormented by thirst, and his lips were black.[22] Mayerne was one of the physicians most closely involved during Prince Henry's final days, and two accounts of his consultation (one in Latin, one in French) survive. In those case records, Mayerne provides a day-to-day description of the course of the illness, which would have been an unusual and innovative medical record in 1611. His detailed account of Prince Henry's symptoms, the conversations and disagreements among the other attending physicians, and the prescribed treatments provide an extraordinarily intimate, detailed portrait of Henry's illness and his physicians' care. Even Sir Walter Raleigh, who was then imprisoned in the Tower, sent a medicinal cordial, "his panacea for all diseases," which did not produce the hoped-for result. Mayerne's scrupulous notes allow us to recognize that Prince Henry died of what was almost certainly the first recorded case of typhoid fever in England.[23] Prince Henry's death unleashed a series of accusations against Mayerne, most of which were likely prompted by professional jealousies, rivalries among physicians, prejudice against him for his foreignness, and

22. Thomas Gibson, "Doctor Theodore Turquet de Mayerne's Account of the Illness, Death and Post-Mortem Examination of the Body of His Royal Highness, Prince Henry of Wales," *Annals of Medical History* 10, no. 6 (1938): 552.

23. See Gibson, 551; and Trevor-Roper, *Europe's Physician*, 171–77.

intense controversy about appropriate treatment. A physician's arsenal of medical therapies, some of which used innovative chemical, mineral, and herbal experimental remedies, included the timing of bleeding or other surgical interventions, and relied on diagnostic judgments—all of which made Mayerne intensely vulnerable to the charges against him. Mayerne's response was to produce reports that documented his treatment at every stage. The king was persuaded by Mayerne's elaborate defense of his procedures, and his royal rebuttal of the accusations was to appoint Mayerne as his first physician.[24] The episode provides rich insight into the social pressures physicians faced and the convergences of political intrigue and medical controversy that accentuated their professional precarity.

In a 1621 sermon, Donne offers an analogy for the wish he shares with his physicians, namely, to understand the hidden operations of illness: "For in experience, when some men curious of naturall knowledge, have made their Hives of glasse, that by that transparency, they might see the Bees manner of working, the Bees have made it their first work to line that Glasse-hive, with a crust of Wax, that they might work and not be discerned" (Ser. 3:232). Like the wax-lined hive, the flesh is a barrier to glimpsing the interior of the human body. To counter that inscrutability, Donne dissects his own body through his observations so that his physicians will be able to see the disease within him. The activity of opening his "infirmities" to his physicians to "anatomise" his body to them (Dev. 267; 9.2), as he puts it, affiliates his self-revelations with the innovations in anatomy inaugurated by the publication of Vesalius's De humani corporis fabrica libri septem.[25] In addition to the numerous new understandings of anatomy it enabled, the Fabrica unleashed into circulation anatomical imagery that saturated the cultural imaginary, changing forever the way people understood their own bodies.[26] Donne famously scaffolds The First Anniversarie as an exercise in anatomy, an analogy that may also index his own sensory and personal memory of attending a dissection.[27]

24. Trevor-Roper, Europe's Physician, 171–77.

25. For a full account of anatomical practices, see Phyllis Allen, "Medical Education in 17th Century England," Journal of the History of Medicine and Allied Sciences 1, no. 1 (1946): 115–43.

26. See Jonathan Sawday, The Body Emblazoned: Dissection and the Human Body in Renaissance Culture (London: Routledge, 1995); Katharine Park, Gender, Generation, and the Origins of Human Dissection (Brooklyn, NY: Zone Books, 2006); and Valerie Traub, "The Nature of Norms in Early Modern England: Anatomy, Cartography, and King Lear," South Central Review 26, no. 1 (2009): 42–81.

27. David H. M. Woollam, "Medical Allusions in the Works of the Seventeenth-Century Poet and Divine," Medical History 5, no. 2 (1961): 144–53, 146–47; Michael

In his iconological study of Rembrandt's *Anatomy of Dr. Nicolaas Tulp*, William Heckscher describes how public anatomies often became festive and theatrical events. Even though he focuses primarily on Amsterdam in the 1630s, his descriptions pertain to England, as he notes, and to Donne's London. Heckscher is attentive to the implications of the spaces used for public and medical dissections, which sometimes included theatrical or religious buildings. He argues that these spatial superimpositions created representations of anatomical dissection that intermingled realms of realism and fantasy.

Donne's references to anatomy in *Devotions* are explicitly Vesalian.[28] Vesalius's radical change was to introduce a practice of anatomy that demanded the anatomist's active, investigative involvement in the dissection. His illustrations of flayed bodies feature compliant corpses, often upright figures arranged in poses that display their exposed muscles and organs to scrutiny. Donne's references to his self-anatomy in *Devotions* are engaged in just these ways. He goes even further, in fact, given that his dissection is an auto-anatomy. Like Berengario da Carpi or Valverde de Amusco's compliant cadavers that part the skin of their own thoraxes, opening the body to the spectators' gaze, or even wield the dissecting knife and their newly flayed skin, Donne participates actively in the investigation of his body's illness (figure 2).

Caspar Barlaeus, the Dutch polymath humanist, wrote of the anatomical theater (figure 3): "This House we found for Death, this hall is rigid with skins forcibly removed. Here, keenly intent, we behold whatever we are inside, and that which is hidden in our bodies' *fabrica* is brought to light. This structure is the seat of the soul, this is the venerable tabernacle of the mind, this insignificant receptacle contains divinity concealed."[29] In *Devotions*, Donne uses his constantly changing bodily condition as the ground for his spiritual awareness. It is as if Valverde's anatomical engraving manifests Donne's effigiation: the cadaver gazes at the pendant shroud of his own flayed skin, in much the same way that Barlaeus's

Neill, *Issues of Death: Mortality and Identity in English Renaissance Tragedy* (Oxford: Oxford University Press, 1997), 102–40; William S. Heckscher, *Rembrandt's Anatomy of Dr. Nicolaas Tulp: An Iconological Study* (New York: New York University Press, 1958), 27–51.

28. Andrea Carlino, *Books of the Body: Anatomical Ritual and Renaissance Learning*, trans. John Tedeschi and Anne C. Tedeschi (Chicago: University of Chicago Press, 1999), 11; William S. Heckscher, *Rembrandt's Anatomy*, 47–49.

29. Quoted in Heckscher, *Rembrandt's Anatomy of Dr. Nicolaas Tulp*, 114. Caspar Barlaeus's poem, "This Anatomical House that can be Visited in Amsterdam," was published in Amsterdam in 1646.

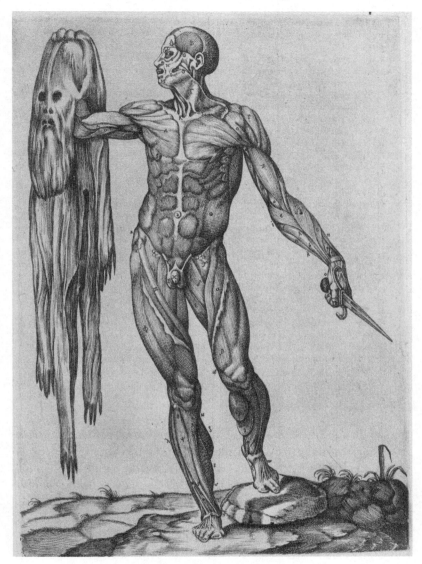

2. Juan Valverde de Amusco, *Anatomia del corpo humano* (1560).
Photograph: The Thomas Fisher Rare Book Library, University of Toronto.

"forcibly removed" skins reveal underneath the "structure of the soul,"
the "tabernacle of the mind." In a 1618 sermon, Donne makes this point
explicit: "we understand the frame of mans body, better when we see him
naked, than apparrelled . . . and better by seeing him cut up, than by seeing him do any exercise alive; one desection, one Anatomy teaches more

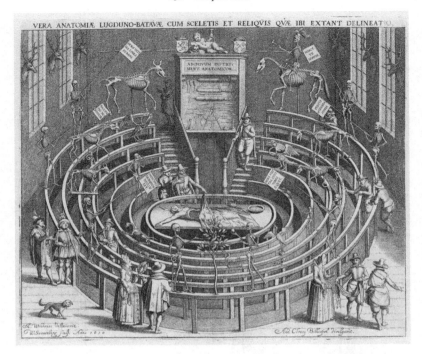

VERA ANATOMIÆ LUGDUNO-BATAVÆ CUM SCELETIS ET RELIQVIS QVÆ IBI EXTANT DELINEATIO.

3. The *Anatomical Theatre of Leiden University* (1610), engraved by
Willem van Swanenberg, after Jan Cornelis Woudanus, published by
Andreas Cloucquius. Photograph: Museum Boerhaave / Wikimedia.

of that, than the marching, or drilling of a whole army of living men. Let
every one of us therefore dissect and cut up himself" (*Ser.* 1:273). Donne's
illness presents a portrait of an inaccessible psychic nature through his
bodily symptoms—the word *symptom* itself resonant with the echo of
its Greek etymology, *mischance*.[30] To follow Donne's description of his
sickness through *Devotions* is to chart the continual translation of each
symptom's migratory expression in his body through intellectual, emotional, and psychic registers toward spiritual understanding. His capacity
to manifest the invisibility of his soul is bound up with his attention to his
corporeal self. Far from seeking to shuck off that bodily self, he clings to
the physicality of his being.

Self-knowledge motivates many early modern anatomy books: the
nosce te ipsum injunction is invoked to authorize the anatomist's explorations of nature's secrets and preempt his potential violation of God's

30. *OED*, s.v. "symptom," n. 1.

mysteries in dissecting the human body. Helkiah Crooke epitomizes this stance in his vernacular anatomical treatise, *Mikrokosmographia*: "by the dissection of the body, and by Anatomy, wee shall easily attaine unto this knowledge. For seeing the soule of man being cast into this prison of the body, cannot discharge her offices and functions without a Corporeall organ or instrument of the body; whosoever will attaine unto the knowledge of the soule, it is necessary that he know the frame and composition of the body."[31] Donne's anatomical conversions shape Expostulation 9, where, having "anatomised" his body to his physicians, he opens his soul to God: "there is no *veine* in mee, that is not full of the bloud of thy *Son* . . . there is no *Artery* in me, that hath not the *spirit of error, the spirit of lust, the spirit of giddines* in it; no *bone* in me that is not hardned with the custom of *sin*, and nourished, and soupled with the *marrow of sinn*; no *sinews*, no *ligaments*, that do not tie, and chain sin and sin together" (*Dev.* 267; 9.2). Through a catalog of emblazoned, synecdochic parts, Donne displays his dissected, opened body to God, translating each structural piece into its spiritual corollary.

In Station 8, we learn that the "King sends his owne Phisician." Some scholars have suggested that Donne was attended by two doctors only: the royal physician, Mayerne, and his friend, primary physician, and son of John Foxe the martyrologist, Dr. Simeon Fox. We suggest, however, following Bald's discussion of an undated letter written to Mrs. Cockayne in which Donne refers to having "Doctor *Fox* and Doctor *Clement* with me," that in Station 7, Dr. Fox is joined by his colleague Dr. William Clement. The arrival of Mayerne at the king's behest then creates the consulting "trinity" of Station 9.[32] Donne's representation of the trinity in *Devotions* thus shuttles between the historical realism of his circumstances and his symbolic transmutation of them.

In Expostulation 9, Donne translates the consultation in which his physicians are engaged into a divine register. Following a long Christian exegetical tradition, he suggests that when God made the first human being, he did so through consultation, and that his "*externall*" works are fashioned by "the whole *Trinity*, and their hand is to every action" (*Dev.* 267; 9.2). Donne then invokes not the heavenly trinity, but "al you blessed, and glorious persons of the *Trinitie* [who] are in *Consultation* now" (*Dev.* 267; 9.2). His "*Trinity*" of earthly doctors debate what they "wil do with this infirm *body*, with this leprous *Soule*, that attends guiltily, but yet comfortably, your determination upon it. I offer not to counsell

---

31. Crooke, *Mikrokosmographia*, 12.
32. Bal. 395–96. See also Bal. 316–17n2.

them, who meet in *consultation* for my *body* now, but I open my infirmities, I anatomise my body to them" (*Dev.* 267; 9.2). Donne's insistence on the repeated "now" locates him in a present in which his physicians have withdrawn to consult, and in which he is suspended, awaiting their verdict. He turns away from his earthly physicians in this hiatus and toward God, "So I do [anatomise] my *soule* to thee, O my *God*" (*Dev.* 267; 9.2), clearly demarcating human and divine realms even as he draws on the physical body to explore his soul. Donne moves through the porous membrane that divides and joins his physical and spiritual life. His bilingual (heavenly and earthly) tropologies link the visible and invisible realms: the trinity of physicians who attended him—Fox, Clement, and Mayerne—are mirrored, overseen, and spiritually augmented by the Holy Trinity.[33] When Donne speaks of the "*holy, and whole Colledge*" (*Dev.* 267; 9.2), it is difficult not to consider the word as analogically hinging a heavenly or Apostolic confraternity and the College of Physicians of London where each of his physicians held membership.[34] The College of Physicians replicates and presages the spiritual collegiality of heavenly consultation, as if their earthly tending manifested Donne's invisible colloquies with God.

The 1634 and 1638 editions of *Devotions* include a frontispiece with an engraving by William Marshall (figure 4). The image reproduces at its center the picture for Donne's marble effigy in Saint Paul's Cathedral. He is wrapped in his shroud, hands clasped across his body as if he were awaiting burial, and his eyes are closed. He is flanked on both sides by two oval inset images illustrating biblical scenes. The lower left image de-

33. See Bal. 516–17 for a discussion of the dating of the letter in which Donne refers to Dr. Fox and Dr. Clement. For Dr. Mayerne's presence during his illness of 1623, see Bal. 452, 454; and David H. M. Woollam, "Medical Allusions in the Works of the Seventeenth-Century Poet and Divine," *Medical History* 5, no. 2 (1961): 148. Stephen Pender notes that Donne had at least two physicians in attendance on him, Fox and Mayerne. See Stephen Pender, "Somiotics: Rhetoric, Medicine, and Hermeneutics in John Donne," PhD diss., University of Toronto (2000), 257n38. F. N. L. Poynter, in "John Donne and William Harvey," *Journal of the History of Medicine and Allied Sciences* 15, no. 3 (1960): 238–42, suggests that the physician the king sends may have been William Harvey. For Mayerne's prescriptions, see Kate Frost, "Prescription and Devotion: The Reverend Doctor Donne and the Learned Doctor Mayerne—Two Seventeenth-Century Records of Epidemic Typhus Fever," *Medical History* 22, no. 4 (1978): 408–16.

34. Simeon Fox was president of the college from 1634 to 1641 and Donne's stepfather, John Syminges, was several times president. See Bal. 37. Harold J. Cook provides a valuable history of the college in *The Decline of the Old Medical Regime in Stuart London* (Ithaca, NY: Cornell University Press, 1986).

picts a canopied, curtained sickbed occupied by a patient. Three attending figures cluster around the bed. The biblical citation above the image
is Psalm 41:3: "The lord will strengthen him upon the bed of languishing:
thou wilt make all his bed in his sickness." The other oval inserts figure
Adam and Eve and the expulsion from the garden, the suffering of Job, and
the supplications of four figures in the lower right-hand oval insert that
illustrate Matthew 26:41: "Watch and pray, that ye enter not into temptation: the spirit indeed is willing, but the flesh is weak." It is tempting to
think that the artist might have been influenced by Donne's description
of his illness in *Devotions*, his spiritual struggles, and his own sickbed and
the three physicians that attended him there. The evocative frontispiece
seems to manifest Donne's thought, as though he were summoning images even with closed eyes, imparting a vision of another world.

Heart Cordials

Stations 11 and 12 mark a pivotal moment in Donne's illness. In Meditation 10, he remarks on the usual sources of diagnostic intelligence—"the
pulse, the *urine*, the *sweat*"—that "all have sworn to say *nothing*, to give no
Indication of any dangerous *sicknesse*" (*Dev.* 270; 10.1). The greatest danger, however, lies in the secret rebellions, the "*Murmuring, murmuring* in
their *hearts*," for these unseen intrigues are "the most deadly, the most
pernicious" (*Dev.* 270; 10.1). Yet his physicians see that "invisibly" and
"insensibly" the "*disease*" has established a "*Kingdome*, an *Empire* in mee,
and will have certaine *Arcana Imperii*, *secrets of State*" (*Dev.* 270; 10.1).
Against these insidious conspiracies the physicians must deploy their art
of discovery, since death, like sin, creeps into our windows, "our *Eyes*,
and *Eares*, the entrances and inlets of our *soule*" (*Dev.* 270; 10.2). Donne's
illness has colonized his body, and his physicians must use their tools of
discovery to eradicate the "conspiracies" that threaten to destabilize his
bodily kingdom. Where magistrates can use torture (the "*rack*") to ex-
tract information, physicians have their "*examiners*," potentially painful
ways of gathering intelligence about the clandestine treacheries foment-
ing within their patients (*Dev.* 270; 10.1).

Donne's erotic poetry alludes in characteristically inventive ways
to the tropology of hearts: hearts are exchanged, broken, extracted,
wounded, possessed by the beloved. The heart is the medium of affective
exchange between lovers, the passional currency of erotic verse. In *Devotions*, the locus of affective exchange is between Donne and his own body.
His physician serves as an intermediary in Station 4, where fear becomes
the affective tender, as contagious as infection. In Station 11, the heart is

4. *Devotions upon Emergent Occasions* (1638). Frontispiece engraved by William Marshall. Photograph: Folger Shakespeare Library, Washington, DC.

the locus not just of self but of life-sustaining health. No longer primarily a generator of erotic passion, it is as an organ vital to the continuation of his life. He becomes newly aware of its murmuring rhythms as a source of essential vitality within his body.

The heart has a long metaphoric history in which its physiological workings are reflective of and intertwined with the figuration of political and social systems. Aristotle gave sovereign status to the heart, but when his writings on animals were lost, Galenic theory supplanted that model by designating the heart, the liver, and especially the brain as shared rulers. During the thirteenth and fourteenth centuries, however, Avicenna's reworking and expansion of Aristotle briefly granted renewed primacy to the heart, evidenced in the writing of Aquinas, who privileged motion. He believed that motion was generated by the soul and expressed through the heart's movement, which in turn created the natural movements of the animal. Because the soul's connection to the body is facilitated by the heart, the heart becomes a natural meeting place for body and soul. Aquinas was an important source for Dante, and his theories influenced Statius's description of the embryo's formation in *Purgatorio*, as we examined in chapter 4. The heart was granted primacy for its linkage to the soul and because it was the first organ to develop.[35]

If illness is a secret rebellion, a plot to establish its kingdom of suffering in Donne's body, it is countered by the presence of a legitimate king in the next station. Station 11 explores the heart as an anatomical organ, as the generator of heat and vital spirits in the body, and as the metaphoric and affective center of the self. Meditation 11 revolves around a classification of the heart derived from Aristotle and the author of the Hippocratic treatise on the heart, *Peri Kardies*, both of whom appoint the heart as the body's principal organ.[36] Aristotle argued that the heart is the first structure with movement to appear in the body, and that it actively assists in the embryo's development. It is also the last organ to fail, for its cessation announces death.[37] Galen modified the traditional primacy of the heart by insisting on the liver's importance, a sharing of corporeal governance that Helkiah Crooke sums up in *Mikrokosmographia*: "the Heart like a

35. Heather Webb provides an instructive account of the shifts in political representations of the heart in her chapter "The Sovereign Heart" in *The Medieval Heart* (New Haven, CT: Yale University Press, 2010), 10–49.

36. Michael F. Frampton, "Aristotle's Cardiocentric Model of Animal Locomotion," *Journal of the History of Biology* 24, no. 2 (1991): 291–330. See also *Peri Kardies: A Treatise on the Heart from the Hippocratic Corpus*, intro. and trans. Frank R. Hurlbutt Jr., *Bulletin of the History of Medicine* 7, no. 9 (1939): 1104–13.

37. Frampton, "Aristotle's Cardiocentric Model," 294.

King maintaineth and cherisheth with his lively and quickening heate, the life of all the partes: the Liver the fountaine and well-spring of most beneficiall humidity or juice, nourisheth and feedeth the whole family of the bodie, as her own proper costs and charges, like most a bountifull Prince."[38] As Crooke puts it, Galen identified the heart as *a* principal part, but not, as Aristotle designated it, *the* principal part.[39] In *Devotions*, Donne follows Aristotelian theory, claiming that the "*Heart* hath the *birth-right*, and *Primogeniture*, and that it is *Natures eldest Sonne* in us, the part which is first born to life in man," and that the other parts and organs have a "dependance upon it" (*Dev.* 273–74; 11.1). The brain, liver, and heart are not a "*Triumvirate*" where sovereignty is shared; rather, "the *Heart* alone is in the *Principalitie*, and in the *Throne*, as *King*, the rest as *Subjects*" (*Dev.* 273; 11.1). But if for Donne, the heart seems to furnish the primary powers and faculties of the self because it is always in motion, it also turns out to be the most vulnerable, the organ "soonest endangered" (*Dev.* 273; 11.1). The heart's solitary sovereignty magnifies its precarity. The brain can hold out longer, and the liver even longer; both can endure "a *Siege*," but the heart will blow up like a "*Myne*" when it is subjected to unnatural heat (*Dev.* 273; 11.1).

It is worth lingering on the strangeness of this imagery. Donne inherits a medical, philosophical, and poetic tradition that personifies the heart. This prosopopoeia rests on an analogy stretching back to Plato's *Republic*, which provided an early influential formulation of the body as political homology.[40] In Donne's hands, however, it is not just that the heart is like a king. Rather, he gives this enigmatic internal organ— which he cannot see and can know only through the analogies that physick and poetry supply—a face, a character, a human role. In his dedicatory epistle to Prince Charles, Donne effusively praises the generosity of his sovereign, King James, affiliating his kingship with Hezekiah, King of Judah, and God the Father. His political analogies have personal and specific historical immediacy (accentuated by James's sending his own trusted physician to care for Donne) that destabilizes the divide between the inside and outside of the body, between the integrity of the self and its social and political surround. Donne's depiction of the heart as a metonymy for the human subject evinces his alarm at its hidden betrayals while also registering the paradox of having such

38. Crooke, *Mikrokosmographia*, 13.

39. Crooke, 367.

40. See Ernst H. Kantorowicz's classic account, *The King's Two Bodies: A Study in Medieval Political Theology* (Princeton, NJ: Princeton University Press, 1957).

importance vested in a tiny organ: "How little of a *Man* is the *Heart*; and yet it is all, by which he *is*: and this continually subject . . . to intestine poysons bred in our selves by pestilentiall sicknesses. O who, if before hee had a beeing, he could have sense of this miserie, would buy a being here upon these conditions?" (*Dev.* 275; 11.1). The physicians must necessarily "intermit" (*Dev.* 274; 11.1) their care of the brain or the liver because these organs may subsist even if compromised, but they cannot live if the heart perishes. The first dictate of nature is "to have care of our owne *Preservation*, to looke first to our selves" (*Dev.* 274; 11.1). Everything depends on the heart's health.

The dramas Donne describes in Meditation 11 are enacted inside his body in unseen, even unfelt ways. The onomatopoeic *"murmuring"* in his heart evokes not actual political conspiracy but the felt dangers of insurrection within his body, as if the conventional political metaphors had been turned outside in. His analogies are laced with intimately observed emotion: the heart, as firstborn son, appears to be busily managing everything for his family, except that he is secretly vulnerable, for "the *eldest* is oftentimes not the strongest of the family" (*Dev.* 273; 11.1). Royal prerogatives are similarly fraught, for those born to a superior place may not be "of stronger parts, than themselves, that serve and obey them that are weaker" (*Dev.* 274; 11.1). Galenic medicine held that the balance of humors in individuals determined temperament and the propensity to health and disease. The tragedy, whether played out as a family dynamic or a political one, is born of the potential discrepancy between an assigned role and its occupant. The heart, like its personifications, can harbor hidden frailties. Donne's earthly king, James I, figures implicitly in *Devotions* as a generous, if not always predictable ruler. His munificence was responsible for Donne's appointment as dean of Saint Paul's in 1621, just two years before his illness.[41] Donne gratefully acknowledges his king and his promotion in the *Devotions'* dedicatory letter to Prince Charles: "*In my* second Birth, your Highnesse Royall Father *vouchsafed mee his Hand, not onely to sustaine mee* in it, *but to lead mee* to it" (*Dev.* 230). In Station 8, the king continues his care when, prompted by grave concern for Donne's health, he sends his personal physician to attend him, as we have already seen. Mayerne had also treated Prince Henry and his arrival at Donne's bedside may have evoked for him, for Donne, and for the king the precarious nature of royal succession, which depended on unseen and uncontrollable bodily forces. Donne's dedication of the *Devotions* to Charles, James I's second

41. The appointment was confirmed by September 13, 1621. See Bal. 366–81.

son and heir apparent, both evokes and conceals this tragic lacuna, a line of succession interrupted by the death of the eldest son. The unspoken charge of Donne's observation was that the "*eldest*" son, Henry, had tragically not been the strongest, and his illness cut short the kingship to which he had been born. The affective elaboration of Donne's metaphors vitalizes the body politic analogy through its internalization of contemporary political allusions within an invisible organ whose emotional vulnerability is palpable.

William Harvey literalizes the historical nuances of Donne's heart analogy in his dedicatory letter to King Charles in *De motu cordis* (1628), where he describes the animal's heart as the "sun of its microcosm" in the same way that the king, Charles I, is the "sun of his microcosm," the "heart of his state."[42] Harvey trained in Padua and followed the Aristotelian tradition of the cardiovascular anatomists Realdo Colombo and Fabricius of Acquapendente, the latter of whom was one of Harvey's teachers.[43] Janel Mueller suggests that Donne's portrayal of the heart's continual activity in Meditation 11—"It is always in *Action*, and *motion*" (*Dev.* 273; 11.1)—may be an allusion to William Harvey's description of ventricular contractions.[44] There are, however, several even more suggestive connections between Donne and Harvey's experiments on the heart and the circulation of the blood. Harvey began to deliver the Lumleian lectures at the College of Physicians in 1616, lectures that were illustrated by the anatomical investigations that he conducted simultaneously.[45] He was appointed physician extraordinary to James I in 1618. In his dedicatory letter to the president of the College of Physicians in London in *De motu cordis*, Harvey notes that having been "confirm'd by ocular demonstration for nine years and more in your sight," and responsive to

42. William Harvey, *De motu cordis*, Dedication to King Charles, *The Circulation of the Blood and Other Writings*, trans. Kenneth J. Franklin (London and Rutland, VT: Everyman, 1993), 3.

43. Walter Pagel, "William Harvey: Some Neglected Aspects of Medical History," *Journal of the Warburg and Courtland Institutes* 7 (1944): 145.

44. *Dev.* 575n.

45. The Lumleian lectures were established in 1582 when John Syminges, Donne's stepfather, was president of the College of Physicians. See F. N. L. Poynter, "John Donne and William Harvey," 234. Luke Wilson provides an insightful account of Harvey's anatomical performances, which he reconstructs from Harvey's recorded lecture notes in *Prelectiones anatomiae universalis*. See Luke Wilson, "William Harvey's *Prelectiones*: The Performance of the Body in the Renaissance Theater of Anatomy," *Representations* 17 (1987): 62–95. See also *William Harvey: Lectures on the Whole of Anatomy*, trans. C. D. O'Malley, F. N. L. Poynter, and K. F. Russell (Berkeley: University of California Press, 1961).

"what is desired by some, and most earnestly required by others," he has determined at last to have his "little Book published."[46] His anatomical demonstrations and theories were in currency for almost a decade before he published the results of his experiments. F. N. L. Poynter argues that it would have been extraordinary for Donne *not* to have known Harvey, to have attended any of Harvey's lectures, or to have at least heard of his work.

As a member of the College of Physicians of London, Harvey was required to swear an oath that registered his allegiance to the Galenic beliefs to which the College adhered. These principles included Galen's teachings about cardiovascular structure and function. Harvey's Proem in *De motu cordis,* however, explicitly opposes Galenic theory, arguing that Galen had conflated the nature of pulse and respiration, heart and lungs. Having laid out in detail the results of his experimentation and the reasons for his divergence from Galen's ideas, Harvey returns at the end of his treatise to Aristotle, affirming the philosopher's according of primacy (as the first organ to develop) and principality (as the source of the animal's power) to the heart.[47] Marjorie O'Rourke Boyle postulates that Aristotle's prescient understanding of cardiac function was derived not from anatomical dissection but from analogical reasoning. Aristotle likened the heart's storage capacity to an amphora of wine. He applied a dynamic principle to it: when it was full, it needed to be poured into another vessel. When it was empty, it was ready to receive more wine. He supplemented his observations about the heart's fluids with parallel insights about its heat-generating capacities. Again, his analogy was to a human artifact, in this case, to the portable clay domed oven common in the Greek household, the *pnigeus.* Aristotle knew that heat was a necessary feature of life for an animal, and he hypothesized that the pulsation of the heart allowed it to regulate its vital heat. Subsequent understanding of cardiac function entailed movement of the blood and its potential for heating and refrigerating the temperature of the heart.[48]

46. William Harvey, *Exercitatio Anatomica de motu cordis et sanguinis in animalibus,* trans. Geoffrey Keynes (1927; reprinted Birmingham: The Classics of Medicine Library, 1978), vii.

47. Harvey, *Exercitatio Anatomica,* 114–15.

48. Marjorie O'Rourke Boyle offers a persuasive account of Aristotle's investigations into cardiac function through his analogical observations of amphorae and ovens. Her argument sheds new light on Harvey's measurement of the fluids in the ventricles: *Cultural Anatomies of the Heart in Aristotle, Augustine, Aquinas, Calvin, and Harvey* (Cham, Switzerland: Palgrave Macmillan, 2018), 1–34.

A 1621 sermon makes Donne's awareness of Harvey's public anatomies and experiments tantalizingly apparent.[49] Donne's text was Proverbs 25:16: "Hast thou found honey? Eat so much as is sufficient for thee, lest thou be filled therewith, and vomit it." The sermon focuses on insatiability and covetousness, and it contains this suggestive passage:

> We know the receipt, the capacity of the ventricle, the stomach of man, how much it can hold; and wee know the receipt of all the receptacles of blood, how much blood the body can have; so wee doe of all the other con-duits and cisterns of the body; But this infinite Hive of honey, this insatiable whirlpoole of the covetous mind, no Anatomy, no dissection hath discovered to us. When I looke into the larders, and cellars, and vaults, into the vessels of our body for drink, for blood, for urine, they are pottles, and gallons; when I looke into the furnaces of our spirits, the ventricles of the heart and of the braine, they are not thimbles. (*Ser.* 3:235–36)

Poynter suggests that Donne's reference to anatomy, dissection, and the measurement of ventricular capacity alludes to Harvey's anatomical experiments in which he measured the volume of fluid in the visceral organs, including the ventricles of the heart. Harvey's ability to demonstrate the blood's circulation ultimately depended on these measurements. Our object here is not to prove that Donne knew Harvey or that he integrated Harvey's groundbreaking discovery of the blood's circulation into his writing, however tantalizing the evidence of their connection might be. It is instead to observe how Donne transmutes the matter of the scientific and medical explorations that were changing the world around him. In this passage, for instance, Donne immediately transposes anatomical measurement into the mind's limitless, unquantifiable insatiability. Harvey's careful measurements become for Donne a metaphor of the mind's resistance to being measured by mathematical calculation. His assessment in *The Second Anniversarie* sums up a cognate dismissal of epistemological certainty: "Thou art too narrow, wretch, to comprehend / Even thy selfe: yea though thou wouldst but bend / To know thy body" (*Ann.* A2:48; 261–63). As fascinating as anatomical exploration of the body was, it could not illuminate the arenas that Donne most hoped to know: the mind and the soul.

---

49. See Poynter's detailed discussion *Prelectiones anatomiae universalis*, edited with an autotype reproduction of the original by a committee of the Royal College of Physicians of London (London, J. & A. Churchill, 1886). Cited in Poynter, "John Donne and William Harvey," 237n9; 240–41.

His catalog of medical riddles in *The Second Anniversarie* epitomizes the futility of trying to master knowledge:

> Knowst thou but how the stone doth enter in
> The bladders Cave, and never breake the skin?
> Knowst thou how blood, which to the hart doth flow,
> Doth from one ventricle to th'other go?
> And for the putrid stuffe, which thou dost spit,
> Knowst how thy lungs have attracted it?
> There are no passages so that there is
> (For ought thou knowst) piercing of substances. (*Ann.* A2:49;
>   269–76)

How the blood moved from the one ventricle of the heart to the other was a central puzzle for anatomists in the early seventeenth century. In *Mikrokosmographia*, Crooke assembles the medical controversies associated with the heart. He grapples with the contentious question of how the vital spirits were generated in the heart and "the ways the bloud goeth out of the right into the left ventricle of the Heart."[50] He remarks dryly that "Anatomists do strive with implacable contention" about how blood is made and conveyed into the left ventricle. He surveys both ancient and later writers and distills the controversy into four opinions, each "repugnant" to the other.[51] Donne is not concerned with these details of the heart's porous septum, pulmonary transit, or even the revolutionary solution that Harvey proposed in *De motu cordis*. What fascinates him are the inscrutable consequences of the problem that binds his list of questions together: how can a substance pass from outside the body to its inside (the bladder stone, phlegm, blood), from one chamber of the heart to the other? This question figures the greater conundrum that shapes *Metempsychosis*, which is structured around the vagrant soul's entrance and exits from its host body. The enigma also frames *Devotions*: how will Donne's soul pass from his human body into its afterlife with God?

In Expostulation 11, Donne depicts his heart in the vivid language and imagery drawn from scriptural and poetic traditions.[52] His heart be-

50. Crooke, *Mikrokosmographia*, 410.

51. He summarizes the positions of Galen, Realdo Colombo, John Botallus, the French king's physician, and Franciscus Ulmus, who wrote an important treatise on the spleen. All of them suggest some kind of channel or porosity that allows for passage (Crooke, 410–14).

52. For discussion of these traditions, see Robert A. Erickson, *The Language of the Heart, 1600–1750* (Philadelphia: University of Pennsylvania Press, 1997); and Eric

comes an organ that can be extracted, ransacked, probed, and bartered. His address to God acknowledges the divine request: "*My God*, my *God*, all that thou askest of mee is, my *Heart*, *My Sonne, give mee thy heart*" (*Dev.* 275; 11.2). Reminiscent of Donne's love poems like "The Legacie" or "The Broken Heart"—which turn on the conceit of the removable, exchangeable heart—his heart here is a hostage to his love for God, vulnerable to seizure by the sickness that threatens to infect it. It is also the locus of his spiritual and emotional self, open to being searched and known in its wickedness and iniquity: "*I the Lord search the Heart*. When didst thou search mine? . . . wouldest thou have my *Heart*?" (*Dev.* 275; 11.2). He worries that his heart is "ill," not just afflicted by the "*venim and Malignitee*" of the disease that threatens him, but from sin and evil. He has known "*stonie*" hearts, hearts that are "*snares*," hearts full of lust, envy, and ambition that causes them to "*burne like Ovens*" (*Dev.* 275–76; 11.2). Yet Donne can find "*wise, perfit* hearts" in God's word, and if his were such a heart, he would indeed be able to give his to God. There is another kind of heart, too, a "*Judas heart*" that has been infiltrated by the devil (*Dev.* 276; 11.2). Donne possesses neither the perfect nor wicked, but instead a middle kind of heart, a "*melting* heart, and a *troubled* heart; and a *wounded* heart, and a *broken* heart, and a *contrite* heart" (*Dev.* 276; 11.2). These afflictions and blows are God's preparation for his heart to be a "*returning* heart," for God to carry it home.

Donne's language straddles the figural and the literal (compressed into the etymological pun of cordial), as if his physicians and their medicines and God's treatments all reflect each other. Station 11 progresses, inward from the social and political surround of the meditation, and then into the emotional heart of scripture that wrestles with God's love and care in the expostulation. In the prayer, Donne moves into the most interior self, a spiritual heart. Donne metaphorizes God's entrance into his heart, however, by borrowing the figurative resources of anatomy and architecture. Donne's body becomes a house, into which he invites God, enjoining him to occupy "every roome of this thy House, my body" and especially "my *Heart*, thy *Bed-Chamber*" (*Dev.* 277; 11.3). He draws on a trope of anatomy, exemplified in Spenser's Castle of Alma, and echoed in his own 1621 sermon, in which Donne describes how measuring the cavities of the body entails looking into "the larders, and cellars, and vaults, into the vessels of our body for drink" (*Ser.* 3:236). Donne plays satirically with this anatomical analogy in *Metempsychosis*, when the mouse creeps into the sleeping elephant's trunk, whose "sinewy Proboscis did remisly

Jager, *The Book of the Heart* (Chicago: University of Chicago Press, 2000).

lie." It enters the elephant's body, walking "as in a gallery," surveying "the rooms of this vast house," moving finally to "the braine, the soules bedchamber," gnawing the "life cords" there (*Sat.* 41; 385–94). The mouse's ingress makes it an agent of death, but when Donne invites God into the bedchamber of his heart, he does so to protect himself against temptations and infections. Donne's language in the prayer hinges on spiritual and earthly registers. His lexical doubleness gestures simultaneously to the infection of sin and bodily infection, divine and bodily cure: God as physician has furnished the "*Cordiall water*" with which he was baptized and the "*Cordiall Blood*" that is the sacrament of communion. These sacramental references offer a potent Christian vocabulary of transformation, to which Donne adds a specifically medical aspect.[53]

Donne's etymological pun on "cordial" straddles figural and literal registers, setting his physicians and their medicines as a resonant counterpoint to God's treatments. His metaphorical play on "cordial" rests, however, on a material physick, the "cordial" of the station's Latin heading, a concoction that his attending physicians administer to keep the "venim and Malignitie of the disease from the Heart" (*Dev.* 273; 11). Just as Donne's earthly physicians are most visible in the station headings, so too are their remedies and treatments most clearly discernible in the station's paratextual frame. Donne reveals in the prayer that the cordial his earthly physicians prepare for him is "assisted" by "the flesh of *Vipers*" (*Dev.* 277; 11.3). In *The Historie of Serpents* (1608), Edward Topsell writes about the concocting of "Theriace, Triacle, and Trochuk" as remedies for serpent bites. The vipers themselves are "mingled" in the making of these medicines because their flesh provides the antidote to their own venom, and they are therefore used as a powerful ingredient for a long list of ailments, including leprosy. Topsell notes that viper flesh is "the most sovraigne remedy of the Plague."[54] In the Expostulation, Donne draws on the specific medical efficacy of the viper cordial, a remedy for leprosy and plague, in his imagery: "as long as I remaine in this leprous house, this flesh of mine, this Heart, though thus prepared *for* thee, prepared *by*

---

53. See, e.g., Richard Kearney, "Carnal Poetics," *New Literary History* 46, no. 1 (2015): 99–124.

54. Edward Topsell, *The Historie of Serpents* (London: William Jaggard, 1608), 302–6, 305. Théodore de Mayerne lists "Aqua Theriacalis" in his *Medicinal Councels* (12), referring his reader to the recipe in his *London Pharmacopoea*, Mayerne's extensive knowledge of vipers and their venom is apparent in "A discourse of the viper and some other poysons, wrote by Sr. Théodore de Mayerne, after discoursing with Mr. Pontæus. Communicated by Sir Theodore de Vaux, M.D. and S.R.S," *Royal Society Philosophical Transactions* 18, no. 211 (1694): 162–66.

thee, will still be subject to the invasion of maligne and pestilent vapours. But I have my *Cordialls* in thy promise; *when I shall know the plague of my heart, and pray unto thee in thy house,* thou wilt preserve that heart, from all mortall force, of that infection" (*Dev.* 276–77; 11.2).

The viper remedies to which Donne refers are recorded in the 1618 pharmacopiae compiled by London physicians. Théodore de Mayerne, William Clement, and Simeon Fox (and William Harvey) were all directly involved in the pharmacopiae, for Mayerne had cultivated a close relationship with London apothecaries that ultimately affiliated them with the College of Physicians. Mayerne's powerful advocacy helped persuade James I in 1617 to grant the apothecaries a charter that established them as a guild separate from the grocers and subordinated to the physicians.[55] The Royal College of Physicians of London then began to regulate physick by compiling a book of remedies that mandated apothecaries to standardize the ingredients and methods for concocting, distilling, and preparing medicine.[56] "Bezoar" water, an antidote or counterremedy, was one of the listed remedies. It was a concoction made up of viper's flesh, like the cordial Donne was given. Mixing herbs, spices, wines, the "filings of unicorns-horn," and a "Troche of Vipers," the remedy strengthened "the heart, Arteries and spirit vitall."[57] Donne praises God for imprinting "all medicinall vertues, which are in all creatures, and hast made even the flesh of *Vipers*, to assist in *Cordialls*, art able to make this present sicknesse, everlasting health; this weaknes, everlasting strength; and this very dejection, and faintnesse of heart, a powerfull *Cordiall*" (*Dev.* 277; 11.3). The cordial originates in a serpent of evil and temptation, and through the pharmacological concoctions of Donne's physicians and through the ministrations of his divine physician, it is translated into its antithesis, a preservation from infection and venom.

Yet as Donne contemplates ingesting the cordial, he is reminded of Nabal in Samuel 25:37, who drank wine, but in the morning, "*his heart dyed within him*" (*Dev.* 276; 11.2). Echoing Lamentations 3:15, Donne charges God with having given him "*Wormewood*," *artemisia absinthium,*

55. Trevor-Roper, *Europe's Physician*, 23–24.

56. Nicholas Culpeper translated and published the pharmacopiae, prefacing it with a brief of the king's proclamation that commanded all apothecaries to follow the guidelines that set out in the *London Dispensatory*. Adhering to these new regulations and practices, will, Culpeper proclaims, eliminate all the "*falsehood, differences, varieties, or uncertainties in making or composing Medicines.*" Nicholas Culpeper, *A Physicall Directory or a translation of the London Dispensatory Made by the College of Physicians of London* (London, 1649), np.

57. Culpeper, *A Physicall Directory*, 81.

an herb notable for its bitterness. If God sends physical illness as a spiritual cure, that divine "medicine" could be a bitter remedy, capable not only of purging his sin but perhaps killing him in the process. When Donne speaks of having had "some diffidence" when he takes the cordial, he registers his moments of fear, of literally feeling his "faith" (from the Latin *fidere*) waver. As Donne and his physicians knew all too well, medical interventions and the remedies of physick could be as dangerous as the illnesses they were designed to cure. To agree to ingest a remedy required trust and faith in his physicians and in God. Unlike Nabal, however, Donne was able to wake up in the morning and find his heart still beating. He proclaims his sense of deliverance: "thou hast cleared a *Morning* to mee againe, and my heart is alive" (*Dev.* 276; 11.2). The measure of his relief is an index of his apprehension about whether he would survive the prescribed treatment.

Animal Physick

The heart cordial that his physicians administer in Station 11 and the pigeons they apply to his feet to *"draw the vapors from the Head"* in Station 12 return us to the operations of Donne's organic soul (*Dev.* 278; 12). These philosophical and metaphorical contiguities are materialized in *Devotions* through a physick that borrows its remedies from plants and animals. Donne had explored these ideas in *Metempsychosis*. The implicit philosophical argument of that poem is that the organic soul is contiguous with the intellective soul. The souls of vegetation and sense undergird, mnemonically inhabit, and continually touch the intellective soul as primordial echoes of a human developmental and precivilized past. They continue to animate the soul of reason, where they manifest in the exercise of perceptual and sensory faculties and in urgencies of the irascible and concupiscible appetitive functions. *Metempsychosis* is marked by Donne's inventive use of anachronism and catachrestic cross-species tropes: his sparrow commits incest; the whale, swordfish, and thresher episodes are threaded with analogies to court life; the perfidiously copulating wolf and dog violate trust, social, and genus categories; and the Petrarchan ape suitor aspires toward sexual integration into another species. But in *Devotions*, Donne also engages through physick a less visible form of crossing the vegetable, animal, human boundaries, a form that the tripartite soul makes manifest. Plants and animals furnished a vast storehouse of ingredients for apothecaries and physicians. Donne alludes to the medicinal resources of plants in his account of the mandrake root in *Metempsychosis*, "the living buried man" whose animal faculties

are immanent, have not yet been activated by the movement of a sensible soul. It is nevertheless a rich pharmacological resource for soporif-
ics, aphrodisiacs, and abortifacients: Eve tears the mandrake from the
earth in the hope that it will "[cool] her child's blood." The mandrake's
"apples" "kindle" desire, while its "leaves, force of conception kill" (*Sat.*
32; 150–68).[58] The sparrow's testicles, dung, and eggs supply sexual aids
that enable "Man to beget, and woman to conceive," a reference to the use
of sparrow testicles, dung, or eggs as aphrodisiacs and fertility aids (*Sat.*
35; 217–18).[59] Animal, vegetable, and mineral supplied the early modern
pharmacopeia with materials for many human needs, from enhancing
natural functions (sleep, procreation, reproduction, digestion and evacu-
ation, managing the passions) to curing the full spectrum of ailments and
diseases that afflicted the population.

The tradition that links animals to health has a powerful classical antecedent in Plutarch's *Moralia*, and it is this theriophilic legacy (to use
George Boas's 1933 coinage) upon which the sixteenth-century Florentine humanist Giovanni Battista Gelli draws in *Circe* (1549).[60] Gelli's
text, which was translated into English in 1557, borrows from and elaborates on Homer: in Gelli's account, Circe has metamorphosed Ulysses's
companions into animals, and although Ulysses tries to persuade them to
return to their human forms, each in turn refuses, preferring their beastly
incarnations. Each animal is animated by an eloquent narratorial voice
that articulates the perspective of a formerly mute animal nature but at
the same time, each creature remembers its earlier human occupation

58. Valeria Finucci catalogs a variety of sources for the aphrodisiac properties of
mandrake in *The Manly Masquerade: Masculinity, Paternity, and Castration in the Italian Renaissance* (Durham, NC: Duke University Press, 2003), 95–97. See also Henry
Cornelius Agrippa, *Three Books of Occult Philosophy* (London, 1650), 1:15, 35.

59. Stephan Batman describes the sparrow as "a full hot bird and lecherous,"
whose flesh when eaten "exciteth to carnall lust," *Batman uppon Bartolome* (London,
1582),12:32; 188. Francis Willughby says that sparrows have large testicles, are "very
salacious," and "are therefore held to be short-lived": *The Ornithology of Francis Willughby*, trans. John Ray and based on Aldrovandi (London, 1678), 249. Poliziano influentially argued in his *Miscellanea* (1489) that Lesbia's sparrow represented Catullus's penis, which may have contributed to the early modern representation of the
sparrow as a symbol of sexual indulgence. For a more general account, see Richard
W. Hooper, "In Defence of Catullus' Dirty Sparrow," *Greece & Rome* 32, no. 2 (1985):
162–78. For Poliziano's commentary, see Julia Haig Gaisser, "Catullus and His First
Interpreters: Antonius Parthenius and Angelo Poliziano," *TAPA* 112 (1982): 102–3.

60. George Boas, *The Happy Beast in French Thought of the Seventeenth Century*
(Baltimore: Johns Hopkins University Press, 1933), 133; John Baptista Gello, *Circes*,
trans. Henry Iden, 1557.

and can insightfully compare its beastly advantages to the shortcomings of its previous human profession. The second of Gelli's ten dialogues stages an encounter between Ulysses and a snake, formerly a physician. The snake-physician coupling plays, of course, on the mythological association between Asclepius and snakes, which are associated with wisdom and enhanced sensory capacities. In this exchange, the snake uses its wisdom to excoriate first the appetites of human beings, whose excessive eating and drinking create disease, and then the profession of physick, which is flawed in its knowledge and corrupt in its practices. The snake argues, following the lines of Plutarch's dialogue, that "Beasts are Rational," that animals are by nature healthier than humans, more able to cure themselves should they become afflicted with sickness. As Gelli's snake asserts, animals intuitively know the herbal remedies for their ailments. The snake expresses from an animal perspective the medical primitivism of such empirics as Leonardo Fioravanti, a sixteenth-century Bolognese physician who believed that humans should emulate beasts since animals supposedly understand instinctively how to cure themselves.

Donne eloquently drew on these beliefs when he anatomized his own perilous illness in *Devotions*:

> We *have* the Phisician, but we *are not* the Phisician. Heere we shrinke in our proportion, sink in our dignitie, in respect of verie meane creatures, who are *Phisicians* to themselves. The *Hart* that is pursued and wounded, they say, knowes an Herbe, which being eaten, throwes off the arrow: A strange kind of *vomit*. The *dog* that pursues it, though hee bee subject to sicknes, even *proverbially*, knowes his *grasse* that recovers him. And it may be true, that the *Drugger* is as neere to *Man*, as to other *creatures*, it may be that obvious and present *Simples*, easie to bee had, would cure him; but the *Apothecary* is not so neere him, nor the *Phisician* so neere him, as they two are to other creatures; Man hath not that *innate instinct*, to apply those naturall medicines to his present danger, as those inferiour creatures have; he is not his owne *Apothecary*, his owne *Phisician*, as they are. (*Dev.* 243; 4.1)

If the animal/human caesura split species according to their souls and the faculties those psyches represented—with human beings figuring on the positive side the superiority of a rational soul, and on the negative, the handicap of their natural propensity to "dis-ease"—beasts and humans were also joined by the psyche they have in common, the sensible or animal soul.

Thinkers from at least the time of Aristotle recognized that humans and animals share psychic, physical, and anatomical characteristics. In the *Fabrica*, Vesalius relies on this anatomical parallel, even as he is also at pains to make various species distinct. Scholars believe that the depiction of the dog and monkey, prominently displayed in the foreground of the famous frontispiece, signals both his continued reliance on (and his departure from) Galenic practice.[61] Vesalius chastises those surgeons and physicians who rely slavishly on inherited Galenic knowledge that was predicated on the practice of using animal dissection for understanding human anatomy: "that it is just now known to us from the reborn art of dissection, from the careful reading of Galen's books, and from the welcome restoration of many portions thereof, that he himself never dissected a human body, but in fact was deceived by his monkeys (granted a couple of dried-up human cadavers came his way) and often wrongly disputed ancient doctors who had trained themselves in human dissections."[62] Although Vesalius corrects many of Galen's errors, the *Fabrica* is nevertheless shaped by the animal/human comparison: "In fact, you will find many things in Galen which he misunderstood even in monkeys, not to mention the most astonishing fact that among the many and infinite differences between the organs of the human body and the monkey Galen noticed only those in the fingers and the flexion of the knee; he would no doubt have missed these as well, had they not been obvious to him without dissecting a human" (3r). The vestiges of human/animal continuity nevertheless deposit themselves in anatomical language, which is apparent in such moments as Vesalius's description of teeth: the name for our "canine" teeth, he says, is "given them because they correspond to the protruding teeth of dogs (in which these teeth are conspicuous)" (1.11.46). When he comes to describe the hyoid bone, that horseshoe-shaped structure that is suspended in proximity to the larynx and tongue, he corrects Galen's terminology. Galen's translators have mistakenly called it "the bone resembling a pig" (1.13, 55), he tells us, but Vesalius renames it "the bone resembling the letter υ [Greek upsilon]," "*corpus ossis hyoidei*" (1.13.55), a fittingly alphabetic distinction of nomenclature for a bone that makes human vocal utterance possible.

Physick derived from animals relies on anatomical similitude and dis-

61. Andrea Carlino, *Books of the Body: Anatomical Ritual and Renaissance Learning*, trans. John Tedeschi and Anne C. Tedeschi (Chicago: University of Chicago Press, 1999), 48–51.

62. Andreas Vesalius, *The Fabric of the Human Body: An Annotated Translation of the 1543 and 1555 Edition of De humani corporis fabrica*, trans. Daniel H. Garrison and Malcolm H. Hast, 2 vols. (Basel, Switzerland: Karger, 2013), 1:6.

tinction. Listing the potential medicinal properties of animals is an ancient practice. Perhaps one of the best exemplars is Pliny, who, in his *Natural History*, offers a vast list of animal parts and how they can be used in
the service of human health. The blood of the elephant, for instance, was
thought to be efficacious in curing rheumatism, shavings of its ivory tusks
mixed with Attic honey could banish "duskish spots" on the face, and
even a touch of its trunk might alleviate the pain of a toothache.[63] The
fat of a lion, mixed with oil of roses, made the skin of the face white and
supple; a camel's brain was good for epilepsy; and camel dung reduced to
ashes and mixed with oil was an excellent prescription for curling or frizz-
ing the hair. Hyenas, which were thought to change sex every other year,
were assumed to be endowed with extraordinary medicinal power, capable as they putatively were of transporting the mind of men and women
and ravishing their senses. The skin from a hyena's head was thought to
cure headaches, and the pith or marrow of a hyena's backbone, mixed
with oil and gall, was supposedly highly beneficial for human nerves.[64]
These extensive and often wildly exotic lists, which were reproduced in
miniature in such bestiaries of the period as Edward Topsell's *Historie of
Four-Footed Beastes* (1607), cataloged the remedies and medicines that
each animal could provide, anatomizing the use of their excrements, their
milk, organs, hair, and skin.[65]

When Donne ingests a viper cordial in Station 11 of *Devotions*, he
literally incorporates the serpent, which becomes curative through medicinal refinement and a complex metaphoric conversion. In the parallel
moment when his physicians place dead pigeons on his feet to draw the
vapors from his head, this remedy sets up a different but no less intricate
identification between animal and human. Francis Willughby recorded
in his *Ornithology* the conventional medical practice of applying pigeons
to parts of the body to move vapors in beneficial directions. As creatures
of the air, birds were thought to exert a metonymic or sympathetic power
on the body's inner vaporous currents. The action of the cure is even
more directly communicated than through analogical sympathy, however. Willughby reports that the pigeon must be cut along the backbone
and then applied directly to the "soals of the Feet, in acute diseases, in
any great defect of spirits or decay of strength, to support and refresh the
patient, that he may be able to grapple with, and master the disease. For

---

63. *The Historie of the World Commonly called, The Naturall Historie of C. Plinius
Secundus*, trans. Philemon Holland (London, 1601), 28.8:310.

64. Pliny, *The Historie of the World*, 28.84:311.

65. Topsell, *Historie of Four-Footed Beasts* (London, 1607).

the vital spirits of the Pigeon still remaining in the hot flesh and bloud, do through the pores of the skin insinuate themselves into the bloud of the sick person, now dis-spirited and ready to stagnate, and induing new life and vigour, enable it to performe its solemn and necessary circuits."[66]

The pigeon remedy has rough affinities both with Paracelsian beliefs in the analogies between the cosmic and human body and with the Galenic principles of spirits. As a creature of air, the pigeon possesses vitalizing spirits and vapors that "insinuate" themselves into the patient's blood through the pores, even as the body's noxious vapors are evacuated through the soles of the feet. Bodily spirits were elementally contiguous with the ambient air and shared a kinship with the atmosphere and the creatures who occupy the air, the birds that Donne calls in *Metempsychosis* the "free inhabitants of the Plyant air" (*Sat.* 35; 215). Donne meditates on the nature of air, in Station 12, describing both the ambient air, which was by turns nourishing and pestilential, and the inner vapors, the *spiritus* or *pneuma*, invisible agents of Galenic physiology that propelled the fungible liquids of the humoral system.[67] He contemplates the paradox that an element so necessary to human survival could with invisible stealth also be an agent of death. Pliny the Elder, who "hunted after the *vapor* of Aetna and dar'd, and challenged *Death* in the forme of a *vapor* to doe the worst, and felt the worst, he dyed" furnishes a potent example of the impossibility of combating air (*Dev.* 278; 12.1). Pliny's fascination with volcanoes prompted him to approach Mount Vesuvius during the catastrophic eruption, first out of curiosity and then to rescue those who were stranded near Pompei, but as Pliny the Younger reported, he succumbed to a cloud of toxic gas and died.[68] Donne metaphorizes the vol-

66. Francis Willughby, *The Ornithology of Francis Willughby* (London, 1678), 183. The book catalogs birds according to Baconian principles of observation. Both Willughby and Ray distinguished their anatomical and biological endeavor from those of Conrad Gessner and others, who included mythological, proverbial, and historical materials. John Hall describes being treated with the same pigeon remedy for great weakness in the aftermath of a "deadly, burning Fever," *Select observations on English Bodies*, 150.

67. William Harvey argues against this Galenic principle in *De motu cordis*, where he differentiates between functions of the heart and the lungs and resists the idea that blood conveys the spirits through the body. Harvey, *De Motu cordis*, 1–15.

68. Donne seems to conflate Mount Aetna and Mount Vesuvius. In fact, Pliny does mention Mount Aetna in his catalog of volcanoes, but we know from Pliny the Younger's letter to Tacitus that his uncle's fatal trip was to Vesuvius, which is Donne's reference. Pliny, *Natural History*, vol. 1, trans. H. Rackham (London: W. Heineman, 1936), 362–63; *Pliny the Younger: Complete Letters*, ed. Peter Walsh (Oxford: Oxford University Press, 2006), 142–45.

canic gas, suggesting that human beings are themselves the "*Well*" that discharges noxious exhalations, spitting out "fiery smoke," spewing the "Suffocating and strangling *dampe*"of human sorrows (*Dev.* 278–79; 12.1). Humans create the volcanic eruptions of illness through their own errors, surfeits, and licentiousness, creating toxic fumes that poison their bodies and minds. These pestilential vapors are apparent in social and political contexts, where they travel as rumor, pernicious language carried on the air, unattributable, invisible, yet spread everywhere and carrying with them the potential to harm or even kill. Donne wonders what he might have done to create these poisonous fumes. Did he create his own melancholy? Was excessive study the cause of his illness? Is it because of his excessive rumination, his "*thoughtfulness*"? Was he not "made to *thinke*?" He knows that he did not actively fabricate the conditions of his sickness, yet he must die for it. He has become his own "*Executioner*" (*Dev.* 279; 12.1).

The dead pigeon prescription was a remedy for a medical crisis, used when the patient was so depleted that they were in mortal danger. Donne remarks in the Expostulation that vapors, like life and death are evanescent, for they "*appeareth for a little time, and then vanisheth away*" (*Dev.* 280; 12.2). Vapors are "*Hieroglyphique*" in Donne's mind, messages for communicating with God. He notes that human beings traditionally used sacrifices, burned offerings that sent smoke toward heaven to convey gratitude and reverence. God's breath is sometimes perfumed and beneficent, but he also sends vapors and smoke to punish, to darken the sun and to generate plagues of locusts. Vapors are a bidirectional channel of communication between heaven and earth. Air signaled the demise of the rebel angels as they fell from heaven, but it became the medium of God's reparation through which the son and then the dove "descended" (*Dev.* 281; 12.2). Expostulation 12 is the crucible through which Donne transforms the dead pigeon of "physick" into the descent of the Holy Spirit. The Latin *Columbâ* in the station heading gestures to the ornithological category of *columbus vulgaris* that for Francis Willughby encompassed both pigeon and dove.[69] Donne's translation of the Meditation's pigeon into the Expostulation's dove expands physick into a theological register. He reminds us that God has afforded "this remedy in Nature, by this application of a *Dove*, to our lower parts, to make these *vapors* in our *bodies*, to descend, and to make that a *type* to us that by the visitation of thy *Spirit*, the *vapors* of sin shall descend, and we tread them under out feet" (*Dev.* 281; 12.2). This reading draws on biblical typological interpretation, but it is also a very particular kind of metaphorical homeopathy.

69. Francis Willughby, *The Ornithology of Francis Willughby*, 180–86.

If the dead pigeon is his physicians' remedy for Donne's melancholy and illness, Donne joins with his physicians to transmute the pigeon into its celestial counterpart, the Holy Spirit, which becomes a message of hope and healing from his divine physician.

When Donne notes that God descended from heaven in the form of a dove at the baptism of his son, the pigeon cure acquires a homeopathic sacramental character. Applying the pigeon to Donne's lower extremities is a sacrifice of physick (a dead bird) that will allow him to redeem himself, to cure himself from sin even as he is potentially cured of his illness: "Let us draw down the *vapors* of our own *pride*, our own *wits*, our own *wils*, our own *inventions*, to the *simplicitie* of thy *Sacraments, and the obedience of thy word, and these* Doves, thus applied, shall make us live" (*Dev.* 281; 12.2). In the prayer, Donne refers pointedly to the sacrificial element. Just as the pigeon's blood will impart its vital spirits into Donne's ailing body, so was the "blood of the Sonne *Christ Jesus*" able to redeem human beings. (*Dev.* 282; 12.3). Donne provides a cognate description of the sacraments as physick in a 1618 sermon. God "prepared and he prescribed this physick, when he was on this earth." Where "other Physitians draw our blood, He makes physick of blood, and of his own blood" (*Ser.* 1.313). The pigeon's blood becomes the dove or Holy Spirit's blood, transmuting it into a eucharistic remedy. Donne recovers in the prayer the dove's creaturely characteristics, its "ordinary" qualities that will assist in following God's "holy *ordinances.*" The etymological resonance between "ordinary" and "ordinance" sets up a kinship between Nature's creatures and God's decrees, between the abundance of the natural world and the physician's purposing of them for medicinal use. God created the dove, Donne says, to "conduce medicinally to our *bodily health.*" It carries "the qualities of it home to my soule" to "imprint there that *simplicity*, that *mildness*, that *harmlessness*, which thou hast imprinted by *Nature* in this *Creature*" (*Dev.* 282, 12.3). This is the action of the pharmacological and medicinal remedies: to transplant the qualities for which a creature is known, the "itness" that defines its creaturely nature, into the human body and soul. It is, we might say, another way to administer ghostly physic, for it works directly on the animal and intellective aspects of the human soul.

6

Translating the Soul

In *The Life of Dr. John Donne*, Izaak Walton claims to have seen many pictures of Donne, "in several habits, and at several ages, and in several postures" (Wal. 79).[1] He recalls the engraving of Donne at age eighteen with the "adornments" that suit youthful fashion and the "giddy gaieties" of that age (figure 5).[2] Walton juxtaposes this "youthful" engraving with Donne's "dying picture," the portrait of an ailing Donne wrapped in his shroud that became the basis for his funeral monument.[3] Walton contrasts the juvenile and "dying" portraits in order to make a point: although Donne was continually attentive to change as his life's informing principle, Walton asserts, his "spiritual employment" as Dean of St. Paul's stabilized the "vertiginous giddiness" of Donne's mind (Wal. 58). For Walton, these portraits capture Donne in postures that encode life stages, habits, and an indication of inner character.[4] Walton uses ekphrastic pictures to capture the idealized qualities he attributes to Donne. He builds his *Life* through these iconic moments, which tend to "arrest" the movement of the biographical narrative and create a hagiographical portrait in the style that Richard Wendorf calls "artifacts of devotion."[5] Whereas Walton's *Life* memorializes Donne in static icons, Donne's own

1. Andrew Hadfield, *John Donne: In the Shadow of Religion* (London: Reaktion, 2021), 15–16, notes that we have an unusually large number of Donne portraits, a relatively uncommon event for a man of his social status.

2. William Marshall's engraving, which was based on a lost miniature that was probably painted by Nicholas Hilliard, was published in *Poems* (London, 1633).

3. A version of that picture was published as the frontispiece of *Deaths Duell*.

4. Richard Wendorf examines the relationship between portraiture and biography in Walton's writings in his study *The Elements of Life: Biography and Portrait Painting in Stuart and Georgian England* (Oxford: Clarendon, 1990).

5. Richard Wendorf, "'Visible Rhetorick': Izaak Walton and Iconic Biography," *Modern Philology* 82, no. 3 (1985): 270.

use of postural or gestural moments in *Devotions* activates the errancy of his mind and the mobility of his narrative. Donne's approach to all aspects of his life, including the process of dying, was to move toward change, to acknowledge his own skeptical inclinations, and to embrace the dynamic aspects of mutability even as he sought to manage the inevitable disruptions of transformation.[6]

As Walton notes, Donne placed his shrouded portrait beside his deathbed, where it became "his hourly object until his death" (*Wal.* 57). It was as if Donne hoped to see himself as he would be after he died, to glimpse his soul unfastened from his body. Walton astutely recognized Donne's motivation to know his unbodied soul when he described *Devotions* as a "Sacred picture of Spiritual Extasies" that "Paraphrased and made publicke" the "most secret thoughts" that "possest [Donne's] Soul" (*Wal.* 41). It is an instructive comment. Like the lovers in "The Exstasie," who as "sepulchrall statues lay; / All day, the same [their] postures were" (*Son.* 59; 18–19), Donne is confined to a supine position for eighteen of twenty-three stations, tethered to a bed by "sharpe sicknesse" (*Dev.* 238; 2.3). His mind and his soul range ecstatically, however, like the "*wandring sportful Soule*" in *Ignatius His Conclave* (*Con.* 5). As he puts it just before he takes to his bed, "*Ascension* is my *Soules* pace and measure, but *precipitation* my *bodyes*" (*Dev.* 236; 2.1). Although his body has fallen into recumbent stillness, his mind roams through the reaches of memory, imagination, and accumulated knowledge. As we saw in chapter 5, however, despite the split implied in "*Ascension*" and "*precipitation*," Donne is deeply engaged with the extent to which the organic soul organizes and lends intelligence to the body, thus enabling its intricate linkages with the intellect and the rational soul. This is why, in *Devotions*, Donne locates his ecstatic prospect as an intermediate state: "God suspends mee betweene *Heaven* and *Earth*, as a *Meteor*" (*Dev.* 241; 3.2). His existence, like that of the "*Humane condition*" in general (*Dev.* 229), occupies a middle space, a space of intrinsication and interanimation. Unlike the lovers of "The Exstasie," in *Devotions*, Donne consistently speculates about his illness and the world through the instrument or "booke" of his body (*Son.* 61; 72). Not yet divorced from his physical self, he hovers between his gesticulat-

6. Donne's skeptical stance is concisely captured in "Satire III": "doubt wisely; in strange way / To stand inquiring right, is not to stray" (*Sat.* 13, 77–78) and and at the end of *Metempsychosis*: "Ther's nothing simply good, nor ill alone, / Of every quality comparison, / The onely measure is, and judge, opinion" (*Sat.* 46, 518–20). For a fuller treatment of the different strands of early modern skepticism, see Anita Gilman Sherman, *Skepticism in Early Modern English Literature: The Problems and Pleasures of Doubt* (Cambridge: Cambridge University Press, 2021).

5. *Poems by J. D. With elegies on the authors death* (1635). Frontispiece portrait engraved by William Marshall, based on a lost miniature, perhaps by Nicholas Hilliard. Photograph: Folger Shakespeare Library, Washington, DC.

ing, suffering, articulate body and an immortal, inscrutable soul that can speak only "soules language" (*Son.* 59; 22).[7]

Devotions is a spiritual picture that turns Donne's body inside out, "effigiating" or creating a picture of his soul, through the symptoms and experiences of his corporeality. Like Spenser's knights in the Castle of Alma, Donne's illness takes him into the house of the soul. His proximity to death occasions speculation about the nature of his soul, his reflexive understanding of his mind, memory, the nature of understanding, and the connection between this intellective, rational soul and his organic souls. His vegetable soul manifests itself through the changes in nutrition, sleep, and purgation that his illness occasions, while his animal soul reveals itself in his compromised locomotion, changing sensations, his emotional life, and his sojourn in the "parlor of the heart" in Station 11. *Devotions* condenses the metaphor of anatomy, which structures *The First Anniversarie*, with the form of the progress, which organizes *The Second Anniversarie* and *Metempsychosis*. Anatomizing his failing body in *Devotions* allows Donne progressively to illuminate the nature of his soul.

In Expostulation 22, Donne declares that the "state of my *body*" is more "*discernible*" than "that of my soule," for God makes his soul visible through the medium of his physical being (*Dev.* 326; 22.2). While his soul is not "sensible," able to be known through the operation of the senses, his body emphatically is (*Dev.* 233; 1.2). But whereas Vesalius's illustrations of flayed bodies in the *Fabrica* display the body's inner workings, Donne's scrutiny of his symptoms—including the weakened sinews that limit or preclude gestural mobility—exposes often disregarded alliances between the bodily self and its properties. These include the orientation of the living body to health and disease, the positioning of the human substance in time and space, and the interface between spoken language and bodily gesture.[8] Put another way, Donne instrumentalizes language

7. Piers Brown, "Donne's Hawkings," *SEL* 49, no. 1 (Winter 2009): 67–86, provides an instructive account of Donne's habit of composing while on horseback. Donne likened his ranging mind to a hawk, a metaphor for the soul's flight and ecstatic communication. In *Devotions*, too, although Donne is physically pinioned by his illness, his mind soars.

8. Oliver Sacks defines a secret, sixth sense, which the Victorians named "muscle sense," the awareness of the relative positioning of limbs and trunk (registered by receptors in the joints and tendons). The receptors enabled a body to feel itself (*prioprio-ceptors*), and the sense was christened "proprioception" in the 1890s. *The Man Who Mistook His Wife for a Hat* (London: Picador, 1986), 68. Our formulation here is also indebted to Pierre Bourdieu's *habitus*, itself a reworking of Aristotle's *hexis*. For Bourdieu, *habitus* is the set of bodily habits and orientations to the world

to enact the philosophical implications of his body's arrangement in space and time through grammatical and tropological expression, elaborating a physics of felt posture or gesture.[9]

In this chapter, we track Donne's use of posture and gesture in *Devotions* as aspects that reveal his inner nature. Our analysis follows Donne's awareness as he moves progressively inward, beginning with the muscles that express posture and gesture, then moving to their implication in the nature of voluntary and involuntary movements in such states as sleep, before concluding at the heart of the matter, where all human lives must end: with the fate of a body abandoned by a soul and the will that knits them together. Adopting an expansive sense of gesture that reaches out to encompass both deliberately composed and elaborately signifying bodily movements and, more unusually, involuntary activities, we argue that Donne accentuates the semiotics of gestures by replicating them in the grammatical and metaphorical aspects of his prose. We examine Donne's reflexive use of parenthesis as a case study. Just as Donne hovers like a meteor between heaven and earth, inhabiting the long pause between conception and death, so too does parenthesis suspend a clause within a sentence. We track how Donne metaphorizes parenthesis as an image of mortal life and of the relationship between a soul and its bodily container. Even as he elaborates the philosophical implications of mortal and eternal life and the intricacies of body and soul intertwining, he enacts his metaphysical speculations in his prose, particularly in his attention to elements of grammatical organization and punctuation. Donne moves between the materiality of his text, his body, and God's presence. The curved arms of the parentheses become the celestial hands that cradle Donne in his sickness. Bodily postures and gestures orient Donne to God, whose divine hands gesture, support, and chastise him and whose terrible and loving face Donne simultaneously yearns and fears to see.

Posture, Gesture, and Voluntary Being

In Renaissance and early modern humanism, posture and gesture were together understood to create a lexicon of bodily communication. Francis Bacon evocatively called such bodily positions "transient hieroglyphs." In

---

that allow for sense-making. See esp. Pierre Bourdieu, *The Logic of Practice*, trans. Richard Nice (Stanford, CA: Stanford University Press, 1990), 69–70.

9. Posture and gesture are tightly imbricated terms. Even though both designate the body's positioning, posture is usually a noun, and even as a verb, it moves toward stillness. Gesture signals movement, even when that motion is consolidated into a noun.

fact, Bacon saw gesture as the basis for a universal language, and he chastised Aristotle for ignoring it, claiming that gesture discloses "the state of the mind and will." He recommended the observation of gesture to James I as a way to discover "dissimulations."[10] In elevating gesture, Bacon was drawing on the long humanistic recovery of ancient Roman rhetorical culture. In *Institutio Oratoria*, Quintilian recognized the supplemental role gesture played in enhancing rhetorical delivery, an aspect promulgated by such early modern rhetoricians as Thomas Wilson, who cites Cicero: "The gesture of man, is the speech of his bodie."[11] Michel de Montaigne was thus picking up on a theme popular in the culture when he catalogs the human body's sign language, which varies, augments, amplifies, and supplements the tongue's utterances. Hands, eyes, heads, eyebrows, shoulder, indeed all movements, possess an eloquence and intelligibility that is "proper to human nature" (Mon. 332; 476). John Bulwer, physician, Baconian natural philosopher, and Donne's later contemporary, intensifies this cultural interest by codifying hand gestures in *Chirologia* and *Chironomia* as what he described as the body's natural, gestural eloquence.[12]

Donne was a participant in this broad cultural investment in the practical and theoretical affordances of gesture. In *Devotions*, he develops an idiosyncratic gestural lexicon that anchors his thinking in the body, allowing his attention to shuttle between gestures and their social, philosophical, metaphorical, and spiritual implications. For instance, his shifts between vertical and horizontal postures are mobilized as verbs of rising and falling that designate physical actions, spiritual orientations, and theological events: God "calld me up, by casting me further downe" (*Dev.* 237; 2.2); "Thy hand strikes mee into this bed; and therefore if I rise againe, thou wilt bee my recompence" (*Dev.* 241; 3.2); "I fall sick of Sin" (*Dev.* 233; 1.2); "I cannot *rise* out of my bed, till the *Physitian enable*

---

10. Francis Bacon, *The Advancement of Learning*, 1605, XVI (3); IX (2). See also Marc Cogan, "Rhetoric and Action in Francis Bacon," *Philosophy & Rhetoric* 14, no. 4 (Fall 1981): 212–33.

11. Wilson, *Art of Rhetorique*, 225. See also, Quintilian, *Institutio Oratoria*, trans. H. E. Butler, Loeb Classical Library (Cambridge, MA: Harvard University Press, 1920–22), Book XI. 3, 245–319.

12. John Bulwer, *Chirologia: Or the Naturall Language of the Hand . . . Chironomia: Or, The Arte of Manuall Rhetoricke* (London, 1644). Bulwer's treatises on hand gestures and voluntary muscles are especially instructive for illuminating Donne's use of gesture. Although Bulwer's treatises were published two decades after *Devotions*, his observations depend on the biblical and Augustinian antecedents in which Donne was himself steeped. On this, see John Wesley, "Original Gesture," *Shakespeare Bulletin* 35, no. 1 (2017): 65–96.

mee" (*Dev.* 319; 21.1). He praises God's eloquence as possessing "*sinewes even in thy milke*" (*Dev.* 310; 19.2), even as he transposes physical stances into verbs as the muscles of his own prose. As we saw in chapter 3, rising and falling are coded as involuntary or voluntary, an incapacity or capacity registered in passive, active, transitive, and intransitive verbs: Donne is struck down by illness, he falls sick, he cannot fall asleep, he cannot voluntarily rise, but God will "raise" him (*Dev.* 268; 9.3), he will lie down, God will "lay" his body in the grave (*Dev.* 302; 17.3).

The Protestant understanding of illness as God's corrective visitation does not fully explain Donne's fascination with the specific operations and failures of the various positions taken by his afflicted body.[13] Yes, he acknowledges that "*affliction* is a *treasure*" that makes one "fit for *God*" (*Dev.* 299; 17.1). And yes, he recognizes the miserable, disease-prone human condition to be a consequence of original sin. Yet he nevertheless ponders the nature of the relationship between sin and bodily illness; he does not accept this relationship as a religious given, the explanation for which is known in advance. If he receives presages of illness in bodily symptoms, why, Donne asks, can he not feel sin's approach in the "*pulse*" of his soul? (*Dev.* 233;1.2). Although human beings are "pre-afflicted" by original sin (*Dev.* 232; 1.1), spiritual and physical health are intricately entangled. As we saw in chapter 4, Donne searches to know the "*root, the fuell, the occasion*" of his sickness, but no Hippocratic or Galenic physician could find it in his physical being, he argues, since it lies deeper than body or soul, in the "*union* of the *body* and *soule*" (*Dev.* 325; 22.2); and it is this "subtle knot" (*Son.* 61; 64) that he tries to "unperplex" (*Son.* 60; 29). In short, although Donne is interested in the religious etiology of what he calls our variable and miserable condition, he is also invested in understanding the living body for its own sake. And the varied positions taken by the body, its participation in the *motus* known as *latio*—the type of change or motion that, as the scholastic thinkers discussed in chapter 2 would have it, occurs when a substance changes location—are integral to the being of that body.

Renaissance and early modern humanism took bipedal uprightness as the posture that defined human prerogatives, the primacy of the intellective soul, and dominion over other living beings.[14] This was the most

---

13. Targoff, *John Donne*, 133–37, outlines this tradition, which tended to ignore the body and concentrate on healing the soul.

14. Other postural habits differentiated human beings from one another according to gender, age, activity, or class: a stooped back announced age, the *pudica* posture of a woman signaled feminine modesty, the raised right hand of the orator pro-

basic orientation of the human body, and Donne treats it extensively in *Devotions*. But he also explores much less obvious positionings that are tied up with the status of voluntary motion as it stands in relation to involuntary and natural motions. If bodily stances and gestural movements in *Devotions*—the orientation of the face, the body's uprightness, gestures of supplication—demarcate the narrative of Donne's illness and the nature of divine-human communication, they also move beyond the semiotics of bodily pose. In Donne's usage, gestural movements mark the subtle, metonymical intersection between the voluntary and involuntary that stands at the gateway between life and death. How does gesture express in bodily movement the inner states of mind and soul? As we noted in the introduction, Donne assumed the posture of death when he posed for his funerary monument, and he prepared for his own final release by crossing his hands over his body and manually closing his own eyelids. Yet as his two-week wait demonstrated, death was not voluntary. He could surrender to dying, but he could not control it through an act of will. Throughout *Devotions*, Donne moves between a proprietary and articulate inhabitation of his willed nature as he suffers through his illness, on the one hand, and his involuntary submission to the symptoms and consequences of illness and God's dominion on the other. He repeatedly models his understanding of his own sickness and approaching death on Christ's acceptance of his suffering and crucifixion: the cross "laid for me by the hand of God, and taken up by me, that is, voluntarily embraced . . . sayes Christ" (*Ser.* 2:301).[15] As we suggested in chapter 3, Donne rehearses this surrender in each station, moving from speculation in the meditations, to active engagement in the expostulations, to the acceptance of God's care in the prayer.

The unpredictable nature of Donne's illness and death situates the ultimate severing of body and soul as beyond his control, subject to God's will. He struggles to achieve a theologically ideal acceptance, epitomized by Christ's acquiescence, yet as often as *Devotions* records Donne's desire to relinquish his will, the book also registers moments of ambivalence and speculations about his own voluntary nature. His depictions of and references to free will, original sin, and predestination are tied up with a rich history, central to which are Donne's responses to the heated debates between Calvinist predestination and an Arminian freedom of the will. In this chapter, however, we direct our attention to the metonymic inter-

---

claimed eloquence. Specific postural characteristics further distinguished individuals and their habits.

15. See also *Ser.* 4:296.

section between the body's voluntary capacities and the felt sensation of losing will that Donne understood to be a property of the organic soul.[16] How are the psychic faculties of will expressed through and in the body's voluntary capacities? Elaine Scarry provides a name for Donne's intellectual and poetic fascination with earthly bodies and his wonderment that God chose to accept the human body by taking it "as his own" in Christ: "volitional materialism."[17] Throughout *Devotions*, Donne refers to God's will and to Christ's acquiescence to it in choosing to die, but he also inhabits the phenomenological sense of feeling the voluntary faculties (and their lack) as a human predicament. The deprivations of his illness reveal the nature of the capacities he has lost. He explores the complexities of his being through this progressive attrition and the fragile, precarious restitution in the stations with which *Devotions* ends. In Station 21, he contemplates rising from his bed, though still weakened by illness and still dependent on God's will: he prays that his body "may learne to *stand*, and to learne by *standing* to *walke*, and *by walking* to *travell*, so my *soule* by obeying this *thy voice* of *rising*, may by a farther and farther growth of thy *grace*, proceed so . . ." (*Dev.* 322; 21.2). This *gradatio* mimics the early human developmental stages of standing and ambulation as achievements of newfound skills, attributable not to the innate bipedal privilege he portrays as a human birthright, but to God's grace. Illness erodes Donne's voluntary capacities over time. But surrendering the will remains a necessarily contradictory endeavor. What does it feel like to capitulate voluntarily to an involuntary state like illness, sleep, or death?

For Donne, gesture marks a juncture between the volitional and the natural, an intersection that had long preoccupied medicine and philosophers of the soul. At least since Galen, physicians and anatomists sought to understand the nature of motion by studying the body's muscles. Don-

16. On the organic soul, see Katharine Park, "Psychology: The Organic Soul," in *The Cambridge History of Renaissance Philosophy*, ed. C. B. Schmitt, Quentin Skinner, Eckhard Kessler, and Jill Kray (Cambridge: Cambridge University Press, 1988), 464–84. Achsah Guibbory provides a superb view of where Donne situated himself in this controversy. Her linkages between Donne's libertine affiliations and Arminianism are especially instructive. See Guibbory, "Reconsidering Donne: From Libertine Poetry to Arminian Sermons," *Studies in Philology* 114, no. 3 (2017): 561–90. Donne remarks on Augustine and the "great quarrel" between the Dominicans and Jesuits on the question of grace and free will in his 1607 letter to Sir Henry Goodyer (*Let.* 15–16).

17. Elaine Scarry, "Donne: "But Yet the Body Is His Booke," *Literature and the Body: Essays on Populations and Persons*, ed. Elaine Scarry (Baltimore and London: Johns Hopkins University Press, 1988), 70–71. For her account of Donne's repeated engagements with philosophical, medical, and poetic versions of consentualism, see 94–96.

ne's attention to the slackened "sinews" and "ligaments" that immobilize him stimulates his thinking about motive power, agency, and the nature of his will, the appetitive faculty of the sensitive soul that governs muscular movement. His loss and recovery of mobility figure as bodily expressions of his initial dismay at, and ultimate acquiescence to, the unknown trajectory of his illness and approaching death.

Gregor Reisch's widely disseminated encyclopedic treatise on natural and moral philosophy, *Margarita philosophica* (1503), includes an instructive account of the soul's voluntary capacity.[18] Reisch was steeped in Platonic and Aristotelian theories of the soul and the learned, thorny controversies they attracted. As a Carthusian monk, his thinking was shaped by Christian and scholastic traditions, as well as Galenic and medieval Arabic writings (Avicenna, Averroës) on Aristotle.[19] Reisch's synthesis of ideas on the soul illuminates the eclecticism of Donne's engagements with faculty psychology in *Devotions*. The place of the will was a vexed question because the will belonged properly to the intellective soul, not the organic soul, which animated living beings through their organs and bodily systems. According to Reisch, who draws frequently on Augustine, the will is a rational, motive power (*potentia*), yet just as the sensitive soul has concupiscible and irascible impulses corresponding to desire and aversion, so does the rational appetite govern motion toward what "reason recognizes."[20] And yet, a version of will also belongs to the sensitive soul as part of the motive faculties, which produce voluntary progressive movement.[21]

Though not categorized as will, volition is central to inhabiting a human body. Galen's treatise *De motu musculorum* charts how motion in the body is produced by muscles contracting. He designates skeletal and facial muscles as the "instrument[s] of voluntary motion," which communicate through nerves to the *psyche*. Involuntary motion, characteristic of the inner and visceral organs, is produced by *physis*, or nature.[22] In his treatise on the muscles of the face, *Pathomyotomia*, John Bulwer asserts that "all *voluntary actions* of the Soul are perform'd by *motion*, and all *mo-*

---

18. Gregor Reisch, *Natural Philosophy Epitomized: Books 8–11 of Gregor Reisch's Philosophical Pearl (1503)*, trans. and ed. Andrew Cunningham and Sachiko Kusukawa (London: Routledge, 2010).

19. Katharine Park, "Psychology: The Organic Soul," 464–67.

20. Reisch, *Natural Philosophy Epitomized*, 239.

21. Park, "Psychology: The Organic Soul," 464–66; Cunningham and Kusukawa, *Natural Philosophy Epitomized*, 217–19.

22. Charles Mayo Goss, "On Movement of Muscles by Galen of Pergamon," *American Journal of Anatomy* 123, no. 1 (1968): 1, 4, 22.

tion necessarily implyth the use of *Muscles*."[23] Bulwer criticized Galen's "myologie," which glances only fleetingly at the voluntary and arbitrary muscular movements, and fails to understand them as powerfully expressive of the affections, the soul, and the will.[24] In his political allegory of the heart in Meditation 12, Donne designates the sinews, which he uses interchangeably with ligaments and muscles, as the *Magistracie*, the legal administration "that ties all together" (*Dev.* 279; 12.1). In "A Valediction: of my Name in the Window," the "Muscle" and "Sinew" "tile" the soul's house (*Son.* 65; 29–30). The ligaments secure his bodily self, but they also effigiate the soul's operations through felt movements or incapacities.

In *Devotions*, the posture that most defines Donne's illness involves the vertical axis, which, from antiquity, encoded rationality and human dominion. In *Mikrokosmographia*, Helkiah Crooke opens his anatomical treatise with the Platonic and Aristotelian belief that human sovereignty, the orientation toward the divine, and rational thought were a natural consequence of erect posture:

> First, man had an upright frame & proportion, that he might behold and meditate on heavenly things. And for this cause, *Anaxagoras* being asked wherefore he was born, he made answere, to behold the heavens and the Starres. Secondly, that the functions and offices of the outward sences, which are all placed as it were a guard in pension, in the pallace of the head, and in the view and presence Chamber of Reason, which is their soveraigne, might in a more excellent manner be exercised and put in practice.[25]

Donne's analysis of being "laid low" by illness in Station 3, "*Decubitus sequitur tandem*," flips Crooke's idealism about human dominion. While the inherent "advantage to Mans body," unlike other "groveling" creatures, is "an upright form, naturally built, and disposed to the contemplation of *Heaven*" (*Dev.* 238; 3.1), it also carries for Donne an innate vulnerability. In an instant a "fever can fillip him downe, a fever can depose him" (*Dev.* 239; 3.1). Any event or illness could topple him by bringing the head, which might have carried a crown, as low as his foot (*Dev.* 239; 3.1). "*Decubitus*" in Donne's Latin station title elicits a Roman posture of reclining on the elbow, an ancient habit associated with relaxation that

23. John Bulwer, *Pathomyotomia* (London, 1649), 4.
24. Bulwer, A3, A3R.
25. Crooke, *Mikrokosmographia*, 5.

Donne explicitly distinguishes from his own.[26] For Donne, to be supine is to court lifelessness. When God came to breathe life into Adam, "he found him flat upon the ground." When God prepares "to withdraw that breath," he again positions the human body "flat upon his bed" (*Dev.* 239; 3.1). According to Donne, human life is bounded by this parenthetical supine posture. God bestows breath, movement, and the illusion of willful control. By contrast, Donne's sickbed is a metonym for his horizontal state. He is paradoxically shackled by the very muscles and sinews that should obey his will, with his "slacke sinewes" acting as the "yron fetters" (*Dev.* 240; 3.2), the "strange Manacles" that bind him to his preparation for death and submission to God (*Dev.* 239; 3.1).

Lying in his bed, assuming the position of his own death, orients him to his mortal end. He says, "[t]here is another *Station* (indeed neither are *stations* but *prostrations*) lower than this bed . . . another *Story*, in the *grave*, the *wombe* of the *Earth*" (*Dev.* 241; 3.2). His supine position superimposes on present time what is to come, as if he were sinking toward his future, his bed giving way to a floor tomorrow and to a grave after that. He proleptically places himself in the tomb that he imagines undergirding his bed, and then projects himself into his own afterlife, speaking posthumously through "the stones" in the voices of the friends who will carry him in their memories (*Dev.* 239; 3.1).[27] Recruiting the word *station* for his own "Story" opposes *station*, etymologically cognate with standing, to *prostration*, a face-down position of supplication or abjection. Donne's prostration summons a classical and early modern tradition of supplication, a gestural lexicon that was anchored in social hierarchies and elaborated in divine and erotic relationships.[28] Donne spent much of his life soliciting the favor of potential aristocratic patrons, a petitioning attitude intensified by his impetuous clandestine marriage and subsequent banishment to Mitcham. *Devotions* announces itself as a supplicatory book, dedicated to Prince Charles and effusive in its gratitude to King James's patronage. That social context mirrors the depiction of his evolving re-

---

26. In Latin, *cubitum*, "elbow," is derived from L. *decumbere*, "to lie down."

27. Hannah Newton details the sickbed as prison metaphor in "Inside the Sickchamber in Early Modern England: The Experience of Illness through Six Objects," *English Historical Review* 136, no. 580 (2021): 530–67, 554.

28. For an analysis of the social and divine languages of courtesy and gesture, see Michael C. Schoenfeldt, *Prayer and Power: George Herbert and Renaissance Courtship* (Chicago: University of Chicago Press, 1991); Frank Whigham, *The Social Tropes of Elizabethan Courtesy Theory* (Berkeley: University of California Press, 1984); Leah Whittington, *Renaissance Suppliants: Poetry, Antiquity, Reconciliation* (Oxford: Oxford University Press, 2016).

lationship with God as his divine physician and sovereign. Although God has removed him from his "upright forme" and "weakened" his "bodily knees" through sickness, he finds a way to bow to God with the "knees of [his] heart" (*Dev.* 241; 3.3).[29] Echoing the penitential Prayer of Manasseh—"Now therefore I bow the knee of mine heart"—Donne captures his spiritual condition in an impossible physical gesture.[30] Whereas Donne's capacity to bend his knee requires the engagement of voluntary muscles, the beating of his heart was understood by ancient physicians to be regulated by *physis*.[31] The play between God's might and Donne's agency—even in submission—is expressed through a metaphor of physick that condenses social gesture. The metaphor also reveals Donne's desire to submit himself both to God's will and to the natural processes of illness in a moment when he has been deprived by nature of the means to express obeisance.

If the body's vertical orientation proclaims human dominion, Donne holds that its frontal plane is equally eloquent. To prostrate one's body, hide one's face, or to turn one's back on an interlocutor is to make gestures of submission, supplication, refusal, or even duplicity.[32] The postural consequence of human uprightness congregates four sensory organs

29. Donne noted the inability of the elephant's knees to bend in *Metempsychosis*: "nature hath given him no knees to bend" (*Sat.* 41; 385). This myth was debunked by Aristotle but continued to circulate in bestiaries. For instance, Edward Topsell, *The Historie of Foure-Footed Beastes* (London, 1607), 196, mentions the erroneous belief and refutes it, although he also says that when elephants age, because of their great weight, they often prefer to rest upright, leaning on a tree.

30. In the King James Bible, the Prayer of Manasseh is located with the apocryphal books, and it occupied various positions in different editions of the Vulgate.

31. Augustine, *On the Trinity*, trans. Stephen McKenna (Cambridge: University of Cambridge Press, 2002), 51 (10.7.9), comments on this catachresis, which he understands as a mistaken conflation of body and mind: "When the mind [animus], therefore, regards itself as something of this kind, it regards itself as a body. And since it is well aware of its superiority, by which it rules the body, it has thus come about that some people asked what there is in the body that is stronger than the body, and they judged it to be the mind, or the whole soul [anima] in general. And so some thought it to be the blood, others the brain, others the heart, but not in the sense of Scripture when it says: 'I will confess to thee, O Lord, in all my heart' [Psalm 110:1] and 'Thou shalt love the Lord thy God with thy whole heart' [Matthew 22:37], since by a catachresis or metaphor this word is transferred from the body to the soul; but they believed that it was actually that small part of the body that we see when the entrails are torn asunder." Donne seizes on metaphorical possibility by using the body to figure the mind's workings.

32. These postures define what anatomists call the coronal plane, an imaginary longitudinal bisection of the human body into anterior and posterior.

in the head and face, making the face the primary conduit of communication, of potential gestural or discursive conversation.[33] In *Devotions*,
Donne is acutely aware of turning his face toward death, a realization he
encapsulates in Meditation 7: "*Death* is in an olde mans dore, he appears,
and tels him so, and *death* is at a yong mans *backe*, and saies nothing"
(*Dev.* 256; 7.1). The back of the body territorializes the vulnerability of the
unseen.[34] As Donne's image of youthful ignorance of shadowing death
suggests, we may be unaware of what lies behind us, even though we may
partially discern it through other senses. In contrast to the "yong man,"
Donne's illness brings him face-to-face with death, which now coheres as
a distinct, personified shape, a being with whom he is in relation throughout *Devotions*. Donne draws on these gestural nuances to represent his
relationship with God: "I have sinned *behind thy backe* (if that can be
done) by wilfull abstaining from thy *Congregation*, and omitting thy *service*, and I have sinned *before thy face*, in my *hipocrisies* in Prayer, in my
ostentation, and the mingling a respect of *my selfe*, in preaching thy Word"
(*Dev.* 294; 15.3). His anatomization of his own sinning—a perversion of
his "wilful[ness]"—anthropomorphizes God, lending the divine a back
and a face that mirrors Donne's own.

In Meditation 19, he uses *prosopographia*—what George Puttenham
calls the "Counterfeit Countenance" (Put. 324)—to augment his figuration of God's gestural body: "But, O *Lord*, I am not *wearie* of thy *pace*,
nor *wearie* of mine owne *patience* . . . To *heare* thy steps comming *towards*
mee, is the same comfort, as to see thy face present with mee" (*Dev.* 313;
19.3). Donne initially draws solace from the sound of footsteps, anticipat-
ing that the divine footfalls will culminate in an encounter of full presence, synecdochized by God's face. The potentially infectious nature of
Donne's illness necessitates seclusion, which quickly becomes a spiritual
difficulty with which he must wrestle. In Expostulation 5, he compares
his solitude to that of a leper, the paradigmatic figure of diseased isolation: "Have I such a *Leprosie* in my *Soule*, that I must die alone; alone
without thee?" (*Dev.* 248–49; 5.2). He comforts himself in his loneliness
by recognizing that God did not appear until he found Jacob alone, and
that isolation is the necessary state for the face-to-face encounter Donne

33. We draw here on Emmanuel Levinas, *Totality and Infinity*, trans. Alphonso
Lingis (Pittsburgh: Duquesne University Press, 1969), 66, who argues that to present
the face to another is to engage in a relational interaction.

34. See David Wills, *Dorsality: Thinking Back through Technology and Politics*
(Minneapolis: University of Minnesota Press, 2008), 12, for the claim that because it
lies behind the visible, the back "names the unseen."

most desires and most fears: when in the "dereliction and forsaking of friends and *Phisicians*, a man is left alone to *God*, *God* may so wrestle with this *Jacob*, with this *Conscience*, as to put it out of *joynt*, and so appeare to him, as that he dares not looke upon him face to face" (*Dev.* 249; 5.2).

The gestural language of *Devotions* echoes the paradoxical postural tropology of "Good Friday, 1613. Riding Westward." Donne's turning of his "backe" to God at the beginning and end frames the poem, incarnating the compass points through the speaker's frontal and dorsal aspects. His backward reliving of Christ's passion in his memory's eye fills the poem's center and the space between East and West. The poem pivots around the speaker's reluctant movement westward: he is "carried towards the West," "hurried" and "whirl'd," on Good Friday, a day when his "Soules forme bends toward the East" (*Div.* 30; 5–10). The poem's gestural poetics conjures the posture of the theophanic encounter God promises to Moses in *Exodus*: God will place Moses in the cleft of a rock and cover him with his hand as he passes. When he removes his hand, Moses will see God's back, but not his face.[35] The speaker in "Goodfriday, 1613" will not be ready or able to look at the face of the Lord ("Who sees Gods face . . . must dye") until his "rusts" and "deformity" are burned off (*Div.* 31; 17, 40). In *Devotions*, Donne's sickness is the lash that eradicates his sins and prepares him for his face-to-face meeting with God. But his approach is gradual, for only through the *"physicke of life"*—the faithful physician friend who reflects and impersonates the divine—can Donne be guided toward the dazzling encounter with God that will mark his mortal end: "That thou may'st know mee, and I'll turne my face" (*Div.* 31; 42).

Sensation and the Rhythms of Sleep

Station 15, "*Intereà insomnes noctes Ego duco, Diesque,*" "*I sleepe not day nor night*" (*Dev.* 291; 15), epitomizes in diurnally condensed fashion the alternation between sensation and its absence, the voluntary and the involuntary, the body and the soul. Donne's insomnia provokes a meditation on sleep and posture, which shuttles between physical and metaphorical expression: "wee lie downe in a hope, that wee shall rise the stronger; and we lie downe in a knowledge, that wee may rise no more" (*Dev.* 291; 15.1). The play between the twinned iterations of "lie downe" and "rise" in the sentence depends on the metaphoric fungibility of sleep and death. Classical and biblical precedents nurtured the Renaissance commonplace that made sleep and death isomorphic, joined as copies of one an-

35. Exodus 33:19–23.

other.[36] A nightly state in which voluntary movement, sensory activity, and the will were apparently suspended, sleep fascinated natural philosophers, for it raised metaphysical questions about the soul and the will. In their writing on muscles, Galen and Bulwer debate the body's movement during sleep and the apparently involuntary nature of somnambulism.[37] Lucretius contrasts the relaxation and slackening of the limbs with the mind's activation in swift, endlessly creative image-making. Even as the breath "lashe[s]" the body from within in sleep, causing it to fall apart "Bit by bit," the mind is scattered and freed to roam.[38] Aristotle defines wakefulness as the capacity to exercise sense perception, sleep as the absence or incapacitation of perception (Ar. 1:721–28). He describes sleep as the "boundary between living and not living" (Ar. 1:1204; 778b), for he held that intermediate states like sleep effected the movement between being and not-being. Treatises on sleep were thus entangled with philosophies of the soul: where did thought, sensation, or even the soul go during sleep?[39] Aristotle defines sensation as "a movement of the soul through the body" (Ar. 1:721; 454a); to suspend sensation must unavoidably involve the soul. He notes in *De Somno* that all sentient animals experience alternating states in which sensation is temporarily fettered (Ar. 1:722; 454a–b). Each bodily part that has a natural function, such as the eyes or the hand, will eventually "overpass" its period of capacity and will become "exhausted." All beings capable of sensation must alternate waking states with a "dissolution of activity" or incapacity (Ar. 1:722; 454b). Rest is necessary to sustain life, but the proper *end* in animal life, according to Aristotle, is the state of waking, since it involves perception and thinking, which "what is best" (Ar. 1:724; 455b). Sleep and waking are ideally alternating symmetrical orders, bound together through a sensory system that conjoins body and soul.

36. Thomas Cogan, *Haven of Health* (London: 1605), 232, provides a typical example of the emphasis on digestion in his remarks on sleep.

37. See Charles Mayo Goss, "On Movement of Muscles by Galen of Pergamon," 17–20; and John Bulwer, *Pathomyotomia*, 30–45.

38. Lucretius, *On the nature of things*, 134–35 (4:915–53). For a fuller discussion of Lucretian influence and the atom/letter analogy, see Passannante, *The Lucretian Renaissance*. See also Fabio Tutrone, "The Body of the Soul: Lucretian Echoes in the Renaissance Theories on the Psychic Substance and Its Organic Repartition," *Gesnerus* 71, no. 2 (2014): 204–36; and Jessie Hock, *The Erotics of Materialism: Lucretius and Early Modern Poetics* (Philadelphia: University of Pennsylvania Press, 2021).

39. For relevant studies, see Daniel Heller-Roazen, *The Inner Touch: Archaeology of a Sensation* (New York: Zone Books, 2007), 65–71; and Jean-Luc Nancy, *The Fall of Sleep*, trans. Charlotte Mandell (New York: Fordham University Press, 2009).

In *Devotions*, the premise of Meditation 15 appears straightforward in its adherence to Aristotelian theory and in its extension of sleep into theological terrain. "Naturall men," Donne tells us, conceived of sleep as having two purposes: first, to refresh the body, and, second, to prepare for death. If the "*Opiate*" of sleep "locks up sense" to revitalize, its second, figurative or "*emblematicall*" purpose is more complex (*Dev.* 291; 15.1).[40] God's intention when he invented sleep was never to provide a figure of death because death was not in the picture until Man "induced *death* upon himselfe" with original sin. In his clemency, however, God then took the "fearefull forme and aspect" of death and "mended it," presenting it to human beings in the "*familiar*," "*agreeable*," and "*acceptable*" form of sleep (*Dev.* 292; 15.1). God sweetens death by putting us into "our *Enemies* hands" (*Dev.* 292; 15.1) whenever we sink into repose—for sleep, like death, is a preparatory state that unhitches rationality and mental life. The misery of Donne's illness is that insomnia denies him the generous mollification of mortality that God offers others, and does so, perversely, just when the "*Creature*" of death is "now before mine *Eies*" (*Dev.* 292; 15.1), when the sick person most longs for respite. We see insomnia from the outside in *Metempsychosis*, where the distraught figure of Eve appears carrying a child whose "moist red eyes / Had never shut, nor slept since it saw light" (*Sat.* 33; 165–66). Eve's desperation prompts her to seek opiates, poppy or mandrake, to "[cool] her childs blood" and induce sleep (*Sat.* 33; 165–68), but in *Devotions* Donne must craft a different kind of consolation.

Station 15 is the felt record of sleeplessness from the inside. If sleep suspends sensation, insomnia extends and heightens sensation through its refusals of sleep. As any insomniac knows, one cannot "fall" into sleep as an act of will. Merleau-Ponty describes the relief when the sleeper surrenders to slumber: "it is as if my mouth were connected to some great lung which alternately calls forth and forces back my breath."[41] Instead of breathing as a voluntary act, the sleeper is breathed, as if cradled in a cosmic ventilator. Donne notes in his sleepless misery that even abject prisoners who have hollowed out their own graves and lie shackled can sink into sleep. Why is he, about to enter an "*Eternitie*" in which there is no distinction of hours, compelled to watch the clock (*Dev.* 292; 15.1)? Why can he not transpose the heaviness of his own heart to his eyelids so that they might be weighted, compelling him to sleep? To recline in

40. The phrase, "locks up sense" comes from *Son.* 58; 16.
41. Maurice Merleau-Ponty, *Phenomenology of Perception* (London and New York: Routledge, 2002), 245.

preparation creates the expectation of restorative sleep, but that "incumbency" also duplicates the position of death.[42] Why is he not then able to make his sleepless suffering *"emblematicall,"* to translate his sleep-deprived condition into meaning by understanding the anguish of his insomnia as a preparation, a *"parasceve"* for a time when in God's presence he will "wake continually and never sleepe more" (*Dev.* 292; 15.1)?

Donne ends the meditation with his lamenting question about the *parasceve*, a word that designates a day of preparation before the sabbath, especially Good Friday in the liturgical calendar. Attempting to understand insomnia as benefit rather than detriment, he recalls biblical figures who in succumbing to the dangers of sleep were overcome: tares or weeds were sown while husbandmen, who should have been vigilant, slept; the watchmen guarding Christ's sepulcher were asleep when his body was supposedly stolen; and the Philistines laid hold of Samson while he slept with Delilah. In other words, God values the watchers. The watcher is a version of the *rex exsomnis*, the wakeful king, who offers a model of vigilant sovereignty.[43] The irony here is that Donne's wakefulness is not an exemplary act of vigilant will. It is an involuntary consequence of his illness. Although Station 15 is framed by the unvarying, intractable nature of insomnia, it is animated both by Donne's desire to anatomize his insomniac vigilance with articulate agency and by his yearning to melt, first into the silent opiate of sleep, and then into the tenderness of God's mercy.

Parentheses of Sleep

The idea of rehearsal, familiar from our discussion of *Deaths Duell*, informs Station 15, and not only in the sense that sleep is a counterfeit image of dying or that insomnia anticipates continual waking after death. Donne ends the expostulation with this enigmatic sentence: "Though then this *absence of sleepe*, may argue the *presence of death* (the *Originall* may exclude the *Copie*, the *life*, the *picture*) yet this gentle *sleepe*, and rest

42. Donne uses this word in his discussion of postures in Meditation 16, and as Mueller notes, he embeds within it multiple puns: reclining, holding an ecclesiastical position, the recipient of the highest university degree, and in Latin, an instructor (*Dev.* 296; 16.1; 584n [394–95]).

43. See Benjamin Parris, "Seizures of Sleep in Early Modern Literature," *SEL* 58, no. 1 (2018): 52; and Rebecca Tortaro, "Securing Sleep in *Hamlet*," *Studies in English Literature, 1500–1900* 50, no. 2 (2010), 407–26. Benjamin Parris has a more extended discussion of insomnia in Spenser and Milton in *Vital Strife: Sleep, Insomnia, and the Early Modern Ethics of Care* (Ithaca, NY, and London: Cornell University Press, 2021).

of my *soule* betrothed mee to thee, to whom I shall bee married *indissolu-bly*, though by this way of *dissolution*" (*Dev.* 294; 15.2). We focus first on the parenthetical phrase. But before we consider the words within this parenthetical phrase, let us pause on the matter of the parentheses. *Parenthesis* shares with *parasceve* the prefix *para*, a particle denoting something analogous or parallel to, but also separate from—a kind of copy. The parasceve and parentheses are joined by their capacity to create states adjacent or prior to something else, an alternate register.

Donne's self-reflexive attention to parenthesis notices it first simply as a typographical mark. Theodor Adorno reminds us that punctuation carries the residue of its history, for they are the vestigial marks of oral delivery, of embodiment.[44] Before it was a punctuation mark, parenthesis was a rhetorical figure. As rhetorical device, it designates the aside or the insertion of a clause that is grammatically independent of the main sentence. In Donne's England, the rhetorical figure of parenthesis is a dissolution of order (*Interpositio*) according to Richard Sherry's account in *A Treatise of Schemes and Tropes*, and in *The Art of English Poesy*, Puttenham classified parenthesis as a form of *hyperbaton*, a rhetorical figure of disorder.[45] Puttenham nicknamed parenthesis "the Inserter," a figure that "graft[s] in the midst of your tale an unnecessary parcel of speech, which nevertheless may be thence without any detriment to the rest" (Put. 252). He cautioned against overuse; a parenthetical insertion should be "nor too thick, nor those that be very long . . . for it will breed great confusion" (Put. 253). As a punctuation mark, parenthesis performs similar work. One of the first recorded use of parenthesis as punctuation occurs in a scribal manuscript of Coluccio Salutati's *De nobilitate legum et medicinae* (1399).[46] John Lennard claims that in its punctuating forms parenthesis first appeared in England in 1494.[47] It was Erasmus who christened the curved arms of parentheses *lunulae* for the crescent shape of the moon.[48] The promise of the waxing and waning rhythm, which is inherent in the Erasmian name for parentheses and accords with Aristotle's conception of sleep as mandated by nature, is refused by Donne's insomnia, which withholds sleep's darkness.

---

44. Theodor W. Adorno, "Punctuation Marks," trans. Shierry Weber Nicholsen, *Antioch Review* 48, no. 3 (1990): 300–301.

45. Richard Sherry, *A Treatise of Schemes and Tropes* (1550), B. iiii.

46. M. B. Parkes, *Pause and Effect: An Introduction to the History of Punctuation in the West* (New York: Routledge, 1992), 48.

47. John Lennard, *But I Digress: The Exploitation of Parentheses in English Printed Verse* (Oxford: Clarendon Press, 1991), 3.

48. Lennard, 1.

A parenthetical utterance mimics the sleeping-waking continuum: a sentence suspends a separate grammatical structure within itself, just as sleep temporarily interrupts sensation, most voluntary movement, and reflexive awareness in human life. Joan Webber shows how Donne's use of parentheses—what she calls "sentence pockets"—provide explanations for metaphor.[49] By analogy, sleep is a pocket in sentient awareness. In an analysis of Sir Philip Sidney's use of the figure in the *Arcadia*, Jenny Mann argues in a related vein that the "engrafting logic" of what many editors consider invisible punctuation is central to the plot and narrative line. Drawing on the paradoxical logic of the Derridean supplement, she claims that parenthesis operates as an interpretive device whose signifying capacities far exceed its function in a line or sentence.[50] In *Devotions*, the insertion creates a relationship of sequential oscillation between the contiguous parts of the sentence, for although they are syntactically touching, they are independent, just as states of sleeping and waking are joined but distinct. The movement between sensory registers furnishes Donne the material for his metaphorical extension into the human-divine register. Just as human mindedness fluctuates between its suspension in sleep and activation in waking, so, too, is there an alternation between material and divine forms of perception. Donne insists, however, that the parenthetical, which he equates repeatedly with mortal life, cannot be discarded, that "sojourning" in the human body is a necessary prelude to what follows: "This life is not a Parenthesis, a Parenthesis that belongs not to the sense, a Parenthesis that might be left out, as well as put in" (*Ser.* 3:288).

Webber observes that Donne's sermons sometimes use parentheses to "interlard" the text of the sermon with scriptural quotation, conjuring another voice, "whom Donne would call the Holy Ghost." His parenthetical asides thus often produce an effect of two voices speaking simultaneously, something akin to what we might now call double consciousness. The style that ensues emphasizes "interior rather than exterior meaning and blurs the esthetic threshold." Webber also suggests that Donne sometimes uses parenthesis to give definition to metaphor. He moves between a metaphor and its translation, weaving, as she puts it, between sign and symbol.[51] We extend Webber's insights by suggesting that Donne self-reflexively translates the very matter of his text in *Devotions*—his typo-

---

49. Webber, *Contrary Music*, 39.

50. Jenny C. Mann, *Outlaw Rhetoric: Figuring Vernacular Rhetoric in Shakespeare's England* (Ithaca, NY, and London: Cornell University Press, 2012), 96–97.

51. Webber, *Contrary Music*, 36–41.

graphical and rhetorical demarcations—into metaphors that enact his relationship with God.

In *Deaths Duell*, Donne cites God's pronouncement "*doe this and thou shalt live.*" The space between the command, "*doe this,*" and the consequence, "*and thou shalt live*" elides death, "the bodily, the naturall death." Although the first part of the sentence seems to "peece" well with the last part, it "never respects, never hearkens after the *parenthesis* that comes betweene, so doth a *good life* here flowe into an *eternall life,* without any consideration, what *manner* of *death* wee dye" (*Ser.* 10:241). Donne frames the interlude—what comes between a human life well lived and its eternal counterpart: the messy, mortal business of dying—as a parenthesis that God has passed over, suppressed. He enumerates the multiple modes of dying: as tender as a gentle illness that unlocks life like an oiled key or as violent as a raging, frantic fever that batters at life's gate (*Ser.* 10:241). God's sentence seems to miss the human complications of embodiment with its innumerable modes of exiting, and Donne thus supplies it as a parenthesis, which encompasses both the theatrical display of his own afflicted, failing body and his lived account of shedding a fleshly body. Whereas *Deaths Duell* is a parasceve of the death that ensued a few weeks later, *Devotions* functions as an extended anatomy of the parenthesis, of mortal life and the fraught process of departing from it.

In a sermon preached to the Countess of Bedford at Harrington House in January 1620, Donne describes human life as "a *parenthesis,* our *receiving* of our soule, and *delivering* it back againe," which "makes up the perfect sentence; Christ is *Alpha* and *Omega,* and our *Alpha* and *Omega* is all we are to consider." "*Alpha* and *Omega*" are "peeces of time" that frame our "*Occasionall*" world." In the cradle, we had no sense of what our lives would look like, and in the grave, our "sense" and memory of them vanishes. If we consider our life as an "*Alphabet,*" Donne proposes, the Book of Job provides an ideal model. Donne's alignment of Job's mortal suffering with the parenthetical interlude between alpha and omega calls on the resonant Lucretian analogy, where atoms recombine as letters in an alphabet with an apparently infinite capacity to reconstitute themselves as new words and sentences.[52] Job's "first letter, his *Alpha,* we know not, we know not his *Birth*; His last letter, his *Omega,* we know not, we know not his *Death*: But all his other letters, His *Children,* and his *riches,* we read over and over againe, How he *had* them, how he *lost* them, and how he *recovered* them" (*Ser.* 3:187–88). Donne uses the figure of parenthesis to contain everything between the alpha and the omega, the book of Job's

52. Lucretius, *The Nature of Things,* 26–27 (1.820–30).

mortal existence. Whereas human life is a parenthesis in God's terms, sleep is an analogous parenthetical interlude within the span of a human life. In mortal existence, death and sleep are copies of each other, capable of being metaphorically substituted for one another. Donne converts insomnia into sleep through a similar process of recombinant inversion: the biblical phrase *"I sleepe, but my heart waketh"* becomes for Donne *"I wake, but my heart sleepeth."* His body is in "a sicke wearinesse," but his soul is in "peacefull rest" with God (*Dev.* 293; 15.2). In doing so, he enters the gentle *"sleepe"* in which he is married *"indissolubly"* to God, but by way of the parenthetical dissolution of his illness and insomnia.

Here is Donne's description of Christ's volitional death in *Deaths Duell*: in assuming human nature, Christ "delivers that *soule* (which was *never out* of his *Fathers hands*) by a *new way*, a *voluntary emission* of it into his Fathers hands" (*Ser.* 10:248). Donne makes explicit a conversion that subtends his metaphorization of parenthesis: the curved brackets are anthropomorphized as God's hands. God cups Christ's soul between the curves of his palms, shaping and supporting through this gesture of tenderness Christ's voluntary acceptance of crucifixion and death. John Bulwer's *Chirologia* is a "manuall" (from the Latin for hand, *manus*) of rhetoric through hand gestures, the basis for the universal system of communication that became sign language, and a language that must include divine gestures.[53] God's hands are the quintessential synecdoche of his presence and divine contact, which Donne repeatedly registers in *Devotions*: his hands hold the power of death (*Dev.* 296; 16.1); Donne commends his spirit into God's hands (*Dev.* 301; 17.3); the Lord's hand made him of dust and will "recollect" the ashes (*Dev.* 233; 1.2); God's hand leads and corrects him (*Dev.* 237; 2.2). In Expostulation 6, Donne notes that *"it is a fearful thing to fall into thy hands*, and that this feare preserves me from all inordinate feare, arising out of the infirmitie of Nature, because thy hand being upon me, thou wilt never let me fall out of thy hand" (*Dev.* 254; 6.2). Falling out of God's hands, being utterly abandoned, is the most terrible eventuality to imagine, as Donne does in his sermon for the Earl of Carlisle and his company in 1622: *"Horrendum est*, when Gods hand is

---

53. On hands, see Elizabeth D. Harvey, "The Touching Organ: Allegory, Anatomy, and the Renaissance Skin Envelope," in *Sensible Flesh: On Touch in Early Modern Culture*, ed. Elizabeth D. Harvey (Philadelphia: University of Pennsylvania, 2003), 81–102. Marjorie O'Rourke Boyle, *Senses of Touch* (Leiden: Brill, 1998); Claire Richter Sherman, *Writing on Hands: Memory and Knowledge in Early Modern Europe* (Carlisle, PA: Trout Gallery, Dickinson College and Folger Shakespeare Library, 2000). Katherine Rowe, "'God's Handy Worke,'" in *The Body in Parts*, ed. David Hillman and Carla Mazzio (London: Routledge, 1997), 287.

bent to strike, *it is a fearefull thing, to fall into the hands of the living God;* but to fall out of the hands of the living God, is a horror beyond our expression, beyond our imagination. That God should let my soule fall out of his hand, into a bottom-lesse pit, and roll an unremoveable stone upon it, and leave it to that which it finds there" (*Ser.* 5:266).[54] The horror that Donne conjures is a world devoid of God's mercy and God's touch. He confronts that possibility during the extreme isolation of his illness; insomnia only heightens his misery and fear. If every ordinary sleep threatens to extend into a death from which one cannot wake, Donne's conversion of insomnia as deprivation to newfound comfort allows him to rest, even in his wakefulness, in God's hands. The parenthetical interlude of material existence—which is, as Prospero puts it in Shakespeare's *Tempest,* a "little life," "rounded with a sleep"—may also be the physical gesture of Donne being held, as Christ was in his voluntary acceptance of death, between God's curved hands.[55]

The Soul's Ears

The phrases with the widest currency in the long afterlife of *Devotions* are from Donne's three stations on bells: Stations 16, 17, and 18. The bells that tolled in nearby Saint Gregory's church—which flanked the southeast angle of Saint Paul's and filled Donne's deanery sick chamber with sound—spoke, Donne tells us, in God's voice (*Dev.* 301; 17.3).[56] The famous aphoristic fragments capture in their mortal resonances the individual embeddedness in a common humanity, a collective community, and the cosmological surround (*Dev.* 299; 17.1). They are to *Devotions* as one human being is to the continent, "a part of the *maine*" (*Dev.* 299; 17.1), but the detached pieces do not fully represent the complexity of Donne's awareness of his acoustic world, his inhabitation of a diminishing sensory body, and the compressed disquisition on the soul that he unfolds in Meditation 18. These three stations provide an occasion to revisit the endeavor of our book. We suggest that they reveal with startling clarity Donne's patterns of thought in *Devotions* and many of the motivations and disavowals that characterize his sustained, eclectic engagements with

54. See Targoff, *John Donne,* 112–14, for an analysis of this passage.

55. William Shakespeare, *The Tempest,* ed. Stephen Orgel (Oxford: Oxford University Press, 1987), 181 (4.1.157–58).

56. J. G. White, *The Churches and Chapels of Old London* (s.n., 1901), 50. Hannah Newton provides a materialist recreation of the early modern sick chamber, "Inside the Sickchamber in Early Modern England: The Experience of Illness through Six Objects," *English Historical Review* 136, no. 580 (June 2021): 530–67.

natural philosophy and medicine. Physics, metaphysics, and physick con-
verge and "interinanimate" each other in Donne's mind as he faces his
imminent death through the increasingly contracted acoustic envelope
of his dying body and his sickroom.[57]

Kate Frost assigns these three stations to Day 5 of the hexameral
week.[58] If we consider them within the trajectory of Donne's illness, we
can place them at the crisis point in his disease. Donne believed he was
dying. His physicians acknowledge that he is entering a critical phase of
his sickness in Station 14, but they are not able to pronounce him out of
danger until Station 19, when, after "*a long and stormie voyage*," they "*see
land*" (*Dev.* 308; 19.1). The bell triad between these two points records
Donne's progressive realization of his imminent death, an awareness mirrored by the sequencing of the three stations. These stations correspond
roughly to the ringing specified in *Constitutions and Canons Ecclesiastical*, in which a first bell tolled for dangerous illness, a second—called the
Passing Bell, the Death Knell, or the Soul Bell—rang for a death, and a
third bell summoned mourners to the funeral.[59] Donne supplements the
conventional pattern by likening a human being to an army in Expostulation 16: the first bell corresponds to the "*vaunt*," the forward portion, or
face, of an army, or in Donne's analogy, the departed soul; the second bell
announces the "*Reare*," the dead body, which is brought to the church
for the funeral and burial; and the third bell is calibrated "to bring him to
mee in the *application*" (*Dev.* 297; 16.2). In other words, the last bell implicates the listener through their shared mortality, an "*application*" with

---

57. For a history of English bells, see H. B. Walters, *Church Bells of England* (London: Oxford University Press, 1912), 152–64. The term "acoustic envelope" comes
from Didier Anzieu, *The Skin Ego*, trans. Chris Turner (New Haven, CT: Yale University Press, 1989), which describes the infant's early aural experience of object
relations and its surround. See also Kaja Silverman's transposition of this concept
to film theory, *The Acoustic Mirror: The Female Voice in Psychoanalysis and Cinema*
(Bloomington: Indiana University Press, 1988). Niall Atkinson's study of acoustic
architecture, *The Noisy Renaissance: Sound, Architecture, and Florentine Urban Life*
(University Park: Pennsylvania State University Press, 2016), demonstrates how
parish bells created aural communities and parishes. Bruce R. Smith's *The Acoustic World of Early Modern England: Attending to the O-Factor* (Chicago: University
of Chicago Press, 1999) offers an important general understanding of London's
soundscape.

58. Frost, *Holy Delight*, 136.

59. See Mueller, *Dev.* 585n [410–11]. See also Walters's discussion of the parish and
doctrinal controversies about the use of church bells for announcing sickness and
death in *Church Bells of England*, 152–64, and John James Raven, *The Church Bells of
England* (London: Methuen, 1906), 112–13.

theological and medical connotations.[60] The death knell Donne hears from his chamber evokes sympathy in its original, etymological sense of the word: a capacity to suffer with another. His sympathy intertwines acoustic registers, conflating the voice of the dead with the bell's ringing: "I heare this dead brother of ours, who is now carried out to his *buriall*, to speake to mee, and to *preach* my *funerall Sermon*, in the voice of these Bells (*Dev.* 298; 16.3).[61] Acoustic resonance joins their souls, a linkage of sound through the medium of air. His identification with the "dead brother of ours" projects his own role as a renowned preacher into the funeral bell, making him an auditor of his own funeral sermon.

That he may also be transcribing his experience in his memory or onto the "sheetes" he kept by his bed makes this moment an act of sympathetic translation in which he is simultaneously listener and author of the insights that would become *Devotions* (*Let.* 249).[62] Sympathy was a concept in flux in the seventeenth century. On the one hand, it described a traditional system of natural philosophical interconnections and resonances that animated the cosmos and made objects responsive to one another. This idea was supplemented on the other hand by an emergent concept of sympathy that focused on human relations and fellow feeling. Donne's auditory connection with the dead draws on both concepts, for the cosmic correspondences come to include the connections among a human community. Donne's *Devotions*, especially the bell meditations, epitomize the idea that all human beings are joined by a powerful current of feeling, a similarity of natures that binds them together. In Prayer 20, Donne contends that "*simpathy*" in "*affections*" is the glue that binds man and woman in marriage. It is also, he asserts, the bond that fastens "this soule and this body in me" (*Dev.* 318. 20.3). Walton drew on the analogy between marriage and body-soul linkage in his memorable ac-

---

60. *OED*, s.v. "application," n., 1.b., "bringing the benefits of redemption to bear on the heart of the believer" and 2.a., "administration" of a "therapeutic treatment or medicinal substance."

61. See Robert W. Reeder's discussion of this passage in relation to the theological controversies generated by extending charity to the newly departed. He argues that Donne prays to hasten the resurrection and the reunion between body and soul rather than seeking the soul's release from purgatory. However, Donne extends this Protestant position by imagining a more Roman Catholic beatific vison of God, which mirrors the "charitable extasie" of dying saints. "'Charitable Extasie' and Prayer for the Dead in Donne's "Devotions upon Emergent Occasions," *Studies in English Literature, 1500–1900* 56, no. 1 (2016): 93–110.

62. This distinction is at the center of Seth Lobis, *The Virtue of Sympathy: Magic, Philosophy, and Literature in Seventeenth-Century England* (New Haven, CT, and London: Yale University Press, 2015).

count of the vision that appeared to Donne while he was abroad with the Drurys in 1612. Donne had been reluctant to leave Ann while she was pregnant and in precarious health, *"for her divining soul boded her some ill in his absence"* (Wal. 39). He was then visited by a *"dreadful Vision,"* in which he saw his wife pass by him twice with *"her hair hanging about her shoulders, and a dead child in her arms."* The apparition confirmed for Walton what he called the *"sympathy of souls"* between them, a force that made sense of this apparently supernatural occurrence. Walton likens this psychic *"sympathy"* to two lutes tuned to one another and capable of creating harmonic echoes over distance (Wal. 40–41). Walton's account of the vision, which he recalls hearing from "a Person of Honour" who knew the "secrets of his soul" (Wal. 42), evokes a pervasive seventeenth-century fascination with magical or occult phenomena and Donne's own depictions of the communication between souls in "The Exstasie," the Valedictory poems, and the *Anniversaries* (Bal. 252). Donne's auditory connection with the dead in *Devotions* draws on both traditional and emerging concepts of sympathy, for his near-death awareness embraces cosmic correspondences as well as powerful emotional connections to the human community he is about to leave. As Donne listens to the bells and imagines the newly liberated soul of the dead man, he contemplates the severing of the sympathetic ligature that binds his own soul to his body. In his listening, he apprehends another unearthly world of sound, full of thunder, organs, cymbals, God's voice, a *"whole Consort"* (*Dev.* 300; 17.2), a congregation of biblical voices that includes Jacob, Moses, Isaiah and Hezekiah—as if the curtain between worlds had become acoustically permeable (*Dev.* 298; 16.3).[63]

In Station 18, the third of these bell stations, Donne begins to imagine himself as dead. His entrance into apparent death is initially an auditory phenomenon. The sound of the bells saturates his hearing so that their now *"faint,"* erratic *"pulse"* becomes progressively internalized, descriptive of his own faltering "pulse" (*Dev.* 302; 18.1). Donne's proximity to the church allows him to hear the *"Psalme"* and "joine with the *Congregation* in it," but he cannot hear the sermon. The bells thus become a *"repetition Sermon"* (*Dev.* 297; 16.2), speaking in a voice he identifies first as belonging to the newly departed, then as the prophets and disciples, but finally

---

63. Donne reiterates some of the superstitious myths associated with bells: they are thought to drive away evil spirits, or they possessed prophetic powers, as was the case of a monastery bell that rang *"voluntarily"* when any member of the community was sick, and on one occasion, rang for an accidental death that had yet to happen (*Dev.* 295; 16.1).

as God's voice, its *"intermitting"* clapper God's tongue: "I humbly accept thy *voice*, in the sound of this sad and funerall *bell*" (*Dev.* 302; 18.1). At first, he thanks God for reminding him in the bell's voice that he is mortal and approaching death, but when he distinguishes God's "*language* in this *voice*," it delivers more dire news: he is "*dead*, in an *irremediable*, in an *irrecoverable* state for bodily health" (*Dev.* 307; 18.3). He understands that the voice belongs not to a condemning Judge, but to the divine physician who brings death as the "*cure* of my *disease*" (*Dev.* 307; 18.3). The conversation between Donne and God, channeled through the language of the Soul Bell, occasions Donne's meditation on the nature of the soul. If, as Donne often proclaimed, God made the "first Marriage" when he joined body and soul in Adam's creation, original sin brought death that was their "Divorce" (*Ser.* 7:257). While it shares its "ecstatic" perspective with the figurations of ecstatic flights and untethered souls in his poetry, Meditation 18 is unique in being anchored in the impending severance of his own being. "Sickness," he says in a later sermon, is "but a fomentation to supple and open his Body for the issuing of his Soule" (*Ser.* 8:190).

Meditation 18 presents a compressed Renaissance psychology, a natural philosophy of the soul. Donne's 1607 letter to Sir Henry Goodyer, which Ramie Targoff calls "Donne's *De Anima*," provided an earlier version of some of these ideas, though the motivations and contexts are different.[64] In the letter, Donne compares letter writing to "a kind of extasie," a "secession and suspension of the soul" (*Let.* 11). Like the lovers' souls in "The Exstasie," this "suspension" allows communication between souls without the medium of the body. Although he wishes each day to provide for his own soul's safe "convoy," his missive is motivated, he says, by wanting to convey thoughts "concerning" Goodyer's soul (*Let.* 12). The great advantage in having a "mans soul," Donne asserts, is that, unlike beasts, human beings are capable of performing an "*Actum reflexum*, and *iteratum*." The noblest aspect of this self-awareness is the capacity to consider and meditate on the soul itself. It is not clear whether Donne's reference to the soul's reflexive function is meant as a gentle admonishment of Goodyer's financial mismanagement, his intellectual habits, or his behavior at court. If so, Donne embeds his oblique advice in a set of philosophical debates that reveal a great deal about his own intellectual

64. Targoff, *John Donne*, 11, 30–31. In his facsimile edition of *Letters to Severall Persons of Honour (1651)*, M. Thomas Hester retains the letter's heading, "*To my honoured friend S T. Lucey*," but his editorial introduction explains John Donne the Younger's alterations and inventions to bolster the prestige of the collection (xvi–xviii). See Targoff, *John Donne*, 187n25, for an account of attribution. See also Bal. 162n2.

propensities. Donne's letter targets three controversial topics in natural philosophy and theology (physick, grace and free will, and the soul) that exemplify the regrettable hardening of intellectual exploration into "dog-maticall truths" (*Let.* 13). He summarizes controversies about the soul: its origins, traducianism, how many souls there are, whether souls are spe-cies specific, infusionism, and the immortality of the soul. His purpose is not to engage in disputation on these topics, but rather to suggest how human reflexivity can counter the "lazy weariness" that afflicts true in-tellectual searching, which involves "painful inquisition" and uncertainty (*Let.* 12–19). His disquisition on the soul performs his own soul's capacity to interrogate both habits of thought that ossify knowledge and also the social and professional behaviors that arise from them.

Donne returns to these topics in Meditation 18. When his own soul is about to be unlatched, he speculates on its nature. He begins with ques-tions. If the soul has departed, "*whither?*" "Who saw it *come in*, or who saw it *goe out? No body*; yet every body is sure, he *had one*, and *hath none*" (*Dev.* 303; 18.1). The soul is, in other words, an enigma, as much to its owner as to observers. Although the soul is the necessary, animating aspect of a body, its vitalizing properties are inscrutable, visible only through the medium of a body when the two are joined, as Donne proclaimed in Para-dox VI: the soul is "enabled by our body."[65] It is equally discernible in its departure, when what it leaves behind is the bodily vacancy and undo-ing he described in "A Nocturnall upon S. Lucies Day" as "things which are not" (*Son.* 85; 18). Like health, which for Donne is known through the erosions of illness, the soul's capacities become conspicuous through absence. Seeking the location of the departed soul, Donne turns to ques-tion "meere *Philosophers*" (*Dev.* 303; 18.1), who though diverse in their beliefs, are all grouped as thinkers who consider the soul a "nothing": the materialist philosophers (Empedocles and Epicurus, who held that the soul was composed of the same elements as the body, but had "no *seperable substance,* that over-lives the *body*"), and those who focused on the similarities between human and animal souls (Aristotle, Galen, and Aquinas articulated different versions of the tripartite soul).[66] Donne's account condenses centuries of philosophical controversy in his haste to contradict these theories of "nothing" and to assert his foundational be-lief about the soul and the nature of his own thought: the defining charac-teristic of the human soul is nothing other than its self-reflexive capacity.

65. Donne, *Paradoxes and Problems,* 11.
66. For Galen and some background on this topic, see, e.g., R. J. Hankinson, "Ga-len's Anatomy of the Soul," *Phronesis* 36, no. 2 (1991): 197–233.

Turning from "meere *Philosophers*" to "*mixt* Men," "*Philosophicall Divines*," he catalogs the controversies that straddle ancient philosophy and Christianity. Having rushed through an encyclopedic array of questions about the soul's nature and its means of entering the body, Donne turns to consider its immortality, and what happens when the soul leaves the body. Does it sequester for a time in purgatory, "*in a place of torment*," or can it pass directly to God's presence? Citing Augustine's letters to Jerome and their exchanges on the nature and salvation of the soul, Donne concurs with Augustine that it is "the *going out*, more than the *comming in*, that concerns us." Given his sense of proximate death, that question takes on new urgency for Donne, evident in the repetition of his first question, now inflected with new anguish: "*Whither?* Who shall tell mee that?" (*Dev.* 303; 18.1). Donne lists everything he does not know about the dead man, as if his death had effaced even the memory of him from the world: the course of his life, his sickness, his death, or where he went. Donne comforts himself in the knowledge that he prayed charitably for his predecessor in death, now gone to "*everlasting rest*, and *joy*, and *glory*" (*Dev.* 304; 18.1)

Targoff understands the analogy of marriage and erotic relations as Donne's central figuration of body-soul relations. Death as the rupture between body and soul is best depicted as a valedictory moment, she claims, allowing the partings of Donne's valedictory poems to rhyme conceptually with his meditations on death. Marriage is certainly one of his recurrent body-soul tropes, but it offers a particular and limited window of understanding. For one thing, that analogy presupposes a soul that is unique, intellective, and immortal. Donne participated throughout his life in the dynamic conversations about the nature of the soul that absorbed ancient and Renaissance philosophers and his contemporaries. Yet as Donne imagines the final dissolution of the soul in Meditation 18, it regresses through the nutritive and sensory aspects of the organic soul, retracing the trajectory of the errant soul in *Metempsychosis*. Targoff dismisses Donne's belief in the transmigration of souls, citing his rejection of metempsychosis in his 1626 sermon for the funeral of Sir William Cockayne: "God doth not admit, not justifie, not authorize such Superinductions upon such Divorces, as some have imagined; That the soule departing from one body, should become the soule of another body, in a perpetuall revolution and transmigration of soules through bodies, which hath been the giddinesse of some Philosophers to think" (*Ser.* 7:257). Donne focuses here on whether souls could pass from one body to another, and his disavowal would have been shaped by his role as Anglican preacher at the funeral of a prominent London alderman. But Donne's dismissal of the idea as "giddinesse" cannot account for the fascination that he evinces for the metaphysical, metaphoric, and speculative dimensions of the transmigration of souls. More importantly, *Metempsychosis* explores the tripartite soul as the intellective soul's relationship to its own nutritive and animal aspects. To acknowledge the organic soul as often and as fully as he does explicitly in *Metempsychosis* and pervasively in *Devotions*, his sermons, and his other poetry reveals Donne's more capacious and eclectic understanding of how the soul animates the body, how the body's organs communicate through and express sensation, movement, reproductive urgency, and the passions.

Whatever consolations await the immortal soul at death, they do not include a merciful fate for the mortal human body it leaves behind. In the second half of the meditation, Donne turns to focus on the dissolution of the soul's dwelling place. Like the heap of ruined bodies the vagrant soul leaves in its wake in *Metempsychosis*, the un-souled dwelling is swift in its ferocious progress toward putrefaction. The dead body first loses its name, the linguistic cement that glues a person into an identity and social position. The body, its limbs "knit by a lovely *soule*," dissolves: what was a clear, sweet river becomes a "*kennell* of muddy land water" by midday and by nighttime, dissolves into the ocean saltwater. The whole "*house*" becomes sand, then dust, then a "*pecke of Rubbidge*." The body's dissolution traces a backward movement that is mirrored in the relationship between nutritive, animal, and intellective souls, Aristotelian theory filtered through Aquinas. Before human beings acquire an immortal soul, they have a "*soule of sense*" and before that, a "*soule of vegetation*." In *Metempsychosis*, the three souls corresponded to the development of human history, stretching from Eden to the early biblical civilizations of Genesis. Meditation 18 reverses that temporal movement as the immortal soul departs, leaving the vestigial organic souls behind, which quickly perish: "no more *vegetation*, no more *sense*." They return to the womb of the earth, where they diminish, are disturbed in the grave by the arrival of another dead body, and turn to dust, blown "with every wind" (*Dev.* 304; 18.1).

The condensed *De anima* of Meditation 18 captures an essential feature of Donne's thinking. Scholars have long disputed his philosophical, medical, theological, and intellectual affiliations and beliefs. Was his sensibility fundamentally Catholic or Protestant? Did he adhere to Galenic or Paracelsian medicine? Did he believe in the transmigration of souls? Did he lament the new philosophy or celebrate it? Donne was drawn throughout his life to the ferment of controversy and argument. He engaged in the debates that animated his contemporaries not because he sought certainty, however, but because these disputes vitalized his own thinking, his understanding of his own being. Donne was not a philosopher, theologian, a natural historian, a medical or legal scholar—despite his attraction to the erudition and intellectual disputations of these and other disciplines or professions. His scathing imagining of the "infected" conversations the enlightened soul might have when it returned from its ecstatic vision summons parodic figures: the "spungy slack Divine[s]" and the weak "wits and tongues of Libellars" at courts (*Ann.* A2:50; 321–34). His mind was fundamentally poetic and metaphorical, his capacity to transmute and transform erudition into images unmatched. In an undated Whitsunday sermon, Donne warns that even those who have knowledge and belief will lose them if do they do not continue to listen, to "heare." He provides a strange medical proof: "there is a way of castration," he remarks, "in cutting off the eares." To sever the veins behind the ears was thought to "disable a man from generation." The "Eares are," he says, "the Aqueducts of the water of life." To excise them is not only to "intermit" ordinary hearing, but also to castrate the soul, since by excising the organs of hearing, the "soul becomes a Eunuch" (*Ser.* 5:55).[67] Donne recapitulates philosophical theories of the soul on his deathbed as the ultimate act of his reflexive soul in a moment when God is speaking through the bell "to my *soule*" (*Dev.* 307; 14.3). It is as if he had grown that auditory organ as his soul, much like the "drowsie souls" "new eare" in *The Second Anniversarie* (*Ann.* A2:51; 339). His ear is the instrument not just of receiving sound, but of hearing the inaudible "soules language" (*Son.* 59; 22), an unending source of intellectual propagation and metaphoric generation.

67. Blaine Greteman cites this passage as an example of Donne's materialist leanings in "'All This Seed Pearl': John Donne and Bodily Presence," *College Literature* 37, no. 3 (2010): 26–42.

Coda

In the imagined anaphoric death scene of *The Second Anniversarie*, Donne apostrophizes his soul: "Think then, my soule, that death is but a Groome, / Which brings a Taper to the outward roome." He enjoins his soul to "think" with him as he envisages what the "Division" of body and soul might feel like as part of the process of dying: "Thinke that they shroud thee up, and thinke from thence / They reinvest thee in white innocence. / Thinke that thy body rots" (*Ann.* A2:43–44; 85–115). Donne's conjuring of this deathbed moment anticipates both the radical rehearsal of his own dying in *Devotions* and his posing for the marble monument that now stands in the south choir aisle of Saint Paul's Cathedral. His physician and friend Simeon Fox advocated for the monument, and Donne not only readily agreed but clearly had a vision of what the effigy would look like and how it could be fashioned. He engaged a carver to make a wooden urn and an artist to draw his picture. Standing on top of the urn, he wrapped his dying body in the shroud, closed his eyes, and turned his face toward the east.[1] Nicholas Stone's marble effigy of Donne was one of the only funerary monuments to have survived the Great Fire of 1666 (figure 6). The flames licked the urn upon which the statue stands, creating scorch marks that still attest to how narrowly it escaped destruction. Donne's involvement in the making of his monument testifies to his keen

1. Helen Gardner, "Dean Donne's Monument in St. Paul's," *Evidence in Literary Scholarship: Essays in Memory of James Marshall Osborne*, ed. René Wellek and Alvaro Ribeiro (Oxford: Clarendon Press, 1979), 29–44, disputed Walton's description, arguing that Donne could not have stood in his ill and weakened state for the time it would have taken to create the image. See also Sarah Howe, "Portraits," in *John Donne in Context*, ed. Michael Schoenfeldt (Cambridge: Cambridge University Press, 2019), 287–305; 296–303; and Philip Cottrell, "John Donne, Undone, Redone: The John Donne Monument Reconsidered," in *Death, Burial, and the Afterlife: Dublin Death Studies*, ed. Philip Cottrell and Wolfgang Marx (Dublin: Carysfort Press, 2014), 33–63.

6. John Donne's Marble Funeral Monument by Nicholas Stone (1631). Saint Paul's Cathedral, London. Photograph: Elizabeth D. Harvey.

awareness of his own afterlife in the human community. If, as he recounts in horrifying detail in *Deaths Duell* and Expostulation 18, the body and its organic soul decay to "*a pecke of Rubbidge*" (*Dev.* 304; 18.1), what remains?

Donne asks this question repeatedly, beginning in the *Songs and Sonets*, and especially in the valedictory poems. Ramie Targoff rightly suggests that the ligature between body and soul was the defining obsession of Donne's life and that its severance is mirrored in the separation of lovers.[2] But "A Valediction: of my Name in the Window" and "A Valediction: of the Booke" also wonder specifically about the capacity for the inscribed name or sent letters to reconstitute or resurrect the departed. Donne imagines resurrection not in a Christian sense of rising from the dead that engages such controversies as mortalism or psychopannychism, although he playfully invokes these ideas. Instead, he imagines the resurrection in a literary sense.[3] What will happen to his name and his writing after he dies? How will his memory and thought be held for posterity? He envisions in his witty address to his beloved in "A Valediction: of the Booke" that the "Myriades / Of letters" they exchange will become a book "as long-liv'd as the elements," that can withstand the destructive force of Vandals and Goths and still preserve the "learning" deposited in its pages: "Sciences, Spheares Music, Angels Verse" (*Son.* 67; 10–27). In the final stanza, Donne uses astronomical metaphors to chart absence: what other way do we have to calculate longitudes, he asks, "But to marke when, and where the darke eclipses bee?" (*Son.* 69; 62–63).

Just as he designed his monument to leave a material vestige saturated with significance, Donne sought to bequeath to readers of *Devotions* a durative sense of what it felt like to be suspended between life and death, hovering on the threshold of a mortal existence from which he was about to depart. The readers of *Devotions* become versions of the hypothetical bystander from "The Exstasie," who—if "refin'd" by love, if capable of understanding "soules language," if "grown all minde," and if standing within "convenient distance"—will be able to apprehend this "dialogue of one" (*Son.* 59–61; 21–24, 74). We have argued that Donne's "dialogue" in *Devotions* was a conversation with numerous named and unnamed invisible interlocutors, figures from biblical, classical, medical, philosophical, and other contexts, both ancient and contemporary. But his primary dialogue was truly a dialogue of one in the sense that he records his interior conversations with God, himself, and his soul in all

2. Targoff, *John Donne*, 1.

3. C. A. Patrides maps this controversy in "Psychopannychism in Renaissance Europe," *Studies in Philology* 60, no. 2 (1963): 227–29. See also Targoff, *John Donne*, 8–9.

the intricate, reflexive modes that we have charted here. Donne's readers participate in his intimate account of illness, of losing bodily capabilities, of being infiltrated by fear, of longing for and being terrified by the dissolutions of impending death. *Devotions*, Donne's marble monument, and Martin Droeshout's engraving in the frontispiece of *Deaths Duell* are all, we suggest, companion pieces, for they are all acts of discursive and visual translation, representations of Donne's processual dying that seek to inhabit and reveal an un-thought, and an as-yet unknown, state. We can read these memorials as embodying different idioms that augment and illuminate each other in Donne's desire for an earthly posterity.

Donne's placement of his shrouded death portrait on the opening page of *Deaths Duell* is an act of visual transposition. Below the shrouded figure was the epigraph Donne wrote: *"Corporis haec Animae sit Syndon, Syndon Jesu"* (May this shroud of the body be the shroud of the soul, the shroud of Jesus.)[4] As the body's wrapping, the shroud at once hides and displays the sunken flesh beneath it. Early modern shrouds were typically bed linens repurposed for burial coverings, and the winding sheet thus stitches sleep and its copy, death, together, a linkage that Donne probes in Station 15.[5] If the body is the soul's winding sheet, and the flesh occludes direct knowledge of its animating principle, death promises to liberate and effigiate the soul. As John Sparrow noted, the repetition of *"Syndon"* may well be a pun on his own name: "sin-done (Donne)," gesturing toward a resurrected state in which his shroud will be discarded, as Christ's was, and his sins will be at last "done."[6] The dissolution of his name will be, Donne suggests, coincident with the purging of sin. This pun echoes the refrain of "A Hymne to God the Father": "When thou hast done, thou hast not done, / For, I have more," which in the last stanza gives way to the redemptive salvation of Christ's rising, banishing sin: "having done that, Thou hast done, / I have no more" (*Div.* 51; 5–6, 17–18).

Donne's monument seems to promise resurrection in its iconographical details. Unlike many of the recumbent sepulchral effigies in the "shrouds"

---

4. Jonquil Bevan, *"Hebdomada Mortium,"* argues that Donne oversaw the preparation of his last sermon, and she details the circumstances that may have delayed its publication.

5. Hester Lees-Jeffries explores the intricate connections between bed linens and winding sheets in the context of early modern textiles and Donne's writings in "'Thou Hast Made This Bed Thine Altar': John Donne's Sheets," in *Domestic Devotions in the Early Modern World*, ed. Marco Faini and Alessia Meneghin (Leiden: Brill, 2019), 269–87.

6. The reference to John Sparrow's pun is discussed in Bevan, *"Hebdomada Mortium,"* 190.

or crypts of cathedrals, Donne's effigy is erect.[7] As he reminds us again and again in *Devotions*, although his illness imprisons him in an "inhuman *posture*" of recumbency, flat on his back in bed, he will "practise" his resurrection by "rising" (*Dev.* 239; 3.1). Donne divided his account of affliction and recovery into twenty-three "Stations," a word derived from the past participial Latin stem *stare*, to stand. The "occasions" of illness and suffering are, as their etymology in the Latin *occidere* suggest, a kind of falling. *Devotions* is architected, then, by the repetitive movements— which begin with birth—of falling and rising, of alternating between occasion and station. Donne reminds us in *Deaths Duell* that we come into the world wrapped in the "winding sheete" that grew from conception in our "Mothers wombe," and that we move through life toward death, to "*seeke a grave.*" We are bound to mortal life by "*cordes* of flesh," umbilical cords of human attachment (*Ser.* 10:233). As Christ's shroud was discarded when he rose from the tomb, leaving behind the imprint of his suffering and crucifixion on the cloth, so Donne envisions his own rising. The shrouded marble monument depicts his body in transition, ready for burial and prepared to rise again to reveal the unshrouded soul in its full light at the resurrection. Joshua Scodel interprets the epitaph that Donne wrote for his monument as beginning with Donne's own name and ending with Christ's: "he beholdeth Him Whose name is the Rising [or "the East"; *Oriens*]." Scodel suggests that "Oriens" is a "a striking and unusual appellation of Christ based on Zechariah 6:12," but the substitution encapsulates Donne's recurrent hope, often expressed in *Devotions*, that his own heavenly rising will be patterned on Christ's resurrection.[8] Donne positioned his body precisely for the picture on which the monument was based: with his eyes closed, he turned his face toward the east, a semiotic of expectation that beyond the relinquishing of his mortal body, he might face God at last so "That thou may'st know mee" (*Div.* 31:42).

Donne's first step in making his marble monument was to commission an urn. As a cinerary vessel designed to hold the ashes of the dead, the urn signals the inevitable dissolutions of the body. Donne imagines, however, that death and fire cannot completely extinguish his voice, for even reduced to dust and ashes, he can engage the power of his soul.

---

7. "Shrouds," usually in the plural, was an architectural term that designated a crypt or vault. It was used specifically for the crypt chapel at Saint Paul's Cathedral. *OED*, s.v. "shrouds," n.1.4.

8. Joshua Scodel, *The English Poetic Epitaph: Commemoration and Conflict from Jonson to Wordsworth* (Ithaca, NY, and London: Cornell University Press, 1991), 127–29.

If I were but meere *dust and ashes*, I might speak unto the *Lord*, for the *Lordes* hand made me of this *dust*, and the *Lords* hand shall recollect these *ashes*; the *Lords* hand was the wheele, upon which this vessell of clay was framed, and the *Lordes* hand is the *Urne*, in which these *ashes* shall be preserv'd. I am the *dust*, and the *ashes* of the *Temple* of the *Holy Ghost*; and what Marble is so precious? But I am more than *dust and ashes*; I am my best part, I am my *soule*. And being so, the *breath* of *God*, I may breathe back these pious *expostulations* to my *God*. (*Dev.* 233; 1.2).

If God is a divine potter who fashions Donne's funeral urn, then that action necessarily echoes the creation of Adam from clay. Donne compresses in the synecdoche of God's hand the actions of making, destroying, collecting, and scattering that shape and un-shape human life. Donne too is a creator, capable of returning the divine breath in the form of "*expostulations* to my *God*." The contiguity between the project of *Devotions* and Donne's monument is conspicuous in this formulation. Even as he acknowledges his own complete subjection to God and his own mortality, he harnesses his soul, "the *breath of God*," as an instrument of speaking, of initiating in the first station a conversation that will become the whole of *Devotions*. It is a striking moment with which to inaugurate *Devotions*, for he represents his voice as continuing to speak even after his death and dissolution. Donne's meditation on the urn extends his early erotically inflected insight from "The Canonization": "As well a well wrought Urne becomes / The greatest ashes, as halfe-acre tombes" (*Son.* 74; 33–34). Monuments may crumble and burn, ashes will scatter and be reduced to dust, but sonnets, expostulations, elegies, sermons are made of breath and air and partake in the ongoing life of the soul.

Donne's depiction of himself in his shroud affiliates his monument with *transi* sculptures, the tomb monuments portraying shrouded, emaciated, sometimes decaying and worm-eaten corpses that first appeared at the end of the fourteenth century. In contrast to *gisants*, funeral effigies depicting the dead in midlife, often dressed in armor or elaborate dress (reminiscent, perhaps, of the "sepulchrall statues" of "The Exstasie" [*Son.* 59; 18]), *transi* sculptures were gruesome reminders of the inevitability of death and the horrors of decay that await all humans.[9] Appropriate to his conception of the transitional passage between states that he figures in

9. See Kathleen Cohen, *Metamorphosis of a Death Symbol: The Transi Tomb in the Late Middle Ages and Renaissance* (Berkeley: University of California Press, 1973); and Marisa Anne Bass, "The *Transi* Tomb and the *Genius* of Sixteenth-Century Netherlandish Funerary Sculpture," *Netherlands Yearbook for History of Art* 67 (2017):

Devotions, to the active process of dying and physical decomposition that the body underwent and the dynamic sense of bodily resurrection that he imagined, Donne's own *transi* monument captures his inhabitation of death as a process. Wrapped in the shroud that will envelop him when he is dead and no longer sentient, he proleptically experiences his own burial when he poses for the monument.

One type of *transi* tomb juxtaposed *gisants* and *transi* figures, the idealized figure above and a cadaverous or decaying corpse beneath it. These statues were often positioned as layered recumbencies, although some tombs depicted the living, idealized figure in erect or kneeling postures. Donne was familiar with the layered *transi* tomb. The Christian humanist John Colet, who died in 1519, was Donne's predecessor as dean of Saint Paul's, and his *transi* tomb was situated on the south aisle of the church next to where Donne's monument now stands. The tomb was destroyed in 1666 but survives in an engraving that features a bust of Colet with the compartment beneath it holding a skeleton.[10] The Herbert tomb at Montgomery Church in Wales may offer an even more influential model for Donne. It incorporates a *transi* figure underneath the *gisants* effigies of Sir Richard Herbert and Magdalene Herbert, and Donne must have known it because he records his journey to visit the Herbert family in their Montgomery castle in "Good Friday, 1613. Riding Westward."[11] Donne's awareness of the double *transi* tomb haunts his representation of his sickbed as subtended by death: "A sicke bed, is a grave; and all that the patient saies there, is but a varying of his owne *Epitaph*. Every nights bed is a *Type* of the *grave*." Donne's metaphoric compression of bed and grave draw on the familiar layering of sleep and death, but adds another element. In his proleptic "entombment" of the sickbed, he imagines not the silence of death, but communicating: "In the *Grave* I may speak through the stones, in the voice of my friends, and in the accents of those wordes, which their love may afford my memory" (*Dev.* 239; 3.1). His capacity to speak back to God through his dissolution into ash and dust is enabled by the divine breath that is his soul; his voice is made possible by memory and human community. Through the "voice" and "accents of those wordes" that they remember, he comes alive again, carried by the translation of his word through the "voice of his friends."

This potent vision of Donne's capacity for his words to live beyond his

---

160–87. For an evocative treatment of the grim ubiquity of death in Donne's life, see Rundell, in *Super-Infinite*, 276–90.

10. Cohen, *Metamorphosis of a Death Symbol*, xii, 126–28, fig. 78.

11. Philip Cottrell, "John Donne, Undone, Redone," 43, Bal. 270, *Dev.* 487.

burial is cognate with his memorialization of Elizabeth Drury in *The Anniversaries*. In "A Funerall Elegie," Donne contrasts her confinement to a monumental tomb, the "Marble chest" her parents provided, with "these memorials, ragges of paper" that will attempt to give life "to that name." Can she "stoope to bee / In paper wrap't; Or, when she would not lie / In such a house, dwell in an Elegie?" (*Ann.* 35–36; 1–18). Being "wrap't" in paper evokes the "sheet," both a shroud and the writing material upon which Donne inscribes his elegy. His hope, which is entangled with his bid for patronage from the Drurys and the doubleness of the elegiac endeavor, is that his poetic commemoration will help restore Elizabeth Drury to her grieving parents and allow his poetic reputation to flourish. He proposes to build her a house of verse, a memorial container more lasting than tombs of stone, that will allow her to continue to live. Donne's project in *The Anniversaries* is echoed in his hopes for *Devotions*. If he is physically wrapped in his winding sheet as he poses for his memorial picture, he also keeps the twenty "sheetes" upon which he composed his meditations (*Let.* 249), for they were, he tells us, his physick.[12] The *Hexastichon Bibliopolae* that prefaces the 1633 edition of Donne's *Poems* and was probably written by publisher, John Marriot, capitalizes on the pun:

> I see in his last preach'd and printed booke,
> His picture in a sheete; in *Pauls* I looke,
> And see his Statue in a sheete of stone,
> And sure his body in the grave hath one:
> Those sheetes present him dead, these if you buy,
> You have him living in Eternity.[13]

Like the house of elegy that Donne imagines building for Elizabeth Drury, and like the poems that John Marriot believes will immortalize their writer, Donne's *Devotions* is a way of speaking beyond the grave about dying, of literally "imprinting" his dying body on the burial sheets that shroud his body.

Sir Christopher Wren, astronomer and scientist, was the architect of the new Saint Paul's, which he built from the ashes of the old cathedral

12. Mathews, ed., *Collection of Letters*, 302–3.

13. John Marriot [?], "Hexastichon Biliopolae," in *Poems, by J.D. with Elegies on the authors death* (London, 1633), sig. A2v. Erin A. McCarthy provides a fully contextualized account of the publication of the 1633 edition and of Marriot's "Hexastichon Bibliopolae": *Doubtful Readers: Print, Poetry, and the Reading Public in Early Modern England* (Oxford: Oxford University Press, 2020): 150–58. Sarah Howe also discusses this verse in "Portraits," 303.

after the Great Fire. His memorial lies in the church's crypt, its "shrouds." Affixed to the wall above the plain black marble slab that marks his grave is an epitaph that ends with these words: "*Lector, Si Monumenta Requiris, Circumspice*" (Reader, if you seek his memorial, look around you). We might well transpose these words to Donne's monument. Although his marble effigy remains in the cathedral, supplemented by its punning epitaph and saturated with postural and iconographic meaning, if you seek his memorial, he is most fully to be found in *Devotions*, in the voice that continues to speak from the stones and dust to God and to his readers.

Acknowledgments

We have been working on this book since the autumn of 2009, for more than fourteen years. Over these years, we have had the good fortune of living with families and among communities that have supported us and our work. We have been recipients of many acts of kindness and generosity that have enabled and enriched this book.

We began working together in 2009 at the University of Toronto, where Tim was a second-year PhD student and Elizabeth was a professor of English. When Tim finished his PhD and moved to Chicago as an assistant professor, we continued our biweekly sessions long distance, and over the years, we have spent more than five hundred hours meeting to discuss Donne, *Devotions*, and this book. It is with profound joy that we usher it into the world now—and just a little sadness. The sadness springs, in part, from the fact that this book has lived alongside us for so long, and has therefore been part of our lives, woven in with many other happenings, both professional and personal: the launching of one academic career and the ending of another, the birth and maturation of children, the death of parents. The various lives lived over the course of these nearly fifteen years have enriched this book in countless ways.

We are grateful to the many friends and colleagues who have supported us over the years. Richard Strier read the whole manuscript with his typical sharp-eyed incisiveness and wit. We would like to thank him for what, at the time, felt like bitter physick, but now, with more hindsight, we see as pure critical honey. Joshua Scodel read many of the book's chapters, and we are exceedingly grateful for his willingness to share the breadth of his learning and for his ability (a gift, really) to truly see what other scholars are trying to do and then to frame his comments correspondingly. We also thank Arnold Brooks, Jeff Dolven, Kathy Eden, Katie Kadue, Jonathan Lear, Ross Lerner, and Ted Tregear for reading various parts of the manuscript and offering excellent feedback, criticisms, and suggestions. Early feedback from audiences at the Center for Renaissance and Reformation Studies at the University of Toronto and, years later, from the Renaissance Workshop at the University of Chicago, was deeply helpful. We thank the participants at those events, especially Philip Gold-farb Styrt, Lynne Magnusson, Mary Nyquist, and Adam Rzepka.

The two anonymous readers for the University of Chicago Press were outstanding. We thank both readers for understanding our book so well and for offering clear-eyed suggestions for how it could be improved. We are grateful for Alan Thomas, whose early belief in the project was crucial, and to Randy Petilos, who shepherded the book through the publication process with sure hands and great wisdom. Our copyeditor, Mark Reschke, was judicious and insightful. Melanie Simoes Santos pro-vided invaluable editorial and bibliographical assistance. Our line editor, Amy Sherman, offered excellent suggestions. We would also like to thank Alyssa Mulé, who read the manuscript and combed it for errors with ex-traordinary skill. We thank Anne Robertson, then dean of the Division of the Humanities at the University of Chicago, who generously provided a subvention for the book.

TIMOTHY HARRISON

As I transition from the *we* of coauthored gratitude to the *I* of these more individual acknowledgments, I need to begin by thanking Elizabeth, who went so far above and beyond in her duties as PhD supervisor that she ended up coauthoring an article and now a book with me. It was such an enormous privilege to be able to learn how to write scholarly prose from someone so expert in its idioms. I literally cannot imagine my intellec-tual or scholarly trajectory without Elizabeth at its heart. Beginning my scholarly career with collaboration as a central feature of my intellectual life has shaped so much of what I now do and also the kind of work I now value.

I am grateful to have worked at the University of Chicago alongside so many inspiring PhD students, with whom I have discussed Donne and his works in graduate seminars, in workshops, or just as part of everyday conversation. I would like to thank Beatrice Bradley, Ryan Campagna, Andrés Irigoyen, Ben Jeffery, Sarah Kunjummen, Sarah-Gray Lesley, Alyssa Mulé, Kashaf Qureshi, and Michal Zechariah. I have learned so much from each of them, and it is a real privilege to be able to think in their company. I benefited enormously from teaching an undergraduate class titled "John Donne's Poetry and Prose" in spring 2023, some insights from which were *just* able to sneak their way into this book, and from teaching Donne's *Metempsychosis* in two iterations of my "Early Modern Natality" graduate class. The University of Chicago has provided me with an astonishingly rich intellectual and social world, and I want to thank everyone with whom I have had the pleasure of working. To my early modern coconspirators, Ellen MacKay and Noémie Ndiaye: I couldn't imagine being on a better, kinder, more brilliant team. Jane Mikkelson has been a real source of inspiration and wonder, first as a PhD student with whom I was working and now as a coauthor on another book project; my work with Jane has helped to flesh out my sense of what collaboration enables and entails. One of the best things I have done since arriving in Chicago is audit courses taught by other professors. I have learned many things from doing so, some of which are present in this book in both implicit and explicit ways. For allowing me to participate in their seminars, I want to thank David Finkelstein, Susan James, Gabriel Lear, Jonathan Lear, Jean-Luc Marion, and Justin Steinberg. Due to their conversation and comradery, my life is made much better by working with Adrienne Brown, Bill Brown, Joel Isaac, Patrick Jagoda, Heather Keenleyside, Jo McDonagh, Mark Miller, Debbie Nelson, Sianne Ngai, Julie Orlemanski, Thomas Pavel, Mark Payne, Zach Samalin, Sarah Pierce Taylor, Chris Taylor, Ken Warren, and S. J. Zhang.

One of the most surprising things to happen during the period when I was working on this book was the truly wonderful pandemic "bubble" that formed between my family; Edgar Garcia, Alexis Chema, and their daughter; and Ben Saltzman, Ashleigh Langs Saltzman, and their children. It makes me happy to think both about that year (when we raised each other's children and it came to seem as though we were family) and about our continuing friendship. It is a testament to how supported I felt in that moment of crisis that I was able to write almost one hundred drafty pages of this book in 2020, of all years (many of them at the "tree house" in the week before I submitted my tenure file). I am also grateful for sustaining friendships with Cristi Alvarado, Joe Stadolnik, Tina Post, and Mark Temelko.

I would also like to thank the rich community of scholars from whom I have learned and laughed over the years, particularly Jason Peters and Ethan Guagliardo, with whom I have been friends for about as long as I've been writing this book. For brilliant conversation about Donne and other things, I want to thank Brian Cummings, Roland Greene, Achsah Guibbory, Russ Leo, David Marno, Jeff Miller, Jerry Passannante, Joanna Picciotto, David Quint, Ayesha Ramachandran, David Simon, and Nigel Smith.

I am also grateful to my parents, Sam and Helen Harrison, and to my brother, Jeff, for their love and ongoing interest in whatever it is that I am doing. It is only later in my life that I am beginning to recognize how amazing it was to grow up in a family in which the question "How should one live one's life?" did not come with a readymade answer. My family-in-law—Ina and Bert Smit, Paulien Smit and Peter Machiel Lotgering, Derk Smit and Anna Zdunek—has been extraordinarily kind and supportive over the years as well: much of this book was written in one or another of their homes in the northern Netherlands—in Groningen, in Sauwerd, or in Winsum, in the latter of which these words were written.

My daughters, Livia and Elise, have lived their whole lives with this book occupying some place in the background of our family life, which brings me joy and delight. I am grateful that the biweekly meetings that stand behind this book enabled them to get to know their "Aunt Elizabeth." My wife, Christina Smit, has been with me since before this book began to be written, and we have grown together over the nearly fifteen years of its composition in ways I could not have imagined in 2009. In the intervening years, we have had two children, immigrated to a new country, struggled to launch careers, and worked to make the place in which we live a real home. Through all of it, our love has remained that around which my life is organized and that according to which my life is oriented. I am proud of Christina and of our family, and in them I see one of Donne's favorite metaphors literalized: they are my world.

ELIZABETH HARVEY

Working with Tim, first as a student and then as a coauthor, has been one of the greatest gifts of my career. The relationship evolved quickly into a collaborative and reciprocal exploration, and our intellectual bond became a friendship that included our families. It has been an ongoing delight to see his children, Livia and Elise, come into the world and to watch them growing up. Tim's prodigious energy, endless curiosity, generosity, and remarkable erudition continually inspire me. Our mutual excitement about Donne has inflected our years of working together. It is perhaps the ultimate joy for any teacher to have learned so much from a student and to have lived through his transformation into an esteemed colleague.

I have received vital support from numerous sources and people during the many years of this book's gestation. I am profoundly grateful to the Folger Institute for a long-term Andrew W. Mellon Fellowship, which allowed me to participate in the extraordinary community of scholars gathered there and to consult their rich collection of Donne materials. The Jackman Humanities Institute at the University of Toronto gave me a glorious year of fellowship and inspiring exchanges of many kinds. The Social Sciences and Humanities Research Council of Canada supported my research in numerous projects that have found their way into this book. My colleagues in the Department of English at the University of Toronto have contributed their keen insight and collegial generosity in formative ways. I am especially grateful to Brian Corman, David Galbraith, Linda Hutcheon, Thomas Keymer, Katherine Larson, Lynne Magnusson, Mary Nyquist, John Rogers, and Paul Stevens. Audiences at RSA and MLA helped me clarify my ideas, and I have benefited from their questions and comments. Many scholars, friends, and colleagues have inspired and sustained me: Ramie Targoff, Lynn Enterline, Paula Blank (1959–2016), Cynthia Marshall (1954–2005), Susan Zimmerman, Piers Brown, Michael Schoenfeldt, Ayesha Ramachandran, Valerie Traub, Garrett Sullivan, Mary Floyd Wilson, Joel Faflak, Jonathan Crewe, Gail Kern Paster, Bruce R. Smith, Theresa Krier, and Margaret Ferguson. I have been fortunate in working with gifted research assistants, Piers Brown, Timothy Harrison, Mingjun Lu, and Katherine Larson, all of whom are now established colleagues in the profession. Conversations with my undergraduate and graduate students over many years have refined and deepened my understanding of Donne's thought.

I thank my colleagues in the psychoanalytic community for their listening and their friendship: Gordon Yanchyshyn, Taras Babiak, Steven Cooper, Chris Trevelyan, and Christina Connell.

Julie Joosten reads everything I write. She is brilliantly fluent in the languages of the soul.

My parents were lovers of literature and words. My mother, Sheila Harvey Tanzer (1928–2022), died during the final stage of writing this book. Caring for her in the last weeks of her life helped me to understand dying as a process. My father, Lawrence Elliot Harvey (1925–88), died tragically and too young many years ago, but his death introduced me to Donne's *Devotions upon Emergent Occasions*. They both live in this book in different ways.

My immediate family has been heroically patient throughout the writing of this book. My children, Nick and Anthea, are unfolding sources of joy and wonder. Nothing that I have done in this life could have happened without the wisdom, generous companionship, and capacious intellect of Mark Cheetham, who lights up my world with his "wildly constant" presence.

Bibliography

Adorno, Theodor W. "Punctuation Marks." Translated by Shierry Weber Nicholsen. *Antioch Review* 48, no. 3 (1990): 300–305.

Agrippa, Henry Cornelius. *Three Books of Occult Philosophy*. London, 1650.

Alighieri, Dante. *Dante con l'espositione di M. Bernardino Daniello da Lvcca, sopra la sua Comedia dell'Inferno, del Purgatorio, & del Paradiso*. Venice: Pietro da Fino, 1568.

Alighieri, Dante. *Inferno*. Translated by Robert Hollander and Jean Hollander. New York: Anchor, 2000.

Allen, D. C. "John Donne's Knowledge of Renaissance Medicine." *JEGP* 42, no. 3 (1943).

Allen, Phyllis. "Medical Education in 17th Century England." *Journal of the History of Medicine and Allied Sciences* 1, no. 1 (1946): 115–43.

Anzieu, Didier. *The Skin Ego*. Translated by Chris Turner. New Haven, CT: Yale University Press, 1989.

Arbesmann, Rudolph. "The Concept of 'Christus Medicus' in St. Augustine." *Traditio* 10 (1954): 1–28.

Aristotle. *The Complete Works of Aristotle*. Edited by Jonathan Barnes. 2 vols. Princeton, NJ: Princeton University Press, 1984.

Atkinson, Niall. *The Noisy Renaissance: Sound, Architecture, and Florentine Urban Life*. University Park: Pennsylvania State University Press, 2016.

Augustine. *City of God against the Pagans*. Translated by R. W. Dyson. Cambridge: Cambridge University Press, 1998.

Augustine. *Confessiones*. Edited by William Watts. Cambridge, MA: Harvard University Press, 1912.

Augustine. *Confessions*. Translated by Henry Chadwick. Oxford: Oxford University Press, 1991.

Augustine. *De Doctrina Christiana*. Edited and translated by R. P. H. Green. Oxford: Clarendon Press, 1995.

Augustine. *On the Trinity*. Translated by Stephen McKenna. Cambridge: University of Cambridge Press, 2002.

Augustine. *The Works of Saint Augustine: A Translation for the 21st Century*. 41 vols. Translated by Edmund Hill. New York: New City, 1995.

Avicenna. *The Physics of the Healing*. Translated by Jon McGinnis. 2 vols. Provo, UT: Brigham Young University Press, 2009.

Bacon, Francis. *The Proficience and Advancement of Learning, Divine and Human*. In *The Philosophical Works of Francis Bacon*, edited by John M. Robertson, 39–176. London: George Routledge & Sons, 1905. Reprint, London: Routledge, 2011.

Bald, R. C. *John Donne: A Life*. Oxford: Clarendon, 1970.

Bardout, Jean-Christophe. "Johannes Clauberg." In *A Companion to Early Modern Philosophy*, edited and translated by Steven Nadler, 129–39. Malden, MA: Blackwell, 2002.

Bass, Marisa Anne. "The *Transi* Tomb and the *Genius* of Sixteenth-Century Netherlandish Funerary Sculpture." *Netherlands Yearbook for History of Art* 67 (2017): 160–87.

Batman, Stephan. *Batman uppon Bartolome*. London, 1582.

Bede. *The Reckoning of Time*. Translated by Faith Wallis. Liverpool: Liverpool University Press, 1999.

Bevan, Jonquil. "'*Hebdomada Mortium*': The Structure of Donne's Last Sermon." *RES* 45, no. 178 (1994): 185–203.

Binda, Hilary. "'My Name Engrav'd Herein': John Donne's Sacramental Temporality." *Exemplaria* 23 (2013): 390–414.

Blount, Thomas. *Glossographia*. London, 1656.

Boas, George. *The Happy Beast in French Thought of the Seventeenth Century*. Baltimore: Johns Hopkins University Press, 1933.

Bolton, Edmund. *The Elements of Armories*. London, 1610.

Bourdieu, Pierre. *The Logic of Practice*. Translated by Richard Nice. Stanford, CA: Stanford University Press, 1990.

Bowra, C. M. *From Virgil to Milton*. London: MacMillan, 1963.

Boyle, Marjorie O'Rourke. *Senses of Touch*. Leiden: Brill, 1998.

Boyle, Marjorie O'Rourke. *Cultural Anatomies of the Heart in Aristotle, Augustine, Aquinas, Calvin, and Harvey*. Cham, Switzerland: Palgrave Macmillan, 2018.

Bredvold, Louis I. "The Naturalism of Donne in Relation to Some Renaissance Traditions." *Journal of English and Germanic Philology* 22, no. 4 (1923): 471–502.

Brooks, Arnold. "A Fault Line in Aristotle's *Physics*." *Ancient Philosophy* 39 (2019): 335–61.

Brown, Piers. "Donne and the *Sidereus Nuncius*: Astronomy, Method and Metaphor in 1611." PhD diss., University of Toronto, 2009.

Brown, Piers. "Donne's Hawkings." *SEL* 49, no. 1 (2009): 67–86.

Bulwer, John. *Chirologia: Or the Naturall Language of the Hand . . . Chironomia: Or, The Arte of Manuall Rhetoricke*. London, 1644.

Bulwer, John. *Pathomyotomia*. London, 1649.

Calvin, Jean. *Commentary on First Corinthians*. Translated by John W. Fraser. Grand Rapids, MI: Eerdmans, 1996.

Carew, Thomas. *The Poems of Thomas Carew*. Edited by Rhodes Dunlap. Oxford: Clarendon, 1949.

Carey, John. *John Donne: Life, Mind and Art*. London: Faber and Faber, 1981.

Carlino, Andrea. *Books of the Body: Anatomical Ritual and Renaissance Learning*. Translated by John Tedeschi and Anne C. Tedeschi. Chicago: University of Chicago Press, 1999.

Cary, Philip. *Augustine's Invention of the Inner Self: The Legacy of a Christian Platonist*. Oxford: Oxford University Press, 2003.

The Cloud of Unknowing. Edited by Phyllis Hodgson. Salzburg: Institut für Anglistik, 1982.

Coffin, Charles M. *John Donne and the New Philosophy*. New York: Columbia University Press, 1937. Reprint, New York: Humanities Press, 1958.

Cogan, Marc. "Rhetoric and Action in Francis Bacon." *Philosophy & Rhetoric* 14, no. 4 (1981): 212–33.

Cogan, Thomas. *Haven of Health*. London: 1605.

Cohen, Kathleen. *Metamorphosis of a Death Symbol: The Transi Tomb in the Late Middle Ages and Renaissance*. Berkeley: University of California Press, 1973.

Conant, James. "Theological Sources of Modern Conceptions of Logic." In *The Logical Alien: Conant and His Critics*. Edited by Sofia Miguens, 376–404. Cambridge, MA: Harvard University Press, 2020.

Conti, Brooke. *Confessions of Faith in Early Modern England*. Philadelphia: University of Pennsylvania Press, 2014.

Conti, Brooke. "Devotional Prose." In *John Donne in Context*. Edited by Michael Schoenfeldt, 256–65. Cambridge: Cambridge University Press, 2019.

Cook, Harold J. *The Decline of the Old Medical Regime in Stuart London*. Ithaca, NY: Cornell University Press, 1986.

Cottrell, Philip. "John Donne, Undone, Redone: The John Donne Monument Reconsidered." In *Death, Burial, and the Afterlife: Dublin Death Studies*, edited by Philip Cottrell and Wolfgang Marx, 33–63. Dublin: Carysfort Press, 2014.

Courcelle, Pierre. *Les Confessions de Saint Augustin dans la tradition littéraire*. Paris: Institut d'Etudes Augustiniennes, 1963.

Crane, Mary Thomas. "John Donne and the New Science." In *The Palgrave Handbook of Early Modern Literature and Science*. Edited by Howard Marchitello and Evelyn Tribble, 95–114. London: Palgrave Macmillan, 2017.

Crane, Mary Thomas. *Losing Touch with Nature: Literature and the New Science in Sixteenth-Century England*. Baltimore: Johns Hopkins University Press, 2014.

Creighton, Michael. *History of Epidemics in Britain*. Cambridge: Cambridge University Press, 1891.

Croll, Morris W. *Style, Rhetoric and Rhythm: Essays by Morris W. Croll*. Edited by J. Max Patrick and Robert O. Evans. Princeton, NJ: Princeton University Press, 1966.

Crooke, Helkiah. *Mikrokosmographia*. London, 1615.

Culler, Jonathan. *Theory of the Lyric*. Cambridge, MA: Harvard University Press, 2015.

Culpeper, Nicholas. *A Physicall Directory or a translation of the London Dispensatory Made by the College of Physicians of London*. London, 1649.

Cummings, Brian. "Donne's Passions: Emotions, Agency and Passions." In *Passions and Subjectivity in Early Modern Culture*, edited by Brian Cummings and Freya Sierhuis, 51–71. Farnham, Surrey: Ashgate, 2013.

Cummings, Brian. *The Literary Culture of the Reformation: Grammar and Grace*. Oxford: Oxford University Press, 2002.

Da Lucca, Bonagiunta. "Voi, Ch'avete mutata la mainera." In *The Poetry of Guido Guinizelli*, edited and translated by Robert Edwards, 58–59. New York: Garland, 1987.

Daston, Lorraine. "Historical Epistemology." In *Questions of Evidence: Proof, Practice, and Persuasion across the Disciplines*, edited by James Chandler, Arnold I.

Davidons, and Harry D. Harootunian, 282–89. Chicago: University of Chicago Press, 1994.

Daston, Lorraine and Peter Gallison. *Objectivity*. Cambridge, MA: Zone Books, 2007.

Davidson, Arnold. *Emergence of Sexuality: Historical Epistemology and the Formation of Concepts*. Cambridge, MA: Harvard University Press, 2001.

Dear, Peter. *Discipline and Experience: The Mathematical Way in the Scientific Revolution*. Chicago: University of Chicago Press, 1995.

Des Chene, Dennis. *Physiologia: Natural Philosophy in Late Aristotelian and Cartesian Thought*. Ithaca, NY: Cornell University Press, 1996.

DiPasquale, Theresa M. "Donne's Naked Time." *John Donne Journal* 29 (2010): 33–44.

DiPasquale, Theresa M. "From Here to Aeviternity: Donne's Atemporal Clocks." *Modern Philology* 110, no. 2 (2012): 226–52.

Docherty, Thomas. *John Donne, Undone*. London: Methuen, 1986.

Dolven, Jeff. *Senses of Style: Poetry before Interpretation*. Chicago: Chicago University Press, 2017.

Donne, John. *Biathanatos a declaration of that paradoxe or thesis, that selfe-homicide is not so naturally sinne*. London: John Dawson, 1644.

Donne, John, ed. *A Collection of Letters Made by Sr Tobie Matthews, Kt*. London, 1660.

Donne, John. *The Complete Poetry and Selected Prose*. Edited by Charles M. Coffin. New York: Random House, 2001.

Donne, John. *Devotions upon Emergent Occasions*. In *John Donne: 21st-Century Authors*, edited by Janel Mueller. Oxford: University of Oxford Press, 2015.

Donne, John. *The Divine Poems*. Edited by Helen Gardner. Oxford: Clarendon, 1959.

Donne, John. *Donne: Poetical Works*. Edited by J. C. Grierson. Oxford: Oxford University Press, 1971.

Donne, John. *The Elegies and The Songs and Sonnets*. Edited by Helen Gardner. Oxford: Clarendon, 1966.

Donne, John. *The Epithalamions, Anniversaries, and Epicedes of John Donne*. Edited by Wesley Milgate. Oxford: Clarendon, 1978.

Donne, John. *Essayes in Divinity*. Edited by Anthony Raspa. Montreal: McGill-Queen's University Press, 2001.

Donne, John. *Essays in Divinity*. Edited by Evelyn M. Simpson. Oxford: Clarendon, 1952.

Donne, John. *Ignatius His Conclave*. Edited by T. S. Healy. Oxford: Clarendon, 1969.

Donne, John. *Iuuenilia or Certaine Paradoxes and Problemes*. London, 1633.

Donne, John. *Letters to Severall Persons of Honour (1651), A Facsimile Reproduction*. Delmar, NY: Scholars' Facsimiles, 1977.

Donne, John. *Paradoxes and Problems*. Edited by Helen Peters. Oxford: Clarendon Press, 1980.

Donne, John. *Pseudo-Martyr*. Edited by Anthony Raspa. Montreal: McGill-Queen's University Press, 1993.

Donne, John. *The Satires, Epigrams, and Verse Letters*. Edited by Wesley Milgate. Oxford: Clarendon, 1967.

Donne, John. *Selected Prose*. Edited by Evelyn Simpson, Helen Gardner, and T. S. Healy. Oxford: Oxford University Press, 1967.

Donne, John. *The Sermons of John Donne*. Edited by Evelyn M. Simpson and George R. Potter. 10 vols. Berkeley: University of California Press, 1953–62.

Donne, John. *Sermons Preached at the Court of Charles I*. Vol. 3 of The Oxford Edition of the Sermons of John Donne. Edited by David Colclough. Oxford: Oxford University Press, 2013.

Donne, John. *The Variorum Edition of the Poetry of John Donne*. Edited by Gary A. Stringer and Paul A. Parish. Bloomington: University of Indiana Press, 2005.

Drummond, William of Hawthornden. *Flowres of Sion, To which is adjoyned his Cypress Grove*. Edinburgh: John Hart, 1630.

Drummond, William. *The History of Scotland*. London, 1655.

Dryden, John. *The Satires of Decimus Juvenalis*, translated by John Dryden. London, 1693.

Dubrow, Heather. *Deixis in the Early Modern English Lyric: Unsettling Spatial Anchors like "Here," "This," "Come."* New York: Palgrave, 2015.

Dziurosz-Serafinowicz, Dominika. "Aquinas's Concept of Change and Its Consequences for Corporeal Creatures." *logos-i-ethos* 36, no. 1 (2014): 173–86.

Eden, Kathy. *Poetic and Legal Fiction in the Aristotelian Tradition*. Princeton, NJ: Princeton University Press, 1986.

Eden, Kathy. *The Renaissance Rediscovery of Intimacy*. Chicago: University of Chicago Press, 2012.

Eden, Kathy. *Rhetorical Renaissance: The Mistress Art and Her Masterworks*. Chicago: University of Chicago Press, 2022.

Edwards, Michael. *Time and the Science of the Soul in Early Modern Philosophy*. Leiden: Brill, 2013.

Eliot, T. S. "The Metaphysical Poets." *TLS* 1031 (1921): 669.

Eliot, T. S. "Whispers of Immortality." In *Collected Poems, 1909–1962*. London: Faber & Faber, 2002.

Ellrodt, Robert. "Angels and the Poetic Imagination from Donne to Traherne." In *English Renaissance Studies Presented to Dame Helen Gardner in Honor of Her Seventieth Birthday*, edited by John Carey, 264–79. Oxford: Oxford University Press, 1980.

Ellrodt, Robert. *Seven Metaphysical Poets: A Structural Study of the Unchanging Self*. Oxford: Oxford University Press, 2000.

Empson, William. "Donne the Space Man." In *Essays on Renaissance Literature*, vol. 1, *Donne and the New Philosophy*, edited by John Haffenden, 78–128. Cambridge: Cambridge University Press, 1993.

Erasmus, Desiderius. "De Copia." In vol. 24 of *Collected Works of Erasmus*, edited by C. Thomson and translated by B. Knott. Toronto: University of Toronto Press, 1978.

Erickson, Robert A. *The Language of the Heart, 1600–1750*. Philadelphia: University of Pennsylvania Press, 1997.

Ettenhuber, Katrin. *Donne's Augustine: Renaissance Cultures of Interpretation*. Oxford: Oxford University Press, 2011.

Finucci, Valeria. *The Manly Masquerade: Masculinity, Paternity, and Castration in the Italian Renaissance*. Durham, NC: Duke University Press, 2003.

Frampton, Michael F. "Aristotle's Cardiocentric Model of Animal Locomotion." *Journal of the History of Biology* 24, no. 2 (1991): 291–330.

Frost, Kate. *Holy Delight: Typology, Numerology, and Autobiography in Donne's*

"Devotions upon Emergent Occasions." Princeton, NJ: Princeton University Press, 1990.

Frost, Kate. "Prescription and Devotion: The Reverend Doctor Donne and the Learned Doctor Mayerne—Two Seventeenth-Century Records of Epidemic Typhus Fever." *Medical History* 22, no. 4 (1978): 408–16.

Gadamer, Hans Georg. *Truth and Method.* Translated by Joel Weinsheimer and Donald G. Marshall. London: Continuum, 1975.

Gaisser, Julia Haig. "Catullus and His First Interpreters: Antonius Parthenius and Angelo Poliziano." *TAPA* 112 (1982): 83–106.

Garber, Daniel. *Descartes's Metaphysical Physics.* Chicago: University of Chicago Press, 1992.

Garber, Daniel. "Physics and Foundations." In *Cambridge History of Science,* vol. 3, *Early Modern Science,* edited by Katharine Park and Lorraine Daston, 19–69. Cambridge: Cambridge University Press, 2006.

Garcia, Edgar. *Emergency: Reading the* Popol Vuh *in a Time of Crisis.* Chicago: University of Chicago Press, 2022.

Gardner, Helen, ed. *The Divine Poems.* 2nd ed. Oxford: Clarendon, 1978.

Gardner, Helen. "Dean Donne's Monument in St. Paul's." In *Evidence in Literary Scholarship: Essays in Memory of James Marshall Osborne,* edited by René Wellek and Alvaro Ribeiro, 29–44. Oxford: Clarendon Press, 1979.

Gascoigne, George. *The Posies of George Gascoigne Esquire.* London, 1575.

Gibson, Thomas. "Doctor Theodore Turquet de Mayerne's Account of the Illness, Death and Post-Mortem Examination of the Body of His Royal Highness, Prince Henry of Wales." *Annals of Medical History* 10, no. 6 (1938): 550–60.

Goldberg, Jonathan. "The Understanding of Sickness in Donne's *Devotions.*" *Renaissance Quarterly* 24, no. 4 (1971): 507–17.

Goss, Charles Mayo. "On Movement of Muscles by Galen of Pergamon." *American Journal of Anatomy* 123, no. 1 (1968): 1–26.

Greene, Roland. *Five Words: Critical Semantics in the Age of Shakespeare and Cervantes.* Chicago: University of Chicago Press, 2013.

Greene, Thomas M. *The Light in Troy: Imitation and Discovery in Renaissance Poetry.* New Haven, CT: Yale University Press, 1982.

Greteman, Blaine. "'All This Seed Pearl': John Donne and Bodily Presence." *College Literature* 37, no. 3 (2010): 26–42.

Grierson, Herbert. *Metaphysical Lyrics and Poems of the Seventeenth Century: From Donne to Butler.* Oxford: Clarendon, 1921.

Guibbory, Achsah. "Reconsidering Donne: From Libertine Poetry to Arminian Sermons." *Studies in Philology* 114, no. 3 (2017): 561–90.

Guibbory, Achsah. *Returning to John Donne.* London: Routledge, 2015.

Guillemeau, Jacques. *A Worthy Treatise of the Eyes.* Translated by W. Bailey. London, 1587.

Guinizelli, Guido. *The Poetry of Guido Guinizelli.* Edited and translated by Robert Edwards. New York: Garland, 1987.

Hackett, Helen. *The Elizabethan Mind: Searching for the Self in an Age of Uncertainty.* New Haven, CT: Yale University Press, 2022.

Hadfield, Andrew. *John Donne: In the Shadow of Religion.* London: Reaktion, 2021.

Hall, John. *Select observations on English Bodies: or, cures both empericall and his-*

toricall performed upon very eminent persons in desperate diseases. Translated by James Cooke. London, 1657.

Hamlin, Hannibal. *Psalm Culture and Early Modern Literature.* Cambridge: Cambridge University Press, 2004.

Hampton, Timothy. "Putting Experience First." *Republics of Letters* 1, no. 2 (2010): 61–66.

Hankinson, R. J. "Galen's Anatomy of the Soul." *Phronesis* 36, no. 2 (1991): 197–233.

Harris, Neil. "The Vallombrosa Simile and the Image of the Poet in *Paradise Lost.*" In *Milton in Italy: Contexts, Images, Contradictions,* edited by Mario de Cesare, 71–94. Binghamton, NY: Medieval & Renaissance Texts & Studies, 1991.

Harrison, Robert Pogue. *The Dominion of the Dead.* Chicago: University of Chicago Press, 2003.

Harrison, Timothy M. *Coming To: Consciousness and Natality in Early Modern England.* Chicago: University of Chicago Press, 2020.

Harrison, Timothy M. "Personhood and Impersonal Feeling in Montaigne's 'De l'exercitation.'" *Modern Philology* 114 (2016): 219–42.

Harvey, Elizabeth D. "'Mutual Elements': Irigaray's Donne." In *Luce Irigaray and Premodern Culture: Thresholds of History,* edited by Elizabeth D. Harvey and Teresa Krier, 66–87. New York: Routledge, 2004.

Harvey, Elizabeth D. "The Touching Organ: Allegory, Anatomy, and the Renaissance Skin Envelope." In *Sensible Flesh: On Touch in Early Modern Culture,* edited by Elizabeth D. Harvey, 81–102. Philadelphia: University of Pennsylvania Press, 2003.

Harvey, Elizabeth D. "Winged Desire: The Erotics of Ensoulment." In *Eros, Family, and Community,* edited by Ruth Fine, Yosef Kaplan, Shimrit Peled, and Yoav Rinon, 67–84. Hildesheim, Zurich, and New York: Georg Olms Verlag, 2018.

Harvey, Elizabeth D., and Timothy M. Harrison. "Embodied Resonances: Early Modern Science and Tropologies of Connection in Donne's *Anniversaries.*" *ELH* 80 (2013): 981–1008.

Harvey, William. "On Parturition." In *The Works of William Harvey.* Introduced Arthur C. Guyton. Philadelphia: University of Pennsylvania Press, 1989.

Harvey, William. *Exercitatio Anatomica de motu cordis et sanguinis in animalibus.* Translated by Geoffrey Keynes, 1927. Reprinted, Birmingham: The Classics of Medicine Library, 1978.

Harvey, William. *William Harvey: Lectures on the Whole of Anatomy.* Translated by C. D. O'Malley, F. N. L. Poynter, and K. F. Russell. Berkeley: University of California Press, 1961.

Haskin, Dayton. *John Donne in the Nineteenth Century.* Oxford: Oxford University Press, 2007.

Heckscher, William S. *Rembrandt's Anatomy of Dr. Nicolaas Tulp: An Iconological Study.* New York: New York University Press, 1958.

Heller-Roazen, Daniel. *The Inner Touch: Archaeology of a Sensation.* New York: Zone Books, 2007.

Henry, Michel. *I Am the Truth: Toward a Philosophy of Christianity.* Translated by Susan Emanuel. Stanford, CA: Stanford University Press, 2002.

The Historie of the World Commonly called, The Naturall Historie of C. Plinius Secundus. Translated by Philemon Holland. London, 1601.

Hirsch, David A. Hedrick. "Donne's Atomies and Anatomies: Deconstructed Bodies and the Resurrection of Atomic Theory." *Studies in English Literature, 1500–1900* 31, no. 1 (1991): 69–94.

Hock, Jessie. *The Erotics of Materialism: Lucretius and early Modern Poetics*. Philadelphia: University of Pennsylvania Press, 2021.

Hooper, Richard W. "In Defence of Catullus' Dirty Sparrow." *Greece & Rome* 32, no. 2 (1985): 162–78.

Howe, Sarah. "Portraits." In *John Donne in Context*, edited by Michael Schoenfeldt, 287–305. Cambridge: Cambridge University Press, 2019.

Hyman, Wendy Beth. "Physics, Metaphysics, and Religion in Lyric Poetry." In *Blackwell Companion to British Literature*, edited by Robert DeMaria Jr., Heesok Chang, and Samantha Zacher, vol. 2, *Early Modern Literature, 1450–1660*, 197–212. West Sussex: Blackwell, 2014.

Ilardi, Vincent. *Renaissance Vision from Spectacles to Telescopes*. Philadelphia: American Philosophical Society, 2007.

Jager, Eric. *The Book of the Heart*. Chicago: University of Chicago Press, 2000.

Jay, Martin. *Songs of Experience: Modern American and European Variations on a Universal Theme*. Berkeley: University of California Press, 2005.

Johnson, Eleanor. "Feeling Time, Will, and Words: Vernacular Devotion in the *Cloud of Unknowing*." *JMEMS* 41, no. 2 (2011): 345–68.

Johnson, Kimberly. "Donne's Poetics of Obstruction." In *John Donne in Context*, edited by Michael Schoenfeldt, 50–57. Cambridge: Cambridge University Press, 2019.

Johnson, Kimberly. *Made Flesh: Sacrament and Poetics in Post-Reformation England*. Philadelphia: University of Pennsylvania Press, 2014.

Johnson, Samuel. *The Lives of the Most Eminent English Poets*. Edited by Roger Lonsdale. 4 vols. Oxford: Clarendon, 2006.

Jonson, Ben. *The Complete Poems*. Edited by George Parfitt. New Haven, CT: Yale University Press, 1982.

Kamholtz, Jonathan Z. "Immanence and Eminence in Donne." *Journal of English and Germanic Philology* 81 (1982): 480–91.

Kantorowicz, Ernst H. *The King's Two Bodies: A Study in Medieval Political Theology*. Princeton, NJ: Princeton University Press, 1957.

Kearney, Richard. "Carnal Poetics." *New Literary History* 46, no. 1 (2015): 99–124.

Koch, Christof. *The Feeling of Life Itself: Why Consciousness Is Widespread but Can't Be Computed*. Cambridge, MA: MIT Press, 2019.

Kretzman, Norman, and Richard Sorabji. "Aristotle on the Instant of Change." *Proceedings of the Aristotelian Society, Supplementary Volumes* 50 (1976): 69–114.

Kuchar, Gary. "Ecstatic Donne: Conscience, Sin, and Surprise in the *Sermons* and the Mitcham Letters." *Criticism* 50, no. 4 (2008): 631–54.

Kuchar, Gary. "Embodiment and Representation in John Donne's *Devotions upon Emergent Occasions*." *Prose Studies* 24, no. 2 (2001): 15–40.

La Primaudaye, Pierre de. *The French Academie*. Translated by T. B. London, 1586.

Lane Fox, Robin. *Augustine: Conversions to Confessions*. New York: Basic, 2015.

Langer, Ullrich. *Lyric in the Renaissance: From Petrarch to Montaigne*. Cambridge: Cambridge University Press, 2015.

Larson, Deborah Aldrich. *John Donne and Twentieth-Century Criticism*. Cranbury, NJ: Fairleigh Dickinson University Press, 1989.

Lear, Jonathan. *Imagining the End: Mourning and Ethical Life*. Cambridge, MA: Harvard University Press, 2022.

Lees-Jeffries, Hester. "'Thou Hast Made This Bed Thine Altar': John Donne's Sheets." In *Domestic Devotions in the Early Modern World*, edited by Marco Faini and Alessia Meneghin, 269–87. Leiden: Brill, 2019.

Lennard, John. *But I Digress: The Exploitation of Parentheses in English Printed Verse*. Oxford: Clarendon Press, 1991.

Lerner, Ross. *Unknowing Fanaticism: Reformation Literatures of Self-Annihilation*. New York: Fordham University Press, 2019.

Levinas, Emmanuel. *Totality and Infinity*. Translated by Alphonso Lingis. Pittsburgh: Duquesne University Press, 1969.

Levitin, Dmitri. *Ancient Wisdom in the Age of New Science: Histories of Philosophy in England, c. 1640–1700*. Cambridge: Cambridge University Press, 2015.

Levitin, Dmitri. *The Kingdom of Darkness: Bayle, Newton, and the Emancipation of the European Mind from Philosophy*. Cambridge: Cambridge University Press, 2022.

Lewalski, Barbara Kiefer. *Donne's Anniversaries and the Poetry of Praise: The Creation of a Symbolic Mode*. Princeton, NJ: Princeton University Press, 1973.

Lewalski, Barbara Kiefer. *Protestant Poetics and the Seventeenth-Century Religious Lyric*. Princeton, NJ: Princeton University Press, 1979.

Lonie, Iain M. "Fever Pathology in the Sixteenth Century: Tradition and Innovation." *Medical History*, Supplement 1 (1981): 19–44.

Lucretius. *The Nature of Things*. Translated by A. E. Stallings. London: Penguin Classics, 2007.

Lucretius. *On the Nature of Things*. Translated by W. H. D. Rouse. Revised by Martin F. Smith. Loeb Classical Library. Cambridge, MA: Harvard University Press, 1992.

Lund, Mary Ann. "Donne's Convalescence." *Renaissance Studies* 31, no. 4 (2016): 532–48.

Lund, Mary Ann. "Experiencing Pain in John Donne's *Devotions upon Emergent Occasions (1624)*." In *The Sense of Suffering: Constructions of Physical Pain in Early Modern Culture*, edited by Jan Frans van Dijkhuizen and Karl A. E. Enenkel, 323–46. Leiden: Brill, 2009.

Luther, Martin. *Luther's Works*. 55 vols. Edited by Hilton C. Oswald. Saint Louis: Concordia, 1973.

McCarthy, Erin A. *Doubtful Readers: Print, Poetry, and the Reading Public in Early Modern England*. Oxford: Oxford University Press, 2020.

Mack, Peter. *Elizabethan Rhetoric: Theory and Practice*. Cambridge: Cambridge University Press, 2002.

Manilius. *Astronomica*. Edited and translated by George P. Goold. Loeb Classical Library. Cambridge, MA: Harvard University Press, 1977.

Mann, Jenny C. *Outlaw Rhetoric: Figuring Vernacular Rhetoric in Shakespeare's England*. Ithaca, NY, and London: Cornell University Press, 2012.

Marchitello, Howard. *The Machine in the Text: Science and Literature in the Age of Shakespeare and Galileo*. Oxford: Oxford University Press, 2011.

Marion, Jean-Luc. *In the Self's Place: The Approach of Saint Augustine*. Translated by Jeffrey L. Koskey. Stanford, CA: Stanford University Press, 2012.

Marion, Jean-Luc. "Qui suis-je pour ne pas dire *ego sum, ego existo*." In *Montaigne: Scepticisme, métaphysique, théologie*, edited by Vincent Carraud and Jean-Luc Marion, 229–66. Paris: Presses Universitaires de France, 2004.

Mariot, John [?]. "Hexastichon Biliopolae." In *Poems, by J.D. with Elegies on the authors death*. London, 1633.

Marno, David. *Death Be Not Proud: The Art of Holy Attention*. Chicago: University of Chicago Press, 2016.

Martz, Louis L. *The Poetry of Meditation: A Study of English Religious Literature of the Seventeenth Century*. New Haven, CT: Yale University Press, 1954.

Mayerne, Théodore de. "A discourse of the viper and some other poysons, wrote by Sr. Theodore de Mayerne, after discoursing with Mr. Pontæus. Communicated by Sir Theodore de Vaux, M.D. and S.R.S." *Royal Society Philosophical Transactions* 18, no. 211 (1694): 162–66.

Mazzoni, Guido. *Theory of the Novel*. Cambridge, MA: Harvard University Press, 2017.

McDuffie, Felecia Wright. *To Our Bodies Turn We Then: Body as Word and Sacrament in the Works of John Donne*. New York: Continuum, 2005.

McGinnis, Jon. *Avicenna*. Oxford: University of Oxford Press, 2010.

Medicinal Councels or Advices, Written Originally in French by Dr. Theodor Turquet De Mayerne, Kt., Englished by Tho. Sherley. London, 1677.

Merleau-Ponty, Maurice. *Phenomenology of Perception*. Translated by Colin Smith. London and New York: Routledge, 2002.

Milgate, Wesley. "The Early References to John Donne." *Notes and Queries* 195 (1950): 290–92.

Monings, Edward. *The Landgrave of Hessen his princelie receiuing of her Maiesties embassador*. London, 1596.

Montaigne, Michel de. *Les Essais*. Edited by Jean Balsamo, Michel Magnien, and Catherine Magnien-Simonin. Paris: Gallimard, 2007.

Montaigne, Michel de. *Essays*. Translated by Donald M. Frame. Stanford, CA: Stanford University Press, 1957.

Mueller, Janel. "The Exegesis of Experience: Dean Donne's 'Devotions upon Emergent Occasions.'" *JEGP* 67, no. 1 (1968): 1–19.

Murphy, Kathryn. "The Anxiety of Variety: Knowledge and Experience in Montaigne, Burton, and Bacon." In *Fictions of Knowledge: Fact, Evidence, Doubt*, edited by Yota Batsaki, Subha Mukherji, and Jan-Melissa Schramm, 110–30. Basingstoke: Palgrave, 2011.

Murray, W. A, "Donne and Paracelsus: An Essay in Interpretation." *Review of English Studies* 25 (1949): 115–23.

Murrin, Michael. "Poetry as Literary Criticism." *Modern Philology* 65, no. 3 (1968): 202–7.

Nance, Brian K. "Determining the Patient's Temperament: An Excursion into Seventeenth-Century Medical Semeiology." *Bulletin of the History of Medicine* 67, no. 3 (1993): 417–38.

Nancy, Jean-Luc. *The Fall of Sleep*. Translated by Charlotte Mandell. New York: Fordham University Press, 2009.

Narveson, Kate. "The Devotion." In *The Oxford Handbook of John Donne*, edited by Jeanne Shami, Dennis Flynne, and M. Thomas Hester, 308–17. Oxford: Oxford University Press, 2011.

Narveson, Kate. "Piety and the Genre of the *Devotions.*" *John Donne Journal* 17 (1998): 107–36.

Neill, Michael. *Issues of Death: Mortality and Identity in English Renaissance Tragedy.* Oxford: Oxford University Press, 1997.

Nelson, Brent. "*Pathopoeia* and the Protestant Form of Donne's *Devotions upon Emergent Occasions.*" In *John Donne and the Protestant Reformation: New Perspectives*, edited by M. Papazian, 247–72. Detroit: Wayne State University Press, 2003.

Newton, Hannah. "Inside the Sickchamber in Early Modern England: The Experience of Illness through Six Objects." *English Historical Review* 136, no. 580 (2021): 530–67.

Nicholson, Catherine. *Uncommon Tongues: Eloquence and Eccentricity in the English Renaissance.* Philadelphia: University of Pennsylvania Press, 2014.

Nicolson, Marjorie Hope. *The Breaking of the Circle: Studies in the Effect of the "New Science" upon Seventeenth-Century Poetry.* Evanston, IL: Northwestern University Press, 1950.

Nightingale, Andrea. *Once Out of Nature: Augustine on Time and the Body.* Chicago: University of Chicago Press, 2011.

Noë, Alva. *Out of Our Heads: Why You Are Not Your Brain and Other Lessons from the Biology of Consciousness.* New York: Hill and Wang, 2009.

Oakeshott, Michael. *Experience and Its Modes.* Cambridge: Cambridge University Press, 1933.

Orlemanski, Julie. "Genre." In *A Handbook of Middle English Studies*, edited by Marion Turner, 207–22. Malden, MA: Wiley-Blackwell, 2013.

Ornstein, Robert. "Donne, Montaigne, and Natural Law." *Journal of English and Germanic Philology* 55, no. 2 (1956): 213–29.

Otten, Willemien, ed. *The Oxford Guide to the Historical Reception of Augustine.* 3 vols. Oxford: Oxford University Press, 2013.

Pagel, Walter. "J. B. van Helmont, *De Tempore*, and Biological Time." *Osiris* 8 (1948): 346–417.

Pagel, Walter, and Pyarali Rattansi. "Vesalius and Paracelsus." *Medical History* 8, no. 4 (1964): 309–28.

Pagel, Walter. *Paracelsus: An Introduction to Philosophical Medicine in the Era of the Renaissance.* New York: Karger, 1982.

Pagel, Walter. "William Harvey: Some Neglected Aspects of Medical History." *Journal of the Warburg and Courtland Institutes* 7, no. 1 (1944): 144–53.

Papazian, Mary Arshagouni. "The Latin 'Stationes' in John Donne's *Devotions upon Emergent Occassions.*" *Modern Philology* 89, no. 2 (1991): 196–210.

Paracelsus. *The Archidoxies of Theophrastus Paracelsus.* In *The Hermetic and Alchemical Writings*, edited by Arthur Edward Waite. London: James Elliott, 1894.

Paracelsus. *The Book Paragranum.* In *Paracelsus: Essential Theoretical Writings*, edited by Andrew Weeks. Leiden; Boston: Brill, 2008.

Park, Katharine. *Gender, Generation, and the Origins of Human Dissection.* Brooklyn, NY: Zone Books, 2006.

Park, Katharine. "Psychology: The Organic Soul." In *The Cambridge History of Renaissance Philosophy*, edited by C. B. Schmitt, Quentin Skinner, Eckhard Kessler, and Jill Kray, 464–84. Cambridge: Cambridge University Press, 1988.

Parkes, M. B. *Pause and Effect: An Introduction to the History of Punctuation in the West*. New York: Routledge, 1992.

Parris, Benjamin. "Seizures of Sleep in Early Modern Literature." *SEL* 58, no. 1 (2018): 51–76.

Parris, Benjamin. *Vital Strife: Sleep, Insomnia, and the Early Modern Ethics of Care*. Ithaca, NY, and London: Cornell University Press, 2021.

Pasnau, Robert. *Metaphysical Themes, 1274–1671*. Oxford: Clarendon Press, 2011.

Passannante, Gerard. *The Lucretian Renaissance: Philology and the Afterlife of Tradition*. Chicago: University of Chicago Press, 2011.

Passannante, Gerard. "On Catastrophic Materialism." *Modern Language Quarterly* 78, no. 4 (2017): 443–64.

Patrides, C. A. "Psychopannychism in Renaissance Europe." *Studies in Philology* 60, no. 2 (1963): 227–29.

Pavel, Thomas. *The Lives of the Novel: A History*. Princeton, NJ: Princeton University Press, 2013.

Pender, Stephen. "Somiotics: Rhetoric, Medicine and Hermeneutics in John Donne." PhD diss., University of Toronto, 2000.

Peri Kardies: A Treatise on the Heart from the Hippocratic Corpus. Translated by Frank R. Hurlbutt Jr. *Bulletin of the History of Medicine* 7, no. 9 (1939): 1104–13.

Petrarch, Francesco. *Selected Letters*. Translated by Elaine Fantham. 2 vols. Cambridge, MA: Harvard University Press, 2017.

Picciotto, Joanna. *Labors of Innocence*. Cambridge, MA: Harvard University Press, 2007.

Plato. *Complete Works*. Edited by John M. Cooper. Indianapolis: Hackett, 1997.

Plato. *Opera omnia*. Edited and translated by Marsilio Ficino. Frankfurt, 1590.

Pogue Harrison, Robert. *The Dominion of the Dead*. Chicago: University of Chicago Press, 2003.

Pliny. *Natural History*. Translated by H. Rackham. London: W. Heineman, 1936.

Pliny the Younger. *Pliny the Younger: Complete Letters*. Edited by Peter Walsh. Oxford: Oxford University Press, 2006.

Porro, Pasqualo, ed. *The Medieval Concept of Time: Studies in the Scholastic Debate and Its Reception in Early Modern Philosophy*. Leiden: Brill, 2001.

Poynter, F. N. L. "John Donne and William Harvey." *Journal of the History of Medicine and Allied Sciences* 15, no. 3 (1960): 233–46.

Prelectiones anatomiae universalis. Edited with an autotype reproduction of the original by a committee of the Royal College of Physicians of London. London, J. & A. Churchill, 1886.

Puttenham, George. *The Art of English Poesy*. Edited by Frank Whigham and Wayne A. Rebhorn. Ithaca, NY: Cornell University Press, 2007.

Quinones, Richard J. *The Renaissance Discovery of Time*. Cambridge, MA: Harvard University Press, 1972.

Quintilian. *Institutio Oratoria (The Orator's Education), Books 6–8*. Edited and translated by Donald A. Russell. Cambridge, MA: Harvard University Press, 2001.

Ramachandran, Ayesha. *The Worldmakers: Global Imagining in Early Modern Europe*. Chicago: University of Chicago Press, 2015.

Raspa, Anthony. Introduction to *Devotions upon Emergent Occasions*, by John

Donne, xiii–lvi. Edited by Anthony Raspa. New York and Oxford: Oxford University Press, 1987.

Raven, John James. *The Church Bells of England*. London: Methuen, 1906.

Reeder, Robert W. "'Charitable Extasie' and Prayer for the Dead in Donne's *Devotions upon Emergent Occasions*." *Studies in English Literature, 1500–1900* 56, no. 1 (2016): 93–110.

Reisch, Gregor. *Natural Philosophy Epitomized: Books 8–11 of Gregor Reisch's Philosophical Pearl (1503)*. Edited and translated by Andrew Cunningham and Sachiko Kusukawa. London: Routledge, 2010.

Robinson, Benedict S. *Passions Fictions from Shakespeare to Richardson: Literature and the Sciences of the Soul and Mind*. Oxford: Oxford University Press, 2021.

Rosenfeld, Colleen Ruth. *Indecorous Thinking: Figures of Speech in Early Modern Poetics*. New York: Fordham University Press, 2018.

Rowe, Katherine. "'God's Handy Worke.'" In *The Body in Parts: Fantasies of Corporeality in Early Modern Europe*, edited by David Hillman and Carla Mazzio, 310–34. London: Routledge, 1997.

Ruestow, Edward G. *The Microscope in the Dutch Republic: The Shaping of Discovery*. Cambridge: Cambridge University Press, 2004.

Rundell, Katherine. *Super-Infinite: The Transformations of John Donne*. London: Faber & Faber, 2022.

Sacks, Oliver. *The Man Who Mistook His Wife for a Hat*. London: Picador, 1986.

Salmon, W. C. *Zeno's Paradoxes*. 2nd ed. Indianapolis: Hackett, 2001.

Sawday, Jonathan. *The Body Emblazoned: Dissection and the Human Body in Renaissance Culture*. London: Routledge, 1995.

Scarry, Elaine. *Literature and the Body: Essays on Population and Persons*. Baltimore and London: Johns Hopkins University Press, 1988.

Schmitt, Charles B. "Experience and Experiment: A Comparison of Zabarella's View with Galileo's in *De motu*." *Studies in the Renaissance* 16 (1969): 80–138.

Schmitt, Charles B. *Aristotle in the Renaissance*. Cambridge, MA: Harvard University Press, 1983.

Schoenfeldt, Michael C. *Prayer and Power: George Herbert and Renaissance Courtship*. Chicago: University of Chicago Press, 1991.

Scodel, Joshua. *The English Poetic Epitaph: Commemoration and Conflict from Jonson to Wordsworth*. Ithaca, NY, and London: Cornell University Press, 1991.

Sgarbi, Marco. *The Aristotelian Tradition and the Rise of British Empiricism: Logic and Epistemology in the British Isles (1570–1689)*. Dordrecht: Springer, 2013.

Shakespeare, William. *The Tempest*. Edited by Stephen Orgel. Oxford: Oxford University Press, 1987.

Shami, Jeanne. "John Donne." In *The Blackwell Companion to the Bible in English Literature*, edited by Rebecca Lemon, Emma Mason, Jonathan Roberts, and Christopher Rowland, 239–53. Malden, MA: Wiley-Blackwell, 2012.

Sheed, Frank. *Theology and Sanity*. New York: Sheed & Ward, 1946.

Sherman, Anita Gilman Sherman. *Skepticism in Early Modern English Literature: The Problems and Pleasures of Doubt*. Cambridge: Cambridge University Press, 2021.

Sherman, Claire Richter. *Writing on Hands: Memory and Knowledge in Early Modern Europe*. Carlisle, PA: Trout Gallery, Dickinson College and Folger Shakespeare Library, 2000.

Sherry, Richard. *A Treatise of Schemes and Tropes.* London, 1550.

Shuger, Debora. *Habits of Thought in the English Renaissance: Religion, Politics, and the Dominant Culture.* Berkeley: University of California Press, 1990.

Shuger, Debora. "The Title of Donne's *Devotions.*" *English Language Notes* 22, no. 4 (1985): 39–40.

Sidney, Philip. *Apologie for Poetrie.* London, 1595.

Sidney, Philip. *Defence of Poesie.* In *Miscellaneous Prose of Sir Philip Sidney,* edited by Katherine Duncan-Jones and Jan van Dorsten, 59–122. Oxford: Oxford University Press, 1973.

Sidney, Philip. *Defence of Poesy.* In *Sidney's "The Defence of Poesy" and Selected Renaissance Literary Criticism,* edited by Gavin Alexander. New York: Penguin, 2004.

Silverman, Kaja. *The Acoustic Mirror: The Female Voice in Psychoanalysis and Cinema.* Bloomington: Indiana University Press, 1988.

Simon, David Carroll. *Light without Heat: The Observational Mood from Bacon to Milton.* Ithaca, NY: Cornell University Press, 2018.

Simpson, Evelyn M. *A Study of the Prose Works of John Donne.* Oxford: Clarendon, 1924.

Siraisi, Nancy. *History, Medicine, and the Traditions of Medical Learning.* Ann Arbor: University of Michigan Press, 2007.

Smith, Bruce R. *The Acoustic World of Early Modern England: Attending to the O-Factor.* Chicago: University of Chicago Press, 1999.

Smith, D. Vance. *Arts of Dying: Literature and Finitude in Medieval England.* Chicago: University of Chicago Press, 2020.

Smith, Julia J. "Moments of Being and Not-Being in Donne's *Sermons.*" *Prose Studies: History, Theory, Criticism* 8 (1985): 3–20.

Sorabji, Richard. *Time, Creation, and Continuum: Theories in Antiquity and the Early Middle Ages.* Ithaca, NY: Cornell University Press, 1983.

Spiller, R. G. "William Drummond of Hawthornden." *Oxford Dictionary of National Biography.* Oxford: Oxford University Press, 2004.

Stein, Arnold. "Donne and the Couplet." *PMLA* 57, no. 3 (1942): 676–96.

Stein, Arnold. "Donne's Obscurity and the Elizabethan Tradition." *ELH* 13, no. 2 (1946): 98–118.

Stock, Brian. *After Augustine: The Meditative Reader and the Text.* Philadelphia: University of Pennsylvania Press, 2001.

Stock, Brian. *Augustine's Inner Dialogue: The Philosophical Soliloquy in Late Antiquity.* Cambridge: Cambridge University Press, 2010.

Strawson, Galen. *The Subject of Experience.* Oxford: Oxford University Press, 2017.

Strier, Richard. "Donne and the Politics of Devotion." In *Religion, Literature, and Politics in Post-Reformation England, 1540–1688,* edited by Richard Strier and Donna B. Hamilton, 93–114. Cambridge: Cambridge University Press, 1996.

Strier, Richard. "John Donne Awry and Squint: The 'Holy Sonnets,' 1608–1610." *Modern Philology* 86 (1989): 357–84.

Strier, Richard. "Radical Donne: 'Satire III.'" *ELH* 60, no. 2 (1993): 283–322.

Strier, Richard. *Shakespearean Issues: Agency, Skepticism, and Other Puzzles.* Philadelphia: University of Pennsylvania Press, 2023.

Strier, Richard. *The Unrepentant Renaissance: From Petrarch to Shakespeare to Milton.* Chicago: University of Chicago Press, 2001.

Suárez, Francisco. *Metaphysical Disputation I: On the Nature of First Philosophy or Metaphysics*. Translated by Shane Duarte. Washington, DC: Catholic University of America Press, 2022.

Tabak, Jessica. "'O Multiplied Misery!': The Disordered Medical Narrative of John Donne's *Devotions*." *JMEMS* 46, no. 1 (2016): 167–88.

Targoff, Ramie. *John Donne: Body and Soul*. Chicago: University of Chicago Press, 2008.

Teskey, Gordon. "The Metaphysics of the Metaphysicals." In *John Donne in Context*, edited by Michael Schoenfeldt, 236–46. Cambridge: Cambridge University Press, 2019.

Teskey, Gordon. *Spenserian Moments*. Cambridge, MA: Harvard University Press, 2019.

Thomas Aquinas. *Selected Philosophical Writings*. Edited by Timothy McDermott. Oxford: Oxford University Press, 1993.

Thomas Aquinas. *Summa theologica*. Translated by Fathers of the English Dominican Providence. 5 vols. South Bend, IN: Christian Classics, 1948.

Thompson, Evan. *Mind in Life: Biology, Phenomenology, and the Sciences of Mind*. Cambridge, MA: Harvard University Press, 2007.

Thompson, Michael. *Life and Action: Elementary Structures of Practice and Practical Thought*. Cambridge, MA: Harvard University Press, 2012.

Topsell, Edward. *Historie of Four-Footed Beasts*. London: William Jaggard, 1607.

Topsell, Edward. *The Historie of Serpents*. London: William Jaggard, 1608.

Tortaro, Rebecca. "Securing Sleep in *Hamlet*." *Studies in English Literature 1500–1900* 50, no. 2 (2010): 407–26.

Traub, Valerie. "The Nature of Norms in Early Modern England: Anatomy, Cartography, and *King Lear*." *South Central Review* 26, no. 1 (2009): 42–81.

Trevor-Roper, Hugh. *Europe's Physician: The Various Life of Sir Theodore de Mayerne*. New Haven, CT: Yale University Press, 2006.

Trimpi, Wesley. *The Poetry of Ben Jonson: A Study of the Plain Style*. Stanford, CA: Stanford University Press, 1962.

Tutrone, Fabio. "The Body of the Soul: Lucretian Echoes in the Renaissance Theories on the Psychic Substance and Its Organic Repartition." *Gesnerus* 71, no. 2 (2014): 204–36.

Tuve, Rosamund. *Elizabethan and Metaphysical Imagery: Renaissance Poetic and Twentieth-Century Critics*. Chicago: University of Chicago Press, 1947.

Van Laan, Thomas F. "John Donne's *Devotions* and the Jesuit Spiritual Exercises." *Studies in Philology* 60 (1963): 191–202.

Vesalius, Andreas. *The Fabric of the Human Body: An Annotated Translation of the 1543 and 1555 Edition of De humani corporis fabrica*. Translated by Daniel H. Garrison and Malcolm H. Hast. 2 vols. Basel, Switzerland: Karger, 2013.

Vickers, Brian. *In Defence of Rhetoric*. Oxford: Clarendon, 1998.

Vidal, Fernando. *The Sciences of the Soul: The Early Modern Origins of Psychology*. Translated by Saskia Brown. Chicago: University of Chicago Press, 2011.

Vogel, Klaus A., and Alisha Rankin. "Cosmography." In *Cambridge History of Science*, vol. 3, *Early Modern Science*, edited by Katharine Park and Lorraine Daston, 469–96. Cambridge: Cambridge University Press, 2006.

Waller, G. F. "John Donne's Changing Attitudes to Time." *SEL* 14, no. 1 (1974): 79–89.

Walters, H. B. *Church Bells of England*. London: Oxford University Press, 1912.

Walton, Izaak. *Lives of Donne, Wotton, Hooker, Etc*. Oxford: Oxford University Press, 1927.

Watson, Robert. *The Rest Is Silence: Death as Annihilation in the English Renaissance*. Berkeley: University of California Press, 1994.

Watt, Ian. *The Rise of the Novel: Studies in Defoe, Richardson, and Fielding*. London: Chatto, 1957.

Webber, Joan. *Contrary Music: The Prose Style of John Donne*. Madison: University of Wisconsin Press, 1963.

Webber, Joan. *The Eloquent I: Style and Self in Seventeenth-Century Prose*. Madison: University of Wisconsin Press, 1968.

Webber, Joan. "The Prose Styles of Donne's *Devotions upon Emergent Occasions*." *Anglia* 79 (1961): 138–52.

Wells, Greg. *John Hall, Master of Physicke: A Casebook from Shakespeare's Stratford*. Manchester: Manchester University Press, 2020.

Wendorf, Richard. *The Elements of Life: Biography and Portrait Painting in Stuart and Georgian England*. Oxford: Clarendon Press, 1990.

Wendorf, Richard. "'Visible Rhetorick': Izaak Walton and Iconic Biography." *Modern Philology* 82, no. 3 (1985): 269–91.

Wesley, John. "Original Gesture." *Shakespeare Bulletin* 35, no. 1 (2017): 65–96.

Whigham, Frank. *The Social Tropes of Elizabethan Courtesy Theory*. Berkeley: University of California Press, 1984.

White, Helen C. *Tudor Books of Private Devotion*. Madison: University of Wisconsin Press, 1951.

White, J. G. *The Churches and Chapels of Old London, with a Short Account of Those Who Have Ministered in Them*. London: C. E. Gray, 1901.

Whitlock, Baird W. "The Heredity and Childhood of John Donne." *Notes and Queries* 6, no. 9 (1959): 348–54.

Whitlock, Baird W. "John Syminges, a Poet's Step-Father." *Notes and Queries* 1991, no. 1 (1954): 421–24.

Whittington, Leah. *Renaissance Suppliants: Poetry, Antiquity, Reconciliation*. Oxford: Oxford University Press, 2016.

Wills, David. *Dorsality: Thinking Back through Technology and Politics*. Minneapolis: University of Minnesota Press, 2008.

Willughby, Francis. *The Ornithology of Francis Willughby*. Translated by John Ray. London, 1678.

Wilson, Luke. "William Harvey's *Prelectiones*: The Performance of the Body in the Renaissance Theater of Anatomy." *Representations* 17 (1987): 62–95.

Wilson, Thomas. *The Art of Rhetorique*. London, 1585.

Woollam, David H. M. "Donne, Disease and Doctors: Medical Allusions in the Works of the Seventeenth-Century Poet and Divine." *Medical History* 5, no. 2 (1961): 144–53.

Yandell, Cathy. *Carpe Corpus: Time and Gender in Early Modern France*. Newark: University of Delaware Press, 2000.

Index

Made in the USA
Monee, IL
05 May 2024

58019276R00154